GLOBAL DIMENSIONS

OF

GENDER AND CAREWORK

GLOBAL DIMENSIONS

OF

GENDER AND CAREWORK

MARY K. ZIMMERMAN

JACQUELYN S. LITT

CHRISTINE E. BOSE

STANFORD SOCIAL SCIENCES

An imprint of Stanford University Press

Stanford, California 2006

Stanford University Press
Stanford, California

Printed in the United States of America on acid-free, archival-quality paper

Library of Congress Cataloging-in-Publication Data

Global dimensions of gender and carework / [edited by] Mary K. Zimmerman, Jacquelyn S. Litt, Christine E. Bose.
    p. cm.
    Includes bibliographical references and index.
    ISBN 0-8047-5323-7 (cloth : alk. paper)—ISBN 0-8047-5324-5 (pbk. alk. paper)
    1. Women—Social conditions—21st century.   2. Women domestics.
3. Women caregivers.   4. Child care workers.   5. Women alien labor.
6. Women—Employment—Foreign countries.   7. Transnationalism.
8. Sex role.   9. Globalization—Social aspects.   I. Zimmerman, Mary K. II. Litt,
Jacquelyn S., 1958-   III. Bose, Christine E.

HQ1155.G56 2006
331.4'8164—dc22   2005026986

Typeset by G & S Book Services in 10/13.5 Minion

Original Printing 2006

Last figure below indicates year of this printing:
15   14   13   12   11   10   09   08   07   06

For our children: Elliot, Kathryn, Ben, and Shaye. You inspire and sustain us as we move back and forth between work and family, breadwinning and caregiving, and public and private lives.

For our godchildren: Shea Judd Hume, Yuko Ishibuchi Hume, and Yara Blancovich-Castillo, whose lives provide exemplars of maintaining family care-work networks while living transnational lives.

CONTENTS

ACKNOWLEDGMENTS

The enthusiasm and encouragement of our colleagues and students have fortified us throughout this project. We are indebted to Owen Pillion for organizing and completing the many details and complexities of putting this manuscript together. His humor and unflappable spirit kept us going. Lori Wiebold-Lippisch meticulously read the entire manuscript during the editing phase. We thank her for such intelligent feedback. Minjeong Kim helped us receive permissions forms and electronic copies of *Gender & Society* articles reprinted here. We are grateful to the University of Missouri, Columbia, and University of Kansas and the University of Kansas Medical Center for providing travel and research expenses associated with this book. We also thank the editorial board of *Gender & Society* and the publications committee of Sociologists for Women in Society for their enthusiastic support of this project. Kate Wahl, from Stanford University Press, has been a delight to work with. Finally, we are deeply grateful to Jim McGlew and Deborah and Gwen Zimmerman for holding family life together as we completed this project.

INTRODUCTION

In the following pages we hope to excite readers with what can be learned about carework by studying it in relation to gender and globalization, about gender by studying the context of globalization and carework, and about globalization by looking through the lens of carework and gender.

WHO SHOULD READ THIS BOOK

This book is for people interested in understanding the changing world around them. It will introduce you to dimensions of globalization that are typically neglected. This is also a book about gender inequalities. It will broaden your awareness of how global politics constrain gender relations, how global policies shape gender inequalities, and how the dynamics of globalization are changing the lives of women and men all over the world. And, finally, it is a book about the changing nature of labor, particularly of domestic work and the care of others, both paid and unpaid. If you have not thought much about these issues, what you are about to read will open your eyes to how fundamentally important they are. If you already have an interest in care or careworkers, you will like this book because it places and analyzes the current dimensions of this work within the broad context of the global political economy.

WHAT THIS BOOK HAS TO OFFER

With this book as a guide, you can explore the relationships between globalization, carework, and gender through both theory and research. You will discover that globalization is intimately connected with carework, and you will come to understand how this important connection serves to reinforce and perpetuate—and, under some conditions, promises to reduce—traditional inequalities between men and women, as well as between socioeconomic classes and racial-ethnic groups.

Most discussions of globalization have little to do with gender or with carework. Yet, multiple crises of care are developing in relation to globalization in locations all over the world: in developing countries, in developed countries, and in response to migration when women leave the former for the latter. Today, hundreds of thousands of women are living transnational lives. These include migrating mothers who live abroad as maids, housekeepers, babysitters, nannies, kitchen workers, sex workers, personal care attendants, and nurses. They contribute financial support not only to their own families but also to the economies of their home countries. The socially prescribed role of women as family caregivers puts them in a pivotal position. They are sought and recruited to fill gaps in care in affluent countries; while, at the same time, when they leave to go abroad, they create similar gaps in care in their own countries. Careworker migrations are leaving behind serious deficits of care that must be addressed—for example, patients and health-care systems in African countries that desperately need nurses; and children and elders in Mexico, Central America, Indonesia, the Caribbean, and the Philippines without mothers or daughters to care for them at home. In most cases, these deficits get attended to through alternative arrangements, but not without significant implications for the countries and the populations involved.

HOW THIS BOOK IS DEFINED

Our approach offers a unique perspective on issues of globalization. We place women's lives at the center in order to see the new global dynamics from their vantage point. Doing this raises new and compelling questions: Why are women so prominent as workers in the new global marketplace? What are the political forces and interests that have made women central participants in globalization? What are the consequences of these developments—for women, for men, for children and other family members, for societies, and for international relations? Applying a woman-centered, feminist approach takes us into the realm of domestic labor and other forms of carework. Through this lens, we also gain new and compelling insights into globalization issues, such as migration, structural adjustment policies, and the changing context of citizenship rights. In short, our feminist perspective helps us uncover hidden aspects of globalization, such as the rise of transnational families and new patterns of long-distance mothering. This serves to broaden our understanding of how globalization is changing our social institutions and our lives. A feminist perspective also means that we will be focusing attention on politics. Following in the tradition of feminist scholars such as Cynthia Enloe, our book will add an entire dimension to the study of international politics that otherwise would be missing. As Enloe recounts in the context of her own work, focusing on women gave her "an inkling of how relations between governments depend not only on capital and weaponry, but also on the control of women as symbols, consumers, workers and emotional comforters" (2000 xvii). In this book we hope to show how globalization depends not only on capital and information, but on the recruitment, participation, and, in some cases, the exploitation of women.

In order for us to begin, the two key concepts of "globalization" and "carework" require some clarification.

The idea of globalization is difficult to pinpoint. It is most commonly used in a business context to indicate the expansion of corporations and markets beyond the boundaries of nations to a worldwide or "global" scale. The idea of globalization also extends to the spreading influence of multilateral organizations, such as the World Bank and United Nations. Within these global networks, information and capital flow quickly; communication is immediate with instantaneous electronic links that bridge both geographic and cultural divides. Global connectedness, therefore, is a primary characteristic of globalization. But, the meaning of globalization goes beyond expanding institutions and communication networks. There is also a new global interdependence—in particular, the fact that political decisions, market transactions, labor shifts, and dramatic events in one part of the world more directly than ever before impact the other parts. To gain an adequate sociological understanding of human groups and societies today, globalization is a key concept. It obliges us to change our vantage point, to move from studying social policies, social institutions, and culture within country- or nation-specific frameworks to studying them as global systems. Specifically, for this book, taking a global perspective means looking at the organization of care labor in terms of worldwide rather than family- or country-specific patterns. It means seeing carework in relation to new and expanded global hierarchies of gender, class, nationality, and race-ethnicity. Where we used to think of local or national structures of gender, class, and racial stratification, we must now think of these inequalities as part of larger, global stratification systems.

We have deliberately chosen the term "carework" to refer to the multifaceted labor that produces the daily living conditions that make basic human health and well-being possible. Carework includes home management, housekeeping, and re-lated domestic tasks such as laundry, clothing repair, and meal preparation. It also includes the care of others—that is, nursing the sick, looking after and nurturing children, and assisting the disabled and elderly. The protective and restorative as-pects of carework connect on a deep level to many human emotions. Accordingly, we expect carework and careworkers to express a personal, affective dimension—for example, to show love, kindness, or concern. This side of carework is under-scored when such work is simply called "caring." We decided to use the word "carework" because it acknowledges these multiple facets, especially the important emotional dimensions involved (i.e., care), coupled with the complexity and physical demands (i.e., work). The concept of carework also honors nearly 40 years of feminist research and scholarship that collectively show carework to be neither "natural" for women to do nor "essential" to their being. In contrast, carework has been linked historically and culturally to women and to femininity, and women have borne the brunt of carrying out this labor across the globe. It has also been systematically devalued. We see this as part of a process of gender struggle over attempts to subordinate women (overlapping with similar struggles based on class and racial-ethnic difference). Within our view, contemporary carework patterns are largely a result of social arrangements, historically rooted in culture and the political dynamics of gender relations.

HOW THIS BOOK IS ORGANIZED

Our book offers a distinctive format in order to help readers through the com-plexity of issues and considerations that emerge when globalization is examined through the lens of gender and carework. First, we have organized the content of the book around a framing idea: that globalization produces "multiple crises of care." This concept and the four specific crises it refers to are introduced in Part 1. They are intended to provide threads of continuity as readers move through the book and encounter each new conceptual and empirical element. Second, we have created a learning strategy that will bring out the full significance of this innovative material. We want to give our readers a strong conceptual basis for analyzing globalization and for understanding its particular significance for gender and carework. At the same time, we want these concepts not to hang suspended in abstraction, but rather to come alive in the situations of everyday actors in every-day life situations. Thus, our learning strategy is to stress the reciprocal utility of theory and research, guiding readers back and forth between the analytical realm of concepts and ideas and the empirical worlds of real groups and real people.

We carry out this learning strategy by dividing our book into four thematic parts. Part 1 introduces our "multiple crises of care" framework and sets the stage for the rest of the book. The remaining parts each focus on a primary theme that defines current scholarship at the intersection of globalization, carework, and gender: Part 2, "Transnational Migration: Citizenship, Social Control, and Carework"; Part 3, "Motherhood, Domestic Work, and Childcare in Global Perspective"; and Part 4, "Valuing Carework through Policy and Culture: Communities, States, and Supranational Institutions."

Each part begins with an integrative essay that introduces readers to the particular theme as well as to the accompanying set of conceptual and research articles. Drawing on the analytic concepts and using the research studies for illustration and elaboration, we explain how the central ideas of the theme relate to the daily realities of gender and carework in a global context. A number of the excerpts have been taken from influential work in the scholarly literature. These selections are theoretical or conceptual and are intended to convey a key idea or particular analytic approach. Other excerpts have been taken from research studies. They are intended to illustrate and elaborate important problems and issues connected to the theme. To gain the full value of each part, we suggest that readers first read the integrative essay and then read the analytic excerpts and research examples.

In sum, our book draws on a wide range of recent work, particularly from feminist scholars, to offer readers a glimpse of the global challenges ahead. Traditional forms of family life and carework are colliding with worldwide economic pressures, in turn encouraging a myriad of changes for families and individuals. Multiple earner households, longer work hours, and transnational migration are just a few examples. Moreover, the international markets, multinational corporations, and supranational governance structures that attempt to organize and regulate these changes are increasingly reaching into the most intimate corners of domestic life. As these current trends continue to grow and develop, we hope the approach represented by this book will help readers to articulate the new ways of thinking that are required if we want to engage and understand our rapidly changing world.

REFERENCE

Cynthia Enloe. 2000. *Bananas, Beaches, and Bases: Making Feminist Sense of International Politics*. Berkeley, CA: University of California Press.

I

GLOBALIZATION AND MULTIPLE CRISES OF CARE

1 GLOBALIZATION AND MULTIPLE CRISES OF CARE

The events since the destruction of the World Trade Center, public debates about outsourcing, exploitative work conditions in developing counties, immigration issues, and crises of work–family balance all underscore our new awareness of living in a world deeply interconnected on a global scale. Sociologists among others are investigating how this global interconnection affects economies, populations, kin, and the environment. But issues of gender are rarely raised in discussions about a global world. We still know remarkably little about how global interconnections are structured by and affect gender relations here in the United States and around the world.

To understand globalization as a gendered phenomenon, one approach we can take is to analyze the hidden and taken-for-granted carework, both paid and unpaid, that holds together and fortifies individual lives and, by extension, entire societies. It is important to investigate this side of globalization; that is, to examine what is happening to everyday tasks of care, support systems, and expressions of love and nurturing as a consequence of the dramatic economic and labor force changes—changes governed not by local communities or even countries or regions, but by global markets and the growing power of worldwide multilateral organizations. These forces, as discussed in Part 1 by authors Saskia Sassen and Grace Chang, have created global cities where high-end jobs are concentrated, as well as a platform of low-end jobs that service and maintain them. As each of the four parts of this book reveals, carework in these new contexts plays a pivotal role in accentuating gender and global inequalities.

One of the key features in globalization is the movement of laborers within and across national borders. Large populations move about—mostly from south to north and from the countryside to large, global cities—in response to the growing difficulty of sustaining income in poorer regions of the world and a lack of social and economic opportunities. Our image of globalization is fixed on high-profile business travel or video conferencing from one global city to another; however, in reality much of the population movement involves workers searching the globe for resources for themselves and their families. When we focus on gender, the human infrastructure composed largely of women and immigrants becomes visible. Within the dominant narrative of globalization—which Sassen criticizes for "concern[ing] itself with the upper circuits of global capital, not the lower ones" (Sassen 2002, 254)—the troubling underside of outsourcing and cheap service work is obscured. To the more critical eye, in contrast, the exploitation of low-wage and immigrant labor (especially women), as well as a myriad of other problems such as pollution, ill health, and poverty, exist beyond the dazzling images of high-rise office and entertainment districts.

We know too little about the gender patterns and the relations of caring that are structured into global population shifts. As Sassen suggests, "it seems reasonable to assume that there are significant links between globalization and women's migration, whether voluntary or forced, for jobs that used to be part of the First World women's domestic role." In writing this book we ask several questions: How has globalization affected women's traditional work of (unpaid) caring and nurturing as well as their employment in jobs that incorporate these same tasks? Why are many migrant women going into jobs that involve forms of carework? What happens to the carework for their own families once women leave? How much of the labor system, especially in global cities, depends on a reserve army of underpaid careworkers? How has the gendered division of labor changed in globalization?

These questions and others form our thinking about the challenges or crises that constitute globalization. We call them "crises of care" to signal the ongoing and serious changes in our social systems of caring that have been wrought by globalization. These crises emerge from the intersection of gender, globalization, and carework and, as we shall see, reveal how local gender inequalities are becoming transformed into global gender hierarchies. In this book, we define and explore four crises of care: (1) the care deficits in families and among kin when women perform paid carework, either locally or in transnational situations, and the complexities global migrants face in managing both "hands-on" care for employers and long-distance care for their own children and families at home; (2) the commodification of care, with carework increasingly defined as a marketable product, bought and sold often in exploitative working conditions and disconnected from relational contexts; (3) the influence of multilateral (supranational) organizations and structural adjustment policies in adjudicating carework arrangements both nationally and globally, often perpetuating inequitable gendered divisions of labor that reduce women's empowerment; and (4) intensifying global stratification systems based on race, class, and gender as a consequence of globalized carework and contributing to the growing gap between rich and poor nations.

This essay begins by considering the analytical readings that frame Part 1. The individual works of Saskia Sassen and Grace Chang provide us with a set of fundamental concepts and understandings that are helpful as we analyze the multiple crises of care. After defining and discussing each crisis, we turn to the four research studies that complete Part 1, showing how they exemplify these carework crises in the context of gender relations and globalization.

ANALYTICAL CONCEPTS

In "Global Cities and Survival Circuits," Saskia Sassen helps us to see the centrality of women workers, particularly women migrants, in globalization. She elaborates characteristics of the "new" international economy under globalization. Her work lays out a basic connection between women and globalization through the concept of the *global city*. Global cities serve as magnets for the migration of women into low-paying jobs, many of which, through service and domestic work, support the high-paying, upper-level positions created in these new urban centers. In large part, workers migrate from "sending countries" in the southern hemisphere to "receiving countries" located typically in the north. Women migrate to seek opportunities; however, many end up providing cheap service labor instead. A key point in Sassen's analysis is that this "new" labor supply of women and immigrants breaks the traditional dynamic that would ordinarily have empowered these workers. When women have entered local labor markets in the past, their new status as wage earners has brought them greater independence, which they have used to renegotiate male domination in traditional relationships and institutions. For women migrants today, this process of empowerment—both individually and in terms of collective action—is impeded by their physical isolation and invisibility. Sassen argues that, while the transformations of the global marketplace hold out some hope for greater autonomy and empowerment for women through labor force participation, the wealth of the global city has not "trickled down." Gendered (and race-based) cultural definitions that devalue women, she asserts, serve to legitimate their exploitation and lack of empowerment in receiving countries.

Sassen also describes the related problem of *informalization* in the global economy, where employers downgrade work by relocating it to residential areas or to workers' homes. In global cities there is a "double movement" that disproportionately affects women and immigrant workers: paid work is shifted from public to somewhat more private settings (i.e., informalized) where labor costs are lower and work conditions and policies more difficult to regulate; and, at the same time, low-paid carework jobs are created out of what was once unpaid work due to the concentration of affluent professionals who purchase care for their households and children. These shifts blur the lines of distinction between what kinds of work are paid versus unpaid and conducted in public versus in private household settings. The trend from unpaid to paid carework and the accompanying changes in the conditions of such work are part of a *commodification of care* through which the informal and unpaid assistance and caregiving of family and friends (typically women) becomes disaggregated into specific tasks and jobs, performed in the market for wages. Commodification of care has profound implications for the level of control that careworkers have over themselves, their bodies, and their work.

Another helpful concept for our analysis of globalization, gender, and carework is Sassen's notion of *survival circuits*. Because of the characteristics of global cities and the transformation of labor markets around these centers, economic survival in many parts of the world falls more and more "on the backs of women." Households, as well as governments, according to Sassen, increasingly depend on migrating women workers for survival. Decisions to migrate are complex: a combination of individual choice, family decisions, economic necessity, and sometimes coercion and deception. As she points out, these circuits are often the product of third parties such as governments or illegal traffickers who, in one way or another, depend on the movement of populations across national borders and remittances sent back home. Her discussion of the dynamics of Third World debt within the context of the *structural adjustment* programs of multilateral organizations, such as the International Monetary Fund and the World Bank, shows that exporting workers and importing their incomes is often a coping strategy to inject more financial resources back into the national economy. The resulting survival circuits "are often complex, involving . . . increasingly global chains of traders and 'workers'" (see Chapter 2).

In "Disposable Domestics" Grace Chang takes a different approach, pulling us directly into the daily world of undocumented domestic workers. Her work argues against the idea of voluntary immigration, showing instead how migrant women workers are effectively imported into the United States from the Third World and channeled into service jobs, specifically in care work or paid reproductive labor (see Chapter 3). Her work focuses our attention on the central place of domestic carework within the broad interface of gender and globalization that Sassen outlines. Chang's research has the additional benefit of sensitizing us to their often-difficult situations and to issues of exploitation (a theme followed in even greater detail in Parts 2, 3, and 4). She points out the inconsistency between the stereotype of undocumented workers as a drain on the U.S. economy (because they use social services and education) and the valuable carework they perform in support of American workers. Chang highlights the contradictory social policies that attempt to limit benefits for undocumented workers and their families and at the same time continue the importation of cheap careworkers' labor to support highly paid dual-earner American families. Her discussion evokes Sassen's observation of the underlying role of third parties in survival circuits, helping to supply affluent countries with cheap female labor. The term *reproductive labor* is often used in the carework literature, referring to the work of raising and caring for children as well as to the housework, caregiving, and nurturance required to sustain the lives of other family members. One of Chang's key points is that the importation of migrant domestic workers into the United States enables a significant reproductive *work transfer*, where middle-class and upper-class women transfer their previously unpaid carework to poor immigrant women in exchange for a relatively low wage. Transfers are also made to documented foreign workers and U.S. citizens; however, the chances for transfers of reproductive work are enhanced because the immigrant careworkers are often undocumented and have few employment options. Chang illustrates how such women serve as valuable supports for highly paid professionals in the global cities of the north. She also describes the potential collaboration of governments in such arrangements through the introduction of guest worker proposals such as the "nanny visa."

Sociologist Arlie Hochschild (2000) has further conceptualized the global work transfer. Drawing on data collected by Rhacel Salazar Parreñas (see her article in Chapter 4), Hochschild observes that carework in a globalized world increasingly involves a pattern—a "chain"—of women leaving their own families in the care of others and migrating to wealthier countries or global cities where they relieve more privileged women of carework by taking care of their children and families. She calls this phenomenon a *global care chain*, defined as "a series of personal links between people across the globe based on the paid or unpaid work of caring" where each careworker depends for carework on another. This parallels Sassen's work on women's migration patterns, up to a point, but Hochschild adds the idea of work transferred between First and Third World women—that is, the transfer of carework between women of different classes (and possibly racial or ethnic groups) in sending countries and between women of different nationalities, classes, and races or ethnicities in receiving countries.

Care chains and work transfers create other crises when women migrate for jobs abroad, leaving a *care deficit* at home. Children, elderly family members, and others who depend on the absent women will lack care until her services are replaced. Care deficits, as shown in the articles by Parreñas, Repak, and Blair-Loy and Jacobs, occur when the inadequacies in care stem from a shortage of paid carework (such as when nurses migrate from one country to another) as well as unpaid carework (such as when mothers leave the countryside for the global city). Men are involved in care deficits as well. As Terry Repak shows, women may migrate in part to escape male violence. Additionally, in some cases, the migrants who cross borders for jobs in carework themselves are males—for example, male Filipino housecleaners in Italy. In other cases, men are forced to assume caregiving at home as a result of new care deficits, which, in turn, may cause further disruption because these roles often contradict cultural understandings of masculinity.

CRISES OF CARE

For the remainder of this essay, we turn to four crises of care that are central to the globalization of carework. To theoretically locate these crises and to ground them in the empirical world of globalization, we draw on the conceptual points that are made by Sassen and Chang. We also provide illustrations through the four research articles that appear in Part 1.

We consider each crisis separately in order to accomplish two objectives. First, we show how the concepts we have identified—global city, informalization, commodification of care, survival circuits, structural adjustment policies, reproductive labor, work transfer, global care chains, and the care deficit—appear together in the context of real people doing carework. While we treat each crisis individually, keep in mind that in reality they overlap and intersect with each other as part of the overall process of globalization. Our second objective is to show how these analytical concepts can be used and corroborated in research. In excerpts from four studies, each a recent sociological investigation of carework, we show the gendered effects of globalization on the lives of women, men, and children. These studies help us connect the theoretical and conceptual issues of globalization, gender, and carework to the level of everyday life. They allow us to view a neglected side of the global economy—the consequences for individuals, their gender relations, families, and personal survival and empowerment. Together they exemplify multiple crises of care, the central themes in this book, and provide an overall perspective, which we will continue to elaborate with greater detail in Parts 2, 3, and 4.

Crisis 1: The Care Deficit

Deficiencies in care are presumably as old as human relations. They occur for individuals and for households and families when care is needed but cannot be provided—perhaps as a result of new care needs related to childbirth, illness, or increasing disability; or perhaps related to labor shortages in the sources of care, either paid or unpaid, such as when a daughter, mother, or wife enters full-time employment away from home, when a caregiver becomes too frail or dies, or when paid careworkers migrate out of a community. Care deficits thus involve a lack of paid care (or affordable paid care) as well as a lack of informal, family care. Finally, care deficits occur individually or as patterned phenomena in groups or populations due to systematic changes such as epidemics, wars, natural disasters, or dramatic social changes.

Care deficits are tied inextricably to women's labor and position in the gendered division of labor. In most societies, women constitute the backbone of carework provision. Changes in their labor force participation, alterations in resources available for childcare and family maintenance, and changing national and international laws all create potential "care deficits" because women's traditional carework patterns and the underlying gender division of labor are threatened.

An example of a large-scale change that affected women's carework took place in the early to mid-1980s when the home care needs of sick individuals rapidly escalated due to changes in U.S. federal policy. Medicare began paying hospitals a fixed amount per diagnosis rather than reimbursing for the actual length of stay. Medicare's policy change created a strong incentive to release hospitalized patients as soon as possible and thereby save money. This signaled a momentous change in hospital lengths of stay and discharge procedures with huge consequences for families and for paid careworkers in the home health-care field (Glazer 1993). Patients who no longer needed intensive hospital care were dismissed regardless of whether they could care for themselves, placing new burdens on family members, especially women. Home health agencies grew, often by providing de-skilled jobs and paying workers minimum wages. In addition, the care deficit resulting from this U.S. policy led to labor recruitment abroad, such as discussed by Grace Chang and illustrated in the studies by Parreñas and Repak. The resulting care deficit and related problems—including ongoing issues of fraud in the home health sector—have plagued the United States for the past two decades. In addition, care deficit issues stemming from this policy change led, in part, to increased legislative support for the federal Family and Medical Leave Act (FMLA) of 1993. Though the FMLA did not provide paid leave, it gave approximately half the workforce the right to take a twelve-week leave of absence for childbirth and caregiving and not lose their job.

Other major care deficits are just one or two policy changes away. For example, according to the U.S. Department of Labor (2005), 78 percent of mothers of school-age children are in the labor force. School hours do not always coincide with work hours, producing patterned care deficits among school-age children in the early morning and late afternoon. Think of how these deficits would swell if schools changed their hours so that classes ended substantially earlier, say at 1 p.m. A huge care deficit would result. Or, consider countries such as Africa, where as many as 30 percent or more of mothers are infected with HIV and cannot take care of their families. The care deficits in these countries are astronomical. Because carework can either be unpaid or paid and, where paid, financed either publicly or privately, care deficits can occur in any or all situations. Indeed, these patterns show the extreme vulnerability of carework in any system of labor.

The dynamics of globalization create care deficits in sending countries due to the global care chains that leave gaps in both paid and unpaid carework. The same dynamics produce deficits in receiving countries when professional workers spend long hours at work rather than at home. And, as we have seen, these patterns are related. Care deficits in the First World create paid carework opportunities for women to migrate as domestic workers. Some migrant women are themselves nurses, creating another set of deficits when they leave their paid jobs in hospitals and clinics.

Globalization can foster large-scale labor force shifts where occupational groups are systematically recruited from poorer to wealthier countries. Women in care occupations are key targets in these efforts; however, careworkers are imported under different terms depending on their circumstances and characteristics. For example, au pairs, usually young white women from Europe, are given government protections and legitimacy, while other domestic workers are not (Zarembka 2004). A notable example of an institutionally supported large-scale labor migration in recent years is the recruitment of African nurses and physicians for work in European countries, particularly in the United Kingdom. The scale of the care deficit related to these migration patterns multiplies quickly when one considers potential consequences when poor African countries—for example, Zimbabwe, Malawi, and Botswana, which have been dealing with catastrophic numbers of people with AIDS—lose large numbers of their doctors and nurses.

According to a recent study by Aiken and colleagues in the journal *Health Affairs* (2004), the numbers of new registered nurses entering the United Kingdom from countries including Zimbabwe, Nigeria, Ghana, Zambia, Kenya, Malawi, and Botswana have increased dramatically in the past five years. "Overall, between 1999 and 2002, the number of foreign-trained nurses based in and eligible to practice in the United Kingdom more than doubled, to 42,000" (Aiken et al., 73). This migration is occurring in a context where there is already a huge gap in the nurse to population ratio between many African countries and the United Kingdom— for example, 847 nurses per 100,000 persons in the United Kingdom compared with 66 per 100,000 in Nigeria and 129 per 100,000 in Zimbabwe. There are similar concerns with respect to the migration of physicians. Overall, the care deficit has assumed crisis proportions in many areas of Africa.

Examples such as these allow us to better understand the dynamics of globalization in relation to the care deficit crisis. To expand our analysis, we now turn to an introductory discussion of four research studies that are included in Part 1, each of which illustrates the key concepts and ideas we have been discussing as well as adding the rich detail and complexity of everyday life circumstances and events.

In the first of these articles, Rhacel Salazar Parreñas analyzes interviews she conducted with 72 Filipina domestic workers, 46 of whom have migrated to Rome and are working there and 26 who are working in Los Angeles. Their accounts richly illustrate what it is like to be part of the global care chain. They show how women migrate to fill the care deficits of these First World cities and how their decisions simultaneously produced care deficits back home in the Philippines. Filipina migrant domestic workers are unusual in that they tend to be middle-class and well-educated women who often leave professional jobs at home for lower-status jobs abroad because of higher wages. They live a contradiction in that their relatively high status at home is the opposite of their low status as domestic workers abroad.

While Parreñas examines how migrant domestic workers perceive their care-work and the status contradictions of living "in the middle" of the care chain, that is, worrying about adequate care for their own children while providing care for the children of others, Terry Repak focuses on the migration process itself. She uses interview and survey data from Salvadorans to study the gendered nature of the recruitment activities that bring Central American women to the receiving city of Washington, DC. Most of these women arrive to work as housekeepers and thereby to address the First World care deficit. In contrast to women migrants from the Philippines, the majority of those Repak interviewed were unmarried and had migrated alone or with their children. These circumstances meant that they helped fill a care deficit in the United States without being likely to leave one at home. Repak's study provides evidence that Washington diplomatic offices, including agencies of the U.S. government, actively assisted in recruitment activities. This finding supports Sassen's observations that women's global migration follows survival circuits, charted not only by individuals but also by institutions.

Mary Blair-Loy and Jerry Jacobs also conducted an interview study in urban America, in this case New York City. The care deficit involved in their study, however, does not promise to be addressed by migrant workers but rather by professional mothers and wives who either have or are considering leaving paid work for unpaid carework at home due to pressure from the global workplace. Some of these women find alternative work structures, still in the high-status sector of brokerage, to help meet the demands of family care and work. In contrast to the other selections, this study shows a different type of globalized worker—the "valorized" and highly paid beneficiary of the global economy. However, when we look at their circumstances through a gender lens, we see that what is happening to them is reinforcing (or at least not negating) the gendered division of labor. Due to globally induced care deficits, some of these high-end workers are faced with having to leave, or alter, their careers. Instead of engaging in a work transfer, these mothers may opt to stay home, placing their own career development and advancement on hold. This study shows that globalization can work to perpetuate and even deepen gender inequality at the high end as well as the low end of the globalization hierarchy.

Arlie Hochschild (2000) suggests that emotions as well as careworkers travel along the global care chain. Long-distance mothers providing caring for employers' children in homes far away from their own children constitute one example. When these women give hands-on expressions of love and affection to the children they work for, Hochschild argues that these positive emotions are being taken or "displaced" from the careworkers' own children back home. Her concept adds an additional and perhaps somewhat startling dimension to the notion of care deficit. We are not used to thinking of affection as a scarce or transferable resource in the same way that we might think of the labor supply. But if Hochschild's hypothesis is correct and there is an emerging global hierarchy of emotional care and love, depriving poorer nations and further enriching wealthier ones, then the changes put into motion by globalized carework may have even more ominous consequences.

A counterargument calls into question some of Hochschild's underlying assumptions. It takes issue with the notion of families in sending countries being deprived of care. While domestic workers and nannies do form meaningful attachments to their employers' children, these feelings of "love" in most situations cannot be equated with (or exchanged for) the attachment they have to their own children. Thus, developing affection for an employing family does not signal that feelings for one's own children back home have been removed or diverted. Embedded in Hochschild's argument is an assumption that women careworkers (in this case, migrants) have a fixed amount of love, which, if given to an employer, must be taken from one's own family. There is no evidence for such a "zero-sum" phenomenon.

Similarly, there are also assumptions concerning the family left behind. Rather than viewing the sending country and family as passive and victimized, seemingly without the means to replace the mother's hands-on affection and caregiving, in actual fact, we know very little about how care deficits are addressed in sending communities and kin networks. Where Hochschild theorizes an emotional deficit as well as a care deficit, it seems equally (or more) likely to argue for the persistence (or transcendence) of love. Migrating mothers continue to love and to communicate that love to their children back home. While they are not there to hug or caress their child, this does not mean that those children have no hugs and caresses (see Part 3). Other family members may well demonstrate affection as they assume care for these children. Litt (2000) has shown, for example, that in the case of working mothers in the United States new networks and relations of care are developed to provide for children in economically vulnerable families. Thus, the boundaries of the nuclear family and the construction of "motherly love" stretch and change in these new relations of care.

The debate over transfers of love and affection destined for children or the elderly in sending countries to their more affluent counterparts in receiving countries underscores a central point of this book—that globalization involves considerably more than labor markets and economic factors. Grace Chang's research illustrates the personal dimensions of this phenomenon within the overall context of the exploitation of migrant domestics. As one of her respondents remarks, "We *love* the children, but the employers just *need* us" (italics added). Whether or not we agree with the idea of an emotional transfer, themes of long-distance mothering and caring appear in a number of articles throughout this book.

Rhacel Parreñas in her article references the terms "diverted mothering" and "displaced mothering" to refer to time and energy channeled from "more rightful recipients" (the women's own children) to the children and families of employers. She notes that this often makes the work of caring for the children of others a more painful experience. On the other hand, Parreñas finds that most of the women she interviewed felt less guilt for leaving their families as a result of "pouring their love" to their employer's family.

An additional dimension of Parreñas's article is the connection between the racial division of labor, discussed by sociologists in reference to labor shifts of domestic work from white women to women of color in the United States, and the global division of reproductive labor currently emerging. She elaborates the racial dimensions of this shift, comparing the historical transfer of carework from white mothers to African American domestic workers in the United States to the current international transfer from employers in northern urban centers to women from the Philippines, Latin America, and the Caribbean. Parreñas's work identifies an international racial division of reproductive labor. Her work documents the growing trend for race, class, and gender inequalities to expand and deepen into global systems of stratifications.

Crisis 2: The Commodification of Care

This crisis refers to the fact that carework is increasingly being organized into services and products that can be bought and sold. Economic theories suggest that the long-term trend of capital is to expand by continuously identifying, marketing, and selling new products. In the late twentieth and early twenty-first centuries, this process of expansion took hold in the domain of human services and carework. It is nothing new for housekeepers and maids to be employed in the homes of the elite few; however, new forms of commodification of care refer to a broader phenomenon that involves a wide range of care tasks and extends well into the middle class. With commodification, carework activities that previously were carried out informally (outside the market) at home or among friends become transformed into discrete "products" and "product lines" and the means of provision into specialized jobs and carework occupations.

Globalization has intensified the commodification of care with mixed consequences. On the one hand, for consumers in affluent countries the availability of care services and workers in the marketplace has increased the ability of high-end workers to pursue work and careers outside the home. At the same time, it has created jobs in carework with the potential for empowering lower-class women and migrants by allowing them to enter the labor force. From this standpoint, the consequences of the commodification of care seem beneficial. Why, then, are we presenting it here as a crisis?

Commodification imposes a bureaucratic, rationalized authority structure over work. When carework is commodified, it is easy for impersonal rules and procedures, rather than personal affection, to take precedence over relationships and nurturing. Moreover, global migration ensures a supply of low-paid carework labor performed by individuals in conditions of limited social and political resources. Careworkers often cannot oppose or actively resist being exploited and find it difficult to leave (Zarembka 2004). Thus, as Chang articulates, many continue to work under conditions that other workers would find intolerable. While the commodification of carework and the related issue of exploitation are not new, they have been intensified by an increasingly globalized economy and the resulting care deficits and worker cross-border migration.

Commodification in the context of globalization and in terms of gender issues can be considered a crisis because, as Sassen has suggested, the idea of service sector jobs as empowering for women who otherwise would not have employment possibilities is attenuated in the context of global care chains and survival circuits. Women and migrants may end up located in harsh conditions from which it is not easy to exit. Rather than economic security and independence, these jobs often bring low wages, unregulated work conditions, and even vulnerability and sexual abuse. In addition, the particular commodification of care in the context of current globalization creates the conditions for suppressing the emotional, nurturing side of carework. By breaking down care tasks into discrete functions, a more highly differentiated and impersonal division of labor is encouraged, so that care becomes specialized and technical rather than holistic and embedded in human relationships. We argue that in this way an overly commodified arrangement for carework threatens the social bonds and cohesion that are necessary for human well-being. This deepens rather than alleviates social divisions.

We also need to recognize that impersonality and fragmentation of care are equally visible among high-end service workers, such as those who work in the upscale environments of global city hotels. When we think of the historical ideal for how hotel guests should be treated, we think of personal and nurturing care, much as a guest would be cared for at home. This is not the case, however, in the highly commodified hotel workplaces studied by Eileen Otis (2004). Her research involved hotel workers in two luxury hotels in two of China's newly global cities. Paying particular attention to the gender dimensions of work, Otis documents the realities of commodified carework in these settings. Interestingly, though the workers she studied were women and care defined by hotel policy as individualized and "intimate," no link was made between this type of personal care and feminine nurturing or caregiving. In fact, commodification in these environments appeared to redefine care away from such a predisposition. According to Otis,

> Female frontline staff . . . memorize the names and titles of each guest, their
> partners and children and even their favorite dishes and drinks. The hotel uses the
> knowledge employees glean at the point of interaction with guests to build
> individual customer computer files containing lists of preferences amounting to, in

some instances, fifty pages of information. The hotel plays on the appeal to its cosmopolitan clientele of being watched and attended to, that is, becoming hyper-visible to a relatively invisible retinue of female frontline workers. Virtual personalism is encapsulated in the hotel's advertising slogan, "We know you intimately." . . . Yet, these forms of deference were never construed by management or workers in terms of a feminine predisposition to care or to nurture. Indeed, workers were not predisposed to this level of service. . . . (2004, 17)

The picture emerging from these settings is disturbing. It seems that commodification with its bureaucratic detail and precision has become so exaggerated that it adds a new layer of employee responsibility and deference. Moreover, it appears as a system of surveillance and discipline. This theme is revisited in Part 2.

A final dimension of the concept of commodification of care is that it highlights the division between paid and unpaid care as well as the continuities and blurred boundaries as carework moves back and forth from unpaid to paid and back again. Earlier we discussed the idea of work transfer, primarily where the unpaid domestic work of affluent women is transferred to paid domestics who are typically women of color. We must also acknowledge that the work transfer can go the other way. Paid carework also can be *decommodified*—that is, taken out of the market. The policy change cited previously that resulted in declining lengths of stay in U.S. hospitals provides a good example here. Prior to the 1983 Medicare payment change, sick patients received paid (professional) care during hospital episodes that lasted as long as the person needed such care. After the policy change, however, patients were dismissed when their medical needs diminished, but before they could take care of themselves. The care that had previously been provided in the hospital was still needed, but the venue changed from hospital to the patient's home, and the care provider shifted primarily to unpaid family members supplemented in some cases by short visits from home health workers. Thus, health carework for these patients was transferred from paid to unpaid and thereby decommodified.

Globalization has arguably encouraged commodification to a greater extent than decommodification of carework. Both the Parreñas and Repak studies provide a detailed look into the processes and consequences of commodification. With respect to the question of whether women migrants are empowered or exploited, the two studies provide somewhat differing accounts. The women migrants from El Salvador that Repak interviewed appear to have found greater autonomy in Washington. They are unique, however, in that most are single women, who did not leave husbands and children behind or engage in the discontinuities of the global care chain. The women in the Parreñas study, in contrast, while benefiting from the relatively higher income abroad, found anguish rather than empowerment in being caught in the middle of the global care chain. Not only did they miss their children at home, they had to endure the status inconsistencies of being middle class in the Philippines and a servant abroad. Neither of these studies reveals the degree of exploitation that Chang presents in her study of migrant domestic women in Los Angeles (see Chapter 3). Such conditions were further compounded by the impersonal, bureaucratic nature of commodified work. For example, Chang describes the anguish of one of the women she studied who "often became very attached to the children she cared for, only to find that she would be dismissed coldly and abruptly when her services were no longer necessary." Her study illustrates the emotionally difficult challenges for caregivers transferring work that at home was embedded in close human relationships to the rationalized context of commodified care in global cities.

The relationship of globalization to decommodification is less apparent. If we think of paid carework being downgraded rather than shifted entirely to unpaid work, however, then the connections become clearer. Sassen argues that in globalization, paid work, especially work performed by women and migrants, is downgraded to residential areas or informal settings such as worker's homes. As a result of this phenomenon, which she terms "informalization," work is less subject to regulation and workers more subject to exploitation. While Sassen is referring to industrial work, a similar process occurs in the case of carework.

Fúlvia Rosemberg's policy analysis of the recent history of early childhood education in Brazil provides an excellent illustration of the dynamic processes of commodification and informalization in the context of globalization, showing the particular implications for women and girls. In 1988, Brazil embarked on improving its system of early childhood education. Leaders promised that the reforms would empower women by increasing the educational requirements for childcare workers and by providing them with greater opportunities to enter the labor market. In the context of global economics, however, these progressive policies were quickly reversed by the World Bank (see the following discussion), which used the argument that the newly upgraded early childhood education centers would cost as much as five times that of preschool programs in private homes. As a result, early childhood programs reverted to a de-skilled and more informal type of care, which, Rosemberg argues, perpetuates gender subordination. Once again, we see the dual dynamic of empowerment and exploitation for careworkers in globalization, with an outcome that to date appears to favor the latter.

Crisis 3: Supranational Organizations and Their Impact in Shaping Carework

Supranational organizations constitute a powerful force in determining the nature of carework. Because of their growing influence and how it is used particularly in the developing world, we consider their presence another of the multiple crises of care connected to globalization. The term *supranational* refers to multilateral organizations—organizations involving more than two nations or parties—that carry the authority to impose rules and standards over their constituents. Because they form a governance structure at a higher level than those of participating nations, their policies can supersede the policies of nations. The European Union, United Nations, International Monetary Fund (IMF), and World Bank are all examples of multilateral organizations that can also be called supranational. While some authors refer to such organizations as multilateral, we use supranational in order to underscore the potential of their policies to dominate and shape carework both within countries and globally. We should also point out that the global political arena also includes nongovernmental organizations (NGOs) such as Amnesty International that are international in scope, working to apply pressure to affect national as well as supranational policies (see Part 4 for examples). Supranational organizations have the power to counteract local grassroots efforts (as well as support them) and influence the internal social agendas of nations, including efforts to redefine and improve the status and conditions of carework. Rosemberg's study of Brazil provides a compelling example of such a situation using the specific case of early childcare and education policy. She argues that outside intervention from supranational organizations is not new, but rather dates back at least to the activities of the United Nations in the mid-1960s. Globalization, however, has increased the legitimacy and reach of multilateral organizations and, accordingly, expanded their policy role.

These developments raise a troubling question. How can individual societies effect positive social change and move forward in areas such as increased status for carework and the empowerment of women, when the policies of multilateral organizations can work against these efforts? These issues are of particular concern for the developing world. Research and analysis in Africa, for example, suggest that structural adjustment policies block the advancement of women by reinforcing traditional roles and activities. Supranational economic organizations, namely the IMF and World Bank, provide loans to countries to enable them to deal with cash flow problems and to modernize economic systems. But these loans come with strings attached; they require increasing the private sector (to generate cash to repay the loans) and decreasing the public sector, scaling back public services and either making them fee-based—for example, medical services—or pushing them back to the home, as in the case of childcare. These "structural adjustments" often disproportionately affect women because decreasing the public services typically means informalizing work or transferring it to women for no pay.

The impact of multilateral organizations is not limited to structural adjustment in debtor nations, however. Their power also extends to advanced economy countries in northern Europe (e.g., Sweden, Norway, Denmark, and Finland), which have instituted welfare state policies that compensate family carework. These policies offer a counterforce against the commodification of care. By shifting responsibility for a significant amount of carework from individual households to the state, policies have discouraged the private market in carework services and have transferred funding from private to public sources. The relation between social policies such as these and carework is examined in greater detail in Part 4.

The Rosemberg study shows how early childhood education in Brazil shifted from largely informal, unskilled, and poorly paid carework to more highly paid work that required advanced education for teachers, and then back again. It illustrates Sassen's notion of the informalization of carework. In addition, it provides a compelling example of the role of supranational organizations in constraining and shaping the nature of carework. Specifically, first the United Nations and then the World Bank imposed guidelines on Brazil that included how to structure early childhood education. Their policies, developed to facilitate economic development, were oriented to saving money and not to the interests of women and girls. Hard-fought Brazilian national policies that upgraded early childhood education and teacher training were overturned. Higher wages and educational requirements for teachers in early childhood programs were substituted with cheaper care at home provided by mothers. Women's "traditional" caregiving roles at home represented cost-savings. The advancement of women and poor children through the programs that were cut was not on the agenda. This and other care crises related to supranational organizations confirm yet another mechanism whereby issues of globalization and carework serve to expand and deepen an international gender hierarchy.

Crisis 4: Reinforcing Race and Class Stratification Globally

The final crisis of care concerns the deepening global divisions on the basis of race and class. We contend that race-ethnicities and socioeconomic divisions need consideration along with the rise of a global system of gender hierarchy as a primary concern of this book. The key question here is, To what extent is globalization helping to move humanity toward a global stratification system of haves and have-nots that is built upon hierarchies of race-ethnicity, class, and gender? We have seen that globalization in many ways encourages and perpetuates traditional gender patterns that devalue and exploit women's work. In addition, the theories and research presented here suggest that, under globalization, other divisions are intensified as well. The new global economy, according to Sassen, elevates or "valorizes" some workers and devalues others. Why do white male professionals constitute the valorized workers while poor women of color perhaps fall deeper into lives of poverty with little autonomy? To answer this question requires that we take an overall look at the various issues discussed to this point, reconsidering them in terms of the race, class, and global divisions they represent.

Parreñas's research raises issues of class, racial, and ethnic stratification because the Filipina workers, both in the United States and Italy, are involved in historical patterns of work transfer that are themselves hierarchically based. The transfer of white women's domestic and reproductive labor to women of color has taken on global proportions, according to Parreñas. Now, she argues, we are faced with an international transfer of reproductive labor and an international system of racial stratification in reproductive carework. Her work also raises the issue of discontinuities in racial and ethnic identity. Through migration, individuals who form the majority population in their home countries suddenly find themselves confronting a new status and a new identity as a "minority" in their receiving country. Part 2 examines these issues in greater detail.

The Rosemberg study also reveals racial stratification issues within the context of supranationals' influence on women's carework. Those most negatively affected by the multilateral policies involving early childhood education in Brazil have been women and girls of color. Thus, global policies have resulted in deepened race stratification in Brazil. Moreover, supranationals undermined Brazilian policies that were designed to counter race and gender inequalities. Repak draws attention to the migration process of Central American women to work as domestics in Washington, DC. Their arrival strengthens and further solidifies the race-class-gender hierarchies of this global city—the pattern where affluent whites hold the top positions with the women of color and migrants who serve and care for them at the bottom. Private agencies working at least in one instance in cooperation with a governmental office facilitated migration. Thus, Repak's work also suggests that mainstream institutions (albeit unintentionally) are helping to build this hierarchy.

As these studies show, far from creating new opportunities that work against historical patterns of race, ethnic, and class discrimination, globalization through the mechanism of gendered carework may, in fact, propel these nation-specific patterns into new and formidable systems of global stratification. We will continue to examine this process in Part 2.

Looking at carework and gender relations within the context of globalization allows us to see that current developments have yielded multiple crises of care. The purpose in this first chapter has been to introduce and discuss these four crises, along with key concepts that are useful in analyzing them. To further illustrate and elaborate the gendered dynamics of these crises, we turn now to the six remaining chapters in Part 1.

DISCUSSION QUESTIONS

1. Part 2 focuses on the consequences of globalization in terms of four crises of care. Identify these and explain how they involve gender as well as carework.

2. What is the connection between the "care deficit" and the concept of "global care chains"? How do these concepts help reveal the significance of carework in globalization?

3. Describe some ways that care is being commodified. Has globalization been accompanied by increased or decreased commodification of care?

4. What are supranational organizations and why are they important in understanding carework and the connections between gender and carework?

5. How is the globalization of carework affecting systems of race, class, and ethnic stratification?

Aiken, Linda et al. 2004. "Trends in International Nurse Migration." *Health Affairs* 23 (1): 69–77.

Glazer, Nona Y. 1993. *Women's Paid and Unpaid Labor: The Work Transfer in Health Care and Retailing.* Philadelphia: Temple University Press.

Hochschild, Arlie. 2000. "The Nanny Chain." *American Prospect* 11 (4): January.

Litt, Jacquelyn. 2000. *Medicalized Motherhood: Perspectives from the Lives of African-American and Jewish Women.* New Brunswick, NJ: Rutgers University Press.

Otis, Eileen M. 2004. "Doing Deference: An Examination of Frontline Service Work and Femininity in China." Paper presented at the 4th Carework Conference, San Francisco.

Sassen, Saskia. 2002. "Global Cities and Survival Circuits," in Barbara Ehrenreich and Arlie Russell Hochschild (eds.), *Global Woman: Nannies, Maids, and Sex Workers in the New Economy.* New York: Metropolitan Books.

United States Department of Labor, Bureau of Labor Statistics. 2005. "Women in the Labor Force: A Databook." Report #985. Washington, D.C.

Zarembka, Joy. 2004. "Modern Day Slavery in the USA: Implications for People of Color." Paper presented at the Commodification of the Body Conference, University of Missouri-Columbia.

2 | GLOBAL CITIES AND SURVIVAL CIRCUITS

Saskia Sassen

This excerpt explains how globalization, and particularly the migration of labor from sending countries in the southern hemisphere to receiving countries in the north, has affected women. It makes clear that these changes hold significant and sometimes contradictory implications for gender equity. Sassen shows how Third World debt and the role played by supranational organizations affect carework to the disproportionate disadvantage of women. The excerpt also discusses concepts that are central in understanding the linkages between gender, carework, and globalization, including global city, informalization of work, survival circuits, and structural adjustment programs.

When today's women migrate from south to north for work as nannies, domestics, or sex workers, they participate in two sets of dynamic configurations. One of these is the global city. The other consists of survival circuits that have emerged in response to the deepening misery of the global south.[1]

Global cities concentrate some of the global economy's key functions and resources. There, activities implicated in the management and coordination of the global economy have expanded, producing a sharp growth in the demand for highly paid professionals. Both this sector's firms and the lifestyles of its professional workers in turn generate a demand for low-paid service workers. In this way, global cities have become places where large numbers of low-paid women and immigrants get incorporated into strategic economic sectors. Some are incorporated directly as low-wage clerical and service workers, such as janitors and repairmen. For others, the process is less direct, operating instead through the consumption practices of high-income professionals, who employ maids and nannies and who patronize expensive restaurants and shops staffed by low-wage workers. Traditionally, employment in growth sectors has been a source of workers' empowerment; this new pattern undermines that linkage, producing a class of workers who are isolated, dispersed, and effectively invisible. . . .

WOMEN IN THE GLOBAL CITY

Globalization has greatly increased the demand in global cities for low-wage workers to jobs that offer few advancement possibilities. The same cities have seen an explosion of wealth and power, as high-income jobs and high-priced urban space have noticeably expanded. How, then, can workers be hired at low wages and with few benefits even when there is high demand and the jobs belong to high-growth sectors? The answer, it seems, has involved tapping into a growing new labor supply—women and immigrants—and in so doing, breaking the historical nexus that would have empowered workers under these conditions. The fact that these workers tend to be women and immigrants also lends cultural legitimacy to their non-empowerment. In global cities, then, a majority of today's resident workers are women, and many of these are women of color, both native and immigrant.

At the same time, global cities have seen a gathering trend toward the informalization of an expanding range of activities, as low-profit employers attempt to escape the costs and constraints of the formal economy's regulatory apparatus. They do so by locating commercial or manufacturing operations in areas zoned exclusively for residential use, for example, or in buildings that violate fire and health standards; they also do so by assigning individual workers industrial homework. This allows them to remain in these cities. At its best, informalization reintroduces the community and the household as important economic spaces in global cities. It is in many ways a low-cost (and often feminized) equivalent to deregulation at the top of the system. As with deregulation (for example, financial deregulation), informalization introduces flexibility, reduces the "burdens" of regulation, and lowers costs, in this case of labor. In the cities of the global north— including New York, London, Paris, and Berlin—informalization serves to downgrade a variety of activities for which there is often a growing local demand. Immigrant women, in the end, bear some of the costs.

As the demand for high-level professional workers has skyrocketed, more and more women have found work in corporate professional jobs.[2] These jobs place heavy demands on women's time, requiring long work hours and intense engagement. Single professionals and two-career households therefore tend to prefer urban to suburban residence. The result is an expansion of high-income residential areas in global cities and a return of family life to urban centers. Urban professionals want it all, including dogs and children, whether or not they have the time to care for them. The usual modes of handling household tasks often prove inadequate. We can call this type of household a "professional household without a 'wife,'" regardless of whether its adult couple consists of a man and a woman, two men, or two women. A growing share of its domestic tasks is relocated to the market: they are bought directly as goods and services or indirectly through hired labor. As a consequence, we see the return of the so-called serving classes in all of the world's global cities, and these classes are largely made up of immigrant and migrant women.

This dynamic produces a sort of double movement: a shift to the labor market of functions that used to be part of household work, but also a shift of what used to be labor market functions in standardized workplaces to the household and, in the case of informalization, to the immigrant community. This reconfiguration of economic spaces has had different impacts on women and men, on male-typed and female-typed work cultures, and on male- and female-centered forms of power and empowerment.

For women, such transformations contain the potential, however limited, for autonomy and empowerment. Might informalization, for example, reconfigure certain economic relationships between men and women? With informalization, the neighborhood and the household reemerge as sites for economic activity, creating "opportunities" for low-income women and thereby reordering some of the hierarchies in which women find themselves. This becomes particularly clear in the case of immigrant women, who often come from countries with traditionally male-centered cultures.

A substantial number of studies now show that regular wage work and improved access to other public realms has an impact on gender relations in the lives of immigrant women. Women gain greater personal autonomy and independence, while men lose ground. More control over budgeting and other domestic decisions devolves to women, and they have greater leverage in requesting help from men in domestic chores. Access to public services and other public resources also allows women to incorporate themselves into the mainstream society; in fact, women often mediate this process for their households. Some women likely benefit more than others from these circumstances, and with more research we could establish the impact of class, education, and income. But even aside from relative empowerment in the household, paid work holds out another significant possibility for women: their greater participation in the public sphere and their emergence as public actors.

Immigrant women tend to be active in two arenas: institutions for public and private assistance, and the immigrant or ethnic community. The more women are involved with the migration process, the more likely it is that migrants will settle in their new residences and participate in their communities. And when immigrant women assume active public and social roles, they further reinforce their status in the household and the settlement process.[4] Positioned differently from men in relation to the economy and state, women tend to be more involved in community building and community activism. They are the ones who will likely handle their families' legal vulnerabilities as they seek public and social services. These trends suggest that women may emerge as more forceful and visible actors in the labor market as well.

And so two distinct dynamics converge in the lives of immigrant women in global cities. On the one hand, these women make up an invisible and disempowered class of workers in the service of the global economy's strategic sectors. Their invisibility keeps immigrant women from emerging as the strong proletariat that followed earlier forms of economic organization, when workers' positions in leading sectors had the effect of empowering them. On the other hand, the access to wages and salaries, however low; the growing feminization of the job supply; and the growing feminization of business opportunities thanks to informalization, all alter the gender hierarchies in which these women find themselves. . . .

THE FEMINIZATION OF SURVIVAL

[I]mmigrant women . . . enter the migration process in many different ways. Some migrate in order to reunite their families; others migrate alone. Many of their initial movements have little to do with globalization. Here I am concerned with a different kind of migration experience, and it is one that is deeply linked to economic globalization: migrations organized by third parties, typically governments or illegal traffickers. Women who enter the migration stream this way often (though not always) end up in different sorts of jobs than those described above. What they share with the women described earlier in this chapter is that they, too, take over tasks previously associated with housewives.

The last decade has seen a growing presence of women in a variety of cross-border circuits. . . . Such circuits, realized more and more frequently on the backs of women, can be considered a (partial) feminization of survival. Not only are households, indeed whole communities, increasingly dependent on women for their survival, but so too are governments, along with enterprises that function on the margins of the legal economy. As the term *circuits* indicates, there is a degree of institutionalization in these dynamics; that is to say, they are not simply aggregates of individual actions.

SHIFTING RESOURCES FROM WOMEN TO FOREIGN BANKS

Debt and debt-servicing problems have been endemic in the developing world since the 1980s. They are also, I believe, crucial to producing the new countergeographies of globalization. But debt's impact on women, and on the feminization of survival, has more to do with particular features of debt than with debt *tout court*.

A considerable amount of research indicates that debt has a detrimental effect on government programs for women and children, notably education and health care. Further, austerity and adjustment programs, which are usually implemented in order to redress government debt, produce unemployment, which also adversely affects women[5] by adding to the pressure on them to ensure household survival. In order to do so, many women have turned to subsistence food production, informal work, emigration, and prostitution.[6]

Most of the countries that fell into debt in the 1980s have found themselves unable to climb out of it. In the 1990s, a whole new set of countries joined the first group in this morass. The IMF and the World Bank responded with their structural adjustment program and structural adjustment loans, respectively. The latter tied loans to economic policy reform rather than to particular projects. The idea was to make these states more "competitive," which typically meant inducing sharp cuts in various social programs.

Rather than becoming "competitive," the countries subjected to structural adjustment have remained deeply indebted, with about fifty of them now categorized as "highly indebted poor countries." Moreover, a growing number of middle-income countries are also caught in this debt trap. Argentina became the most dramatic example when it defaulted on $140 billion in debt in December 2001—the largest ever sovereign default. Given the structure and servicing of these debts, as well as their weight in debtor countries' economies, it is not likely that many of these countries will ever be able to pay off their debts in full. Structural adjustment programs seem to have made this even less likely; the economic reforms these programs demanded have added to unemployment and the bankruptcy of many small, nationally oriented firms.

It has been widely recognized that the south has already paid its debt several times over. According to some estimates, from 1982 to 1998, indebted countries paid four times their original debts, and at the same time their debt increased four times.[7] Nonetheless, these countries continue to pay a significant share of their total revenue to service their debt. Thirty-three of the officially named forty-one highly indebted poor countries paid $3 in debt service to the north for every $1 they received in development assistance. Many of these countries pay more than

50 percent of their government revenues toward debt service, or 20 to 25 percent of their export earnings.

The ratios of debt to GNP in many of the highly indebted poor countries exceed sustainable limits; many are far more extreme than the levels considered unmanageable during the Latin American debt crisis of the 1980s. Such ratios are especially high in Africa, where they stand at 123 percent, compared with 42 percent in Latin America and 28 percent in Asia.[8] Such figures suggest that most of these countries will not get out of their indebtedness through structural adjustment programs. Indeed, it would seem that in many cases the latter have had the effect of intensifying debt dependence. Furthermore, together with various other factors, structural adjustment programs have contributed to an increase in unemployment and in poverty. . . .

INSTITUTIONALIZED SURVIVAL CIRCUITS

Exporting workers is one means by which governments cope with unemployment and foreign debt. . . . The Philippines Overseas Employment Administration (POEA) has played an important role in the emigration of Filipina women to the United States, the Middle East, and Japan. Established by the Filipino government in 1982, POEA organized and supervised the export of nurses and maids to high-demand areas. Foreign debt and unemployment combined to make the export of labor an attractive option. Filipino workers overseas send home an average of almost $1 billion a year. For their parts, labor-importing countries had their own reasons to welcome the Filipino government's policy. The OPEC countries of the Middle East saw in the Filipina migrants an answer to their growing demand for domestic workers following the 1973 oil boom. Confronted with an acute shortage of nurses, a profession that demanded years of training yet garnered low wages and little prestige, the United States passed the Immigration Nursing Relief Act of 1989, which allowed for the importation of nurses.[9] And in booming 1980s Japan, which witnessed rising expendable incomes but marked labor shortages, the government passed legislation permitting the entry of "entertainment workers. . . ."[10]

The Philippines may have the most developed programs for the export of its women, but it is not the only country to have explored similar strategies. After its 1997–1998 financial crisis, Thailand started a campaign to promote migration for work and to encourage overseas firms to recruit Thai workers. Sri Lanka's government has tried to export another 200,000 workers in addition to the 1 million it already has overseas; Sri Lankan women remitted $880 million in 1998, mostly from their earnings as maids in the Middle East and Far East. Bangladesh organized extensive labor-export programs to the OPEC countries of the Middle East in the 1970s. These programs have continued, becoming a significant source of foreign currency along with individual migrations to these and other countries, notably the United States and Great Britain. Bangladesh's workers remitted $1.4 billion in each of the last few years. . . .[11]

CONCLUSION

The same infrastructure designed to facilitate cross-border flows of capital, information, and trade also makes possible a range of unintended cross-border flows, as growing numbers of traffickers, smugglers, and even governments now make money off the backs of women. Through their work and remittances, women infuse cash into the economies of deeply indebted countries, and into the pockets of "entrepreneurs" who have seen other opportunities vanish. These survival circuits are often complex, involving multiple locations and sets of actors, which altogether constitute increasingly global chains of traders and "workers."

. . . Both in global cities and in survival circuits, women emerge as crucial economic actors. It is partly through them that key components of new economies have been built. Globalization allows links to be forged between countries that send migrants and countries that receive them; it also enables local and regional practices to go global. The dynamics that come together in the global city produce a strong demand for migrant workers, while the dynamics that mobilize women into survival circuits produce an expanding supply of workers who can be pushed or sold into those types of jobs. The technical infrastructure and transnationalism that underlie the key globalized industries also allow other types of activities, including money-laundering and trafficking, to assume a global scale.

1. For more detailed accounts of each of these configurations please see my "Towards a Feminist Analytics of Globalizations," in Saskia Sassen, *Globalization and Its Discontents: Essays on the Mobility of People and Money* (New York: The New Press, 1998); and my article, "Women's Burden: Countergeographies of Globalization and the Feminization of Survival," *Journal of International Affairs*, vol. 53, no. 2 (Spring 2000), pp. 503–24.

2. Indeed, women in many of these settings are seen, rightly or wrongly, as better cultural brokers, and these skills matter to global firms. In the financial-services industry, women are considered crucial to interfacing with customers, because they are believed to inspire more trust and thereby to make it easier for individual investors to put their money in what are often known to be highly speculative endeavors. See Melissa Fisher, "Wall Street Women's 'Herstories' in Late Financial Corporate Capitalism," in *Constructing Corporate America: History, Politics, Culture*, ed. Kenneth Liparito and David B. Sicilia (New York: Oxford University Press, 2002).

3. I have developed this at length in *Globalization and Its Discontents*.

4. Pierrette Hondagneu-Sotelo, *Gendered Transitions: Mexican Experiences of Immigration* (Berkeley: University of California Press, 1994); Sarah Mahler, *American Dreaming: Immigrant Life on the Margins* (Princeton, N. J.: Princeton University Press, 1995).

5. Michel Chossudovsky, *The Globalisation of Poverty* (London: Zed/TWN, 1997); Guy Standing, "Global Feminization Through Flexible Labor: A Theme Revisited," *World Development*, vol. 27, no. 3 (1999), pp. 583–602; Aminur Rahman, "Micro-credit Initiatives for Equitable and Sustainable Development: Who Pays?" *World Development*, vol. 27, no. 1 (1999), pp. 67–82; Diane Elson, *Male Bias in Development*, 2nd ed. (Manchester, UK: Manchester University Press, 1995). For an excellent review of the literature on the impact of the debt on women, see Kathryn Ward, "Women and the Debt," paper presented at the Colloquium on Globalization and the Debt, Emory University, Atlanta (1999).

6. On these various see Diana Alarcon-Gonzalez and Terry McKinley, "The Adverse Effects of Structural Adjustment on Working Women in Mexico," *Latin American Perspectives*, vol. 26, no. 3 (1999), 103–17; Claudia Buchmann, "The Debt Crisis, Structural Adjustment and Women's Education," *International*

Journal of Comparative Studies, vol. 37, nos. 1–2 (1996), pp. 5–30; Helen I. Safa, *The Myth of the Male Breadwinner: Women and Industrialization in the Caribbean* (Boulder, Colo.: Westview Press, 1995); Nilufer Cagatay and Sule Ozler, "Feminization of the Labor Force: The Effects of Long-term Development and Structural Adjustment," *World Development*, vol. 23, no. 11 (1995), pp. 1883–94; Erika Jones, "The Gendered Toll of Global Debt Crisis," *Sojourner*, vol. 25, no. 3, pp. 20–38; and several of the references cited in the preceding footnotes.

7. Eric Toussaint, "Poor Countries Pay More Under Debt Reduction Scheme?" (July 1999), www.twnside.org.sg/souths/twn/title/1921-cn.htm. According to Susan George, the south has paid back the equivalent of six Marshall Plans to the north (Asoka Bandarage, *Women, Population, and Crisis* [London: Zed, 1997]).

8. The IMF asks HIPCs [Heavily Indebted Poor Countries] to pay 20 to 25 percent of their export earnings toward debt service. In contrast, in 1953 the Allies canceled 80 percent of Germany's war debt and only insisted on 3 to 5 percent of export earnings debt service. These general terms were also evident as Central Europe emerged from communism. For one of the best critical examinations of globalization, see Richard C. Longworth, *Global Squeeze: The Coming Crisis for First World Nations* (Chicago: Contemporary Books, 1998).

9. About 80 percent of the nurses imported under the new act were from the Philippines. See generally, Satomi Yamamoto, "The Incorporation of Women Workers into a Global City: A Case Study of Filipina Nurses in the Metropolitan New York Area" (2000).

10. Japan passed a new immigration law—strictly speaking, an amendment of an older law—that radically redrew the conditions for entry of foreign workers. It allowed professionals linked to the new service economy—specialists in Western style finance, accounting, law, et cetera—but made the entry of what is termed "simple labor" illegal. The latter provision generated a rapid increase in the entry of undocumented workers for low-wage jobs. But the new law did make special provisions for the entry of "entertainers."

11. Natacha David, "Migrants Made the Scapegoats of the Crisis," ICFTU Online (International Confederation of Free Trade Unions, 1999). www.hartford-hwp.com/archives/50/012html.

DISPOSABLE DOMESTICS: IMMIGRANT WOMEN WORKERS IN THE GLOBAL ECONOMY

Grace Chang

This excerpt highlights the connections between the daily working conditions of immigrant women domestics and the economic interests and policies of the First World countries that receive them. It brings to life the way in which careworkers face economic and cultural exploitation and the forces that perpetuate these conditions. These issues help inform the current policy debate over whether the United States should establish temporary or guest worker programs.

The nomination of Zoë Baird for US Attorney General in 1993 forced a confession that provoked a public uproar: Baird admitted to employing two undocumented Peruvian immigrants, as a baby-sitter and a driver, in clear violation of the immigration law prohibiting the hiring of "illegal" aliens. Responses to Baird's disclosure indicate that her "crime" is a pervasive phenomenon.[1] Deborah Sontag reported in the *New York Times* that two-career, middle-class families employing so-called illegal immigrants to do child care and domestic work is so common that employment agencies routinely recommend undocumented immigrants to their clients. As the director of one Manhattan nanny agency said, "It's just a reality of life that without the illegal girls, there wouldn't be any nannies, and the mommies would have to stay home and mind their own kids."[2] Another agency's director said bluntly, "It all comes down to money. . . . The reason that people hire immigrants without papers is that they're looking to save. If they want legal, they can get it, but it costs."[3] According to a survey of 18 New York agencies, "illegal" workers earned as little as $175 a week and "legal" workers as much as $600.[4]

Thus, the uproar surrounding Baird was not so much a response to the discovery that some people flouted the law by employing undocumented workers. This was hardly news. Rather, the public outcry was a reflection of resentment that this practice was so easily accessible to the more privileged classes while other working-class working mothers struggled to find any childcare. As one critic of Baird commented, "I don't think it's fair. I raised my kids while I was working. I worked days. My husband worked nights at the post office. Our in-laws filled in when they had to."[5] Another woman pointed out: "Average working mothers don't make nearly what she makes, and yet we are obligated to follow the law."[6]

What was conspicuously absent from most of the commentary on the Baird controversy was concern for the plight of the undocumented workers themselves. Two other news stories involving immigrant women working in private households appeared in a California newspaper the same time Baird's situation was making headlines across the nation; yet these stories did not receive comparable attention. The first of these involved Claudia Garate, who immigrated from Chile at age 19 in order to take a job as an au pair for a professional couple. Garate testified before the state Labor Commissioner in Sonoma County that she slept on the floor and worked on call twenty-four hours a day, seven days a week as a maid, baby-sitter, cook, and gardener for $50 a month. Garate's employers held on to her visa and passport and withheld her pay for 13 months, claiming they would deposit it in a bank account for her. The second case involved Maria de Jesus Ramos Hernandez, who left her three children in Mexico to work as a housekeeper in California. Once here, her employer repeatedly raped her, telling her that he had paid her way here and would have her jailed if she did not submit to him.[7]

Evidence indicates that while Garate's and Hernandez's cases may have been extreme, abuse of undocumented women working in private households is not uncommon. Lina Avidan, then-program director for the San Francisco-based Coalition for Immigrant and Refugee Rights and Services (CIRRS), said, "I have clients who work . . . seven days a week doing child care from 6 a.m. to 10 p.m. [for] $200 a month. Clearly, they are working in the homes of the wealthy and they're not even getting minimum wage."[8] A 1991 CIRRS survey of Chinese, Filipina, and Latina undocumented women in the San Francisco Bay area revealed that the majority (58 percent) of the employed undocumented Latinas surveyed held jobs in housecleaning and in-home care of children or the elderly, while the remainder worked in service jobs or factories. They were usually earning between $250 and $500 per month. Forty percent of these women were supporting between one and three people on these wages, while 38 percent were supporting between four and six.[9] Members of Mujeres Unidas y Activas (MUA), a support group for Latina immigrant domestic workers, report that they commonly endure conditions approaching slavery or indentured servitude.[10]

These statements are echoed by immigrant domestic workers in Los Angeles years after the Zoë Baird episode has passed. Patricia Tejada fled from El Salvador in 1988 because of the war, leaving her three children and husband behind. She worked as a baby-sitter and housekeeper for the next four years in Los Angeles to try to save enough money to bring her family to join her. She recalls spending many nights crying, wondering how her children were and whether they were safe. Throughout those years, she often became very attached to the children she cared for, only to find that she would be dismissed coldly and abruptly when her services were no longer necessary: "We love the children, but the employers just need us. When they don't, they say, 'We don't need you anymore,' " she says with a wave of her hand.[11]

Another woman, Amalia Hernandez, who fled El Salvador with her four cousins, found her first job working in Los Angeles as a live-in nanny caring for a newborn infant. Although Amalia had been offered $80 per week, she was paid $50 instead to work from 6 a.m. until midnight, most days. In her next job, she was supposed to be paid $100 per week, but was told by her employer for a year and a half that her salary was being saved for her. When she asked for her pay, the employer told his wife to throw her out. Amalia left the house with only one month's pay and a bunch of "hand-me-down" clothes. Although she tried to take the employer to small claims court, the employer won the case by insisting that Amalia was a very bad worker and threatening in the courtroom that she would call the INS to deport her. Amalia recalls that she hardly spoke any English at the time and was frightened by her employer's threats.

She describes her current employment situation as tolerable. She takes care of three children, ages four, two, and two months. In a typical day, she begins at 6 a.m. preparing breakfast, gives the children lunch for school, brings the four-year-old to preschool for half a day, cleans the house, does laundry, and cooks dinner. Essentially, she works around the clock every day while "the lady stays home all day and gets angry if I sit down." Suffering from an injury sustained on the job, Amalia is in constant pain carrying the baby around, up and down the stairs all day. She wishes she could go to the doctor for the injury but is afraid she will lose her job if she takes time off to do so. She is paid $275 per week and has random times off, given at her employer's whim.[12]

Taken together, these accounts indicate that middle-class households often make exploitative use of immigrant women to do childcare and domestic work. They also suggest the advances of many middle-class white women in the workforce have been largely predicated on the exploitation of poor, immigrant women. While middle- and upper-class women entrust their children and homes to undocumented immigrant women, the immigrant women often must leave their own children to work. Some leave their children with family in their home countries, hoping to earn enough to return or send money back to them.[13] Thus, middle- and upper-class women are readily able to find "affordable" care for their children at the expense of poor immigrant women and their children. The employment of undocumented women in dead-end, low-wage, temporary service jobs makes it possible for middle- and upper-class women to pursue salaried jobs and not have to contend with the "second shift" when they come home.

Several scholars have analyzed the systematic use of people of color and immigrants as expendable workers or as a reserve labor army in the United States. Robert Blauner's theory of internal colonialism, developed in *Racial Oppression in America*, proposes that the state channels people of color into a colonized labor force within the United States by restricting their physical and social mobility and political participation. Elaborating on this model in *Race and Class in the Southwest*, Mario Barrera observes that immigration policies allowing for the "recruitment" or importation of foreign laborers are coupled with policies denying these laborers the rights of citizen workers, thus rendering them more easily exploitable.[14] In *Inside the State: The Bracero Program, Immigration and the INS*, Kitty Calavita proposes that the state formulates immigration policy not only to accommodate capital's demands for cheap labor, but to fulfill its own agenda. Calavita says that the state seeks to maximize the utility of immigrants as laborers while minimizing its own costs and responsibilities associated with maintaining a surplus labor army of immigrants.[15]

Clearly Proposition 187 [a California legislative initiative passed in 1994 and later largely dismantled that denied public education to undocumented children and an array of public benefits and social services to undocumented persons] and the Personal Responsibility Act [also known as the Personal Responsibility and Work Opportunity Reconciliation Act (PRWORA), a federal law signed by President Clinton in 1996 to reform the U.S. welfare system] suit well the agenda of limiting state costs and responsibilities for immigrant workers. These act in conjunction with immigration policy allowing for the recruitment or direct importation of immigrants as expendable commodities. A number of examples of migrant contract-labor programs in recent US history illustrate how the state fulfills this agenda, maintaining a reserve labor force of immigrants without having to provide citizen-worker rights or benefits. The Bracero program involved hundreds of thousands of Mexican, primarily male, migrant workers imported to labor in agriculture in the American Southwest in the 1940s through 1960s. While the conventional wisdom is that contract labor programs are a thing of the past, such programs are not merely a phenomenon of distant history, as many people may think. Furthermore, efforts to resurrect something closely resembling the Bracero program are underway in a number of industries. Recently, a proposal was made to bring in female migrants as domestic, child-care, or elderly-care workers under a special, temporary worker visa called the "nanny visa."

In 1953, a group of women in El Paso, Texas, organized the Association for Legalized Domestics. Contrary to what its name suggested, this group was composed of Anglo women who were housewives calling for a program to facilitate hiring Mexican women to work for them as maids. The association proposed that potential workers could be screened for age, health problems, and criminal records. Employees were to earn a minimum wage of $15 a week and were to be given room, board, and one and a half days off on weekends. A group of Chicana women working as maids in El Paso organized to try to block these efforts. They protested that the housewives merely wanted to import Mexicana women to work for lower wages, while local workers were readily available but demanded higher wages. Ultimately, the association's efforts to enlist government support in obtaining cheap "household help" were frustrated when the Department of Justice rejected the proposal.[16]

Forty years later, proposals with much the same goals as those of the El Paso housewives' association emerged in the wake of the Zoë Baird controversy. When Baird lost the nomination for US attorney general because she had employed two "illegal aliens" as a baby-sitter and a driver, she attempted to defend herself, claiming: "I was forced into this dilemma to care for my child. . . . In my hope to find appropriate child care for my son, I gave too little emphasis to what was described to me as a technical violation of the law."[17]

Apparently, this did garner the sympathies of many people. While some condemned Baird for what was seen as a flagrant violation of the law and a white-collar crime, others flocked to her defense. Many argued that what she did should not be considered a crime, that the law should be changed to make it easier (and legal) for working women or two-career couples to do what she had done. Writing for the *New York Times*, Deborah Sontag reported: "Many say, at the least, that household employers should be exempt, or that household workers should get a special visa."[18] Sontag quoted sociologist Philip Kasnitz: "A law that forces thousands of illegal immigrants and middle-class families to engage in criminal activity desperately needs to be reformed."[19] Soon after the Baird controversy began to quiet down, proposals began to be circulated to allow private household employers to legally hire those who might otherwise be "illegal" immigrant workers.

The federal Commission on Immigration Reform held meetings in February 1993 to hear testimony on the need for some type of immigration program for domestic workers, child-care workers, and home-health aides (all encompassed under the rubric of "homecare workers"). . . . One plan proposed to create a new classification for home-care workers within the existing unskilled labor visas. . . . A second plan proposed to require the Department of Labor to determine when there was a shortage of domestic (that is, citizen or resident) workers and then to allow potential or current employees to apply for visas themselves. . . .

Responses to the Baird controversy indicate that neither heightened "awareness" nor fear of the law have influenced household employers to change their practices or attitudes about the use of immigrant workers, undocumented or otherwise. One woman explained that she would continue to flout the law, employing an undocumented Peruvian as a housekeeper: "After Zoë Baird, my husband and I discussed whether it was now an issue for us, and decided that neither of us will ever run for office."[20] Another woman, seeking specifically to hire an "illegal" immigrant, said: "I want someone who cannot leave the country, who doesn't know anyone in New York, who basically does not have a life. I want someone who is completely dependent on me and loyal to my family."[21] These comments should give us pause before considering home-care worker visa proposals relying on the good graces or ethics of household employers to uphold their employees' rights. . . .

Immigrant women workers may battle internalized forces, as well. Dominant US ideology identifies women as caretakers and women of color/Third World women especially as servants to nurture and clean up after First World elites. This may reinforce roles often defined for immigrant women in their home countries as dutiful daughters, mothers, and wives, raised in cultures emphasizing respect for elders and the protection of children. Explains Maria Griffith-Cañas, who emigrated from El Salvador and worked in convalescent homes for many years before she began organizing home- and health-care workers in SEIU Local 250: "You see minorities as the ones tending because our cultures say that we care for elders."[22]

The workers she organizes now in nursing homes around the East Bay tell of grueling work conditions at the same time that they express great emotional attachment to and concern for their patients. A typical day shift begins at 7:30 a.m. and ends at 3:30 p.m., with a half-hour lunch break, and usually entails tending to six or seven patients each for two to three hours, including waking, bathing, toileting or "diapering," dressing, and seating them in wheelchairs for lunch by 11 a.m., then returning them to bed. Many have done this work as CNAs for years, earning from $5.39 per hour as a starting wage to a maximum of $7 per hour, earned by one woman who had worked in the industry for nine years.

Many of the workers are somewhat elderly themselves, and are tested by the physically demanding nature of the work. . . . When asked to name the most difficult part of their job, workers responded that they worried about the quality of care that was possible to give within such short time periods; there were too many patients assigned to staff. One woman responded that the hardest thing for her is when a patient she has cared for and grown close to over a long period of time is moved or dies. . . . Even amidst their employers' assaults on them, many of the workers at Casa San Miguel could not bring themselves to leave their patients.

My aim here is not to suggest that immigrant women are in need of feminist consciousness-raising or politicization, but to suggest that immigrant women's culturally inscribed values and identities may play into the hands of employers eager to capture these women's "labors of love" for themselves, their dependents, and clients. Thus, employers are able to exploit immigrant women's beliefs and roles that may be deeply engrained. When these ideologies are formalized in government policy and employer practice, immigrant women are doomed to become disposable workers.

In stark contrast to care workers' attachments to and concern for their clients, employers often refuse to acknowledge or take responsibility for the human and workers' rights of the undocumented people who live and work in their midst. If policy makers and employers of immigrant workers—who are often one and the same—are going to insist that we solve the "illegal immigration" problem, then they must take responsibility for their own complicity in this system. . . .

While the proposals for a home-care worker visa ultimately did not gain momentum, similar policy proposals will undoubtedly arise again. When they do, it will be crucial that provisions are made to ensure fair wages and conditions for household workers and some means of holding employers accountable to these standards. Without these, immigrant women are in danger of becoming the new "braceras"—a pair of arms to rock the cradle or scrub the floors for their employers, then go home tired and empty-handed to their own children.

1. The *San Francisco Chronicle* reported that, although no precise figures exist, "experts believe a large percentage of the estimated 3 million undocumented workers now residing in the United States are employed in child-care and domestic work." See "Hiring of Aliens Is a Widespread Practice," *San Francisco Chronicle*, January 15, 1993, p. A-6.

2. Deborah Sontag, "Increasingly, Two-Career Family Means Illegal Immigrant Help," *New York Times*, January 24, 1993, p. A-1.

3. Sontag, "Increasingly, Two-Career Family Means Illegal Immigrant Help," p. A-13.

4. Sontag, "Increasingly, Two-Career Family Means Illegal Immigrant Help," p. A-13.

5. Felicity Barringer, "What Many Say About Baird: What She Did Wasn't Right," *New York Times*, January 22, 1993, p. A-1.

6. Barringer, "What Many Say About Baird," p. A-10.

7. Carla Marinucci, "Immigrant Abuse: 'Slavery, Pure and Simple,'" *San Francisco Examiner*, January 10, 1993, pp. A-1, A-8.

8. Marinucci, "Immigrant Abuse."

9. Chris Hogeland and Karen Rosen, "Dreams Lost, Dreams Found: Undocumented Women in the Land of Opportunity" (San Francisco: Coalition for Immigrant and Refugee Rights and Services, Immigrant Women's Task Force, 1991), pp. 10–11.

10. Carla Marinucci, "Silence Shields Abuse of Immigrant Women," *San Francisco Examiner*, January 11, 1993, pp. A-1, A-10.

11. Interview with Patricia Tejada (pseudonym), Los Angeles, California, February 16, 1998.

12. Interview with Amalia Hernandez (pseudonym), Los Angeles, California, February 15, 1998.

13. The CIRRS report suggested that the availability of "underground" service jobs for women in housecleaning, child care, and the garment industry encourages women to migrate alone or without families. As one respondent, Rosa, explained: "I am very worried because we left the children with my parents, who are very old. We have not been able to send money home as planned because everything costs so much here." See Hogeland and Rosen, "Dreams Lost, Dreams Found," p. 5.

14. Robert Blauner, *Racial Oppression in America* (New York: Harper and Row, 1972); Mario Barrera, *Race and Class in the Southwest: A Theory of Racial Inequality* (Notre Dame, IN: University of Notre Dame Press, 1979).

15. Kitty Calavita, *Inside the State: The Bracero Program, Immigration, and the INS* (New York: Routledge, Chapman and Hall, 1992).

16. Mary Romero, *Maid in the U.S.A.* (New York: Routledge, 1992), p. 91; citing *El Paso Times*, September 25, 1953, and *El Paso Herald Post*, October 12, 15, and 30, and November 9 and 18, 1953.

17. "Baird Apologizes for Illegal Hiring," *New York Times*, January 20, 1993, pp. A-1, A-12.

18. Sontag, "Increasingly, Two-Career Family Means Illegal Immigrant Help," p. A-13.

19. Sontag, "Illegal Immigrant Help," p. A-13.

20. Sontag, "Illegal Immigrant Help," p. A-13.

21. Sontag, "Illegal Immigrant Help," p. A-13.

22. Interview with Maria Griffith-Cañas, March 16, 1996.

4 | MIGRANT FILIPINA DOMESTIC WORKERS AND THE INTERNATIONAL DIVISION OF REPRODUCTIVE LABOR

Rhacel Salazar Parreñas

This article introduces the concept of an "international transfer of caretaking" in which affluent women in global cities purchase the carework services of migrant Filipina women at relatively low wages. These migrants in turn employ lower-paid domestic workers to care for their children and families back home. Parreñas argues that this three-tier system constitutes an international division of reproductive labor in which women are stratified based on race, class, and nationality. She explores the contradictions and social consequences for the Filipina migrant careworkers in the middle of this global care chain.

Looking at the migration and entrance of Filipina women into domestic work, this article documents the creation of a division of reproductive labor in the global economy. This particular division of labor occurs among working women and arises out of the demand for low-wage service workers in postindustrial nations. By reproductive labor, I refer to the labor needed to sustain the productive labor force. Such work includes household chores; the care of elderly, adults, and youth; the socialization of children; and the maintenance of social ties in the family (Brenner and Laslett 1991). Relegated to women more so than men, reproductive labor has long been a commodity purchased by class-privileged women. As Evelyn Nakano Glenn (1992) has observed, white class-privileged women in the United States have historically freed themselves of reproductive labor by purchasing the low-wage services of women of color. In doing so, they maintain a "racial division of reproductive labor," which establishes a two-tier hierarchy among women (Nakano Glenn 1992).

Two analytical goals motivate my query into the structural relationship between the politics of reproductive labor and the flow of Filipina domestic worker migration. First, I return to the discussion of the commodification of reproductive labor initiated by Nakano Glenn (1992) to extend her discussion to an international terrain. In this way, my analysis of the division of reproductive labor considers issues of globalization and the feminization of wage labor (Sassen 1984, 1988). Second, I extend discussions of the international division of labor in globalization from a sole consideration of productive labor to include analyses of reproductive labor. By analyzing the structural relationship between reproductive labor and the feminization of the migrant labor force, I show another dimension by which gender shapes the economic divisions of labor in migration.

The globalization of the market economy has extended the politics of reproductive labor into an international level. As I show in this article, the migration and entrance into domestic work of Filipino women constitutes an international division of reproductive labor. This division of labor, which I name the *international transfer of caretaking*, refers to the three-tier transfer of reproductive labor among women in sending and receiving countries of migration. While class-privileged women purchase the low-wage services of migrant Filipina domestic workers, migrant Filipina domestic workers simultaneously purchase the even lower-wage services of poorer women left behind in the Philippines. In other words, migrant Filipina domestic workers hire poorer women in the Philippines to perform the reproductive labor that they are performing for wealthier women in receiving nations. . . .

Contemporary labor migration is situated in the globalization of the market economy. As Saskia Sassen has further indicated, globalization has sparked the feminization of migrant labor. Contributing an insightful theoretical framework on the position of women in the global economy, Sassen (1984, 1988) establishes that globalization simultaneously demands the low-wage labor of Third World women in export processing zones of developing countries and in secondary tiers of manufacturing and service sectors in advanced, capitalist countries. The case of women in the Philippines provides an exemplary illustration. While Filipina women comprised 74 percent of the labor force in export processing zones by the early 1980s (Rosca 1995), they constituted more than half of international migrants (55 percent) by the early 1990s (Asis 1992).

In globalization, the penetration of manufacturing production in developing countries creates a demand for women to migrate to advanced, capitalist countries. First of all, the manufacturing production (e.g., garment, electronics, and furniture) that remains in the latter set of countries must compete with low production costs in developing countries. This results in the decentralization and deregulation of manufacturing production (i.e., subcontracting or homework). Second, multinational corporations with production facilities across the globe, by and large, maintain central operations in new economic centers, or what Sassen (1994) refers to as "global cities," where specialized professional services (e.g., legal, financial, accounting, and consulting tasks) are concentrated. For the most part, global cities require low-wage service labor such as domestic work to maintain the lifestyles of their professional inhabitants. Notably, many of the low-paying jobs created in advanced, capitalist countries are considered traditional "women's work." As a result, many of the immigrants who respond to the increasing demand for low-wage workers in advanced, capitalist countries are women. . . .

METHOD

This article is based primarily on open-ended interviews that I collected with 46 female domestic workers in Rome and 26 in Los Angeles. . . . Both destinations also have particular colonial ties to the Philippines. While the United States maintains economic dominance in relation to the Philippines, Italy enjoys cultural dominance indirectly through the institution of the Roman Catholic Church. As a consequence of these macro-historical links, Filipinos have come to represent one of the largest migrant groups in both the United States and Italy (Caritas di Roma 1995; Portes and Rumbaut 1996). By 1990, the flow of legal migration from the Philippines was, next to Mexico, the second largest in the United States and the third largest, next to Morocco and Tunisia, in Italy (Campani 1993; Portes and Rumbaut 1996).

My sample of domestic workers in Rome and Los Angeles reveals women who are mostly mothers with a fairly high level of educational attainment. Contrary to the popular belief that Filipina domestic workers are usually young and single (Catholic Institute for International Relations 1987), my study shows a larger number of married women. In Los Angeles, only 5 of 26 interviewees are never-married single women, while in Rome, less than half of the women I interviewed (19) are never married. Women with children living in the Philippines constitute the majority of my sample in both Rome and Los Angeles: 25 of 46 in Rome and 14 of 26 in Los Angeles.

Because they perform jobs that are considered unskilled, domestic workers are often assumed to lack the training needed for higher status jobs in the labor market. In the case of Filipina domestics in Italy and the United States, the prestige level of their current work does not in any way reveal their level of educational training. Most of my interviewees had acquired some years of post secondary training in the Philippines. In Rome, my interviewees include 23 women with college degrees, 12 with some years of college or post secondary vocational training, and 7 who completed high school. In Los Angeles, my interviewees include 11 women with college diplomas, 8 with some years of college or post secondary vocational training, and 5 with high school degrees. Even with a high level of educational attainment, Filipina women migrate and enter domestic work because they still earn higher wages as domestic workers in postindustrial nations than as professional workers in the Philippines. . . .

REPRODUCTIVE LABOR IN SENDING AND
RECEIVING NATIONS

Migrant Filipina domestic workers depart from a system of gender stratification in the Philippines only to enter another one in the advanced capitalist and industrialized countries of the United States and Italy. In both sending and receiving nations, they confront societies with similar gender ideologies concerning the division of labor in the family; that is, reproductive labor is relegated to women. Yet, in the receiving nation of either Italy or the United States, racial, class, and citizenship inequalities aggravate the position of migrant Filipinas as women. . . . Nakano Glenn's (1992) formulation of the racial division of reproductive labor suggests that the demand for low-wage service workers, particularly domestic workers, arises not solely from the concentration of highly specialized professional services in global cities, as Sassen has argued correctly, but also from persisting gender inequalities in the families of these professionals. To fully consider the politics of reproductive labor in the migration of Filipina domestic workers, I now expand and reformulate the concept of the racial division of reproductive labor by placing it in a transnational setting. In doing so, I situate the increasing demand for paid reproductive labor in receiving nations in the context of the globalization of the market economy.

Globalization has triggered the formation of a singular market economy. As such, production activities in one area can no longer be understood solely from a local perspective. Likewise, I argue that reproduction activities, especially as they have been increasingly commodified, have to be situated in the context of this singular market economy. In this sense, I insist that reproduction activities in one area have concrete ties to reproduction activities in another area. With the feminization of wage labor, global capitalism is forging the creation of links among distinct systems of gender inequality. Moreover, the migration of women connects systems of gender inequality in both sending and receiving nations to global capitalism. All of these processes occur in the formation of the international division of reproductive labor.

This division of labor places Nakano Glenn's (1992) "racial division of reproductive labor" in an international context under the auspices of Saskia Sassen's discussion of the incorporation of women from developing countries into the global economy. It is a transnational division of labor that is shaped simultaneously by global capitalism, gender inequality in the sending country, and gender inequality in the receiving country. This division of labor determines the migration and entrance into domestic service of women from the Philippines.

The international transfer of caretaking is a distinct form of the international division of labor in which Filipina domestic workers perform the reproductive labor or the "private sphere" responsibilities of class-privileged women in industrialized countries as they leave other women in the Philippines to perform their own. This international division of labor refers to a three-tier transfer of reproductive labor among women in two nation-states. These groups of women are (1) middle-class women in receiving countries, (2) migrant Filipina domestic workers, and (3) Filipina domestic workers in the Philippines who are too poor to migrate.

Under the international transfer of caretaking, women's migration from the Philippines is embedded in the process of global capitalism. At the same time, gender is also a central factor of their migration. The process of migration for women involves escaping their gender roles in the Philippines, easing the gender constraints of the women who employ them in industrialized countries, and finally relegating their gender roles to women left in the Philippines.[1]

The international transfer of caretaking refers to a social, political, and economic relationship between women in the global labor market. This division of labor is a structural relationship based on the class, race, gender, and (nation-based) citizenship of women. In the international transfer of caretaking, Filipina domestic workers do not just ease the entrance of other women into the paid labor force but also assist in the economic growth of receiving countries. Patricia Licuanan (1994, p. 109), in reference to households in Hong Kong and Singapore, explains,

> Households are said to have benefited greatly by the import of domestic workers. Family income has increased because the wife and other women members of working age are freed from domestic chores and are able to join the labor force. This higher income would normally result in the enlargement of the consumer market and greater demand on production and consequently a growth in the economy.

In the article "Economy Menders," Linda Layosa (1995, p. 7), the editor of the transnational monthly magazine *Tinig Filipino*, describes the international transfer of caretaking:

> Indeed, our women have partially been liberated from the anguish of their day-to-day existence with their families and from economic problems, only to be enslaved again in the confines of another home, most of the time trampling their rights as human beings. . . . We have to face the reality that many of our women will be compelled to leave the confines of their own tidy bedrooms and their spotless kitchens only to clean another household, to mend other's torn clothes, and at the same time mend our tattered economy.

In her description, she falls short of mentioning who takes up the household work that migrant Filipina domestic workers abandon upon migration. Most likely, they are other female relatives, but also less privileged Filipina women, women unable to afford the high costs of seeking employment outside of the Philippines. Thus, migrant Filipina domestic workers are in the middle of the three-tier hierarchy of the international transfer of caretaking.

The case of Carmen Ronquillo provides a good illustration of the international transfer of caretaking.[2] Carmen is simultaneously a domestic worker of a professional woman in Rome and an employer of a domestic worker in the Philippines. Carmen describes her relationship to each of these two women:

> When coming here, I mentally surrendered myself and forced my pride away from me to prepare myself. But I lost a lot of weight. I was not used to the work. You see, I had maids in the Philippines. I have a maid in the Philippines that has worked for me since my daughter was born twenty-four years ago. She is still with me. I paid her three hundred pesos before and now I pay her one thousand pesos.

> I am a little bit luckier than others because I run the entire household. My employer is a divorced woman who is an architect. She does not have time to run her household so I do all the shopping. I am the one budgeting. I am the one cooking. [Laughs.] And I am the one cleaning too. She has a 24- and 26-year-old. The older one graduated already and is an electrical engineer. The other one is taking up philosophy. They still live with her. . . . She has been my only employer. I stayed with her because I feel at home with her. She never commands. She never orders me to do this and to do that.

The hierarchical and interdependent relationship between Carmen, her employer in Italy, and her domestic worker in the Philippines forms from the unequal development of industrialized and developing countries in transnational capitalism, class differences in the Philippines, and the relegation of reproductive labor to women. The case of Carmen Ronquillo clearly exemplifies how three distinct groups of women participate in the international transfer of caretaking. While Carmen frees her employer (the architect) of domestic responsibilities, a lower paid domestic worker does the household work for Carmen and her family.

Wage differences of domestic workers illuminate the economic disparity among nations in transnational capitalism. A domestic worker in Italy such as Carmen could receive U.S. $1,000 per month for her labor:

> I earn 1,500,000 lira (U.S. $1,000) and she pays for my benefits (e.g., medical coverage). On Sundays, I have a part-time (job), I clean her office in the morning and

she pays me 300,000 lira (U.S. $200). I am very fortunate because she always gives me my holiday pay (August) and my thirteenth month pay in December. Plus, she gives me my liquidation pay at the end of the year. Employers here are required to give you a liquidation pay—equivalent to your monthly salary for every year you worked for them, but they usually give it to you when you leave but she insists on paying me at the end of the year. So, in December, I always receive 5,400,000 lira (U.S. $3,600).

The wages of Carmen easily afford her a domestic worker in the Philippines, who, on average, only earns the below-poverty wage of U.S. $40 per month. Moreover, the domestic worker in the Philippines, in exchange for her labor, does not receive the additional work benefits Carmen receives for the same labor, for example, medical coverage. Not surprisingly, migrant Filipina domestic workers, as shown by their high level of educational attainment, tend to have more resources and belong in a more comfortable class stratum than do domestic workers in the Philippines. Such resources often enable Carmen and other migrant Filipina women to afford the option of working outside of the country.

THE OVERLOOKED PARTICIPANTS: CHILDREN AND WOMEN IN THE PHILIPPINES

The private world remains devalued, as poor people become the wives and mothers of the world, cleaning the toilets and raising the children. The devaluing of certain work, of nurturance, of private "domestic" work, remains: rearing children is roughly on a par—certainly in terms of salary—with cleaning the toilet. (Katz Rothman 1989, p. 252)

While the devaluation of "rearing children" could be lamented as a tragedy for children, the experiences of the different groups of children (and elderly) in the international transfer of caretaking should be distinguished between those who remain cared for and those who are not and those who regularly see their parents/children and those who cannot. The fact that "rearing children is roughly on a par ... with cleaning the toilet" means that migrant Filipina domestic workers usually cannot afford the higher costs of maintaining a family in industrialized countries due to their meager wages. In the United States, where people of color have traditionally been caregivers and domestic workers for white families, mothering is diverted away from people of color families. Sau-ling Wong (1994, p. 69) defines *diverted mothering* to be the process in which the "time and energy available for mothering are diverted from those who, by kinship or communal ties, are their more rightful recipients." Historically, a married Black domestic worker in the

United States "typically saw her children once every two weeks, leaving them in the care of the husband or older siblings, while remaining on call around the clock for the employer's children" (Wong 1994, p. 71). Now, in an international context, the same pattern of diverted mothering could be described for Filipina, Latina, and Caribbean domestic workers as many are forced to leave their children behind in the country of origin (Colen 1995; Hondagneu-Sotelo and Avila 1997).[3] The question then is, Who cares for these "other" children?

In the Philippines, it is unusual for fathers to nurture and care for their children, but, considering that not all migrant Filipina domestic workers hire domestic workers, some are forced to give in to the renegotiations of household division of labor led by the migration of their wives. Other female relatives often take over the household work of migrant Filipinas. In these cases, non-egalitarian relations among family members should be acknowledged considering that for female family members left in the Philippines, "the mobility they might achieve through migration is severely curtailed" (Basch, Glick Schiller, and Szanton Blanc 1994, p. 241). However, hired domestic workers—a live-in housekeeper or *labandera* (laundry woman who hand washes clothes)—also free migrant Filipina domestics of their household labor. Almost all of my interviewees in both Rome and Los Angeles hire domestic workers in the Philippines. This should not be surprising considering that the average wage of domestics in the Philippines is considerably less than the average wage of migrant domestics.

In discussions of the international division of (productive) labor, women who cannot afford to work as domestic workers in other countries are equated with those who do so. For example, migrant Filipina domestic workers and female low-wage workers in the Philippines are considered to be equally displaced in global capitalism. Maya Areza, who dreams of retiring in the Philippines after a few more years in the United States, reminds us of the structural inequalities characterizing relations among women in developing countries when she states,

> When I retire I plan to go home for good. I plan to stay at my parents' house. . . . I would just lounge and smoke. I will get a domestic helper who I can ask to get my cigarettes for me. . . . My children and my cousins all have domestic workers. You can hire one if you have money. It's cheap, only one thousand pesos ($40). Here, you earn $1,000 doing the same kind of work you would do for one thousand pesos there! I won't have a problem with hiring one.

Because migrant Filipina domestic workers are usually in the middle of the hierarchical chain of caretaking, they maintain unequal relations with less privileged women in the Philippines. Under the international transfer of caretaking, the unequal economic standing of nation-states and discrepancies in monetary currencies are prominent factors that distinguish the position of female low-wage workers in advanced, capitalist, and developing countries. They differentiate, for example, the position of domestic workers in the United States and Italy from domestic workers in the Philippines. Migrant Filipina domestic workers surely take advantage of these differences in wages and maintain a direct hierarchical relationship with the domestic workers whom they hire in the Philippines. In the international transfer of caretaking, domestic workers (e.g., housekeepers and laundry women) hired by families of domestic workers abroad are the truly subaltern women.

THE SOCIAL CONSEQUENCES OF "BEING IN THE MIDDLE"

So far, I have established the formation of the international division of reproductive labor. As a structural process that determines the migration of Filipina domestic workers, this division of labor also results in particular social consequences that are embodied in the lived experience of its participants. In this section, I illuminate the social consequences of "being in the middle" of this division of labor. The process in which reproductive labor is transferred to migrant Filipinas is not as smooth as it sounds. For many, the process involves multiple contradictions in their positions in the family and the labor market.

To illuminate the consequences of "being in the middle," I return to the story of Carmen Ronquillo. Before migrating to Rome, Carmen, who is in her mid-40s, had worked for 15 years as a project manager of the military food services at Clark Air Force Base. With the closure of this U.S. military base in 1992, Carmen thought that she could not find a job that offered a comparably lucrative income in the Philippines. Therefore, Carmen decided to follow her sister to Rome, where she could earn much more as a domestic worker than as a professional in the Philippines. Seeking employment in Italy was a huge investment for her family. Carmen paid an agency U.S. $5,000 to enter Italy without a visa. The high costs of migration from the Philippines suggest that this option is usually limited to those with financial means. Consequently, labor migration for Carmen and the many other middle-class women who can afford to leave the Philippines usually entails the emotional strains brought by their downward mobility to the lower status job of domestic work. As Carmen describes,

> My life is difficult here. Would you believe that here I am a "physical laborer"?
> When I was working in the Philippines, I was the one supervising the supervisors.
> [Laughs.] So, when I came here, especially when I cleaned the bathrooms, I would
> talk to myself. [Laughs hysterically.] I would commend and praise myself, telling

myself, "Oh, you clean the corners very well." [Laughs.] You see, in my old job, I would always check the corners first, that was how I checked if my workers had cleaned the place well. So, sometimes I would just cry. I felt like I was slapped in the face. I resent the fact that we cannot use our skills especially because most of us Filipinos here are professionals. We should be able to do other kinds of work because if you only do housework, your brain deteriorates. Your knowledge deteriorates. Your whole being is that of a maid.

As reflected in the bitter attitude of Carmen toward domestic work, a central contradiction of being in the middle of the international transfer of caretaking is the experience of *conflicting class mobility*. For migrant Filipinas, domestic work simultaneously involves an increase and decrease in class status. They earn more than they ever would have if they had stayed as professional women in the Philippines. Yet, at the same time, they experience a sharp decline in occupational status and face a discrepancy between their current occupation and actual training. For the women "in the middle," this discrepancy highlights the low status of domestic work.

Vanessa Dulang, an office worker in the Philippines and domestic worker in Rome since 1990, describes the gains and losses that migrant women such as herself incur from the limited labor market option of either staying in the Philippines or working as a domestic outside of the country:

Life is hard in the Philippines. You don't earn enough. Nothing will happen to you if you stay there. Even though you are a maid here, at least you are earning money. What I couldn't buy in the Philippines, I could buy here. . . . But work is difficult. You bend your back scrubbing. You experience what you would never experience in the Philippines. In the Philippines, your work is light but you don't have any money. Here you make money, but your body is exhausted.

In the spatial politics of globalization—unequal development of regions—the achievement of material security in the Philippines entails the experience of downward mobility in other countries. According to Basch, Glick Schiller, and Szanton Blanc (1994, p. 234), this decline in social status in migration generally pushes migrants to build "de-territorialized national identities." They cope with their marginal status in the receiving country by basing their identities on the increase in their class status in the country of origin. In the same vein, migrant Filipina domestic workers resolve their conflicting class mobility by stressing their higher social and class status in the Philippines. They do just that by hiring their very own domestic workers or perceiving themselves as rightful beneficiaries of servitude. In this way, they are able to mitigate their loss of status in migration. As Joy Manlapit of Los Angeles tells me,

When I go back, I want to experience being able to be my own boss in the house. I want to be able to order someone to make me coffee, to serve me food. That is good. That is how you can take back all the hardships you experienced before. That is some thing you struggled for.

Gloria Yogore, her counterpart in Rome, finds similar comfort in the knowledge of the higher social status she occupies and will occupy once she returns to the Philippines:

In the Philippines, I have maids. When I came here, I kept on thinking that in the Philippines, I have maids and here I am one. I thought to myself that once I go back to the Philippines, I will not lift my finger and I will be the *signora*. [Laughs.] My hands will be rested and manicured and I will wake up at 12 o'clock noon.

Ironically, migrant Filipina domestic workers find comfort from the contradiction of the simultaneous decline and increase in their class background by stressing the greater privilege that they have and will have in relation to poorer women in the Philippines.

Another consequence of being in the middle is the experience of the *pain of family separation*. Being in the middle is contingent on being part of a transnational household, meaning a household whose members are located in two or more nation-states. Among my interviewees, 41 of 46 women in Rome and 20 of 26 women in Los Angeles maintain such households. I placed my interviewees categorically under this type of household structure on the basis that their remittances sustain the day-to-day living expenses of their immediate and extended families in the Philippines. Almost all of the never-married single women without children in my sample (14 in Rome and 6 in Los Angeles) are, in fact, part of transnational households. Notably, only 1 single woman does not send remittances to the Philippines regularly.

Emotional strains of transnational family life include feelings of loss, guilt, and loneliness for the mothers and daughters working as domestics in other countries. Plagued by the *pain of family separation*, women like Carmen struggle with the emotional strains of family separation in their daily lives:

My son, whenever he writes me, he always draws the head of Fido the dog with tears on the eyes. Whenever he goes to mass on Sundays, he tells me that he misses me more because he sees his friends with their mothers. Then, he comes home and cries. He says that he does not want his father to see him crying so he locks himself in his room. When I think of them [her children] is when I feel worst about being here. I was very, very close to my two children. . . . Whenever I think of my children, I am struck with this terrible loneliness.

Being in the middle of the international division of reproductive labor entails geographical distance in families and consequently emotional strains for "lonely" mothers and "miserable" children in the Philippines.

Another contradiction of being in the middle of the international division of reproductive labor or the international transfer of caretaking is the fact that women in the middle must care for someone else's grandchildren, children, or parents while unable to care for their own. In contrast to the two other social consequences that I have previously described, this is not unique to the transnational situation of migrant domestic workers. It has been observed in the United States with non-migrant domestics (Katzman 1978). However, it does reflect one of the structural constraints faced by Filipina domestic workers in the process of globalization: The choice of maximizing their earnings as transnational low-wage workers denies them the intimacy of the family. Thus, care giving is made a more painful experience. As Christina Manansala, a domestic worker in Rome since 1990, states, "Of course it is hard to take care of other children. Why should I be taking care of other children when I cannot take care of my own child myself?" Another domestic worker in Rome adds,

> Sometimes when I look at the children that I care for, I feel like crying. I always think about how if we did not need the money, we would all be together and I would be raising my children myself. (Analin Mahusay, children are three and five years old)

The pain of care giving leads to another contradiction and that is the experience of *displaced mothering* or more generally, *displaced caretaking*, which is also a social consequence that is not unique to the international division of reproductive labor.

Unable to take care of their own families, migrant Filipina domestic workers, like the non-migrant domestics forced into "diverted mothering" in the United States, find themselves needing to "pour [their] love" to their wards. As Vicky Diaz, a mother in Los Angeles who left five children between the ages of 2 and 10 years old in the Philippines 10 years ago, describes her relationship to her ward, "The only thing you can do is give all your love to the child. In my absence from my children, the most I could do with my situation is give all my love to that child." Trinidad Borromeo of Rome finds similar comfort from "pouring her love" to her elderly ward, "When I take care of an elderly, I treat her like she is my own mother." Notably, some women develop an aversion to care giving, like Ruby Mercado of Rome, who states, "I do not like taking care of children when I could not take care of my own children. It hurt too much." However, most of my interviewees do indeed feel less guilt for leaving behind their families in the Philippines when caring for and "pouring [their] love" to another family. Ironically, as mothering is transferred to domestic workers, those without children, such as Jerrisa Lim of Los Angeles, begin to feel that they know what it is like to mother: "After doing child care, I feel like I experienced what it is like to be a mother. It is hard to have children. There are pleasures that go with it. That is true. But it is hard." The idea that domestic work involves the act of "pouring love" suggests that a certain degree of emotional bonds to dependents in the family, including children and elderly persons, are passed down in the transfer of caretaking. By operating in the realm of emotion, the commodification of caretaking is further heightened in globalization.

CONCLUSION

The hierarchy of womanhood—based on race, class, and nation—establishes a work transfer system of reproductive labor among women—the international transfer of caretaking. It is a distinct form of transnational division of labor that links women in an interdependent relationship. Filipina domestic workers perform the reproductive labor of more privileged women in industrialized countries as they relegate their reproductive labor to poorer women left in the Philippines. The international division of reproductive labor shows us that production is not the sole means by which international divisions of labor operate in the global economy. Local economies are not solely linked by the manufacturing production of goods. In globalization, the transfer of reproductive labor moves beyond territorial borders to connect separate nation-states. The extension of reproductive labor to a transnational terrain is embedded in the operation of transnational families and the constant flow of resources from migrant domestic workers to the families that they continue to support in the Philippines. While acting as the primary income earners of their families, migrant Filipina domestic workers hire poorer domestic workers to perform the household duties that are traditionally relegated to them as women. In this way, they continue to remain responsible for the reproductive labor in their families but at the same time, as migrant workers, take on the responsibility of productive labor.

The formulation of the international division of reproductive labor treats gender as a central analytical lens for understanding the migration of Filipina domestic workers. It shows that the movement of Filipina domestic workers is embedded in a gendered system of transnational capitalism. While forces of global capitalism spur the labor migration of Filipina domestic workers, the demand for their labor also results from gender inequities in receiving nations, specifically the relegation of reproductive labor to women. This transfer of labor strongly suggests that despite their increasing rate of labor market participation, women continue to remain responsible for reproductive labor in both sending and receiving countries. At both ends of the migratory stream, they have not been able to negotiate directly with male counterparts for a fairer division of household work but instead have had to rely on their race and/or class privilege by participating in the transnational transfer of gender constraints to less-privileged women.

Ironically, women in industrialized (Western) countries are often assumed to be more liberated than women are in developing countries. Yet, many women are able to pursue careers as their male counterparts do because disadvantaged migrant women and other women of color are stepping into their old shoes and doing their household work for them. As women transfer their reproductive labor to less and less privileged women, we can see that the traditional division of labor in the patriarchal nuclear household has not been significantly renegotiated in various countries in the world. This is one of the central reasons why there is a need for Filipina domestic workers in more than 100 countries today.

NOTES

1. Notably, in the Philippines, older (female) children, not fathers, are more likely to look after younger siblings while their mothers work (Chant and McIlwaine 1995). In addition, daughters are traditionally expected to care for aging parents.

2. I use pseudonyms to protect the anonymity of my informants.

3. In most other receiving nations, migrant Filipinos are deterred from family migration by their relegation to the status of temporary migrants or their ineligibility for family reunification (Constable 1997).

REFERENCES

Asis, Maruja M. B. (1992). The overseas employment program policy. In *Philippine labor migration: Impact and policy*, edited by G. Battistella and A. Paganoni. Quezon City, Philippines: Scalabrini Migration Center.

Basch, Linda, Nina Glick Schiller, and Christina Szanton Blanc. (1994). *Nations unbound: Transnational projects, post colonial predicaments, and deterritorialized nation-states*. Langhorne, PA: Gordon and Breach.

Brenner, Johanna, and Barbara Laslett. (1991). Gender, social reproduction and women's self-organization: Considering the U.S. welfare state. *Gender & Society* 5 (3): 311–33.

Campani, Giovanna. (1993). Immigration and racism in southern Europe: The Italian case. *Ethnic and Racial Studies* 16 (3): 507–35.

Caritas di Roma. (1995). *Immigrazione. Dossierstatistico '95*. Roma: Anterem Edizioni Ricerca.

Catholic Institute for International Relations [CIIR]. (1987). *The labour trade: Filipino migrant workers around the globe*. London: Catholic Institute for International Relations.

Chant, Sylvia, and Cathy McIlwaine. (1995). *Women of a lesser cost: Female labour, foreign exchange and Philippine development*. London: Pluto.

Colen, Shellee. (1995). "Like a mother to them": Stratified reproduction and West Indian child care workers and employers in New York. In *Conceiving the new world order: The global politics of reproduction*, edited by F. D. Ginsburg and R. Rapp. Berkeley: University of California Press.

Constable, Nicole. (1997). *Maid to order in Hong Kong: Stories of Filipina workers*. Ithaca, NY: Cornell University Press.

Hondagneu-Sotelo, Pierrette, and Ernestine Avila. (1997). "I'm here, but I'm there": The meanings of Latina transnational motherhood. *Gender & Society* 11 (5): 548–71.

Katz Rothman, Barbara. (1989). *Recreating motherhood: Ideology and technology in a patriarchal society*. New York: Norton.

Katzman, David M. (1978). *Seven days a week: Women and domestic service in industrializing America*. New York: Oxford University Press.

Layosa, Linda. (1995). Economy menders. *Tinig Filipino*, June 7.

Licuanan, Patricia. (1994). The socio-economic impact of domestic worker migration: Individual, family, community, country. In *The trade in domestic workers: Causes, mechanisms, and consequences of international migration,* edited by N. Heyzer, G. Lycklama á Nijeholt, and N. Weerakoon. London: Zed.

Nakano Glenn, Evelyn. (1992). From servitude to service work: The historical continuities of women's paid and unpaid reproductive labor. *Signs: Journal of Women in Culture and Society* 18 (1): 1–44.

Portes, Alejandro, and Rubén Rumbaut. (1996). *Immigrant America: A portrait.* 2nd ed. Berkeley: University of California Press.

Rosca, Ninotchka. (1995). The Philippines' shameful export. *The Nation* 260 (15): 522–27.

Sassen, Saskia. (1984). Notes on the incorporation of Third World women into wage labor through immigration and off shore production. *International Migration Review* 18 (4): 1144–67.

———. (1988). *The mobility of labor and capital: A study in international investment and labor.* New York: Cambridge University Press.

———. (1994). *Cities in a world economy.* Thousand Oaks, CA: Pine Forge Press.

Wong, Sau-ling. (1994). Diverted mothering: Representations of care givers of color in the age of "multiculturalism." In *Mothering: Ideology, experience, and agency,* edited by E. Glenn, G. Chang, and L. Forcey. New York: Routledge.

5 LABOR RECRUITMENT AND THE LURE OF THE CAPITAL: CENTRAL AMERICAN MIGRANTS IN WASHINGTON, DC

Terry A. Repak

In this excerpt, Terry Repak uses survey and life history data to provide an in-depth account of the gendered processes in both sending and receiving countries through which care labor is recruited. Her focus is on domestic workers from Central America who are aggressively recruited by Washington, DC, elites. Gender is a main factor in the social and economic conditions in sending countries that influence the decision to migrate as well as the reluctance to return.

Since the early 1960s, Washington, DC, has attracted over 200,000 Central Americans—many of them undocumented, and a majority of the original migrants women.[1] The finding that 70 percent of Central American migrants in the 1960s and 1970s were women (Cohen 1980; Repak 1988) evokes a number of insights into gendered patterns in the migration process. One of the major implications of this study is that Latin American migration cannot be understood as a homogeneous entity, as gender-based migrations such as the movement of Central Americans into the Washington area display different causes and consequences from more thoroughly documented Mexican and Dominican cases, among others (Cornelius 1988; Grasmuck and Pessar, 1991; Portes and Bach 1985; Wallace 1986). The migration of Central Americans into the Washington area does not follow ordinary settlement patterns because the initial migrants chose to settle in a city without a large established Latin American population, unlike migrants to cities in California and in Texas (Cornelius 1988; Rodriguez 1987; Wallace 1986).

The life histories recounted in this article illustrate the extent to which gendered labor recruitment and the establishment of gender-based social networks operated as determining factors in the decision to migrate and the eventual choice of destination. In-depth interviews also reveal the unusual degree of autonomy shown by Central American women in the decision-making stages of the migration process. The findings discussed here draw on three primary sources: a pilot sample of fifty Central American men and women, the majority of whom were located through social service agencies in Washington, DC; a larger random survey of 100 Central American households; and interviews with thirty directors and representatives of social service agencies in Washington, DC. The interviews and surveys were conducted from 1988 to 1990. . . .

Washington's development into a "world city," or a point from which global economic activities are coordinated (Sassen-Koob 1986), and the growth and diversification of the local economy since the 1960s resulted in an economic boom that created escalating demands for unskilled and semi-skilled labor. Tight labor market conditions persisted throughout the 1980s, forcing wages well above the minimum wage for entry-level jobs. For example, twice the number of jobs opened up in the Washington area from 1970 to 1980 as the number of people moving into the region and the overall unemployment rate for the metropolitan area reached a low 2.7 percent in May 1988 (Gladwell 1988; Grier 1988; Knight 1988). Throughout the 1980s, Washington had the highest average household income of any major metropolitan area in the country: $50,000 after taxes (Grier 1988). The Washington, DC, area experienced a major labor shortage during this period, despite the massive entry of women into the regional labor force since the early 1970s. Currently, Washington has the nation's highest proportion of women in the workforce at 69 percent, which has created an insatiable demand for day-care providers over the past two decades.

The need for service workers, and particularly for domestics and baby-sitters, became acute with the shift out of these occupations by African American women since the 1960s. Power (1990) found that nationwide 37.5 percent of employed Black women were private household workers in 1960, but by 1989 only 3.5 percent of employed Black women remained in domestic service (p. 1). These women were hardly forced out of domestic service because of the availability of immigrant women who would work for lower wages. Instead, Power (1990) explained that

> Black women have achieved a dramatic improvement in their occupations distribution in the past three decades largely through a movement out of service and into clerical occupations. Among Black women who work full time year round, improved occupational distribution has been reflected in a rapid increase in their median income relative to white women's, increasing from fifty-one percent of white women's income in 1955 to ninety-eight percent in 1975. (p. 2)

Because of its large proportion of women in the workforce, Washington has a high percentage of children under five years of age receiving in-home care (at 11 percent, compared with U.S. census figures of 5.3 percent nationwide). Since informal-sector jobs are generally underreported in census data, the actual figure is probably well above 11 percent.

As news of this surfeit of jobs spread, Washington began to attract refugees and immigrants from all parts of the globe in recent years. By the mid-1980s, the region was home to the second largest group of Salvadorans in the United States (after Los Angeles), the third largest concentration of Central Americans, the fourth largest group of Koreans, and the largest group of Ethiopians outside of Africa (Pressley 1987). Many recent arrivals chose to migrate to Washington because it is the capital city and because news spread rapidly about the favorable job market in the region. But none of the other groups have approached the numbers of Salvadorans and other Central Americans who made their way to Washington over the past three decades.

METHOD

Two principal groups form the basis for this study: a pilot sample of fifty individuals from Central American countries who were located primarily through social service agencies, and a main sample of 100 Central American households that were randomly selected for an extensive survey (although a completely random survey of a largely undocumented population is impossible as Cornelius [1982, p. 5] explained). Fieldwork for the project involved different methods to complement survey data with interviews and ethnographic material.

Lengthy tape-recorded interviews were conducted with informants, and a snowball sampling method was used as initial respondents were asked to suggest the names of relatives or friends who might participate. This method was employed at the onset of the research because of the intention to compare roughly equal numbers of documented with undocumented Central Americans, as well as more recent migrants with earlier arrivals. Aware of the potential pitfalls of drawing conclusions from a nonrandom snowball sample,[2] I used this information primarily to frame the questions for a survey that could be used to gather data from a wider population of Central Americans, and to enrich quantitative data with personal histories. . . . An attempt was made to re-interview as many of these initial informants as possible five years later (in 1993), and two-thirds of them were eventually contacted.

On the basis of information obtained in the pilot sample, the neighborhoods and apartment buildings in the Washington area where Central American families reside were identified for a more random survey of 100 households. Ten apartment buildings or complexes with a high proportion of Central American residents were selected in the District of Columbia and the Maryland and Virginia suburbs. Three Salvadoran research assistants visited the buildings, making several attempts to contact tenants in targeted apartments. Interviewers used a standardized questionnaire written in Spanish that collected detailed background information. The refusal rate was low (approximately 30 percent) most probably because of the presence of interviewers from the same country as the respondents.

REASONS FOR CHOOSING TO LIVE IN WASHINGTON, DC

The following life history aptly illustrates the diverse forces that lured the initial Central American migrants to the Washington area. Rosa Lopes is a Salvadoran woman who worked as a housekeeper for a family from the USAID (U.S. Agency for International Development) when they were stationed in San Salvador. When the family's tour of duty was finished, they invited Rosa to return with them to Washington, DC, to continue working as their housekeeper. The family sponsored Rosa for her green card, and soon she was able to send money to bring her husband Javier to Washington as well. Arriving in the late 1960s, Javier found a job as a tailor in one of Washington's exclusive men's stores. In 1971, Javier and Rosa invited his niece Teresa (who was working as a domestic in San Salvador) to join them in Washington. Another American family that was looking for a housekeeper asked Rosa if she knew of any candidates for the position, and in this way Rosa arranged a job for Teresa. Eventually, after living and working with various families in the Washington suburbs as housekeeper, Teresa moved into her own apartment with a companion.

In 1980, Javier and Rosa learned that two other nieces were having trouble finding work in San Salvador. Maria was forced to abandon her studies when the university was closed by the government as civil war escalated. In all her attempts to secure a job in El Salvador, she was frustrated by the sexual advances and expectations thrust on her by prospective employers. She felt that her opportunities to secure employment without sexual harassment would be better in the United States, even if she had to work as a maid.

Similarly, Carmen lost her job in 1980 when her factory was closed because of increased fighting. Like their cousin Teresa, both Maria and Carmen were single women with few prospects for gainful employment in El Salvador; all three made the decision to migrate without the permission or aid of fathers or spouses. After paying for their passage to the United States, Rosa arranged a job for Maria as a live-in housekeeper with an American family (who agreed to sponsor her for legal residence), and she allowed Carmen to live with her and Javier while she cleaned houses for a year. Carmen found most of her jobs through Rosa's network of friends. Maria invited her fiancé from San Salvador to join her once she became a permanent resident, and Carmen in turn brought her sister (with her three children) and two brothers to Washington. By 1990, thirty-five members of this extended family had made their homes in the Washington area.

As seen in this family history, women were favored in recruitment efforts by Washington's diplomatic and professional families in need of domestics and babysitters. When respondents from my samples were grouped according to the time of their migration, 70 percent of those who came to Washington in the early pre-1980 phase of the Central American migration were women. Close to one-third of the respondents in the pilot sample who went to Washington before 1980 said that they were recruited to work or had jobs arranged from them in that city. This type of recruitment assumed a number of different forms. Lucia Herrera, a single mother who had been abandoned by her partner, was working as a housekeeper for a family from the U.S. State Department stationed in San Salvador. When the family planned their return to Washington, they invited Lucia to work for them there. At the time, Lucia and her daughter were living in her parents' crowded household and Lucia was constantly lectured by her four older brothers on how to raise her daughter. She resolved to remove her young daughter from this oppressive living situation because it allowed them both few opportunities to mold their own futures. Lucia decided to accept the offer to go to the United States for her daughter's sake, against her brothers' advice.

In several other cases, diplomatic families stationed in Washington sent representatives to El Salvador and to Guatemala to recruit women who were willing to take jobs as live-in housekeepers. In one case, a private agency based in New York worked through the U.S. Embassy in San Salvador to recruit a woman who agreed to accept a job as a domestic for a family living in New York in the 1960s (she and her son later moved to Washington). In all but one of the above cases, the women were part of the initial influx of Central American migrants to the Washington area in the 1960s and 1970s. In several other households, women came after 1980 when relatives living in Washington arranged positions for them as live-in housekeepers with professional Washington families. Three women migrated to work for diplomats stationed in Washington after their sisters (who were already working in that city) were asked by employers to contact prospective migrants.

Approximately 20 percent of respondents in the survey sample said that they were recruited by an employer or had a job arranged for them on behalf of an employer in Washington before their migration. . . . However, a large percentage of respondents in the sample were not the first members of their families to migrate and a majority of these respondents arrived in the Washington area after 1980.

The offer of a job in the United States frequently appealed to women seeking better opportunities for themselves and their children, particularly if they had no ties to male partners and if they were responsible for the support of other members of their households. Several women also said that they decided to leave El Salvador to escape partners who were abusive or who wasted money on other women. Others, like Julia Mendez, were desperate to leave El Salvador after they received death threats. Julia related how she was assaulted twice by men who were dressed like soldiers in her province of San Miguel in 1986. Julia's cousin, who had worked for three years for a Salvadoran family living in Washington, gave Julia the address of her former employers, and Julia took it on herself to travel to the U.S. capital alone. She contacted the family her cousin had worked for as soon as she arrived, and they agreed to take her on as their live-in housekeeper. In such cases, employers favored Central American women as domestics, partly because of the proximity of these countries to the United States and because they were recommended through social networks. Increasing economic and cultural ties between the United States and the Central American countries since 1960 (via media and social networks) had allowed the distances between the two regions to shrink.

CONSEQUENCES OF MIGRATIONS IN WHICH WOMEN PREDOMINATE

The most striking feature to emerge from the in-depth interviews with women in the pilot study was the high proportion of women who made the decision to migrate on their own without the collaboration or assistance of male partners or fathers. Twenty-two of the thirty women interviewed said that they did not follow or accompany a male partner when they moved to the United States but migrated on their own or brought a child/children along. Only five of the thirty women were married and accompanied husbands at the time of their migration (two others accompanied fathers and one a male companion). Nearly half of the women were single and migrated to the United States alone, and ten women were single mothers who had been abandoned by their partners or who were divorced (seven brought their children along). Thus, a majority of the Central American women who went to Washington made the decision to migrate on their own accord and with inducements similar to those that drew male migrants to other parts of the United States. This is a marked contrast from earlier Dominican and Mexican migration patterns where women tended to migrate after men to reunite the family (Grasmuck and Pessar 1991; Hondagneu-Sotelo 1992).

Gender lies both at the center of the decision to migrate as well as the reluctance to return, as Pedraza (1991) notes. Studies of Mexican migrants in California as well as Jamaicans and Dominicans in New York found a near unanimous preference among women for permanent settlement in the United States in opposition to men's desire for return migration, as women struggle to maintain the gains they won with migration and employment (Foner 1986; Grasmuck and Pessar 1991; Hondagneu-Sotelo 1992). Few of the Central American men and women interviewed in Washington engaged in this gender struggle over return migration. Because of the high incidence of female-headed households in countries such as El Salvador and Guatemala, Central American women's participation in wage labor was hardly a novelty. Many of the women in the pilot sample migrated to the United States as single women or single mothers specifically to improve their occupational position or earnings. Five years after the initial interviews with the women in the pilot sample were conducted, two-thirds of the respondents were reinterviewed and only two had returned to their country of origin. Half of the women in the pilot sample remain single mothers or single women without children. Among those who are married or living with a male companion, half the women met their partners in the United States and therefore formed or negotiated their roles on their own terms within this "first world" culture. Because of the continuing civil strife in their countries of origin, men and women appear to be in agreement that the circumstances for return migration are less than optimal, particularly for their children.

Several other trends emerge with a migration pattern in which women predominate, along with certain idiosyncrasies that surface due to the fact that many of the early Central American migrants were recruited or invited to the Washington area for specific jobs. Foremost is the fact that the migration pattern appears to result in permanent immigration and settlement. Women who were recruited to work in Washington brought more family members along with them (or eventually sent for them) than male recruits did, and all of the women claimed to have arrived in the United States with legal documents. A majority of them said that they had attained permanent resident status by the time of the interview, an assertion that was verified at the social service agencies where they were interviewed. The respondents in the pilot sample who said that they had been recruited to work in Washington were all young single women (some of them with children) who migrated to the United States legally, brought or sent for family members soon after their arrival, and decided to reside permanently in the United States. The relatives they sent for also migrated to the United States legally, found jobs quickly through the initial migrant's network and became permanent residents. . . .

A focus on gender is essential to understand the link between micro- and macro-forces that propel most international migrations. This is particularly true in the case of the Central American migration to Washington, where gendered labor recruitment of Central American women was necessary to fill the shrinking pool of domestic servants and baby-sitters at a time when increasing numbers of U.S.-born women wished to enter the wage labor force. In the same way that the economic activities of societies and the division of labor are differentiated on the basis of gender, the structural forces attracting women migrants in larger numbers than men to particular labor markets in the United States are inherently gender specific as well.

1. Figures on the number of Central Americans in Washington vary because of the large number of recent and undocumented migrants among them. *The Washington Post* reported in 1987 that an estimated 80,000 Salvadorans alone lived in the District of Columbia, and up to 100,000 more resided in the surrounding suburbs (Pressley 1987). At its annual Festival of American Folklife in 1988, the Smithsonian Institution estimated that approximately 200,000 Salvadorans resided in the metropolitan area. Official figures from the 1990 census counted over 230,000 residents of Hispanic origin in the metropolitan area, but representatives of the city's social service agencies claim that this is an undercount because many undocumented persons refused to respond to the census.

2. As Grasmuck and Pessar (1991) noted, "The snowball sample, being unrepresentative, involves the risk of unrecognized biases in regard to other variables. It is possible, however, to evaluate the overall representativeness of a snowball sample by comparing it on key variables with other representative samples of the subject population" (p. 58).

REFERENCES

Cohen, Lucy. 1980. Stress and coping among Latin American women immigrants. In *Uprooting and development: Dilemmas of coping with modernization*, edited by C. Coelho and P. Ahmed. New York: Plenum.

Cornelius, Wayne. 1982. Interviewing undocumented migrants: Methodological reflections based on fieldwork in Mexico and the United States. UCSD Program for U.S.-Mexican Studies, San Diego.

————. 1988. Los migrantes de la crisis: The changing profile of Mexican labor migration to California in the 1980s. Paper presented at the Conference (1988) on "Population and Work in Regional Settings," El Colegio de Michoacan, Zamora. Michoacan.

Foner, Nancy. 1986. Sex roles and sensibilities: Jamaican women in New York and London. In *International migration: The female experience*, edited by R. Simon and C. Brettell. New Jersey: Rowman and Allanheld.

Gladwell, Malcolm. 1988. Shortage of employees hampers area firms. *The Washington Post*, Business-I, 18 August, p. 1.

Grasmuck, Sherri, and Patricia Pessar. 1991. *Between two islands: Dominican international migration*. Berkeley: University of California Press.

Grier, George. 1988. *Special report: Greater Washington's labor shortage*. Washington, DC: Greater Washington Research Center.

Hondagneu-Sotelo, Pierrette. 1992. Overcoming patriarchal constraints: The reconstruction of gender relations among Mexican immigrant women and men. *Gender & Society* 6:393–415.

Knight, Athelia. 1988. DC on way to full employment. *The Washington Post*, 30 July, p. A-1.

Pedraza, Silvia. 1991. Women and migration: The social consequences of gender. *Annual Review of Sociology* 17:303–25.

Portes, Alejandro, and Robert L. Bach. 1985. *Latin journey: Cuban and Mexican immigrants in the United States*. Berkeley: University of California Press.

Power, Marilyn. 1990. Occupational mobility of Black and white women service workers. Paper presented at the second annual Women's Policy Research Conference, Washington. DC: Institute for Women's Policy Research.

Pressley, Sue Ann. 1987. Area melting pot getting fuller. *The Washington Post*, 13 December, p. A1.

Repak, Terry. 1988. They came on behalf of their children: Central American Migrants in Washington, DC. U.S. Department of Labor Working Paper DO. 3. Washington, DC.

————. Forthcoming. *Waiting on Washington: Central American workers in the nation's capital.* Philadelphia: Temple University Press.

Rodriguez, Nestor. 1987. Undocumented Central Americans in Houston: Diverse populations. *International Migration Review* 21:4–25.

Sassen-Koob, Saskia. 1986. New York City: Economic restructuring and immigration. *Development and Change* 17:85–119.

Wallace, Steven. 1986. Central American and Mexican immigrant characteristics and economic incorporation in California. *International Migration Review* 20:657–71.

6

MULTILATERAL ORGANIZATIONS AND EARLY CHILD CARE AND EDUCATION POLICIES FOR DEVELOPING COUNTRIES

Fúlvia Rosemberg

Translated from Portuguese by Ann Puntch

Fúlvia Rosemberg's historical analysis in this excerpt details how the structural adjustment policies and overall economic agenda of multilateral organizations (which we prefer to designate as supranational organizations) reversed early childcare and education policies in Brazil. These outside influences had a profound impact both on the nature of carework and on the chances for women's advancement.

[C]ontemporary proposals for early child care and education (ECCE) attributed to the process of globalization have existed in underdeveloped countries since the 1970s. These proposals, put forward by multilateral organizations, encourage programs for the children of developing countries with low state investment, low-quality services, and the inadequate remuneration of women's labor. Thus, they reinforce ideologies of traditional family values, which create and sustain the domination of gender, class, race, and age. Multilateral organizations' ECCE guidelines fail to promote equity in socio-economics, gender, and race as they promised to do and, in the majority of cases, result in incomplete, poor-quality ECCE coverage. This, in turn, provokes new processes of exclusion. Up until 1996, public and contracting day care systems in Brazil were maintained independent of official or state regulation or supervision by the social assistance sector. Day care workers— for whom there were a variety of terms, many linked to the domestic sphere, that is, "nanny," "nursemaid," and "attendant"—did not need any prior educational or professional training under this system because their work was identified either as an extension of maternal care or as charitable activity. In contrast, preschool in Brazil has typically been administered in connection with the educational system and has required professional training at least equivalent to that for midlevel teaching. Different from day care centers, preschools functioned only half time, offering little backup for children of working mothers. The preschool teaching profession is composed almost exclusively of women and is poorly remunerated;

it is the worst paid level of the teaching profession in the Brazilian educational system (Rosemberg 2002).

The function of care was not formally recognized in teacher training, only educating small children. A long, uneven, history first led by the women's movement and later by the pro-children and pro-ECCE groups (Pro Day Care Movement 1970–1980 and the Inter-Forum Movement for Child Education) has attempted to build a new conception of ECCE that includes both care and education for small children. The search for this type of integration responds to the political ideal of social equality of gender, class, and race. On one hand, the care of small children as a professional activity requiring previous training, a work contract, salary, and a decent workplace places value on women's work. On the other hand, equalizing day care centers and preschools encourages mothers' participation in the labor market and also the well-being of small children. This is especially the case for those who use public services, since the division of the systems (of day care separate from preschool) has historically meant maintaining two different services: for the poor, day care of lower quality than preschool and for the more affluent and wealthy, better-quality services.

In the following . . . analysis, [I consider] two significant periods of multilateral influence on ECCE policy in Brazil and the consequences of these interventions in dramatically altering ECCE programs with important implications for women and carework.

In Brazil, several authors have shown how the demand for ECCE constituted a cause to which different factions of the women's and feminist movements rallied in the 1970s and 1980s, especially those linked to the Catholic Church, the Left political parties, academics, and consciousness-raising groups (Campos, Rosemberg, and Ferreira 1992). At the same time, the Brazilian feminist movement played a fundamental role in building a concept of ECCE as a right of (and not benevolence toward) working mothers and small children. The process of establishing contemporary Brazilian ECCE, however, could not manage to write its own national history since it suffered strong pressure from multilateral organizations, which found national allies (including governments).

Developed countries have been able to construct their own history with little outside interference. They constitute the majority stockholders in the multilateral organizations and exert pressures rather than suffering them. The history of contemporary ECCE policies in the developing countries is quite different. In addition to their marked internal economic inequalities (which maintain a large number of women as domestic employees who provide care for small children), they have experienced strong outside pressure, largely from multinational organizations. In Brazil in the 1970s, this influence came especially from the United Nations Educational, Scientific, and Cultural Organization (UNESCO) and UNICEF, organizations that developed and disseminated the non-formal or community-based model for child care and education, that is, low-cost public investment including the use of voluntary or semi-voluntary (low-paid) work by women without professional training. . . .

FINDINGS

The following research findings are organized into two periods: the earlier UNICEF and UNESCO proposals for ECCE in developing countries and the contemporary World Bank proposals. . . .

UNICEF AND UNESCO PROPOSALS FOR ECCE IN DEVELOPING COUNTRIES: 1970 TO 1985

The new concept of ECCE, developed and proposed by UNESCO/UNICEF, reached Brazil between 1965 and 1972, during a period of military dictatorship when ECCE coverage was reduced and concentrated in the private sector. At the time, there was little academic discussion or national debate and, therefore, no possibility of questioning or perfecting the model that was being disseminated by the multilateral organizations and adopted by the federal government.[1] More important, the local community had no experience with ECCE, and the percentage of Brazilians who had used ECCE programs was insignificant. Since the model did not include specialized professional training for teachers and had adopted the ideology that any woman could care for and educate children in organized programs, services were expanded without adding new national competence for this massive endeavor. The recognized model of an institution for children was that of a poor quality elementary school centered on the female teacher. Thus, in Brazil's pedagogical plan, the model for ECCE came from a (stereo)type of the traditional, impoverished elementary school.

The data available for the period show substantial increases in the first ECCE enrollment in 1983 and 1984. . . . Especially in the Northeast, states extended enrollment, mainly to children older than six, by using the labor of female teachers who were not educated for the task and who received low wages. . . . The expansion placed older children in ECCE programs—children who, according to the constitution, should have been in elementary school. Second, the expansion was made possible due to the work of unqualified women teachers whose low salaries reduced public investment. This process of inclusion and exclusion needs to be noted, paying attention to the complex dynamic of gender subordination and social and racial discrimination that left marks on the profile of Brazilian children attending ECCE programs.

Together with the entry of 397,739 new first enrollments in 1984, more than 14,528 teaching positions requiring less than secondary-level training (the level of school training for preschool and elementary schoolteachers) were created in the ECCE system. . . . Not only did unqualified teachers absorb the increased enrollments in ECCE during this period but the impact of this model is evident in the almost continuous increase in ECCE educators with only a primary-level education. . . . The failure to professionalize the teacher corps in ECCE was accompanied by the inverse phenomenon in elementary teaching. In 1985, 14.4 percent of elementary school teachers had not completed professional education; in 1987, this number fell to 11 percent, and it reached 10.3 percent in 1993. Thus, the devaluing of ECCE seems to be accompanied by a trend (although weak) to upgrade elementary teaching. ECCE programs admit and retain children with the highest rates of exclusion from elementary education, that is, poor and Black children. Joining these two observations leads me to the main analytic conclusion for this period. ECCE in Brazil does not perform only the functions consigned to it in developed countries (to care for and educate small children). Rather, it took on a new one: that of being a poor alternative to elementary education, retaining poor and Black children who would be candidates for repetition in the early grades of compulsory education. Here, we are very far from sharing a global vision of ECCE. But among developing countries, we do share the same experience: poor ECCE for poor children.

I would argue that importing the low-cost ECCE model to Brazilians had a nefarious impact: gender inequality as well as race and class exclusion. In basing itself on the principle of women's hidden ability to be child caretakers and educators, the low-cost model employed women who had a very particular repertory for what ECCE would be. The model available to them was the school they had known as children, which many of them had abandoned. Brazilian ECCE came to be, in many cases, an anticipation of obligatory schooling, even proposing to teach children literacy in addition to keeping them in a protected space for a certain period. This impoverished model of ECCE penetrated the poorest regions with the aim of compensating for deficiencies. These poorest regions of Brazil, defined as priorities, are also those in which the proportion of Blacks is high. Thus, Brazilian ECCE results in the exclusion of young, elementary-age children. In addition, the model does not support the right of mothers to work, demonstrated by the lack of vacancies for infants (considered to be expensive care) or for full-time care.

Furthermore, this non-formal model exploits female teachers in multiple ways: It pays them low wages, it fails to invest in their professional training, it offers a precarious work environment, and it offers obstacles to unionization and building a professional career.

In the 1990s, the World Bank entered the scene, reviving the old proposals of UNESCO.

THE ENTRY OF THE WORLD BANK: 1990 TO PRESENT

The end of the Brazilian dictatorship in 1985 was followed by an intense period of social mobilization in the context of designing a new constitution. The women's movement and the "pro-Constitution children's movement" participated in this mobilization (Campos, Rosemberg, and Ferreira 1992; Rosemberg 1999). These social movements developed a proposal for the constitution to recognize ECCE, which was approved in 1988. During this period, multilateral organizations had little interest or activity in the area of Brazilian ECCE. UNESCO was directing its activities more toward Africa (Rosemberg 1998), UNICEF was giving visibility to new themes such as "street children" and "child prostitution" (Black 1996; Rosemberg and Andrade 1999), and education had not yet become a priority for the World Bank (Torres 1996).[2] After the constitution was adopted, a new team with a proposal for a new national ECCE policy occupied the ECCE office in the Ministry of Education. Its proposal departed from the low-cost model, taking on the goal of expanding coverage with quality of service (Brazil / Ministry of Education 1993, 21).

Among the seven directives contained in this proposal, two stand out: (1) that there be equality between day care centers and preschools, both having the function of caring for and educating small children as an expression of children's right to education and the protection of maternal work, and (2) the proposal for equivalent educational training at the high school and university levels for day care and preschool teachers. The implementation of these proposals was interrupted in 1994 by a new federal government (of Fernando Henrique Cardoso), which incorporated the guidelines of the International Monetary Fund into its plan for economic and social policy, especially educational policies, influenced by the World Bank (Tommasi, Warde, and Haddad 1996). . . .

The World Bank established that resources should be concentrated on primary education, arguing that the rates of return on public investment in primary education will be higher than at other levels of instruction (Coraggio 1996). Following these directives, Brazilian educational reforms of the 1990s targeted social spending away from secondary education and ECCE, decentralized education, privatized education by creating a consumer market for educational services, and deregulated it in the sense of the federal government's "letting go" of the process of education (Haddad 1998, 48–49). With respect to elementary education and ECCE, this has meant municipal financing and management with control over the product through national curricula and the evaluation of results. Investing in elementary education resulted in a decrease in the rate at which ECCE programs were being established, especially the educational training of child educators. It also meant reducing federal resources destined for ECCE, which was reflected in the fact that there was almost no increase in the rates of attendance during the period from 1995 to 1999 (Rosemberg 2002).

The World Bank entered the ECCE arena beginning in the late 1980s.[3] Its specific line of action was called early child development. Since the World Bank was focusing on developing countries with the expectation of developing a massive service, it adopted proposals for non-formal and low-cost programs such as those UNESCO and UNICEF had proposed in earlier decades, practically without alteration. And just as had happened with UNESCO and UNICEF, the low-cost models were not only seen as non-problematic but they were elevated to the level of an ideal model, often supported by arguments of respect for national, local, and cultural diversity. Thus, what is good for developed countries is not good for developing countries.

How does this translate into recommendations? One excerpt from a book by Mary Eming Young (1996, p. 40), the World Bank senior public health specialist on ECCE, provides an answer:

> Expenses for early child development programs can be divided among the following needs: Site. Center-based programs have been estimated in some studies to cost up to five times as much as preschool programs in private homes, even where minimal home improvement costs are reimbursed. Any home that can provide a safe space, minimum sanitation facilities, and a kitchen is sufficient.

Young proposed family day care for the expansion of services to poor children, one of the forms of work that most reinforces gender subordination (Mozère 1998). Thus, on one hand, early child development programs proposed by the World Bank are presented as levers to overcome gender domination (by allowing mothers to work outside the home). On the other hand, early child development programs base themselves on gender subordination in proposing family day care as a model for expanding the offer.

The Brazilian government incorporated a perspective very similar to this in its first version of the National Plan for Education (*Plano Nacional de Educação*) developed after the vote on the new national law for education (in 1996). This plan takes a giant step backward by defining different goals for day care centers and preschools, a throwback to the historical dichotomy of day care for the poor: preschool for the rich. It defends keeping children younger than three in the home environment and advocates "non-formal" programs destined to create conditions for these children to remain in the family (Brazil/Ministry of Education 1997, p. 15). In other words, this Ministry of Education document welcomes programs that train mothers who stay at home caring for and educating their children, instead of center-based ECCE. This perspective is still more clearly formulated in the party platform of the president of the republic for the 1998 electoral campaign, which returned him to office:

> One should not underestimate the capacity of mothers of families, even those with little schooling, to do many day care tasks themselves, if they are carefully oriented. For this reason, no country intends to universalize day care for children, on the contrary, remaining with their mothers has been encouraged by support programs and maternal child care guidelines. (Partido Social Democrata Brasileiro 1998, p. 78)

As we have seen, programs of this type present at least three kinds of negative impacts on women's autonomy: They make it difficult for working mothers of small children to participate in the labor market; they encourage the continuation of domestic employees working in the home to care for the children of working mothers, the worst paid and most stigmatized work in Brazil; and they discourage the professional development of ECCE teachers.

The Ministry of Education guidelines, strongly influenced by the orientation of the World Bank, met with a coalition of academics, unionists, and other professionals who were prepared, mobilized, and living under a democratic regime. So the debate about ECCE and other areas of education was, and continues to be, intense (ANPEd 1998). We managed to win this battle; the present national plan for education has been reformulated. Now, however, a new danger has been spotted. The Inter-American Development Bank has become interested in ECCE in developing countries. Its new proposal for Brazil is anxiously awaited.

This Brazilian case study illustrates the gendered impact of the pressure of multilateral organizations in constructing national ECCE policies for the developing countries. Since ECCE policies and programs have a significant impact on people's lives, especially poor Blacks, women, and children, it is necessary to be alert to the twists of these proposals. Often, proposals are dressed up in updated or progressive terminology—such as "community participation," "cultural respect," "gender sensibility," "in the best interest of children," and "globalization"—that deflects critical attention. In this sense, I warn those in the developed world interested in carework, especially ECCE, to be cautious about generalizing globalization. A just criticism of the values intrinsic in modernity could make way for the implantation of even more unjust and exclusionary ECCE models in the developing world in the name of respect for what is local. The difference between the wealth of the North and the poverty of the South may conceal a common aspiration: to have good, sufficient ECCE programs that allow mothers to work outside the home with tranquility and include women educators who become professionals, receive decent salaries, work in adequate places, and produce good care for children.

1. It would be possible to question the premise that the country did not have resources to invest in ECCE. During the same period, there was intense use of public resources (with international loans) to build roads and airports and even to expand higher education.

2. I use quotation marks around the expressions "street children" and "child prostitution" to signal my criticism of the emphasis given to children and not to the adults who exploit them. I consider child prostitution to be a special case of sexual abuse by adults against children (Rosemberg and Andrade 1999).

3. The World Bank has disseminated and exported its canons for ECCE to many developing countries. Such canons are not exclusively theirs. Since the Jomtien Conference, they have shared this canon with other signatories, including the United Nations Educational, Scientific, and Cultural Organization (UNESCO) and UNICEF. As we know, the elaboration of the resolutions of the Jomtien Conference relied on the participation of "international" advisors (Chabbott 1998). In the case of ECCE, the Consultative Group on Early Child Care and Development (an American nongovernmental organization) was the nongovernmental organization that has most cooperated with the multilateral organizations and was the main consultant to Jomtien. In the intense searches I have carried out, I found almost no evaluation of the impact of the activities and proposals of the multilateral organizations, especially UNESCO and UNICEF, on ECCE policies for the developing world. In a general way, UNESCO and UNICEF have been protected from the sharp criticisms of the World Bank's social policies in recent years. For some exceptions, see Hancock (1989), Penn (2002), and Rossetti-Ferreira, Ramon, and Silva (2002).

ANPEd. 1998. *Parecer da ANPEd sobre a proposta elaborada pelo MEC do Plano Nacional de Educação.* São Paulo, Brazil: Associação Nacional de Pós-Graduação em Educação.

Black, M. 1996. *The children and the nations: The story of UNICEF.* Potts Point, Australia: P.I.C. Pty Ltda.

Brazil/Ministry of Education. 1993. *Política de educação infantil.* Brasília, Brazil: Ministry of Education.

Brazil/Ministry of Education/SG/SEEC. 1977. *Sinopse estatística do ensino de pré—1 grau 69/75.*

Campos, M. M., F. Rosemberg, and I. Ferreira. 1992. *Creches e pré-escolas no Brasil.* São Paulo, Brazil: Cortez.

Chabbott, C. 1998. Constructing educational consensus: International development professionals and the World Conference for All. *International Journal of Educational Development* 18:107–18.

Coraggio, J. L. 1996. Propostas do Banco Mundial para a educação: Sentido oculto ou problema de concepção? In *O Banco Mundial e as políticas educacionais,* edited by L. de Tommasi, M. Warde, and Sergio Haddad. São Paulo, Brazil: Cortez, PUC-SP, Ação Educativa.

Haddad, S. 1998. Os bancos multilaterais e as políticas educacionais no Brasil. In *A estratégia Dos Bancos Multilaterais para o Brasil,* edited by A. Vianna Jr. Brasília, Brazil: Rede Brasil.

Hancock, G. 1989. *Lords of poverty.* New York: Atlantic Monthly Press.

Mozère, L. 1998. Les métiers de la crèche. Entre competences fèmenines et savoirs spécialisés. *Cahiers du Gedisst* 22:105–24.

Partido Social Democrata Brasileiro. 1998. *Programa do PSDB para a presidência.* São Paulo, Brazil: Partido Social Democrata Brasileiro.

Penn, H. 2002. Primeira infância: A visão do Banco Mundial. *Cadernos de Pesquisa* 115: 7–24.

Rosemberg, F. 1998. *Educação infantil na UNESCO. Preliminary research report.* São Paulo, Brazil: FCC.

———. 1999. *Educar e cuidar como função da educação infantil no Brasil: Perspectiva histórica.* São Paulo, Brazil: FCC/PUC-SP.

———. 2002. *Panorama da educação brasileira contemporânea.* São Paulo, Brasil: Interamerican Development Bank/FCC.

Rosemberg, F., and L. Andrade. 1999. Ruthless rhetoric. *Childhood* 1:113–31.

Rossetti-Ferreira, M. C., F. Ramon, and A. P. S. Silva. 2002. Políticas de atendimento à criança Pequena nos países em desenvolvimento. *Cadernos de Pesquisa* 115:65–100.

Tommasi, L. de, M. J. Warde, and S. Haddad. 1996. *O Banco Mundial e as políticas educacionais.* São Paulo, Brazil: Cortez/PUC-SP/Ação Educativa.

Torres, R. M. 1996. Melhorar a qualidade da educação básica? As estratégias do Banco Mundial. In *O Banco Mundial e as políticas educacionais,* edited by L. de Tommasi, M. Warde, and S. Haddad. São Paulo, Brazil: Cortez/PUC-SP/Ação Educativa.

Young, M. E. 1996. *Early child development: Investing in the future.* Washington DC: World Bank.

7

GLOBALIZATION, WORK HOURS, AND

THE CARE DEFICIT AMONG STOCKBROKERS

Mary Blair-Loy and Jerry A. Jacobs

This excerpt shows the impact of the technological and economic forces of globalization on gender relations both in families and in the workplace. Focusing on the lives of U.S. stockbrokers, Blair-Loy and Jacobs show that the pressures from global markets and international competition have changed work hours, creating conditions for a care deficit at home. This has disproportionately affected women, leading them to make decisions that reinforce a male breadwinner/female caregiver division of family labor and that perpetuate gender inequality.

Recent research has examined the relationships between globalization and the work of caring for children, the elderly, and other vulnerable members of society. This literature has examined "global care chains," international links between people "based on the paid or unpaid work of caring" (Hochschild 2000). Much of this research explicitly studies the Third World end of the chain, focusing on the nannies and housekeepers from developing countries who provide some of the carework for First World families, often while they pay a fraction of their wages for a nanny in their home country to care for their own children (Hondagneu-Sotelo 2001; Salazar Parreñas 2001). Other studies, focusing on dual-income families in the First World, implicitly address the other end of the chain (e.g., Hochschild 1989, 1997). This research has revealed that global care chains are dependent on a gendered division of labor, in which women are primarily responsible for family care in developing and developed nations. This research has also traced connections between the caregiving work of women from developing nations and the labor force participation of U.S. women.

Yet there has been virtually no research on how specific pressures of the global economy affect the prospects for caregiving among the highly skilled, well-heeled, First World financial professionals. This is the lacuna our article tries to fill.

We study stockbrokers because their jobs have been greatly affected by the revolutions in communications and computing that are key to the globalization process. On one hand, stockbrokers have flourished in the global economy (Sassen 1998) and by many measures would be considered members of the financial and technological elite. On the other hand, these high-end "servants of globalization"

(Salazar Parreñas 2001) face job insecurity as a result of severe volatility in the financial services industry. They are also experiencing new pressures from increased competition, a faster work pace, and the prospect of an extended trading day.

This article tries to answer the question, What is the state of carework among brokers and their families? Stock brokerage remains a highly compensated, male dominated industry, with many men able to support stay-at-home wives. In this segment of the industry, a sharply gendered division of labor characterizes many families. The number of female brokers increased during the 1990s as employment opportunities expanded (Securities Industry Association [SIA] 1998). Our data suggest that increased work demands and time pressures reduce the time brokers have for family caregiving while also encouraging female brokers to cut back on their professional commitments to fulfill family responsibilities. Yet we also find that the same forces creating new work patterns and time pressures for brokers also create the possibility for alternative work structures that allow for a better balance between work and family. The net effect of these processes on the demand for paid caregivers from developing nations is not clear.

The financial services area is one of the industries in the United States most affected by global and domestic competition (Berger et al. 2000; Fraser 2001; Powell 2001). . . . New technology is making access to overseas markets easier and more seamless than ever before. Yet it has also contributed to a 24-hour day for the securities industry. As it is always trading time somewhere in the world, the part of the day normally reserved for family and personal time is disappearing.

Many overseas markets are developing systems that allow them to trade any country's stocks at any time, day or night. Bonds already trade 24 hours a day. The New York Stock Exchange (NYSE), traditionally a leader in foreign stock trading, is expecting new competition from a single pan-European stock exchange that may open sometime in the near future. The NYSE faces further competition from electronic exchanges in the United States, on which securities trade 24 hours a day. In response, the NYSE and the NASDAQ Exchange are planning a future extension of their trading hours into evening trading sessions known as extended-hours trading.

Currently, the NYSE is open from only 9:30 a.m. to 4:00 p.m. Eastern Standard Time. For years, the NYSE and the NASDAQ Exchange have resisted lengthening the trading day with extended-hours trading due to concerns about market liquidity and stability, investor protection, and overly long days for finance professionals. But increasing globalization of securities, coupled with the growing number of individuals who actively manage their own stock portfolios using low-cost, electronic trading systems, is pressuring these venerable institutions to change. . . .

DATA AND METHOD

In the summer of 2000, we conducted in-person interviews with executives, stock-brokers, managers, and other employees in four securities firms ($N = 87$). This article primarily uses results from 61 stockbrokers and branch managers, supplemented by interviews with 6 spouses of broker respondents. The four firms were selected for their variety along dimensions of size, market segment, and geographical location. Each firm is typical of one type of NYSE member firm. Nationwide, NYSE firms account for the vast majority of the assets, capital, and revenue of the securities industry and employ almost half the securities industry workers (SIA 1999)[1]. . . .

We met most respondents in their offices, generally in the afternoon after the major exchanges had closed for the day. We asked a range of semistructured questions covering career backgrounds, typical workdays, work demands, technology, online trading, the proposed extended-hours trading, and work-family balance. Interviews were tape-recorded, transcribed, and coded.

Although we cannot claim our data are strictly representative of the retail side of securities firms, we suspect that the patterns uncovered here likely characterize many securities workers in firms similar in size to the ones included in this study.[2] Our sample is male dominated. In three firms, between 12 and 14 percent of our respondents are women. These figures are similar to the overall proportion of female brokers in the industry. . . .[3]

EMPLOYMENT AND CAREGIVING AMONG STOCKBROKERS

Brokers work long hours. Respondents in our four firms already work an average of 10 hours a day plus occasional work on weekends. The majority report that the pace of work has increased in recent years, in part due to the increased competition and new opportunities wrought by new technologies and globalization. For instance, one broker says that the market has grown "more intense" in the past 5 to 10 years. Another says that the pace is "much more frantic than it was" as he struggles to keep up with the explosion in new financial products and new technologies.[4]

Similarly, several respondents told us that their job never really ends. For example, one female broker says that she can keep her hours manageable during the week only if she also works on the weekend. A male broker says, "It's in a business that's so intellectually challenging and complicated that it's hard to, it's hard to walk away from it, because you're never done." He says that although he has never felt caught up during his entire eighteen years in the industry, the pace has grown more intense in the past five years. Another agrees: "At this kind of job you're on call 24 hours a day, I think. . . . So it never really stops."

Another man agrees: "Well, remember you're always in work mode in this job. I mean there's never a time when you're not." He does not regard this as a conflict with family or personal responsibilities, however, because it is the "lifestyle" one must accept in return for a generous, commission-based income. "You get a lot of money in this job. And so as a result you're kind of always on call." This broker is single and has no children. His apparent lack of family care responsibilities likely contributes to his stoical attitude about the extensive demands of his work.

In contrast, a married, female broker-manager with children says that she comes home in the evening, spends time with her family, and then does work on her laptop after her children are in bed. She also works from home on the weekend. Sally Bergman, the wife of another broker, told us that even when her husband is home, he is constantly checking the market in his home office.

> He wakes up about a half hour to 45 minutes before I do. He gets himself coffee, sits in his office for about 30 to 40 minutes, and spends all his time on the computer. Checking what the markets have done, what's going on, checking reports . . . and then he probably spends about another hour in the evening. . . . On the weekends, he spends a lot of time with it on. . . . He keeps one screen on that has live quotes from around the world, so he just keeps checking on that throughout the day.

DEFICIT OF FAMILY CAREGIVING BY BROKERS

Given this absorbing and time-intensive work, it is unsurprising that the brokers and managers in our sample spend little time with their families. For example, one broker leaves for work before his young son is up and often gets home just a half hour before his son's bedtime. A male broker with four children spends just an hour on family responsibilities in a typical day. A male branch manager leaves home before 6:30 a.m. and gets home at 6:30 or 7:00 each evening.

We later interviewed this broker's wife, who stays home caring for their toddler. She told us something he had not mentioned: They had a baby due in one month. She said that since their first child happened to be born on a Friday, her husband spent that weekend at home helping her. She does not know if he will take any time off when the second child is born: "I've asked him and I haven't gotten an answer yet. Even for a couple days—and to watch [our toddler] more than anything else, I guess."

Nine respondents explicitly volunteered that they prioritized work over family responsibilities. But even those who proclaimed the importance of family over work still squeezed in family time around their consuming work obligations. One broker said tersely, "The family has adjusted to my business style; let's put it that way." Another broker insists that time with family is very important, and so they have dinner as a family every night. However, this family dinner must wait until 8 p.m., when he gets home from work. He says that if he arrives home any earlier, his wife wonders what went wrong.

One of the six spouses we interviewed is male. Mondays through Thursdays, he works long days, while his mother cares for his preschool daughter and for his school-aged son. He cooks dinner every night and stays home with the children on Fridays. He says that although his wife works long hours, they have been fortunate. With help from his mother and his four-day-a-week schedule, "it isn't too hard to handle her extra hours."

The other five broker spouses we interviewed were women. According to them, their husbands spend very little time on childcare or housework. One wife, employed full-time, says she shoulders most of the domestic responsibilities. She reports that she does the cooking, grocery shopping, and the laundry. With a touch of sarcasm, she adds, "I don't think my husband knows where the washer and dryer are, actually. But they are right in our basement." Describing a typical evening, she says that after coming home from work, she makes dinner while her three children are "usually climbing on my legs." She reports that during that time, her husband is generally looking for the remote control to the television set.

Another wife, Sally Bergman, took a tone that was less sarcastic and more enthusiastic about her husband's involvement. When it comes to housework, she says, "I primarily do it all. Without a doubt. And he would be the first one to tell you that, right off the bat." But she praises the energy her husband puts into caring for their son.

> He's a very, very hands-on father, so that alone gets big bonus points. Every Saturday morning, he takes my son on the train for a train ride. . . . They just ride the rails for about two hours!. . . He'll take him all the way into the city. They'll go into his office, because my two-year-old loves the big elevator. It shoots straight up! So, you know to a two-and-a-half-year-old, that's the end all of excitement!

From her perspective, she is fortunate that her husband is willing to take their son into the office with him on a weekend morning.

In fact, many brokers seem to feel that their responsibility for family care is appropriately limited to leisure-related activities on weekends and during short vacations. Most do not seem to view the work of caregiving as a constant, ongoing activity for which they have primary responsibility. Several respondents said they relied on weekends as their only time away from the job. For example, one man explained,

> I've not yet figured out how to be real successful in a rapidly changing environment without putting in more hours than I would prefer. But I don't tend to work too much on weekends. I'll take work home, but I hardly ever have to come in. So that's been my major change since I started to have a family and have kids. I'm at least home on weekends for them.

Others cite weekends as their chance to get away from work and spend uninterrupted time with their families. For instance, one female broker complained that even when she is home with her two young children, she is often "busy doing things, and it's not always quality time with my kids; it's catching up on grocery shopping and cleaning the house. So there's a lot that I'm doing that's still not focused on family." She tries to "curb doing work on the weekends" and spend Saturdays and Sundays relaxing with her family on their boat.

Some brokers explained that since their business is unceasing, they take very short vacations. For example, one man said that his family's longest vacation is usually in conjunction with the Fourth of July or Labor Day so that he only has to miss four days of work. Others mentioned that longer vacations are only possible when the market is doing well. Otherwise, clients would contact them and expect them to take care of business.

SELF-CARE

Several male brokers we interviewed discussed the need to escape from the stress of work and of family. Some seemed to find spending time with their families more stressful than being at work and strove to protect what one man called "sanity time" for themselves. This time includes playing golf, working out at the gym, and going out with friends. One broker explained,

> I don't want to spend too much time away from home, but I don't want to spend too much time at home. . . . I work hard . . . but then I also have to take care of myself, so I exercise. So I don't come home [right after work] and feel like I'm going straight from work to home, and I'm taking care of a new baby, and I didn't have time for me. And I don't want to feel resentful for that.

Some of the wives we interviewed seem to wish their broker husbands would spend less time on "sanity" time and more time with their families. For example,

Cindy Smith slowly admitted that her husband spends a lot of time on the golf course and not much time with their young son: "He golfs a lot. [Long pause.] I would be happier if. . . . He only takes care of our son on weekends once or twice a month."

None of the female brokers we interviewed explicitly discussed setting aside personal time. The female brokers with children seemed to have more direct, day-to-day responsibility for child rearing and were more likely than their male counterparts to discuss the litany of things they do with their children after work. One woman went so far as to say that she came to work to unwind. "I come here to relax and have a cup of coffee in peace. I find my home life is a lot more stressful."[5]

In sum, demanding job responsibilities restrict the time brokers have available for family caregiving. Respondents feel that the volume and pace of work is increasing. Workdays are long, vacations are short, and some brokers feel compelled to keep track of the market all weekend. Parents report spending relatively little time with their children, and these reports are buttressed and elaborated on by the broker spouses we interviewed. Unsurprisingly, female brokers in our sample seem to do more family caregiving than do male brokers. The next section focuses on the implications of these intensive work demands for gender equality at work and at home.

IMPLICATIONS FOR GENDER INEQUALITY

The majority of married brokers in the sample are the sole or major breadwinners. Among married men in the sample, 66 percent have wives who are homemakers or who just hold part-time jobs. Among married fathers, 75 percent have wives who are homemakers or are employed part-time. The male brokers' heavy breadwinning responsibilities increase the pressure on brokers to work long hours.

For example, one man discusses the pressures he feels as the sole breadwinner.

> I leave the house at 6:30 every morning. Maybe earlier. So I don't see my family as much as I'd like to. But I think that, you know, you have to pay those dues to go forward. And it's worked out well. So, you know, I mean the bottom line is somebody's got to pay the bills in life. I would love to sit home with my child and wife but that's not really, that's not gonna happen.

This respondent works in one of the three commission-based firms in our study. The more hours commission-based brokers spend serving clients and prospecting for new ones, the more money they can bring home. The financial rewards for hardworking financial consultants are potentially very high, which induces them to put in longer hours.

Among the families of the men in the sample, brokers' wives are encouraged to stay home to do the domestic work that enables their husbands' long hours and corresponding lucrative earnings. This process reinforces a domestic division of labor in which the husband is the breadwinner and the wife is the caregiver. For example, one broker we interviewed calls himself a "workaholic." He generally stays at the office until 8:00 or 9:00 p.m. He said that he achieved work-family balance by moving from the suburbs to a Manhattan apartment near his office so that he could go home for dinner and then return to work at night. This schedule allows him to see his children before they go to bed. He said that he was "traditional" and, when he married, had looked for a wife who wanted to stay home with the children.

Some of the wives we interviewed discussed the benefits of staying home to support their husbands' earning potential. Cindy Smith complained about her husband's long hours but then acknowledged the benefits of his high income.

> I hate to sound so superficial, but his job is so lucrative that it's sort of hard to turn your nose up at it. You know, we're, we're very, very grateful. Ah, because the job he does has allowed us to do more things than I'd ever thought I'd be able to accomplish at this young age. And give things to our children. . . . You know, we have security that I never imagined we would.

Her husband's job demands make it desirable for the family to have a homemaking spouse, while his high earnings make this option affordable.[6]

Long work hours make it tremendously challenging for brokers in the commission-based firms to be involved family caregivers themselves. These work demands likely also serve as a barrier to women's entering or staying in the occupation. Twenty-one percent of our broker sample is female, which is probably a higher proportion of women than are in the brokerage occupation overall. An SIA (2001) study of 48 firms found that just 14 percent of brokers and 12 percent of branch managers are women.

Unlike the male respondents, who are likely to have a wife at home or who is working just part-time, women in our sample are either single or married to full-time employed husbands. Men in the sample are somewhat more likely than women to be married (79 percent vs. 62 percent) but overwhelmingly more likely to have children (69 percent vs. 38 percent). Only 5 of 13 female brokers in the sample are parents, and 2 of these 5 women work part-time.

The two part-timers are grateful for their reduced-hours schedules and credit them for allowing them to manage both their work and their family responsibilities. One woman says that although it is stressful to try to squeeze five days of work into three, it is basically "working out, you know, for me, I really shouldn't have any complaints. . . . It's a great way to kind of do both. Yeah, I feel very lucky to have the schedule I do."

Three women without children say they hope to cut back to part-time when they do have children. For example, one woman reports, "My ideal vision" is that

> I'm gonna be home not working two days a week. . . . That's how it's all structured. I don't know if it will truly happen that way, . . . [but] I'm not willing to sacrifice my family and my personal goals for business.

Whether they can negotiate a part-time schedule after they have children remains to be seen. . . .

FUTURE EFFECTS OF EXTENDED-HOURS TRADING

Work pressures will likely increase further with the advent of extended-hours trading sponsored by the NYSE and NASDAQ. While the implementation of extended trading hours has so far been postponed, low-cost online brokerage accounts, Internet investing sites, and electronic communication networks are responding more quickly and flexibly to this demand for longer trading days than are the traditional brokerages and the major stock exchanges. Electronic communication networks have recently developed Web-based trading platforms that electronically execute trades for individuals in after-hours sessions, and they have developed systems that can execute trades 24 hours a day. Several brokerage houses also offer online trading in addition to their traditional services. Some firms offer online trading only during regular market hours, but others allow online trades to be executed in the after-hours market, electronic communication networks that are open after the major stock exchanges have closed. Two of our firms offer online and after-hours trading, and a third firm has launched a pilot program of these services.

In the currently available after-hours market, volume and liquidity are low,[7] and most brokers do not find it necessary to follow it closely into the night. Yet an extended-hours trading system sponsored by the NYSE and NASDAQ will be a different matter. It is not clear when extended hours will be implemented, but we think it is just a matter of time. When that occurs, extended-hours sessions will likely increase interest and volume in after-hours trading. These current and proposed developments may all lengthen what is already a long day for securities professionals and further limit the time they can devote to family caregiving.

One broker, musing about the possible effects of extended-hours trading, says, "It's gonna be a real experiment to see how we can ultimately cater to our clients' needs. . . . I can't imagine coming home from work and then watching the market all night." Another broker first says he would refuse to work later in the evenings.

> I already work too much. I leave in the morning when [my son] is still in bed. And there's many nights, because I do take evening appointments, or I'll have a meeting here in town, that I won't get home until seven, eight o'clock, and I've got half an hour and he's in bed.

But later in the interview, he concedes that if the major markets do stay open later, he would have to keep an eye on them. To make this idea more palatable, he imagines doing this from home rather than from the office.

Sally Bergman predicts that the real victims of extended-hours trading, when it is implemented, will be brokers' families.

> [Extended-hours trading] would destroy family life for so many people. . . . There are some brokers who coach basketball and . . . do things like that. And that just eliminates any time. The people who are going to lose are brokers' families.

Extended hours are viewed particularly negatively by commission-based brokers. These brokers will likely have to be available to clients during large swings in the stock market or when dramatic financial news is announced, even if these developments occur during nonstandard hours. The commission-based firms we studied are struggling with a hybrid of traditional elements (semiautonomous broker responsibility for his or her own stable of clients) and global expectations.

To meet the demands of a global economy, traditional firms cannot simply expect their brokers to work longer days. For example, one man at the New York City–based firm complains that he already works 10 to 11 hours a day.

> [If extended hours are introduced], to work a 14-hour day in this industry for five days a week would probably lead to burnout. So I don't see how I could personally be here 'til 9:00 every night. I don't think I could. . . . I'd have no life during the weekday. That's no way to live. . . . I'd probably look to go [work] elsewhere. That's how adamantly I feel about it.

Similarly, a woman at the wirehouse adamantly opposed the idea of introducing extended trading. "I think it stinks!. . . I'm able to juggle [now] but extended hours would really be a big problem for me. As I think for most people, I think we, I, work enough!"

If extended hours are introduced, these firms will be left scrambling to develop the staffing resources—such as shifts and teams—to handle it. For example, an executive at the New York City–based firm announced flatly that extended-hours trading "is not going to happen." He then went on to admit that if extended trading was in fact introduced, he would have no idea how to accommodate it.

> Now, I don't see the broker being in the office all day long. . . . I don't think I'll be able to staff an office that way without going to shifts. If I go to shifts, that means I have to increase the number of salespeople [brokers] I have, when my space is already the same. . . . I don't believe I'm going to go to two double shifts, where I'm going to [make] two people share a desk. I don't see that happening . . . without going into serious expenses to do that.

In sum, commission-based brokers expect that extended-hours trading will further intensify their work demands. They resent the notion that they may have to spend even longer hours at work. Yet their managers may be ill equipped to handle these changes when they occur. . . .

In our U.S. sample, generous earnings make it possible for the majority of male, married brokers to support homemaking or part-time-employed wives. Yet these high earnings come with the price of exposure to the wild fluctuations of the equities markets. The boom years culminating in the market peak of 2000 gave way to an enduring bear market that continues as this report is being written. Firms have slashed the number of retail brokers as stock prices have declined and trading volumes have plummeted. Thus, while at times it is fair to characterize brokers as the winners in the globalization process, many also become victims of the volatility of globalization as well. Brokers who are economically supporting their spouses are particularly vulnerable as they do not have the earnings of a spouse to help cushion a period of low earnings or unemployment.

Much research on global care chains has explored connections between the caregiving labor of women from developing nations and dual-earner couples in the United States. In contrast, this article shows how specific pressures for securities professionals, including longer work hours due to new technology, competition, and globalization, reinforce a male breadwinner/female caregiver division of labor within First World families. In the commission-based firms, most male brokers who have children rely on their wives to provide the caregiving they cannot. The family's economic dependence on the male broker's income reinforces the pressure to work long hours and to spend even less time at home. At the same time, the tremendous challenge of combining commission-based financial consulting with caregiving work helps sustain the male domination of the broker occupation.

Broadly, our findings illustrate how the specific demands and rhythms of paid work help define the gender division of labor on the job and thereby influence the amount and kind of caregiving within the family. . . . The ongoing implementation of a 24/7 global trading system will require major changes in the way work is conducted by stockbrokers. It is clearly impossible for any individual to work 24/7. Some division of labor is needed. . . . Brokerage houses are not the first institutions to face the demands of a 24/7 workweek: Hospitals, police forces, and factories have developed systems for addressing this issue. The evolution of work in the financial securities industry will shed light on the choices being made in response to the technological and economic forces of globalization. These choices will affect wages, economic opportunities for women, and the nature of caregiving for decades to come.

1. About 280 of the 7,400 firms registered with the Securities and Exchange Commission are New York Stock Exchange (NYSE) members. In 1999, these NYSE firms accounted for 85 percent of the assets and 72 percent of the total revenue of all securities firms (Securities Industry Association 1999). We did not interview anyone in very small firms, which are unlikely to be members of the NYSE.

2. These interviews are a part of a larger study of the securities industry. We are currently analyzing a quantitative survey of securities professionals based on a random sample of a national listing ($N = 600$). This quantitative analysis suggests that our qualitative results are not idiosyncratic for this industry.

3. In a Securities Industry Association (2001) study of 48 firms, which together employ 49 percent of securities professionals, 14 percent of brokers and 12 percent of branch managers are women.

4. In a companion article analyzing a quantitative survey of 600 securities workers, we find that three-quarters of this sample reported that their work pace had increased significantly in the previous two years (Blair-Loy and Jacobs 2002).

5. This parallels Hochschild's (1989) report of a "leisure gap" between employed husbands and wives and her finding that wives tend to shoulder most of the "second shift."

6. The median income for retail brokers overall in 2000 was $141,000, with income in the $200,000 to $500,000 range not uncommon (Weinberg 2001).

7. Low volume and liquidity mean that there are small numbers of buyers and sellers in the after-hours market. This makes it harder to execute trades, increases volatility and risk, and limits the appeal of after-hours trading.

Berger, Allen N., Robert DeYoung, Hesna Genay, and Gregory F. Udell. 2000. Globalization of financial institutions: Evidence from cross-border banking performance. In *Brookings-Wharton papers on financial services*, edited by Robert E. Litan and Anthony M. Santomero. Washington, DC: Brookings Institution.

Blair-Loy, Mary, and Jerry Jacobs. 2002. Work and family concerns among stockbrokers. Unpublished paper, Washington State University, Pullman.

Fraser, Jill Andresky. 2001. *White collar sweatshop: The deterioration of work and its rewards in corporate America*. New York: Norton.

Hochschild, Arlie. 1989. *The second shift: Working parents and the revolution at home*. New York: Viking.

———. 1997. *The time bind: When work becomes home and home becomes work*. New York: Metropolitan Books.

———. 2000. The nanny chain. *American Prospect* 11 (4). Available from http://www.prospect.org/print/V11/4/hochschild-a.html.

Hondagneu-Sotelo, Pierrette. 2001. *Domestica: Immigrant workers cleaning and caring in the shadows of affluence*. Berkeley: University of California Press.

Powell, Walter W. 2001. The capitalist firm in the twenty-first century: Emerging patterns in Western enterprise. In *The twenty-first-century firm: Changing economic organization in international perspective*, edited by Paul DiMaggio. Princeton, NJ: Princeton University Press.

Salazar Parreñas, Rhacel. 2001. *Servants of globalization: Women, migration, and domestic work*. Stanford, CA: Stanford University Press.

Sassen, Saskia. 1998. *Globalization and its discontents*. New York: New Press.

Securities Industry Association (SIA). 1998. *Fact book*, edited by Grace Toto and George Monohan. New York: Securities Industry Association.

———. 1999. *Fact book*. New York: Securities Industry Association.

———. 2001. *Report on diversity strategy, development and demographics: Key findings*. New York: Securities Industry Association.

Weinberg, Rick. 2001. Brokers' median pay topped $366K last year. *Registered Representative Magazine Online*, 13 August.

II

TRANSNATIONAL MIGRATION: INFLUENCES
ON CITIZENSHIP, SOCIAL CONTROL,
AND CAREWORK

8 TRANSNATIONAL MIGRATION: INFLUENCES ON CITIZENSHIP, SOCIAL CONTROL, AND CAREWORK

The nature of global carework and the many carework crises we have discussed in this book are greatly influenced by women's transnational migration for jobs. When women travel to another country, their work options can be limited or expanded either by their home nation or their destination country, both of which control the transnational migration process through the use of citizenship and labor regulations. Therefore, migration is not only about movement from one geographic place to another, it also is about gaining and losing rights and opportunities.

In this essay we explain some of the concepts that help illustrate how migration and citizenship have shaped who performs paid and unpaid carework and under what conditions it is done. We begin with a description of current migration patterns. Then, we describe three outcomes of migration: (1) fluidity between paid and unpaid carework over a woman's life course and across geographic space; (2) careworkers' limited citizenship rights and their experiences of surveillance by governments and employers; and (3) marginalization of transnational migrants based on the interconnections of gender, class (usually their social class in the new country and not their class status at home), and nationality (especially highlighting presumed racial-ethnic characteristics).

TRANSNATIONAL MIGRATION

In 1990, for every 100 men who migrated internationally, 91 women did so, making women about 47 percent of the global international flow of people. These rates vary regionally from a high of 123 women migrants per 100 men in Eastern Europe, to a low of 67 women per 100 men in Western Asia, but most regions—Africa, the Caribbean, South America, and Southern and Eastern Asia—all have women's migration rates near the global average (United Nations 2000). The overall equality in migration rates can be attributed to the increased number of women who now migrate on their own as "contract workers"—people who go to another country for a specified time period, often to work in fields like domestic or childcare work, entertainment, food and lodging services, or on assembly lines.

These women workers have become an increasingly important source of income for their families since the 1980s (United Nations 2000). For example, Saskia Sassen reports that remittances are the third largest source of foreign currency in the Philippines and make up one-third of the foreign currency transactions in Bangladesh (Sassen 2002, 270). These temporary workers are considered *transnational migrants* and not immigrants, because they do not intend to, and indeed, they are not allowed to, remain in the countries they move to.

Two excerpts in this book, by Sassen and Chang, present the key feature of women's migration for the global economy: migration creates new labor supplies. Not surprisingly, the demand for women's labor has resulted in a feminization of migration both among rural to urban migrants within a single country—such as when women travel to find work in urban-based manufacturing export processing zones—and among countries that have large amounts of out migration, such as the Philippines, which exports many of its citizens to the newly industrializing countries of Asia as well as to developed countries like the United States or Japan. Indeed, low-wage carework is one major segment in the labor market that is open to immigrant women, especially in global cities, so that the bottom of many nations' occupational distributions is becoming internationalized. However, because these jobs are located in employers' homes, this major sector of the labor market tends to remain invisible and difficult to organize because of its geographically scattered nature.

Furthermore, as Cynthia Enloe indicates in her excerpt, since World War II, many governments have "acted as if an 'immigrant worker' was male. An 'immigrant's family' was [supposedly] composed of the wife and children of that male worker. This portrait does not match the facts . . . [but] this portrait of a masculinized immigrant workforce encouraged policy-makers to see restrictions on women immigrants as a means of preventing male immigrant workers from putting down roots" (see Chapter 9). Minjeong Kim describes how barriers to settlement affect married international students. When married men come from Korea to the United States to study, their wives are barred from seeking employment and are forced into unpaid carework—thus discouraging the family from staying in the United States longer than necessary. Even after a husband's degree is earned and if he obtains a U.S. job with an H1 visa, his wife cannot be employed for several years, until she obtains permanent resident status, unless she finds an employer who will sponsor her own H1 visa. Restrictions on the migration of male workers' wives have even carried over into similar restrictions on women who migrate for work, regardless of their marital status. For example, as Shu-Ju Ada Cheng describes, women from the Philippines, who migrate to do carework in Taiwan, are not allowed to marry or to become pregnant—if they do, they lose their jobs and are deported—because the Taiwanese government does not want immigrant families putting down roots.

Focusing on women's migration highlights three important global carework dynamics that are centered on the concepts that we introduce in this chapter. The first is the shifting, but overlapping, nature of care in women's lives—during different life stages and in different national settings—between paid and unpaid work. Articles by Kim and by Denise Spitzer and colleagues, for instance, reveal different ways that women's unpaid carework can be increased by family migration. These changes are related to the concepts of the international division of paid labor and the international division of reproductive labor. The second dynamic is created by the powerful influence of national governments in shaping women's carework. We explore how formal citizenship rights are legally constructed by states, how these rights are shaped by the actions of other citizens into the day-to-day experience of substantive citizenship, and how, as a result, women frequently experience only partial citizenship. Nation states can limit workers' rights through legal othering, direct control, or enlisting the aid of employers. For example, the articles by Cheng and Kim, respectively, show how Taiwan's and the United States' immigration policies explicitly limit some women's employment and their citizenship rights. Rebecca Raijman and her colleagues bring to light how undocumented Latina immigrants in Israel actively resist limitations on their employment by working illegally. Finally, migration reveals the dynamic, and often explicit, interplay between gender, class, and national origin (e.g., race or ethnicity) in determining who performs carework. Thus, in Cheng's article we learn that educated women from five South Asian countries are the only migrants who can be legally hired as paid careworkers in Taiwan.

SHIFTING THE BALANCE BETWEEN PAID AND UNPAID WORK

Most research on women's work outside of the United States is based on case studies of a single country, usually drawn from three major global industries—the service industry (including carework, paid domestic work, tourism, and sex work); the manufacturing industry (usually focusing on factory workers in export processing zones); or international marriage, often referred to as the mail-order bride industry, but which could also be thought of as transnational housework or global unpaid carework. When we place women's transnational migration at the center of the global economy, we see the similarities between paid service work and women's unpaid carework, as well as the overlapping nature of and shifting balance, over the course of a woman's life, between performing unpaid family carework, being a paid careworker, and becoming an employer of paid careworkers.

As Maria Mies, Veronika Bennholdt-Thomson, and Claudia von Werlhof (1988) observed, there has been an international trend towards the "housewifization" of all labor—an interesting term that incorporates several aspects of the relationship between paid work and women's unpaid work at home. First, paid work is becoming increasingly feminized, with new jobs drawing more on women's than men's labor. Second, paid work is increasingly organized like women's housework—with jobs that require flexible schedules and are occupationally segregated. Third, many of these jobs, like market vending, factory outwork, or off-the-books childcare, are in the informal sector of the global economy that is rapidly expanding but, like housework, is not regulated by national labor laws, thus increasing informalization of work in many individual countries (as discussed in Part 1). Finally, since women's traditional tasks are stereotyped as unskilled—although they are not—companies or individual employers can more easily pay less and provide less job security. In other words, economic restructuring and the *international division of paid labor* in a global assembly line have created new jobs that have many of the characteristics of women's paid carework and unpaid carework and housework, which is not surprising since women are the source of new labor in most countries worldwide.

In addition, scholars like Rhacel Parreñas and Pierrette Hondagneu-Sotello, whose work appears in this book, have illustrated that there is an *international division of reproductive carework* labor that occurs when women from developing countries migrate internationally to more developed ones to perform paid carework for other women, then use these earnings to hire someone back home (often a rural-to-urban migrant or another family member) to take care of their own families (see Part 3 for an expanded discussion of this process). Thus, the differences between live-in or live-out domestic work are blurring because a transnational migrant cannot return to her own family at night, although live-out work still provides her more autonomy. This new interrelationship among women is known as a carework chain or circuit, which literally transfers care labor from developing to developed countries and from rural to urban areas. In so doing, it also creates new challenges for the migrating woman as she moves from unpaid carework for her own family to paid carework for another family.

Therefore, paid and unpaid carework are *not* dichotomous, and as Nona Glazer (1993) has shown for the United States—the line between them is porous. Some forms of work—like post-operative health care—have shifted back and forth between being done by paid employees to being performed unpaid by family members. This same approach, looking at the links of paid and unpaid work, is useful in thinking about the gendered nature of carework on an international level because it forces us to see how, due to migration patterns and the rise of women's paid employment across the globe, the unpaid carework of women in one country can become the paid carework of women from another country, although it can also move back again to unpaid work.

Two articles in Part 2 provide examples of how migration can easily shift women's energies from unpaid carework for their own families to paid carework or domestic work for other families—especially if they migrate without husbands or as single women. Cheng describes the outcomes for Filipinas who migrate legally to Taiwan, while Raijman and colleagues do so for Latinas who work illegally in Israel. Whether or not their migration was legal, the women confront similar and severe restrictions on their paid work. In addition, both groups suffer problems with staying connected to their families, either because they have left children behind in their home countries in the care of others or because their long overseas work stints mean they will forfeit the opportunity to marry and have families of their own.

The other two case studies focus on what happens to couples that migrate together, often increasing women's unpaid carework. Kim's report on Korean student couples in the United States shows how middle-class women are forced to shift their priorities from the paid work they often performed in their homeland into full-time unpaid carework, since U.S. immigration regulations do not allow them to be employed. Meanwhile, Spitzer and colleagues show that even when Asian women who migrate to Canada can and do enter paid employment, their family carework burdens are significantly increased by migration. As Enloe suggests, "being a foreign-born wife and being a foreign-born domestic worker often become strikingly similar under restrictive immigration laws" (see Chapter 9).

GLOBALIZATION FROM ABOVE: STATE CITIZENSHIP REGULATIONS

The next dynamic of carework that is revealed through the lens of transnational migration—the role of nation states and citizenship—requires understanding several concepts. As described in our introduction, globalization is characterized by global interdependence, and political or labor market decisions in one country affect other parts of the world. Therefore, studying women who migrate to do carework means that we must also look at the effect of a destination country's migration or labor market regulations on residents of other countries.

Richard Falk (1993) argues that the concept of globalization encompasses the coexistence of two sorts of globalization or interconnectedness. "There is *globalization-from-above*, reflecting the collaboration between leading states and the main agents of capital formation" (p. 39; *emphasis added*). This form of globalization, by developed countries such as the United States, Japan, Germany, or Great Britain along with international institutions like the World Bank or International Monetary Fund (IMF), tends to increase global stratification. Meanwhile "*globalization-from-below* . . . consists of an array of transnational social forces animated by environmental concerns, human rights, hostility to patriarchy, and a vision of human community . . . seeking an end to poverty, oppression, humiliation, and collective violence" (p. 39; *emphasis added*)—this form of globalization, comprised of activist groups in civil society, tends to decrease global stratification while increasing state and corporate accountability. Falk's class-based perspective on globalization from above is an important one, because it exhorts us to look at global patterns of carework as structured by economic market demands, and the regulations of national governments or multinational organizations about citizenship and employment—as well as the more typically reported patterns of carework experienced by individual women (or by the households that hire them) when transnational migration decisions are made. Furthermore, Falk's approach encourages us to look for workers' activism on their own behalf and explore the role of social movement groups that have challenged national governments, pushing them to enhance the citizenship or employment rights of domestic workers and careworkers and fostering globalization from below by creating successful organizations like the National Union of Domestic Employees (NUDE) in Trinidad and Tobago or Intercede (The International Coalition to End Domestics' Exploitation) in Canada.

Market demands and international debt policies have a large impact on women's carework. As Enloe's excerpt indicates, when nations borrow money from the IMF or the World Bank, loan restrictions, known as structural adjustment requirements, are placed on the debtor governments. Among the typical requirements are keeping wages down, cutting social services, reducing health and education budgets, and eliminating food subsidies, all of which make women's daily carework harder. As described in other parts of this book, the "politics of international debt won't work in their current form unless mothers and wives are willing . . . to adopt cost-cutting measures" at home (see Chapter 9). This problem is exacerbated if men travel overseas in search of better-paying jobs. Then the wives who remain behind are transformed into temporary single mothers, with increased domestic work and carework at home.

In Part 2, we examine what happens when migration is thrust upon women by structural adjustment, usually because overseas jobs are not available for men. Then women migrate to work as nurses, maids, and entertainers; and governments rely on their remittances to help repay foreign creditors. Governments do not merely count on some of these overseas earnings being sent home. There are controls on migration-for-work experiences that can be hidden or explicit in national regulations. For example, the government of the Philippines *requires* overseas workers to send a certain percentage of their pay home, and if they do not do so their permission to work abroad can be withdrawn.

Such restrictions on migrants and on migration are often accomplished through definitions and practices of formal citizenship. *Citizenship* has had diverse meanings across time and region. For example, the news media may label someone as a "global citizen." This term is used to describe a wide variety of people including humanitarians working to help tsunami victims, for ecological sustainability, or to conquer AIDS, and it can refer to financial and corporate elites, with few ties to any particular nation, whose primary goal is to make a profit for their firm (Falk 1993). Our focus is not on these forms of global citizenship, but rather it is on citizenship within a single country—because when people migrate for work in other nations, citizenship regulations and norms in their home nation and in the host country shape the type and nature of paid and unpaid carework that is available to them.

In the excerpt from her book *Unequal Freedom* (see Chapter 10), Evelyn Nakano Glenn describes the two main components of citizenship in a nation. *Formal citizenship* is created through law and policy. It defines rights and responsibilities, and it creates a legal structure that legitimates the recognition (or denial) of individuals as citizens. Many women who migrate to take jobs as careworkers have only partial or no formal citizen rights in the nation where they live and their status shapes the nature of the work that is available to them. Raijman and her colleagues provide an example of women with few rights in their study of undocumented Latinas working as domestics in Israel. Their illegal status and inability to obtain formal Israeli citizenship excludes them from most jobs regardless of their previous employment or current skills and segregates them into domestic work. It is easy to exploit these women, for example by withholding back wages, since they worry more about being deported for having overstayed their tourist visas than about trying to claim the wages that are owed to them.

Kim's article also illustrates a formal exclusion from the right to work, applied to wives of international students in the United States. However, in this case, rather than working illegally, the outcome is different. The Korean students' wives that she describes feel forced into intensive mothering and a life focused on carework, even though many of them held jobs back home. Their choices are different than the workers in Israel because they did not migrate in order to work and because their families are less impoverished.

However, even in cases when women are legal labor migrants, their jobs can be restricted according to their nationality, and furthermore, they may be excluded from permanent settlement. In essence, their civil rights are limited and they have only *partial citizenship*. Such exclusion is usually reserved for workers who are expected to take on marginalized jobs. For example, Shu-Ju Ada Cheng's article describes how Taiwan's 1992 Employment Service Law limits foreign workers to three unskilled labor occupations—domestics, caregivers, and construction or manufacturing workers—as well as six white-collar job categories. Since only workers from the Philippines, Thailand, Indonesia, Malaysia, and Vietnam are eligible for the unskilled jobs, there is an implicit association between low skill and race or nationality. In other words, racial-ethnic occupational segregation and stereotyping are fostered by the Taiwanese government's immigration restrictions, making the performance of carework more difficult for the workers.

This process is extended into a *legal othering*, which is how Cheng refers to the extensive regulations that accompany work permission. Foreign laborers must have regular health exams every six months and cannot change jobs or employers, cannot bring family members, and cannot marry other foreigners or locals. These racial-nationality restrictions are also gendered: Women must take regular pregnancy tests and are supposed to be deported if they become pregnant. Cheng argues that Taiwan's controls on immigrant women's bodies are a way to maintain the current "ethnoscape," or the racial-ethnic composition of the country. Formal citizenship laws are clearly controlling and limit how paid carework is done and by whom.

The legal devaluation of migrant domestics from the Philippines is reflected in their social devaluation. Cheng provides examples from handbooks for Taiwanese housewives that describe migrant domestics as technologically backward and poor, as having different and often lesser work ethics, and as either oversexualized (Filipina domestics) or desexualized (Thai and Indonesia domestics). This discourse is similar to that found in colonizing countries about the supposedly inferior inhabitants of their colonies. Thus, South Asian domestic workers are essentialized as culturally and racially different "wailao" or foreign labor—and that difference is considered "undesirable" or culturally marginal—while native-born Taiwanese domestics are uniformly thought to be better and "more like us."

Believing these stereotypes about South Asian migrant domestics, Taiwanese employers enforce additional restrictions on them, as described below, and thus employers become complicit with the government as social control agents both by limiting workers' civil rights and by buying into an ideology that devalues these workers.

The second component is *substantive citizenship*, or the ability to exercise one's formal rights. For individuals, this requires access to a minimum level of economic security and resources so that people can take advantage of the rights to which they are entitled. At a societal level, this requires that local and national government officials, as well as ordinary people, enforce these rights.

Cheng's study of Filipina domestics clearly illustrates the loss of substantive citizenship when ordinary citizens—Taiwanese employers and employment agencies—enforce and extend their government's exclusionary practices. Since employers must pay a guarantee deposit to cover the cost of deporting a worker who runs away or does not finish her work contract, they impose restrictions to be sure the deposit is refunded. Their strategies include confiscating domestic worker's passports, forced savings (withholding earnings and putting them in a bank account), restricting mobility outside the employer's home so that they cannot easily network with other domestic workers, and monitoring worker's sexuality—strategies which limit workers' private lives as well as how they perform their jobs, and practices that are applied unequally to women and men. Thus inequality among women, according to social class and nationality, becomes institutionalized in the global economy.

RACE-ETHNICITY, GENDER, CLASS, AND CAREWORK LABOR

In her excerpt, Glenn makes the case that racial-ethnic, gender, and class stratification are embedded in and intertwined with citizenship and labor systems in the United States. The articles in Part 2—on Taiwan, Israel, Canada, and also on the United States—demonstrate that similar dynamics occur on a global level. We can see these intersections of race-ethnicity (or national origin), gender, and social class in the dynamics of global carework by looking at social controls on migration and migrants, differentially applied citizenship regulations, and labor market structures.

A country's policies on migration can limit carework opportunities based upon a woman's country of origin. Both Raijman and Cheng argue this happens so that nations can simultaneously acquire needed workers on a temporary basis, while maintaining a country's perceived racial-ethnic composition. The articles by

Raijman and Kim both describe complete prohibitions on work by Latino migrants to Israel and by Korean students' wives in the United States, respectively. In the face of comparable barriers to employment, Latinas opt to work illegally in Israel, while Korean international students' wives retreat into unpaid carework. The difference in the Latinas' and Koreans' strategies is based on a third factor, social class, which is reflected in their reasons for migration. Latinas migrate to Israel, by themselves, explicitly to find jobs and increase their families' incomes at home. Many are single mothers. In contrast, the Korean women, who are usually college graduates themselves and former business and professional workers, migrate with their husbands and for their husbands' graduate education. They hope to be employed or continue education while in the United States, but that is not their motivation for migration.

Regardless of whether a migrant's employment is legal, the level of state control and *surveillance* is much higher on paid carework than on unpaid carework. Stringent regulations apply in both legal (e.g., for Filipinas in Taiwan) and illegal (e.g., for Latinas in Israel) contexts, and the work is heavily monitored. While it may not be surprising that the undocumented Latina domestics and careworkers in Israel feared deportation, Cheng shows that Filipinas who legally worked in Taiwan had similar worries, since they could be deported for getting pregnant or getting married while there.

In contrast, unpaid carework gains little legal attention and is regulated primarily through marriage laws rather than by labor laws. Some women migrate from former communist countries (such as Poland or Russia) or from troubled economies in Asia (such as Thailand, Vietnam, or the Philippines) as mail-order brides, or perhaps e-mail brides, to marry men from developed countries or newly industrializing nations. Frequently, such women are motivated by economic need; meanwhile men are seeking traditional marriages in which wives focus their activities on unpaid domestic work and carework, and these future husbands want to believe stereotypes that "exotic" Asian women will be home-oriented. Unfortunately, most studies of migration and carework labor do not include these marriage migrants in their analyses, perhaps because they are unaffected by labor regulations. One could argue that, like the international students' wives who are also ignored in migration studies, these women may end up performing extensive unpaid carework. Surprisingly, some of these migration-for-marriage agreements involve indirect payments for the wives' family carework when new husbands agree to send remittances to the women's families back home. Such cases could be construed as unregulated payment for unpaid carework.

Like class and gender, nation of origin, which is the basis for ethnicity and is tied to racial composition, is embedded in labor market systems. The intersection of racial ethnicity or nationality with gender and class is most clearly visible in Cheng's description of Filipina's carework labor in Taiwan: Women from only five countries are eligible to migrate for domestic work and carework jobs there, and only men from these same countries can migrate for construction work. Furthermore, since those jobs also are considered low-skill and dirty, class is intertwined with race and gender. While this division of labor is internal to Taiwan, it also creates an international division of paid labor across countries, according to race, class, and gender, or as Parreñas labels it in her excerpt, an international division of reproductive labor. While Parreñas highlights the hierarchical relationships among women, Cheng demonstrates the role of the nation state in structuring these connections.

Finally, Glenn argues that racial-ethnic or nationality groups may be excluded from different aspects of citizenship—although not necessarily from all aspects simultaneously. The articles on unpaid carework provide two illustrations of this partial citizenship. Kim's research on the Korean wives of Korean students in the United States provides an example of the link between the two forms of citizenship and women's work. As international students, men enter the United States on F1 visas, but their wives' F2 (dependents') visas do not allow them to work, regardless of their previous jobs in Korea. The students' wives have the right to enter full-time undergraduate or graduate programs, but since 9/11 they are not allowed to go to school on a part-time basis. Therefore, their formal citizenship rights are limited. Without kin to watch their children, and without the ability to earn tuition money, their educational rights are rarely exercised. Thus their substantive citizenship also is limited, and without other options, they are forced into becoming full-time careworkers for their families—freeing their husbands from any household responsibility, but limiting the women's own options.

Chinese and South Asian immigrant women in Canada, who are caregivers for family members with chronic illnesses, also are pushed into performing increased amounts of carework, according to Spitzer's research, because of government cutbacks in programs and health services. Immigrant women must do this intensive unpaid carework while simultaneously taking on more paid work than they previously had done in order to cover increased family expenses. Wives' workload is shaped by the *gendered nature of caregiving*—sons did little carework for their elderly parents and other female relatives, who might help wives with these tasks, were not usually available since family networks had been ruptured by migration. Wives were similarly burdened by the *ethnic nature of caregiving*—because family members who were trying to preserve traditional (gender) norms insisted that any outside help had to be culturally and linguistically appropriate, especially for elders with health-care problems. Therefore, wives bore the primary burden of care and public aid programs were rarely used. Migration made these problems particularly noticeable to the women because the situation had been different at home: Women from China were used to having support from their work units, and women from South Asia either had had servants, or were afforded time off from work and had help from other women family members because there was no state system of support. In Canada, the funding and cultural inadequacies in health services limited their substantive citizenship in the realm of rights to health care.

CONCLUSION

In sum, migration is significant to the global economy because it creates new labor supplies and, increasingly, that labor supply is composed of women. However, the job opportunities for women migrants are often limited to low-wage carework. That work remains low wage, in part, because carework is often characterized and essentialized as based on women's so-called natural traits. These false beliefs provide a rationale for considering carework unskilled labor and as not deserving higher pay. In addition, women who migrate to perform paid carework are usually taking over the unpaid carework of other, often upper-middle-class and differently raced women, establishing a class and racial-ethnic–based inequality among women both in the local and the global economies. Examining carework through the lens of transnational migration and in the context of "globalization from above" reveals several other key features.

First, for several reasons there is often fluidity between paid and unpaid work in women's lives. Since paid and unpaid carework are not mutually exclusive, women who migrate for paid work continue to nurture their families at home even while working overseas, as described in Part 3 on transnational motherhood. Furthermore, stringent regulations on paid carework allow women to migrate for a limited time period, so at some point they must return to their home countries and unpaid carework. In other cases, women find themselves asked to change marital and pay status. For example, some single Filipinas working overseas as domestics find themselves pushed into marrying the elderly men whom they care for— merely so a family can save money on carework expenses. Finally, in other cases, women migrate to marry, but like Filipinas who migrate to wed South Korean farmers, they find themselves simultaneously doing both unpaid family work and unpaid family farm labor as well.

Second, the global carework labor market is structured by national citizenship and marriage regulations and not just by individuals' choices. For some migrants, like careworkers in Israel or international students' wives in the United States, paid work is prohibited and few citizenship rights are available. Other paid careworkers are recruited by employment agencies in developed or newly industrializing countries from a limited set of developing countries that are usually defined by immigration laws. Once women arrive to work under these temporary labor contracts, strict surveillance is applied to them—often including confiscation of their passports, required regular health and pregnancy tests, limited opportunities to get out of the house and socialize with other careworkers, and postponed pay—all of which limit their substantive citizen rights and result in partial citizenship.

Third, the articles included in Part 2 illustrate that gender is interconnected with race-ethnicity, nation, and class in shaping carework labor systems on a transnational level—not just within nations. One consequence of globalized carework is that the inequalities among women are intensifying and global stratification systems are strengthened, rather than undermined. Middle- and upper-class women in the United States and other developed countries benefit from these migration chains, obtaining low-cost help with domestic work and carework that is still defined as their responsibility. In the past domestic workers or careworkers might have been women of color or working-class women who had resided in the United States for long periods of time. Increasingly, today careworkers are transnational migrants, who are redefined as women of color once they are within U.S. borders. These are some of the issues that we take up in Part 3.

DISCUSSION QUESTIONS

1. Part 2 focuses on the ways in which citizenship, migration, and labor regulations limit and shape women's opportunities to perform paid and unpaid carework, especially as "viewed from above." In what ways do the readings suggest that women resist these restrictions, as "seen from below"?
2. How does migration alone versus migration with a family member influence carework? Does a migrant woman's marital status make a difference to her carework?
3. Why do governments control who may enter their nation and what work transnational migrants may perform? What forms of control and surveillance are used?
4. Describe some of the ways in which gender and race-ethnicity (or nationality) intersect in shaping the carework of transnational migrants.

Falk, Richard. 1993. "The Making of Global Citizenship," pp. 39–50 in Jeremy Brecher, John Brown Childs, and Jill Cutler (eds.), *Global Visions: Beyond the New World Order*. Boston: South End Press.

Glazer, Nona. 1993. *Women's Paid and Unpaid Labor: The Work Transformation in Health Care and Retailing*. Philadelphia: Temple University Press.

Mies, Maria, Veronika Bennholdt-Thomson, and Claudia von Werlhof. 1988. *Women: The Last Colony*. London: Zed.

Sassen, Saskia. 2002. "Global Cities and Survival Circuits." In Barbara Ehrenreich and Arlie R. Hochschild (eds.), *Global Woman: Nannies, Maids, and Sex Workers in the New Economy*. New York: Henry Holt.

United Nations. 2000. *The World's Women 2000: Trends and Statistics*. UN Publication Number E.OO.XVII.14. New York: United Nations.

9 "JUST LIKE ONE OF THE FAMILY": DOMESTIC SERVANTS IN WORLD POLITICS

Cynthia Enloe

In this excerpt on the international flow of domestic workers, Enloe shows how structural adjustment policies influence women to migrate overseas for carework jobs. She argues that earlier restrictions on the migration of male workers' wives have carried over into similar restrictions on women who migrate for work, regardless of their marital status.

DOMESTIC SERVANTS AND THE IMF

Women seek domestic-servant jobs outside their own countries for many reasons. While those reasons may be the result of distorted development—elite corruption, dependence on exploitative foreign investors, refusal to implement genuine land reform—the women who emigrate usually speak in more immediate terms. They need to earn money to support landless parents or an unemployed husband. They are the sole supporter of their children. They are afraid that if they don't emigrate they will have no choice but to work as prostitutes. They cannot find jobs in the fields for which they were trained. Civil war has made life at home unbearable. They have sisters and schoolmates who have gone abroad and promise to help find them work. These may be private calculations, but they help governments trying to balance their trade and payoff their international debts.

International debt politics has helped create the incentives for many women to emigrate, while at the same time it has made governments dependent on the money those women send home to their families. The International Monetary Fund, which serves as a vanguard for the commercial banking community by pressuring indebted governments to adopt policies which will maximize a country's ability to repay its outstanding loans with interest, has insisted that governments cut their social-service budgets. Reductions in food-price subsidies are high on the IMF's list of demands for any government that wants its financial assistance. Keeping wages down, cutting back public works, reducing the numbers of government employees, rolling back health and education budgets—these are standard IMF

[handwritten note:] opposite of what has really worked for any country that has developed.

prescriptions for indebted governments. They usually attract support from at least some members of the government itself, especially in the finance ministry.

These policies have different implications for women and men in the indebted country, because women and men usually have such dissimilar relationships to family maintenance, waged employment, public services and public policy-making. If a government does decide to adopt the IMF package, feeding a family and maintaining its members' health will become more taxing. Food will cost more, while income coming into the household is likely to fall. Senior government officials often fear that if they implement the IMF policies, they will lose their popular support. Daily life will become so hard that large sectors of the public will take the risk of openly calling for the regime's removal. Thus policy-makers make their own calculations: they need the IMF loans to maintain international credibility; but if they swallow the IMF pill whole, they may not be around to benefit from that credibility. Crucial to this political calculation, though not acknowledged, is the absorption capacity of individual households: how much financial belt-tightening can each family tolerate?

This question depends on the skill and willingness of women—as wives and single mothers. . . . Thus the politics of international debt is not simply something that has an impact on women in indebted countries. The politics of international debt won't work in their current form unless mothers and wives are willing to be- have in ways that enable nervous regimes to adopt cost-cutting measures without forfeiting their political legitimacy. It is the recognition of this strategic link between financial policy, regime stability and women's domestic responsibilities that has made women activists in Third World countries the leading theoreticians in developing a distinctly feminist analysis of international debt politics. . . . [1]

The women and men who send this money home go abroad to do quite different sorts of jobs. The men emigrate to work as seamen and construction workers. . . . The women whose home governments rely on them for remittances go abroad to work as nurses, maids, entertainers and prostitutes.

This gendered labor export system is built on the personal relationships between women and the men in their families. . . . [W]omen's lack of access to the resources necessary to cope while their husbands are away can make a man's absence impossibly stressful. The problems of a woman whose husband has left home to take a job on a Kuwaiti tanker are not just those of a single adult; she is a woman in a patriarchal society. Government officials who need those men to earn money overseas count on their wives to cope with the burdens. The politics of international debt are in no small measure the politics of these women's coping. . . .

Sri Lanka and the Philippines are the two countries today whose economic stability is most dependent on feminized migrant labor. Sri Lankan and Filipino women who leave home to work abroad have become economically more important than their male counterparts. Some of the Filipino women are recruited to work as nurses, some as entertainers. But the greatest number work as domestic servants. Their governments have relied on feminized labor at home—on plantations, in tourist resorts, in Export Processing Zones—to stay financially afloat. Now they also depend on women's overseas earnings to keep foreign creditors and their financial policeman, the International Monetary Fund, content.

"DOWN BIG YARD": MAIDS AND THE STATE

Primrose is a 35-year-old Jamaican woman working as a domestic worker in Toronto, Canada. . . . After eight years Primrose had come to the conclusion that the white women—and their often demanding children—for whom she kept house were only part of the problem. The Canadian and Jamaican governments, were also to blame for the conditions domestic workers had to cope with. . . .

Primrose, like other Caribbean, Latin American, Asian and British women working in Canada as domestic servants, comes face to face with the Canadian government in the form of the Immigration Department. "She is a hassle, but Immigration is also a hassle, and you never know when they might decide to send you home."[2] Pressing an employer for back pay or time off is risky. If the employer is having marital troubles with her husband and isn't getting sufficient household money to pay the salary due, the domestic worker is reluctant to go to the Immigration Office to get help in enforcing her contract.

"I have a girlfriend and every time she has to go down to Immigration she say, 'I'm going for sentence now. Down big yard.' So if I'm going tomorrow, I'll say, 'I'm going for sentence,' and they'll say, 'Good luck!' because any time you going down there is problems. If the government wanted to do something about it, they could.[3] . . .

The 1980s was a turning point. The Canadian parliament had tightened its immigration laws during a period of rising unemployment and increasing public debate about racial tensions. For their part, immigrant domestic workers began to develop their own organizations: Domestic Workers United and Intercede, the International Coalition to End Domestics' Exploitation. Intercede, a group of Caribbean and Filipino women, focussed its attention on Canadian immigration law, for as long as domestic workers were made vulnerable by immigration regulations, they would be too weak to effectively bargain with their employers. In other words, a person who hires a woman to clean or mind her children is never in simply a personal relationship with that woman: her discretion is conditioned by the government's immigration regulations and its bureaucracy's way of administering those rulings.

In 1981 Intercede persuaded the Canadian parliament to change the law so that foreign domestic workers on temporary visas would have the same rights under labor law as Canadian citizens. . . .

In Britain, France, Saudi Arabia, Japan and the United States immigrant domestic workers' relationships with each other and with their employers are shaped in large part by political debates over immigration. These debates, so indicative of a society's own national identity and what it thinks of its place in the international system, are usually riddled with assumptions about male and female citizenship. Broadly speaking, many governments since World War II have acted as if an "immigrant worker" was male. An "immigrant's family" was composed of the wife and children of that male worker. This portrait does not match the facts, for governments have depended on immigrant women to work in hospitals, to clean office buildings, hotels and airports, to mind children and to operate sewing machines during the decades of post-war economic expansion. . . . The facts notwithstanding, this portrait of a masculinized immigrant workforce encouraged policy-makers to see restrictions on women immigrants as a means of preventing male immigrant workers from putting down roots.

. . . Being a foreign-born wife and being a foreign-born domestic worker often become strikingly similar under restrictive immigration laws.[4]

1. A. Lynn Bolles, "IMF Destabilization: The Impact on Working Class Jamaican Women," *Transafrica Forum*, vol. 2, no. 1, Summer, 1983, pp. 63–76; Gita Sen and Caren Grown, *Development Crises and Alternative Visions: Third World Women's Perspectives*, New York, Monthly Review Press, pp. 59–66; *Women's World*, published by ISIS, special issue on the "Debt Crisis," no. 17, March, 1988; Maria de los Angeles Crummett, "Women in Crisis: Paying the Costs of 'Adjustment' in Rural Mexico," typescript, Department of Economics, Barnard College, Columbia University, NY, 1988; conversations with Peggy Antrobus, Women and Development Program, University of the West Indies, Barbados, in Cambridge, MA, spring, 1987. Peggy Antrobus is developing a detailed analysis of the gendered implications of the global economic crisis.

2. This quote and material surrounding it is drawn from Makeda Silvera, *Silenced*, Toronto, Williams-Wallace Publishers, 1983; the quote appears on p. 100.

3. Ibid.

4. Women, Immigration and Nationality Group (WING), *Worlds Apart: Women Under Immigration and Nationality Law*, London, Pluto Press, 1985, pp. 137–9; Yasmin Alibhai, "For Better or for Worse," *New Statesman and Society*, January 6, 1989, pp. 22–3. For a feminist analysis of the 1988 US Immigration Reform Act, see Annette Fuentes, "Immigration 'Reform': Heaviest Burdens on Women," *Listen Real Loud*, American Friends Service Committee, 1988.

10 | FROM *UNEQUAL FREEDOM: HOW RACE AND GENDER SHAPED AMERICAN CITIZENSHIP AND LABOR*

Evelyn Nakano Glenn

> In this excerpt Evelyn Nakano Glenn describes the two main components of citizenship in a nation: formal citizenship, which is created through law and policy, and substantive citizenship, which is the ability to exercise one's formal rights. Many women who migrate to take jobs as careworkers have only partial or no formal citizen rights in the nation where they live, and their status shapes the nature of the work that is available to them. Glenn makes the case that racial-ethnic, class, and gender stratification are embedded in and intertwined with citizenship and labor systems in the United States. Other articles in Part 2 illustrate how this intersection in citizenship and labor systems regulates carework around the globe.

EXPLAINING EXCLUSION

Citizenship is not just a matter of formal legal status; it is a matter of belonging, including recognition by other members of the community. Formal law and legal rulings create a structure that legitimates the granting or denial of recognition. However, the maintenance of boundaries relies on "enforcement" not only by designated officials but also by so-called members of the public. In the South, for example, segregation of public conveyances was enforced not only by white drivers and conductors but also by white passengers, who imposed sanctions on blacks whom they perceived as violating boundaries. Contrarily, men and women may act on the basis of alternative schemas of race, gender, and citizenship that differ from those in formal law or policy. For example, in the Southwest, in an era when full citizenship rested on white racial status, Mexicans were designated as "white" by the U.S. government, but many Anglos did not recognize the official "whiteness" of Mexicans and often refused to consider them "Americans" entitled to political and civil rights. . . .

Still, because excluded groups by definition have often lacked resources and access to courts and other formal venues to mount such challenges, much of their opposition has taken place in informal or "disguised" ways and in informal sites. These less formal types of contestation have been even more neglected by scholars of citizenship than formal challenges. . . .

Citizenship is constituted through a process that involves not only beliefs and activities of various elements of the elite but also those of ordinary people, including those denied recognition and rights. . . .

I focus on how the boundaries and meanings of citizenship are reinforced, enacted, and contested in ways related to race and gender at the local level and in everyday interaction. This focus clarifies the distinction between formal and substantive citizenship, and it avoids an overly monolithic view of oppression by revealing the variability and unevenness in the race-gender boundaries of citizenship.

Formal citizenship is that embodied in law and policy, while substantive citizenship is the actual ability to exercise rights of citizenship. Substantive citizenship involves two issues. One has to do with a capacity to exercise rights to which one is formally entitled. T. H. Marshall made this point when he argued that social citizenship—the right to a modicum of economic security, education, and other resources—was necessary to realize one's civil and political rights. For example, the right to bring suit in court (a civil right) is only possible if individuals have access to legal representation.[1] The second issue has to do with enforcement or lack of enforcement of formal citizenship rights by the national, state, or local government or by members of the public. Racialized and gendered citizenship is created when theoretically universal citizenship rights are differentially enforced. For example, universal suffrage may be guaranteed by the Constitution, but historically the right to vote has been differentially protected. . . .

Different groups may also be excluded from different facets of citizenship. Several aspects of citizenship should be differentiated. At the most general level is the notion of citizenship simply as belonging—membership in the community, sometimes defined as the nation. Within this meaning, however, there are several sub-meanings, including the notion of *standing* (being recognized as a full adult capable of exercising choice and assuming responsibilities); the notion of *nationality* (being identified as part of a people who constitute a nation, whether corresponding to the boundaries of a nation state or not); and the notion of *allegiance* (being a loyal member of the community). A given category of people may be excluded from one of these meanings of citizenship but included in other meanings.

A second set of distinctions has to do with different kinds of rights that go with belonging. The most widely used model is T. H. Marshall's tripartite model of civil, political, and social citizenship. . . . An additional facet that I will touch on is one that recent scholars have called cultural citizenship. Cultural citizenship refers to the right to maintain cultures and languages differing from the dominant ones without losing civil or political rights or membership in the national community.[2] . . .

For nonwhite people and women, citizenship has always been a malleable structure, molded by the efforts of dominant groups seeking to enforce their own definitions of citizenship and its boundaries, and by the efforts of subordinated groups to contest these definitions and boundaries. Thus the meaning of citizenship has evolved over time, has varied by place, and has differed for different people. It is out of struggles at the local level that regionally and historically specific formal and substantive citizenship has emerged.

To understand how citizenship has been shaped by race and gender and in turn how it has helped create and maintain race and gender inequality, we have to study citizenship, not in isolation, but in relation to race-gender formation in other institutions in the society—the family, schools, political parties, and the labor market. Of these institutions the one most closely entwined with the formation of American citizenship has been the labor system, to which we now turn. . . .

LABOR AND CITIZENSHIP

Coercion continued to structure the work of men and women of color long after it became technically illegal to subject a citizen to voluntary or involuntary servitude. This was closely correlated with two factors: the character of regional economies where large numbers of workers of color were concentrated (and to which they had often been recruited), and segregation of the labor market that confined people of color to certain industries. The division between free and coercive labor regimes correlated to a significant extent with the division between more advanced capitalist industries and the less advanced preindustrial sector. . . .

These coercive labor practices can be seen as violating the intent and spirit of the Thirteenth Amendment and antipeonage laws, and therefore as deviating from the supposed American commitment to freedom. . . . However, when such practices were challenged in courts, the liberal theory of contract actually helped legitimate debt bondage. It did so by positing a theoretical equality between employer and worker that ignored the employer's economic power to affect the worker's ability to give voluntary consent. U.S. court decisions in the Gilded Age often . . . protected employers' rights to impose economic constraints that had the effect of preventing workers from leaving their jobs and from exercising autonomy in their "private" lives. In essence, the courts did not recognize debt bondage as a form of peonage. Only in the 1930s did the efforts of organized labor succeed in bringing about a shift to "modern" labor relations based on collective bargaining and legislative regulation.[3]

THE OBLIGATION TO WORK

It was not just liberal law and belated feudalism that reinforced coercion in the labor system. Even more fundamentally, American concepts of citizenship supported the legitimacy of forced labor under certain circumstances. This is because of what some historians have identified as a central element of American citizenship, namely the obligation to work and earn. Judith Shklar has argued that, along with the ballot, "the opportunity to work and be paid an earned reward for one's labor" is the main source by which individuals gain public standing, by which she means respect and recognition as a full member of society. In her formulation, to be a citizen in good standing one must be economically independent, that is, an "earner"—a "free remunerated worker, one who is rewarded for the actual work he has done."[4] Originally, this meant being neither a slave (who works but does not earn) nor an aristocrat (who does not work); implicitly, it also meant not being a woman (whose work is owed to and owned by the male head of her family).

The latter half of the nineteenth century saw fundamental shifts in the U.S. economy (from a small producer economy to capitalist industrialization) and expansion of civil and political citizenship (with the abolition of slavery and peonage and expanded suffrage). Ownership of one's labor and the ability to freely sell it, rather than ownership of productive property, became the basis for claiming independence. Within this definition, at least theoretically, free labor status was universalized. Despite this theoretical freedom, however, people of color and white women continued to be viewed as dependent and to find themselves subject to more intensive exploitation and restrictive controls than white men.

Why and how has the U.S. labor system maintained inequality and coercion despite a theoretically free labor system? The answers are complex. With regard to inequality and lack of mobility, one part of the answer in the case of white women was the continuing reliance on the household for reproduction and subsistence activity and women's responsibility for this labor. As a result, women continued to be defined as economically dependent on male breadwinners and their unpaid labor was considered an obligation rather than being voluntary. For men and women of color, the main structural mechanisms ensuring exploitability and lack of mobility in the labor market were occupational stratification and segregation.

women's choice

NOTES

1. Marshall, T. H. 1964. "Citizenship and Social Class," in *Class, Citizenship, and Social Development*. New York: Doubleday: p. 107.

2. Rosaldo, Renato. 1994. "Cultural Citizenship in San José, California," *PoLAR* 17 (November): 57.

3. Orren, Karen. 1991. *Belated Feudalism: Labor, the Law, and Liberal Development in the United States*. New York: Cambridge University Press: pp. 15–19, 211–215.

4. Shklar, Judith N. 1991. *American Citizenship: The Quest for Inclusion*. Cambridge, MA: Harvard University Press: p. 64.

11 | RETHINKING THE GLOBALIZATION OF DOMESTIC SERVICE: FOREIGN DOMESTICS, STATE CONTROL, AND THE POLITICS OF IDENTITY IN TAIWAN

Shu-Ju Ada Cheng

This article on domestic service in Taiwan shows how the state has an impact on transnational women migrants' work, even in an age of global interdependence. The Taiwanese government recruits women from only five countries for domestic and carework, restricts the contractual terms under which the women do this work using legal othering, extensive surveillance, and delimited partial citizenship rights, and then engages employers to help in its gendered and raced efforts of labor control.

The globalization of domestic service has drawn much scholarly attention during the past several years. In this article, I argue that domestic service, while increasingly associated with a gendered transnational labor system globally, is constantly reconstituted as a new labor regime locally. The state mediates the globalization of domestic service, and national policies continue to shape the welfare of foreign domestics as governed subjects. The state remains integral to the gendered analysis of carework.

Taiwan became one of the major labor-receiving countries in Asia in the mid-1980s. The entry of foreign labor became a public concern, which compelled the Taiwanese government to legalize a labor importation scheme in 1991. In 1992, migrant women were first legalized to work as domestics. Since then, domestic service, as a state-sanctioned legal occupation, has been under state control.

I examine the case of Taiwan to demonstrate the role of the state in shaping the experience of foreign domestics. My central argument focuses on the relationship between the household and the nation, through which the tension between the state and globalizing processes becomes intensified and shapes the lives of foreign domestics. . . . The household practices of Taiwanese employers indirectly facilitate the state's control over foreign domestics as alien subjects and assist the state's agenda in policing national borders. Bringing state practices, popular discourse, and the rhetoric and practices of Taiwanese employers together, I demonstrate that they collectively constitute a regulatory regime constraining the lives of foreign domestics and perpetuating gender inequality.

In this age of global interdependence, the state continues to exercise influence. The management of foreign domestics within households of employment is not only important for labor control but also central to the state's administration over its alien subjects. It expresses the state's anxiety over a changing demographic landscape. It is ultimately integral to the state's control over its national borders and over the future contour of the nation. The case study of Taiwan is important because it demonstrates the centrality of the state to the organization of national and global systems of care. It offers us the opportunity to reexamine the role of the state in mediating a transnational and highly gendered labor system.

THEORETICAL FRAMEWORK: ARTICULATING THE HOUSEHOLD AND THE NATION

Domestic service . . . challenges essentialist conceptions of gender and of universal womanhood since "many women employers simply perpetuate the sexist division of labor by passing on the most devalued work in their lives to another woman—generally a woman of color" (Romero 1992, 131). Yet domestic service is also an institution through which gender ideology and sexual inequality operate. The globalization of domestic service further illustrates the state's appropriation of women's labor and the gendered nature of all national systems of care. When women from developing nations migrate to developed or other developing nations to care for other people's families, they leave the care of their children and elders to their female relatives or other domestics. At the same time, passing on housework to women from other countries does not necessarily facilitate the liberation of women employers in labor-receiving countries. Local women continue to be deemed responsible for the maintenance of their households in local communities. Women at both ends of the migration process bear the cost of social reproduction while respective governments are spared the burden of fully compensating their reproductive labor. In short, while the globalization of domestic service simultaneously manifests and reproduces the prescribed gender division of labor both within and across national borders, it also points to the state's appropriation of care labor and the lack of official recognition for women's carework as equally important as productive factors to national economies.

Researchers have examined the globalization of domestic service from various angles. . . . Most studies of the globalization of domestic service have come from three major theoretical paradigms. The first is the international division of labor perspective. Researchers assert that the globalization of domestic service reproduces gendered and racialized divisions of labor in global capitalism and that it constitutes a transfer of labor between developed and less developed regions and nations. . . .

Furthering and complicating this international division of labor perspective are studies on the transnational nature of female labor migration. The international division of labor perspective retains the nation as the unit of analysis and stresses the inequitable distribution of reproductive labor between countries of unequal development. In contrast, the transnational perspective focuses on the interconnected dynamics of global capitalism. It highlights the interdependence of women situated at unequal points along social, economic, and national hierarchies, as well as the different effects of global restructuring of care on these women. . . .

A third theoretical paradigm, without dismissing the force of global economic restructuring, stresses the intervention of the state and the impact of state policies. Both Chin (1998) and Chang (2000) focused on the maneuvering of the state amid global forces and explored how state policies shape household politics under the context of globalization. . . .

My work builds on these latter studies on the importance of the state in the globalization of domestic service. . . . I am particularly interested in how the question of the nation is codified into state policies and translated into concrete household practices. . . . [I]t is necessary to examine how nationalist politics, reflected through state policies, dictate the particular experience of foreign domestics within the household as well as society as a whole. In other words, the linkage between the household and the nation needs to be fully explored.

METHODOLOGICAL APPROACHES

This article is based on a six-month ethnographic research project on the experience of Filipina domestics in Taiwan. I stayed in Taiwan from July to December 1999 and was mainly based in Taipei. For my overall research project, I used multiple methodologies. I collected firsthand sources and reviewed materials written in the local language. . . . In addition, I conducted formal in-depth interviews with thirty-five Filipina domestics, twelve Taiwanese employers, three government officials, four employment agencies, and five local labor groups. In addition to conducting in-depth interviews, I regularly attended the religious gatherings of Filipina domestics. I alternated between two churches for this part of the research, and I focused on one of them for participant observation. I also regularly went to a detention center to interview undocumented workers and attended a couple of court proceedings regarding the case of an undocumented Filipina domestic.

I will demonstrate how the state shapes the experience of foreign domestics through examining state practices, popular discourse, and the rhetoric and practices of Taiwanese employers. For the section on state practices, I reviewed relevant laws as well as legislative reports . . . among them dating back to the late 1980s. . . . For the section on popular discourse, I utilized materials from the newspaper reports, official manuals, magazine articles, and nonacademic books . . . and . . . [f]or the section on the rhetoric and practices of Taiwanese employers, I used narratives from formal interviews with them. . . . The use of data from multiple methodologies enables me to articulate the interlocking control of the regulatory regime at discursive, material, and institutional levels.

My goal is to demonstrate the structural effects of the regulatory regime on the lives of foreign domestics. I decided not to include the voices of foreign domestics ` in order not to distract from the theoretical debate. . . .

STATE PRACTICES OF CONTROL AND EXCLUSION: THE INSTITUTIONALIZATION OF OTHERING

To understand state practices of control and exclusion in Taiwan, it is necessary to examine the complex fusion of racial and nationalist politics embedded in the process of labor importation. . . .

It is important to note that foreigners have always worked in Taiwan as missionaries, English teachers, and white-collar professionals, and in other occupations. These foreigners usually have come from regions of high socioeconomic development, such as Japan, the United States, Canada, and Europe. Their presence has not stirred extensive public debates, nor has it compelled the state to institutionalize their legal status. It was not until the mid-1980s that the sheer numerical expansion of foreigners from South and Southeast Asia triggered all forms of discourses and control mechanisms about them. It was then that the term *wailao*, "foreign labor" in Chinese, emerged in the process and that foreign labor was gradually constructed as a social problem. Interestingly, this occurred at the same time that the struggle for an independent Taiwanese national identity intensified. . . .

The emergence of the term *wailao* and the characteristics associated with it deserve particular attention. *Wailao*, a generic term for foreign workers of both sexes, does not refer to all foreigners working in Taiwan. It mainly refers to foreign workers from South and Southeast Asia. While foreigners are always considered different, it is the undesirable difference of this particular group of foreigners that calls for public concern. Wailao are in demand for the so-called 3K (dirty, dangerous, and unskilled) jobs and for the relief of labor shortages, but dirty, dangerous, and unskilled has also come to symbolize what this group of foreign laborers means to Taiwan. Foreign workers from South and Southeast Asia are often described as racially, culturally, and religiously different from the Taiwanese. The imaginary differences of these wailao become analogous to their assumed poverty, criminality, lower work ethics, and backwardness. As the source of social evils, foreign workers are often regarded as the culprit of crimes, prostitution, contagious diseases, and racial/ethnic conflict. Interestingly, foreignness is usually articulated to be the major reason for their undesirable difference. While foreignness is juxtaposed with national, cultural, and racial differences, what constitutes the racial distinction between foreign workers and Taiwanese is usually left unarticulated. The emphasis on foreignness as well as national and cultural differences simultaneously subsumes the implicit articulation of physical differences, the marker of which is skin color. . . .

In August 1992, the Taiwanese government finally legalized the importation of foreign domestics. By the end of 2000, there were more than 11,000 domestics working in Taiwan. This number includes only documented workers. Women have also entered the country to work as domestics through the category of caregiver, a response to the government's freeze on importing of foreign domestics. Foreign women in both categories are required to do what is generally considered domestic work. If we add the number of caregivers, the total number of migrant women doing domestic work increases to more than 26,000 in 1998.

The legal grounds for regulating foreign labor did not exist until May 1992, when the government ratified the Employment Service Law, which is the central legal instrument for the regulation and employment of foreigners. The Employment Service Law stipulated that foreigners could be employed in nine categories of work. The first six categories are white-collar and respectable occupations, including occupations such as managers, college teachers, athletes, performers, entertainers, and missionaries. The last three categories, generally considered lower and unskilled, include domestics, caregivers, and laborers working in the construction and manufacturing industries. The term *wailao* usually applies to workers imported through the last three categories. For these categories, only laborers from the Philippines, Thailand, Indonesia, Malaysia, and recently Vietnam are eligible for employment. Even though the categories appear to be skill oriented, the eligibility for employment is nation specific. Foreign workers of these nationalities are considered racially and culturally different, and this produces an implicit association of skill, nationality, and race.

Taiwan's foreign labor policy reflects the state's anxiety over a changing ethnoscape within its national boundaries and reveals its deep-seated concern over the development of national identity. According to immigration regulations, foreign workers need to obtain records of good health and good conduct prior to their entry. They are not allowed to work in different jobs or for different employers unless certain irregular circumstances occur.[1] They are not allowed to bring family members during their employment, nor are they allowed to marry either other foreigners or locals. Both men and women have to submit to health examinations every six months. For women, the health examination includes a pregnancy test. They are supposed to be deported if they become pregnant and/or give birth to a child. In other words, the exclusion of foreign labor from permanent settlement has been crucial to state control.

The treatment of wailao, as opposed to other categories of foreigners, is particularly intrusive. The monitoring and surveillance of both their bodies and their emotions are integral to the state's attempt to police national borders and ultimately to control the racial/ethnic composition of its citizenry. More important, the invasiveness of state regulations over decisions concerning human sexuality, such as marriage and pregnancy, has particular impact on migrant women. The regulation of their sexual activities and reproductive decisions reflects the gendered as well as racial nature of immigration policies. The control of women's bodies becomes a means through which the state realizes its particular racial/nationalist project.

State practices of control and exclusion depend on Taiwanese employers and employment agencies for enforcement. Since Taiwanese employers have intimate contact with foreign workers, they bear the responsibility of containing alien labor at home, usually with the assistance of employment agencies. The government imposes on employers the responsibility of ensuring that foreign workers do not violate immigration regulations, for example, by running away or getting pregnant. Specific mechanisms enable and sanction the transfer of power and authority from the state to employers. For example, the employers have to pay a guarantee deposit whose purpose is to defray the living and deportation cost if a foreign worker runs away and is caught. The government returns the whole amount of the deposit to the employers when the foreign workers finish their contracts and return home. The employers lose their deposit if a worker runs away. They also lose their quota for foreign labor and do not regain their quota until the workers are found. Employers are also required to pay a security fee, which is a tax for the employment of foreign labor, held until these workers leave the island.

Since employers are concerned that foreign workers might run away, many impose strict programs of management and surveillance. It is common for employers or employment agencies to confiscate workers' passports. Employers also withhold a certain percentage of workers' earnings and deposit it in the bank. The withheld earnings, euphemized as "forced savings" and sanctioned by the Taiwanese government, are returned to workers after they finish their contracts. Oftentimes, to ensure that foreign workers comply with immigration regulations, employers and employment agencies resort to restricting workers' mobility. For example, some Taiwanese employers prohibit foreign domestics from going out on Sundays. To make sure that they stay home at all times, one employer in my sample did not give his domestics any house keys. Therefore, with the sanction of the state, Taiwanese employers are able to exert overarching authority over foreign labor and serve as indirect agents of control for the state.

Taiwanese employers' control over foreign domestics is gendered, thus rendering their migration experience qualitatively different from that of male migrant workers. The private nature of domestic service enables employers to exert the most invasive scrutiny over domestics and to adopt very coercive measures against them. For foreign domestics, no clear boundary exists between work and home. They are subject to the surveillance of their employers at all times. Working in isolated households, they are unable to establish social networks for collective resistance. Furthermore, the Taiwanese government does not allow migrant women to become pregnant or give birth. The burden of regulating the sexual behavior of migrant women falls on the employers. Taiwanese employers thus expand their control to include these intimate matters. Their anxiety over the sexual activities and reproductive decisions of foreign domestics constitutes the core of the discipline and surveillance of these women workers, which I examine in the next section.

Taiwanese employers and employment agencies thus become governmental instruments in regulating alien labor, masking indirect state control. Therefore, the practices of Taiwanese employers within their households reflect not only interpersonal dynamics but also the dictates of state policies and broader nationalist politics. . . .

POPULAR DISCOURSE ON DOMESTIC SERVICE: FOREIGN DOMESTICS AS THE UNDESIRABLE DIFFERENCE

Foreign domestics in Taiwan mainly come from the Philippines, Thailand, Indonesia, and Malaysia. In October 1999, Vietnamese women were also allowed to enter Taiwan for work as domestics, becoming the fifth group of foreign labor eligible for employment on the island. However, Filipinas have dominated the field of domestic service in Taiwan since the legalization of labor importation. Beginning in the early 1990s, newspapers and magazines in Taiwan have regularly included columns and articles on the training, management, and disciplining of foreign domestics. In addition to academic studies (Lan 2000; Y. Li 1995; Lin 1999; Wang 1996, 1997), several nonacademic books (M. Li 1998; Wei 1998) have also been published on the topic of foreign domestics, Filipina domestics in particular. These columns, articles, and books provide useful information for Taiwanese who plan to employ or have employed foreign domestics. They cover immigration regulations, importation procedures, and the selection of employment agencies. They advise Taiwanese employers on how to train their domestics in the maintenance of households, such as preparing Chinese food, cleaning the house, and taking care of children. They contain information on interpersonal relationships, household dynamics, and possible conflicts derived from racial and cultural differences. They suggest strategies to resolve any problems that might occur from the employment of foreign domestics, and they also discuss possible influences of these domestics on children.

Foreign domestics are consistently constructed as undesirably different from native Taiwanese yet essential to Taiwanese families in popular discourse. There are three major themes through which foreign domestics are constructed as others in Taiwan. These themes include the invocation of the colonial discourse, the production of national myths, and the simultaneous sexualization and asexualization of foreign domestics. Next, I elaborate on these three central elements of popular discourse.

Sanitizing Alien Species, Civilizing the Darkness

The first theme is the invocation of the colonial discourse. One major mechanism in the othering of foreign domestics is the representation of them as savages in need of being civilized and modernized. With the legalization of foreign domestics, words of wisdom have emerged to caution against the perils and the traits associated with wailao. Words of wisdom usually consist of the following logic: Poverty has driven migrant women to work abroad as domestics. Since they come from poor countries, their education, hygienic practices, and physical conditions tend to be inferior. Accordingly, their individual and collective characteristics are also less than satisfactory. . . . Foreign workers' skills, education, and training become irrelevant in comparison. The socioeconomic backgrounds and class statuses of individual Filipinos are secondary to their collective status as migrant labor, which is synonymous with being poor, uneducated, and uncivilized.

Preconceptions about the poverty and the associated backwardness of foreign domestics are central to the discourse on domestic service. Strategies to modernize them and combat their backwardness are integral to the informational repertoires. . . . Technological backwardness, like cultural backwardness, is considered as a consequence of poverty.

Emphasizing the transmission of household skills is central to the construction of foreign domestics as uneducated and uncivilized. . . . For Taiwanese employers, training foreign domestics to do housework and to operate household appliances constitutes a process of reeducating, modernizing, and civilizing. As a result, overseas employment becomes an act of kindness by employers, through which foreign domestics are given the opportunity to become modernized, in sync with Taiwanese women. Hiring a foreign domestic becomes a gesture of goodwill and a form of charity by Taiwanese employers.

Selling National Myths, Strategizing Control of Alien Laborers

The second rhetorical theme is the invention of national myths. Central to the invention of national myths is the emphasis on the different national and cultural characteristics of various groups. Foreign domestics and foreign workers are often assumed to embody distinctive characteristics, undesirably different from Taiwanese nationals. They are also presumed to have different work ethics that require various strategies of control. . . .

Filipino workers tend to be seen as aggressive, disobedient, and militant yet well educated. Thai and Indonesian workers tend to be seen as obedient, docile, and loyal yet less intelligent and less educated. Similarly, Filipina domestics tend to be viewed as intelligent, independent, shrewd, and calculating yet disobedient and militant. Indonesian and Thai women tend to be seen as docile, obedient, reserved, and loyal. . . .

The emphasis on differences among foreign workers is important for several reasons. To distinguish workers of different nationalities from one another further accentuates their essentialized characteristics. The association between national traits and the quality of labor becomes instrumental in diversifying, segregating, and stratifying the labor market. It allows employment agencies to have multiple sources of labor. It also helps confine workers of different nationalities to their own niches at work and creates competition among them. The segregation and separation of workers from different countries allows better control by all agents of power, thus effectively suppressing labor militancy and coalition building. . . . In addition, these differences commodify labor. In other words, for Taiwanese employers, choosing domestics becomes a choice among objectified products with different essentialized traits. These assumed differences also enable Taiwanese employers to deploy diverse strategies of control to ensure their domestics' servility. Most important, the focus on difference heightens the distance between foreign workers and Taiwanese, and it furthers the otherness of foreign labor.

Sexualizing the Exotic, Domesticating Alien Creatures

The third mechanism is the simultaneous sexualization and asexualization of foreign domestics. Since the legalization of foreign domestics, Taiwanese employers *debased*
have been cautioned about Filipina domestics' seductive, sensuous, and hypersex- *animal-*
ual nature. These sexualized images generally are not applied to foreign domestics *like*
of other nationalities, such as Indonesian and Thai women. These women tend to
be seen as more conservative, respectful, reserved, and asexual due to their cultural
upbringing and religious traditions, while Filipinas tend to be seen as promiscu-
ous, seductive, and sexual as a result of their association with the West. Sexualized
images of Filipina domestics tend to stir concern among Taiwanese employers
regarding their sexual activities and reproductive decisions. The state's proscrip-
tion of pregnancy and childbirth creates tremendous stress for both Taiwanese
employers and foreign domestics in Taiwan. For foreign domestics, pregnancy
signifies the termination of their labor contracts and their immediate deportation.
To prevent the untimely deportation of domestics, Taiwanese employers intervene
to scrutinize their lives. . . .

By incorporating sexuality and reproduction as relevant concerns for
Taiwanese employers, popular discourse on domestic service accentuates the
sexuality of Filipina domestics and produces them as sexual others. Sexualizing
Filipina domestics, juxtaposed with the asexualization of domestics of other nationalities, tends to obscure their vulnerability to various forms of sexual abuse
within households of employment. The sexualization of Filipina domestics
facilitates the incorporation of their sexuality as an integral part of their control by
employers. The surveillance of foreign domestics' sexuality as a legitimate management strategy points to the gendered nature of household practices. And this
intrusive surveillance helps relieve the state of its anxiety over the reproduction of
alien labor and serves as indirect state control. . . .

These discursive themes, consistent with the paradigm of undesirable
difference in legal othering, contribute to the representation of foreign domestics
as others in popular discourse.

THE APPROPRIATION OF THE OTHER AND HOUSEHOLD
PRACTICES: THE ROLE OF TAIWANESE EMPLOYERS

In this section, I present findings from my interviews with Taiwanese employers.[2]
I demonstrate how certain Taiwanese deploy rhetoric similar to the popular discourse on foreign domestics and how the rhetoric of the other is appropriated to

justify household practices of control. . . . I use pseudonyms in the following discussion for the sake of confidentiality.

The official rhetoric is that the importation of foreign domestics should liberate Taiwanese women from the burden of household chores and enable them to join the workforce. Yet based on the experience of female Taiwanese employers in my sample, the employment of foreign domestics did not have direct bearing on their participation in the labor force. Among the 12 households I studied, all the women employers had worked prior to their hiring domestics. One woman worked for the family business, while the rest of them held regular employment in the formal sector. One decided to leave work after her first child was born and reentered the workplace after she had hired Filipina domestics. Ten of the Taiwanese women worked and continued to be employed before and after they had employed Filipina domestics. Eight also had had experiences with Taiwanese domestics before employing Filipinas. Many Taiwanese employers turned to foreign domestics because they provided the best solution for cheap labor.

Some Taiwanese employers persistently mentioned the undesirable difference of foreign domestics during our interviews. This undesirable difference was articulated in multiple forms. Some employers emphasized the cultural similarities between Taiwanese employers and Taiwanese domestics. Mrs. Chen, who had employed both Taiwanese and Filipina domestics, used this particular approach. . . . She repeatedly emphasized that her previous Taiwanese domestics were better compared with her current domestic. . . . "Taiwanese domestics usually have our traditional values. They work hard. They are more like us, more like our own family members."

Undesirable difference could be expressed through the juxtaposition of the superiority of Taiwanese employers and the inferiority of foreign workers. Mrs. Chen invoked the collective character of Taiwanese people to articulate her own struggle with the family business: "Taiwanese people are more diligent and hardworking. . . . There is a reason why Filipino people have to go abroad."

Undesirable difference could also be articulated through the emphasis on the stage of economic development in the Philippines. The rhetoric of poverty emerged persistently. One male employer, A-Ho, stressed the poverty of the Philippines and of Filipinos to account for their status as migrant labor: "Foreign workers are usually poor in their own countries. They come here to make money. Not all of them work hard, though." Another female employer, Mrs. Lin, expressed her perception of Filipinos as poor: "I feel sorry for them. . . . Some of them have good education. They cannot get jobs there. . . . The country is poor, so they have to send people out to work." For these employers, poverty becomes the marker that explains their differential statuses and their distinctions as Taiwanese employers and foreign workers.

Most often, the undesirable difference of foreign domestics is articulated through the notion of essentialized national and cultural characteristics. Another employer, Mrs. Hsia, compared Filipino workers with workers from other countries:

> My husband has experience dealing with Thais and Filipinos. . . . He thinks that Thais are more innocent and honest. . . . Filipinos usually have better education. They speak English. They might be more intelligent and easier to train. . . . They are more aggressive than other foreign workers.

When Mrs. Chen complained about her current Filipina domestic, the comments were associated with her perception of Filipinos as a collectivity. She invoked the notion of national character and cultural distinctions to describe her domestic's performance as a worker: "I think it is just their national characteristics, their culture. That is how they are, they way they do things." The narratives of these Taiwanese employers mirror the rhetoric of government officials and legislative members, who consistently call attention to the undesirable difference of foreign workers. Their narratives also parallel the representation of foreign domestics as the other in popular discourse.

The notion of undesirable difference is often deployed to justify employers' household practices of control. This particular group of employers tends to exercise invasive and intense forms of control over their foreign domestics. A-Ho insisted that his children address their Taiwanese domestics in respectful terms while allowing them to address foreign domestics by their first names. When I pressed him about why he treated his Taiwanese and Filipina domestics differently, A-Ho responded, "It is mainly because Filipina domestics have low social status in Taiwan. If you treat them better, or different from their current status here, you will have problems controlling them.". . .

Food allocation and eating order are central mechanisms through which the Taiwanese employers delineated household hierarchy. Both A-Ho and Mrs. Chen maintained that domestics should eat only after employers had finished their meals. A-Ho went further to mark their hierarchical statuses. He insisted that a certain amount of food be set aside for domestics in designated dishes. . . .

Taiwanese employers convey authority and control by dictating how household tasks should be done. Both Mrs. Chen and Mrs. Hsia gave detailed instructions as to how the floor should be cleaned. Mrs. Chen insisted that her domestics kneel on the floor to clean and wax it. Mrs. Hsia insisted that her domestics clean and wax the floor following a certain order of rooms. Kneeling to clean the floor particularly signifies the servile nature of domestic service. The use of time is another critical mechanism that employers use to define power. A-Ho and his wife had full-time employment and did not stay home during the day. They usually gave the domestic a list of tasks to be completed for the day before they left. They required the domestic to record specifically how she completed the tasks and how she spent time doing housework each day in a notebook. They went over the notebook with the domestic. They also examined the quality of her performance. For example, they would use their fingers to check for dust in the apartment. Several employers, including A-Ho, Mrs. Chen, and Mrs. Pan, instructed their domestics to return to their rooms at a designated time toward the end of the day. The domestics of these employers had to stay within sight to be called on for service. They mentioned that it was difficult to request service from domestics once they entered their rooms to rest.

Controlling foreign domestics' social networks is particularly central to Taiwanese employers. While all Taiwanese employers are concerned that their domestics might run away, employers who deploy rhetoric of the other tend to use extreme forms of surveillance. A-Ho, Mrs. Chen, and Mrs. Hsia did not allow domestics to make phone calls in the house. A-Ho, Mrs. Hsia, and Mrs. Lin accompanied domestics when grocery shopping instead of letting them run errands on their own. They made sure that domestics had minimal contact with the outside world, and they were extremely concerned about their association with other workers. They did not want them to go to church on Sundays either. Mrs. Hsia required the domestic to return home right after the church service. Mrs. Chen used extra pay to convince her domestic to stay on Sundays. A-Ho designated a weekday as the rest day. For them, church provides the domestics with dangerous and unwelcome information and networks. . . .

It is important to note that the ability of Taiwanese employers to impose tight control lies in their status as a sponsor for foreign workers and Filipinas' status as live-in domestics. Employers can ultimately threaten to deport their domestics if they do not comply with their demands. Deportation is in fact a state-sanctioned mechanism of ensuring workers' submission and docility. The alien status of foreign domestics and their lack of citizenship rights often subject them to intense control and discipline at home. In other words, state control eases the process of labor discipline, while labor control ensures the implementation of government regulations.

LIBERATION OR RECONSTITUTION: CHANGING MEANINGS OF HOMEMAKING AND PRIVATE SPHERE

The globalization of domestic service has had various implications for the Taiwanese society. It has produced the dual effects of professionalizing and exoticizing homemaking. What is interesting, though, is that the production of foreign domestics as others has simultaneously led to the elevation of Taiwanese employers. Homemaking is no longer simply physical and emotional labor conducted by Taiwanese women. It is now a domain of service contracted to and carried out by foreign women who require supervision, training, discipline, and management. Taiwanese female employers are no longer simply homemakers. Maintaining households has now taken on the façade of a profession for them. The category of foreign domestics constitutes a particular field of knowledge, and the supervision of foreign domestics requires skills, information, and experience. Foreign women are now service providers, while Taiwanese women are household managers, supervising foreign domestics and their performance in maintaining households. Homemaking has become a professional occupation for them. In other words, the globalization of domestic service facilitates the reconstitution and redefinition of household labor.

The professionalization of homemaking further entrenches the gendered nature of domestic labor. The Taiwanese female employers I interviewed emphasized that they continued to be the ones responsible for the maintenance of their households. They are seen as the main caretakers of the family, and they are responsible for hiring and supervising foreign domestics. . . .

The globalization of domestic service also heightens the othering of foreign domestics. . . . Yet the emphasis on national and cultural differences accentuates the foreignness and diminishes the racialness of alien labor. It disguises the embedded racial inequality within domestic service and schemes of labor importation. Naming them as foreign domestics and stressing their exotic nature also de-emphasizes their experience of racial discrimination and the racialized nature of Taiwan's immigration policy. . . . In other words, the legalization of domestic service has transformed the private sphere, in which homemaking traditionally exists, into a public sphere susceptible to state regulation. The private sphere, in which domestic service is performed, has become a domain where state policies and nationalist politics play out.

CONCLUSION: RETHINKING THE GLOBALIZATION OF DOMESTIC SERVICE

The case of Taiwan contributes to the expansion of the race-gender-class analysis central to previous studies on domestic service. Most important, it offers an important non-Western perspective to the scholarship on the globalization of domestic service. While the globalization of domestic service reflects and reproduces the unequal gender division of labor locally and globally, it also illustrates the gendered nature of social arrangements of care. The transfer of reproductive labor from middle-class Taiwanese women to foreign domestics only perpetuates the system of gender inequality that persistently relegates women to the realm of carework and devalues women's caring labor.

Furthermore, household dynamics are not solely shaped by unequal power relationships between two women. Embedded within the tension between the native employer and the alien domestic are also the politics of citizenship and of national identity. The experience of foreign domestics in Taiwan testifies to the continued importance of the state in mediating the globalization of domestic service. . . .

The globalization of domestic service constitutes the transfer of reproductive labor within global capitalism. However, the case of Taiwan shows that one cannot talk about a global system or a transnational process without examining the role of the state. While domestic service has become associated with a transnational labor force, it is always reconstituted and localized with new meanings. The state continues to reconfigure the national system of care, and state policies continue to shape the welfare of foreign domestics as governed alien subjects.

1. The irregular circumstances include the death or emigration of the employer, the closing of the factories, or the inability of the employer to pay salaries for more than three months.

2. I acquired some of the Taiwanese subjects initially through personal networks. Later, I obtained contact information about other Taiwanese employers through a snowball sampling method. I studied a total of 12 Taiwanese households. I conducted two interviews with five employers. Only one of the employers I interviewed was male. For four households, I also interviewed other members within the family. The age of Taiwanese employers in my sample ranges from 28 to 65 years. Their current and previous occupations vary, including a marketing engineer working in the computer industry, secretaries at local or foreign-owned businesses and in educational institutions, a teacher, and a trader. One of them owns a business, and one works for the family business. All of these Taiwanese employers are of middle and upper-middle-class standings, and they consider themselves as such. The majority of them have a university or junior college education. Two employers have master's degrees, and two of them are only high school graduates.

Chang, Grace. 2000. *Disposable domestics: Immigrant women workers in the global economy*. Cambridge, MA: South End.

Chin, Christine B. N. 1998. *In service and servitude: Foreign female domestic workers and the Malaysian "modernity" project*. New York: Columbia University Press.

Lan, Pei-chia. 2000. Global divisions, local identities: Filipina migrant domestic workers and Taiwanese employers. Ph.D. diss., Northwestern University, Evanston, IL.

Li, Mei-lan. 1998. *Wei chi nu yung mia kuang chia* (Foreign domestics, wonderful housekeepers). Taipei, Taiwan: Yuan liu.

Li, Yi-kun. 1995. Why do they not act: A study on different acting strategies of migrant workers. Master's thesis, Fu-Jen Catholic University, Hsin Chuan, Taiwan.

Lin, Chin-ju. 1999. *Filipina domestic workers in Taiwan: Structural constraints and personal resistance*. Taipei: Taiwan Grassroots Women Workers' Centre.

Romero, Mary. 1992. *Maid in the U.S.A.* New York: Routledge.

Wang, Hui-ching. 1996. *Work stress and coping amongst Filipino female domestic helpers in Taiwan*. Taipei: Taiwan Grassroots Women Workers' Centre.

Wang, Li-ru. 1997. Examining policies of foreign domestic workers and women's labor. Paper presented at the Conference of Foreign Labor and State Development, Taipei, Taiwan, April.

Wei, In-chun. 1998. *Our Filipina domestic—Nora*. Kaohsiung, Taiwan: Chia chi szu.

12

INTERNATIONAL MIGRATION, DOMESTIC WORK, AND CARE WORK: UNDOCUMENTED LATINA MIGRANTS IN ISRAEL

Rebeca Raijman, Silvina Schammah-Gesser, and Adriana Kemp

Because of blocked opportunities in their homelands, undocumented Latina migrant women take domestic and carework jobs in Israel that they would not have taken in their home countries. This search for economic betterment leads Latina migrants to risk working illegally in Israel, forcing them to live under constant surveillance, with few citizenship rights, and to remain on the margins of Israeli society. While they take these jobs to secure a better future for their children, they are forced to leave them behind, thus subverting the traditional definition of motherhood by replacing unpaid carework for their families with paid carework.

Drawing on the experiences of undocumented non-Jewish Latina women in Israel as a case study, this article has a twofold purpose: First, we offer an analysis of the fundamental dilemmas faced by migrant women, who, besides being segregated in the labor market by gender, race, class, and nationality, live in perpetual fear of being arrested by state authorities and deported, and second, we delve into the strategies that migrant women develop to cope with their situations.

Although the dilemmas and strategies analyzed in the article are resonant with the female labor migration experience in general, our focus on non-Jewish undocumented migrant women in Israel is novel. Previous research in Israel has mainly concentrated on Jewish migrant women and the "occupational cost" they pay when migrating to Israel (Raijman and Semyonov 1997; Remennick 1999). However, because of their Jewish origin, these migrants' status is substantially different from that of non-Jewish labor migrants. The latter are not entitled to citizenship, not even to "permanent resident" status, and are therefore bound to remain excluded from the dominant regime of incorporation in the host country (Kemp et al. 2000; Raijman and Kemp 2002). . . .

THEORETICAL BACKGROUND: GENDER,
DOMESTIC SERVICE, AND INTERNATIONAL MIGRATION

The incorporation of migrant women into domestic service and care work is not only the result of migratory circumstances (a lack of language proficiency, inadequate cultural orientation, and incompatible occupational skills), but rather it reflects the fact that domesticity is one of the few occupations open to migrant women due to gender segregation in the labor market of developed countries (Glenn 1986; Salazar Parreñas 2001). That is, in addition to their migrant status, immigrant women experience further difficulties in the labor force as a result of the "double negative" effect of gender and birthplace (Boyd 1984; Raijman and Semyonov 1997; Robinson 1991).

This situation is more acute in the case of undocumented migrant women, thus adding a significant dimension to their disadvantages in the receiving society. Because of their illegal status, they are excluded from most jobs regardless of their human capital, and they cannot enter occupations for which they have qualifications. The structural constraints within the labor market of the host country compel women to enter the domestic and carework sector. Likewise, their status as undocumented migrants makes female workers particularly vulnerable to discrimination, exploitation, and abuse. These are especially acute in the sphere of domestic and care work in which duties are conducted in isolated households that are closed to public scrutiny (Cheng 1996, 2003; Salazar Parreñas 2001; Wong 1996). Under these conditions, the experience of downward occupational mobility becomes gendered....

In addition to the occupational cost exacted from downward mobility (as women who work at domestic jobs) and their illegal status, women also face the emotional distress associated with the separation from their families, especially those who leave children behind in their countries of origin....

[F]or migrant mothers, who leave their children in their homelands, the need arises to switch from an ideology of "family in one place" (glorifying the idea of privatized mothering) to a new rhetoric of transnational motherhood (emphasizing the breadwinner role) (Hondagneu-Sotelo and Avila 1997, 548). Thus, transnational motherhood openly subverts traditional conceptions of mother-child bonds nurtured daily within the home and conventional views that employment and mothering are mutually exclusive. Adjusting to their new role as "overseas mothers" capable of caring for their children by "remote control" forces women to face the paradox that to provide their children with a better future, they are forced to leave home....

Building on previous work by Hondagneu-Sotelo and Avila (1997), Hondagneu-Sotelo (2001), and Salazar Parreñas (2000, 2001), we focus on three main dilemmas faced by undocumented non-Jewish Latina women in Israel. The first is that to break the cycle of economic stagnation and blocked mobility in their homelands, migrant women are forced to take low-status jobs (e.g., domestic work), often positions that they would never have taken in their countries of origin, despite uncertainty about possible economic outcomes (Salazar Parreñas 2000, 2001). The second relates to the search for economic betterment, which leads Latina migrants to risk living and working illegally in the host country and forces them to remain "aliens" and relegated to the margins of society. The third dilemma concerns their role as mothers, who, to secure a better future for their children, are obliged to leave them behind, thus subverting the traditional definition of "motherhood" that emphasizes the presence of the mother at home (Hondagneu-Sotelo and Avila 1997).

Although the second dilemma (the cost of being illegal) is related to the costs of international migration and may apply equally to migrant men and women, the first and third dilemmas (downward occupational mobility and the transnationalization of motherhood) derive from gender segregation in the labor market, the new globalized gendered economy of care, and the gendered domestic division of labor in migrants' countries of origin. . . .

THE ISRAELI SETTING

Overseas labor migration is a recent phenomenon in Israel. As a self-defined Jewish nation-state, Israel actively encourages immigration of Jews from practically every corner of the globe and is both institutionally and ideologically committed to their successful absorption. The legal platform for the Jewish character of the state . . . confers on all Jews, and only Jews, the right of immigration, while the latter grants them Israeli nationality virtually automatically. At the same time, Israel is an ethnically divided society, with a population of approximately 83 percent Jews and 17 percent Arabs.

Labor Migration: The Israeli View

Although labor migrants have become an integral part of the economy, they are placed at the bottom of the labor market and the social order. They suffer from the worst working conditions and are generally excluded from the welfare and benefit system accorded to Israeli citizens. Furthermore, since the end of 1995, Israel's declared policy toward migrant workers has been to reduce their number drastically, by arresting and deporting migrant workers without work permits. The overall goal set by the minister of labor was to reduce the proportion of migrant workers to just 1 percent of the labor force. . . .

Although Israel has a democratic regime, its labor migration policy resembles the patterns of labor migration regulation and control in the Gulf system and in the newly industrialized countries in South East Asia, where laws and regulations governing labor migration are much stricter than those prevailing in Western labor-importing countries. Similar to the Gulf states and to Taiwan, in Israel work permits are granted to employers, to whom the migrant worker is indentured, thereby maximizing employers' and the state's control over the foreign population. The state does not allow residence without a work permit; does not recognize any right of asylum or any right of family reunification; does not guarantee access to housing, social benefits, or medical care; and carries out a blatant deportation policy that allows the arrest and expulsion of undocumented migrants at any time by simple administrative decree. In that sense, Israel's labor migration policy reflects the state's continuous anxiety over a changing ethnoscape that may pose a threat to its Jewish character. . . .

Domestic Service in Israel

The history of domestic service in Israel is one of ethnic succession. Since the establishment of the state in 1948, several ethnic groups entered this occupational niche. . . . By the mid-1990s, the arrival of foreign workers radically changed the ethnic composition of the domestic sector. Filipino migrants were legally recruited by professional (recruitment) agencies to care for the elderly and handicapped, while other migrant women such as Latinas and Black Africans were increasingly incorporated as cleaning and care workers through informal channels.

The existence of a Latina labor force in the domestic service sector (in which the majority of undocumented Latinas work) is a recent phenomenon in Israel. No large, established (non-Jewish) Latin American community existed prior to the arrival of these women in the early 1990s. The entry of Latin American migrant women into the domestic sector is characterized by two informal patterns of recruitment. One way is through Latin American Jewish families living in Israel. Family members or friends residing in the sending country act as recruiters, and the Israeli family sends funds for a plane ticket and other expenses. The Latino migrants come as "counterfeit tourists" and remain in Israel after their tourist visas expire. As tourists, they can stay legally in the country but do not have the right to work. When their visas expire (after three months), they become illegal residents and run the risk of being caught and deported by the Israeli authorities.

The second recruitment pattern involves migrants' own social networks. Pioneering Latino labor migrants in Israel laid the foundations for a social network serving present-day economic migrants from Latin America, mostly from the "southern cone." Individuals in the countries of origin respond to "invitations" from friends and family already living and working in Israel. Others decide to engage in similar experiences, swayed by the rumors of earning "easy" money in Israel, which encourage people to come and "make it in the Holy Land."[1] Relatives and friends already residing in Israel help others to join the migration process by providing them with help and information during their initial period after arrival. . . .

Method

Data collection was based on 44 in-depth interviews with migrant women, as well as informal conversations during visits to households and in other social gatherings. Interviews were guided by a semi-structured questionnaire, including items relating to pre-migration background, reasons for migration, occupational history in Israel, patterns of residence, income, leisure time, social networks, and community participation. Supplementary questions were posed to immigrant mothers, including topics relating to child-rearing arrangements in their home countries, monitoring strategies used by transnational mothers, their role as the sole wage earner (especially in the case of single-parent families), and the social stigma attached to migrant mothers who leave their families behind. Besides the interviews, we also conducted focus groups with transnational mothers in which women discussed the topics listed above. All names used in this article are pseudonyms.

We used a multiple-entry snowball sampling technique to detect and construct a sample of undocumented Latina labor migrants in Israel, thus avoiding the danger of interviewing limited personal social networks. We conducted fieldwork in various social and institutional settings (such as soccer games, salsa clubs, chess clubs, religious services, social clubs, organized tours, fairs, kindergartens, schools, etc.), thereby broadening the range of interviewee profiles.

Approximately 40 percent of the women in our sample had come from Colombia, the largest group among Latino migrants in Israel. Almost a quarter had migrated from Ecuador, and the rest were from Bolivia, Peru, Chile, Uruguay, Argentina, Brazil, and Venezuela. The majority of the women had arrived in Israel after 1993, and for most of them, their current stay in Israel was their first trip to this country.

LATIN AMERICAN LABOR MIGRATION TO ISRAEL

Sociodemographic Characteristics

The majority of Latina labor migrants in Israel are undocumented (96 percent). They average 35 years of age, confirming what other studies have shown, that migrants are concentrated in the middle labor force ages. These migrant women are evenly distributed along marital status categories: one-third is single, one-third is married, and one-third are divorced or widows. Almost half of all migrant Latinas left their children behind in their countries of origin under the care of husbands, parents, or other family members. These Latinas in our sample report an average of 11.5 years of formal education, and 15 percent hold a postsecondary degree. The majority (75 percent) was in the labor force in their countries of origin, and two-thirds worked in pink-collar occupations (clerks and sales), mostly in retail and public sectors. Only a minority (10 percent) worked in domestic service prior to migration. This fact suggests that for most of the sampled Latina migrants, migration involves some kind of downward occupational mobility.

The major motivating factors for migration were wage gaps (between their home countries and Israel) and a lack of opportunities for upward social and economic mobility in the sending societies. The average income of the women in their countries of origin amounted to no more than U.S. $250 per month. These levels contrast sharply with the expected income to be earned in Israel, which amounts to around $1,000 or $1,200 per month. This means that the economic incentives for migration to Israel are very strong because most women expect to earn three times what they would get at home.

THE COSTS AND DILEMMAS OF WOMEN'S LABOR MIGRATION

The Burden of Occupation Downward Mobility: *Aquí nos toca duro: Allá era la señora aquí soy la sirvienta* (We Are Really Having a Hard Time: Over There We Were Ladies and Here We Are Servants)

Undocumented Latina migrants in Israel told us that the income they earn is also intended to bolster their family status at home. However, the mismatch between their skills and the jobs they perform still remains a major source of distress. That is because for the majority domestic work is the only option available in the host labor market.

Among these Latinas, the negative connotations attached to this type of work stem not only from the nature of the work itself, and the context of the work (especially in the case of live-in arrangements), but also because in Latin America domestic workers are located at the bottom of the social ladder. Even the term of reference, *las sirvientas* (the servants), with its class connotation of social distance and inequality, reflects their marginal status.

Consequently, for the majority of these women, taking a cleaning job was traumatic, even though they saw their stay in Israel as a transitional experience. This feeling was more pronounced among newly arrived migrants who, for the first time, took a live-in job (*internas*) in private households. The trauma of having to work as *internas* is exemplified in the words of Veronica, a 24-year-old Latina, who prior to her arrival had completed the second year of her studies in the faculty of dentistry in Ecuador. She came to Israel following her mother and aunt, who had also taken cleaning jobs. In Quito, Veronica worked as a clerk earning $100 per month to finance her studies.

For Veronica, the cool and calculated assessment of the prospects of earning around $1,000, compared with the meager $100 per month she got at home, won out. Still, no matter how prepared she was to endure the new working conditions, she felt a real shock on her arrival:

> I started right away working as a live-in caretaker of an old man. The first week was a nightmare. For someone like me who had never done this type of job and, on top of it, in a completely unknown country and without knowing a single word in Hebrew! . . . I was supposed to be at his side round the clock and stay at home. I could not help but cry the whole week. The disappointment of initially seeing Tel Aviv with tourists' eyes and then turning to the real thing, to what you have come to. . . . Even though I knew that cleaning was the only type of job available for me and Mom, I could not stand seeing my mother or myself working as servants. It was degrading. . . .

The experience of downward mobility is further deepened among migrant women taking live-in positions. Many, like Veronica, reported the feeling of "being locked up" (*encerradas*), feelings that were exacerbated if their employers did not speak Spanish. Furthermore, the private nature of the work and the asymmetrical relations of power inherent in the employer-employee relationship mean that migrant women have few if any options to negotiate their working conditions. Due to their isolation, they are initially unaware of the salary range for this type of work, and many of them have settled for much lower wages than they should. In several cases, women report being paid only one-fifth of the highest salary available in the sector. In more extreme situations, employers (using the excuse that it is for the sake of the worker's own economic interests) retain the worker's salary, promising to deposit it in a savings account until considerable sums mounted up. Some employers even confiscate passports to prevent workers from changing jobs. As reported in the interviews, there are cases in which workers never got their salaries or passports returned to them.[2] Yet very few Latinas have considered the possibility of taking legal action against their employers due to the fear associated with their non-legal status.

Be that as it may, with tenure in the country and the establishment of social networks, many female domestic workers have managed to move from live-in to live-out domestic service and to rent an apartment with friends or family members. These new residential arrangements allow them to have multiple employers, usually attending to two houses per day, an average of 12 hours of work per day (many of them work seven days a week). Although having multiple employers enables them to earn more money, they also incur extra expenses (e.g., rent, food, utilities). Nevertheless, live-out arrangements are viewed by migrant women as a substantial improvement in their quality of life, allowing them to control their time and private life, to mix with the Israeli society, to learn the Hebrew language, and to get firsthand information regarding both the Latino community and the wider Israeli context (see Hagan, 1998, and Hondagneu-Sotelo, 1994, for similar findings regarding the U.S. case).

Yet their employment remains unstable, and domestic workers are still vulnerable to their employers' demands, as their contracts are limited to mere verbal agreements. Under these conditions, Latina migrants are permanently seeking and maintaining a large number of jobs with the result that job searching is not merely a limited strategy for employment but part of the job itself. Despite the fragility of domestic work conditions, social interaction with other migrant women in different settings (church, salsa nightclubs, soccer games, and other informal social or community gatherings) helps these women develop a particular set of values, practices, and collective advice that act as a basic work culture, thereby establishing a more structured framework to their position as domestic workers (Salzinger 1991).

With the passage of time, many Latinas realize that what they considered a temporary job has turned into a dead-end position with no prospect for change. The frustration is even greater for those who understand that returning home is no longer a viable alternative, given the endemic socioeconomic and political problems in their countries of origin. They feel lost: *"No somos de aquí, ni somos de allá: somos parias."* ("We belong neither here nor there. We are pariahs.")

Being at the crossroads, many are planning to migrate to a European country (primarily Spain). This step is seen as an alternative strategy—as the opportunity to become a legal resident in Israel is almost nonexistent, and the hope of finding a more suitable job, if not for them at least for their children, is doomed to failure....

For many women, the autonomy and economic independence their new income allows provide sufficient incentive for enduring the costs of occupational downward mobility. Some of them become the major source of financial support not only for their children but also for their extended family. Yet seeing themselves as economic providers and considering the prospects of enjoying the fruits of their efforts in their countries of origin are not the only way to cope with downward mobility. Despite their extreme marginality and absolute exclusion, migrants develop other modes of dealing with the painful reality resulting from their marginal positions . . ., one central strategy among Latina migrant women becomes participation in ethnic associations, especially religious organizations.

The Cost of Being Illegal: *Diosito, haznos invisibles a los ojos de la policía* (God, Make Us Invisible to the Eyes of the Police)

This saying was the climax of a "petition" prayer offered by a group of Evangelical Latino migrants who regularly meet to celebrate their weekly mass in a shabby old house turned into a church, near the old Central Bus Station in Tel Aviv, where most undocumented labor migrants live. . . . Able to experience some kind of relief and empowerment through religious rites, these women desperately craved a miracle.

Because Latino migrants in Israel must join the local labor force without work permits, they are forced to remain at the margins of the host society. As undocumented residents and workers in the informal sector of the economy, they do not have access to employment benefits, although they are supposed to be protected by local labor laws (Raijman and Kemp 2002). Employers can exploit this asymmetrical situation to their own benefit in a number of ways. As already mentioned, prearranged rates of payment may be lowered, earnings may be paid much later than previously agreed, or earnings may not be paid at all. Although undocumented workers have the right to claim their share, they rarely take this option even when nongovernmental organizations are ready to act on their behalf. As a rule, they prefer to lose their money and change jobs rather than take legal action that may entail the risk of being caught by the police and deported. . . .

Viviana, a labor migrant from Bolivia, shared her consternation regarding her illegal status.

> I live with tension. We never have a moment of peace. We are not free to act and interact as normal people. People take advantage of this situation. Take for instance the question of renting an apartment. You know that they charge you more just because you are illegal and you cannot say a word. I already left two apartments and my money guarantee was not returned. Again, I couldn't complain. If you need a medicine, you cannot get it because illegal workers don't have medical insurance. Most employers do not want to pay for that.

Since the beginning of the deportation policy in 1995, as police arrest and deportation campaigns became a daily routine, illegality has become the daily nightmare for every migrant. Suddenly, home and street turned into dangerous places. Fearing arrest and deportation, migrants tried to avoid even the most casual encounter with the police. "I never take the same path on my way back home. Even the Tel Aviv marketplace that was a meeting place for Latinos on Friday afternoon has become a taboo place. You never know who is haunting you" (Gloria).

Police raids targeting the old and new Central Bus Station area in Tel Aviv led many migrants to move out to the surrounding areas with a lower concentration of foreign workers, hoping to reduce the chances of being caught. . . .

In other cases, many women working as live-out domestics considered the possibility of taking a live-in position as a strategy to avoid being arrested on their way to work. It is particularly striking that for undocumented migrants in Israel, the fear of arrest and deportation exceeds their anxiety about terrorist attacks and the deteriorating security situation in the country. . . .

Still, for most the fear of deportation and the need to find a shelter from the vicissitudes of everyday life bring labor migrants, especially migrant women, to the Catholic churches and the Evangelical churches newly established by the migrants themselves. . . .

Redefining Motherhood in the Context of International Migration: *Para procurar por el bien de los hijos uno se debe separar de ellos* (To Secure the Future of Our Children We Have to Leave Them Behind at Home)

Migrant mothers redefine their roles and conceptions of family life as they are forced to deal with great temporal and spatial separation from home and to endure novel arrangements for child raising. The concept of transnational motherhood helps understand the manner in which the meaning of motherhood shifts, to adapt to the new circumstances created by international migration in the era of globalization (Hondagneu-Sotelo and Avila 1997, 549). . . . As overseas mothers, they are breaking away from the "cult of domesticity" and the rigid role models rooted in Latin American traditions as well as in Spanish Catholicism (Hondagneu-Sotelo and Avila 1997). . . .

An ideology that places mothers solely in the "private" realm creates serious conflicts for migrant mothers who are forced to work far away from home (Glenn 1994). Consider the case of Marta, a divorced mother who came to Israel from Latin America three years ago, leaving behind two adolescent children in the care of her mother and sisters, as the father had cut all ties with her and evaded his economic responsibilities. . . .

> We are at a crossroads. On the one hand, we are supposed to be at home looking after the well-being of our family and children. On the other hand, the economic needs push us to look for a better future abroad . . . because, you know, that in Latin America it is impossible to make it. You cannot have everything at once. Sometimes you have to choose. In our case we have to make the best of a bad job and go to work. What else is left for us? I do miss my children. I always think about them. . . . What are they doing right now? Who is taking care of them? My mother was right in saying that they need me. But what can I do? You cannot have your cake and eat it.

Estela, a Black Latina single mother who left her eight-year-old boy with her family in Colombia, expressed a similar dilemma. She pointed out that coming to Israel was a difficult decision to make:

> [You have to decide] either to go out, fight for life, and make a living, or stay at home with the children but without the possibility of having a better future. It is especially difficult if you are a single or a divorced mother, as in my case. If I had a husband to share the burden with me, it would have been a completely different story. I would never have left.

While aware that their redefinitions of the female role, family life, and child-rearing arrangements transgress traditional family conventions in their home countries, these women propose a new conception of motherhood, in which taking economic responsibility is as important as—or even more important than—their daily presence in the home. As Marta told us,

> We have been taught that mothers are to stay with their kids. That is why we may feel bad about leaving our children. But I am a different type of mother. I have left them but they are having a little bit more than other children there [in her country of origin]. My mother thinks that I am irresponsible, but why? I am here working and I am not avoiding my duties. I am the same mother I was before, even a better one because I can help them. My commitment as a mother has not changed.

Sometimes, reference to the "sacrifice" of downward occupational mobility helps diminish the fears and anxieties caused by the transition to transnational mothering and the criticism that may rise from home, as made explicit by Yolanda, a separated migrant woman from Bolivia:

> In Bolivia I used to sell jewelry but I only made $60 a month. . . . When I decided to separate from my husband I realized that migration was the only available

alternative for me in order to earn a living for me and my children. Since my arrival I have been working in domestic service. It is hard for me. In Bolivia I had a maid myself!! It is even harder to be away from my children! But for me it is the only possible way to economic independence.

The emphasis on their economic role helps migrant mothers reevaluate their own definitions of mothering, as expressed in the words of Rocío, a divorcee who left her four-year-old daughter with her sister in her home country:

Very few mothers are ready to make the sacrifice of those women who go abroad and leave their children behind. It takes a mother to dare to do so. Many women don't do anything in order to overcome the difficult situations. Instead, those who leave [their children] really give their best [for them]. Uno se siente mas madre. [One feels more of a mother.]

In making the assessment of the costs and benefits of mother-child separation, Estela is convinced that the sacrifice is worthwhile:

We are not with our children but this is a sacrifice for their own benefit. We miss many things [by being far away] but we are doing more, helping more. I am a responsible mother because I am taking charge of the economic well-being of my son as well as my family. I am doing my bit. I feel at ease with my conscience because I am doing my best to support my child.

The articulation of a new rhetoric of transnational motherhood proves to be critical as women attempt to make sense of their new situations. Notwithstanding their discursive significance, transnational practices of motherhood and child care have to meet two conditions to become a fully legitimate and viable strategy for migrant mothers. The first condition, as we have already shown, is economic need. The second is to have a suitable family arrangement for the children. All the women we interviewed emphasize the fundamental role their families have in raising their children. They concurred that without the willingness of their families (mothers, sisters, brothers) to care for them, they could not have come to Israel and stayed for lengthy periods of time. Thus, when the arrangements are satisfactory and the well-being of the child is guaranteed, the separation is considered as a viable option.

Still, separation is not accepted in all cases as a legitimate solution. When the home arrangements fail and their children are not taken care of properly, migrant mothers are confronted with a new dilemma. . . .

Most women agree that the first option is to search for an adequate alternative arrangement for the children in the home country since the priority for transnational mothers is to remain in Israel and earn money. The second option is to bring the child to live with them in Israel. . . .

If these two options are not viable, the appropriate way to cope with the situation would be to return home. Transnational mothers openly criticized those migrant mothers who know that their children are not receiving proper care at home but decide to remain in Israel. There is a line that cannot be crossed when it comes to motherhood: the well-being of the children. . . .

CONCLUSIONS

We suggest that while the cost of being illegal may apply equally to migrant men and women, downward occupational mobility and the transnationalization of motherhood are distinctly gendered as they derive from gender segregation in the labor market, the new globalized gendered economy of care, and the gendered domestic division of labor in migrants' countries of origin. Not only are the dilemmas gendered, but also the particular strategies chosen by migrants tend to be patterned along distinct gender lines. . . .

We argue that Latina migrants' participation in religious activities opens an alternative path for social mobility and a public space, perhaps the only one available to undocumented migrant women, where they can acquire visibility within their community. Churches offer Latina migrants a space for the production of a "sense of belonging" within the experiential context of uprootedness and marginality. The significance of religious activities and participation for Latina migrants should be understood against the backdrop of the constant threat of arrest and deportation and the ability of migrant churches to provide, albeit only for fragmented moments, a protected space for doubly disadvantaged migrant women.

Transnational mothering rhetoric is another important strategy that Latina migrants use in their attempts to cope with family life disruption. . . . As we have shown, a redefinition of mothering that stresses the economic responsibility for their children as equally important to—or even more important than—their daily presence at home becomes a central strategy that legitimizes separation from their children. . . .

In some cases, the lengthy disruptions in family life lead to the routinization of the separation, meaning that transnational mothers are forced to come to terms with the fact that they do not raise their own children. Separations may last longer than the women had originally planned as they keep on delaying their return home. . . .

Whatever the costs and dilemmas migrant women face in Israel, in the final analysis many of them critically evaluate the chances they have of becoming permanent residents in Israel. . . . Even the term by which they are known, *ovdim zarim* (foreign workers), with a biblical connotation of profanity, exemplifies their marginal position.

Unwillingness to accept labor migrants is expressed through exclusionary immigration policies (especially severe limitation of family reunion and refusal to grant residence status), restrictive naturalization rules, and a double standard: an exclusionary model for non-Jews (foreign workers) as opposed to an "acceptance-encouragement" model for Jews. The ethno-national nature of the state and the absence of an egalitarian idea and practice of citizenship for non-Jews make Israel a society without prospects for the incorporation of non-Jewish immigrants.

NOTES

Author's Note: This research was supported by the Israeli Science Foundation founded by the Israel Academy of Sciences and Humanities. The authors wish to thank five anonymous reviewers for their helpful comments and Christine Bose for her editorial suggestions. We are also grateful to Tamara Barsky, Alejandro Paz, and Valentin Nabel for their efficient research assistance and to Deborah Bernstein for her careful reading and helpful suggestions.

1. Being the "Holy Land," Israel uniquely attracts Christians from all over the world aspiring to visit as pilgrims. As the millennium approached, many migrants expressed their wish to settle in Israel, yearning for the coming of the Messiah (Raijman et al. 2001; Raijman and Kemp forthcoming; Schammah-Gesser et al. 2000).

2. Similar findings were reported by Cheng (2003, 173–75) in her analysis of state control and foreign Filipina domestic workers in Taiwan.

Boyd, M. 1984. At a disadvantage: The occupational attainment of foreign-born women in Canada. *International Migration Review* 18:1091–120.

Cheng, S. A. 1996. Migrant women domestic workers in Hong Kong, Singapore and Taiwan: A comparative analysis. *Asian and Pacific Migration Journal* 5:139–52.

———. 2003. Rethinking the globalization of domestic service: Foreign domestics, state control and the politics of identity in Taiwan. *Gender & Society* 17 (2): 166–86.

Glenn, E. Nakano. 1986. *Issei, Nisei, war bride.* Philadelphia: Temple University.

———. 1994. Social constructions of mothering: A thematic overview. In *Mothering: Ideology, experience, and agency,* edited by Evelyn Nakano Glenn, Grace Chang, and Linda Rennie Forcey. New York: Routledge.

Hagan, J. M. 1998. Social networks, gender, and immigrant incorporation: Resources and constraints. *American Sociological Review* 63:55–67.

Hondagneu-Sotelo, P. 1994. *Gendered transitions: Mexican experiences of immigration.* Berkeley: University of California Press.

———. 2001. *Domestica. Immigrant workers cleaning and caring in the shadows of affluence.* Berkeley: University of California Press.

Hondagneu-Sotelo, P., and E. Avila. 1997. I'm here, but I'm there. The meanings of Latina transnational motherhood. *Gender & Society* 11:548–71.

Kemp, A., R. Raijman, J. Resnik, and S. Schammah-Gesser. 2000. Contesting the limits of political participation: Latinos and Black African migrant workers in Israel. *Ethnic and Racial Studies* 23 (1): 94–119.

Raijman, R., and A. Kemp. 2002. State and non-state actors: A multi-layered analysis of labor migration policy in Israel. In *Public policy in Israel,* edited by D. Korn. London: Lexington Books.

———. Forthcoming. Consuming the Holy Spirit in the Holy Land: Evangelical churches, labor migrants and the Jewish state. In *Consumption and market society in Israel,* edited by Y. Carmeli and K. Applebaum. Oxford, UK: Berg.

Raijman, R., A. Kemp, S. Gesser, and J. Resnik. 2001. *Searching for a better future: Latino labor migration.* Discussion paper 105. Tel Aviv, Israel: Tel Aviv University, Golda Meir Institute for Social & Labor Research.

Raijman, R., and M. Semyonov. 1997. Gender, ethnicity and immigration: Double-disadvantage and triple-disadvantage among recent immigrant women in the Israeli labor market. *Gender & Society* 11 (1): 108–25.

Remennick, L. 1999.Women with a Russian accent in Israel: On the gender aspects of migration. *European Journal of Women's Studies* 6 (4): 441–61.

Robinson, K. 1991. Housemaids: The effects of gender and culture on the internal and international labor migration of Indonesian women. In *Intersexions: Gender/class/culture/ethnicity*, edited by Gill Bottomley, Marie de Lepervanche, and Jeannie Martin. Sydney, Australia: Allen & Unwin.

Salazar Parreñas, R. 2000. Migrant Filipina domestic workers and the international division of reproductive labor. *Gender & Society* 14 (4): 560–81.

———. 2001. Servants of globalization: Women, migration, and domestic work. Stanford, CA: Stanford University Press.

Salzinger, L. 1991. Maid by any other name: The transformation of "dirty work" by Central American immigrants. In *Ethnography unbound: Power and resistance in the modern metropolis*, edited by Michael Burawoy et al. Berkeley: University of California Press.

Schammah-Gesser, S., R. Raijman, A. Kemp, and J. Reznik. 2000. "Making it" in Israel? Non-Jewish Latino undocumented migrant workers in the Holy Land. *Estudios interdisciplinarios de America Latina y el Caribe* 11 (2): 113–36.

Wong, D. 1996. Foreign domestic workers in Singapore. *Asian and Pacific Migration Journal* 5:117–38.

13 "FORCED" INTO UNPAID CAREWORK: INTERNATIONAL STUDENTS' WIVES IN THE UNITED STATES

Minjeong Kim

This article examines the carework experiences of migrant South Korean women who are prohibited from working for wages in the United States because they are considered legal dependents of their husbands who are considered "temporary migrants," coming to the United States to study. Restrictive laws mean that these international students' wives cannot be employed as they had been at home, and that they can only go to school themselves if they can afford to attend full-time. Since this is very difficult to do, most are forced into full-time carework, which reduces their substantive citizenship and creates unequal gender relations within their families.

International students' wives (ISWs) are women who come to the United States because their husbands come to study for master's or doctoral degrees in U.S. academic institutions for their own career advancement. ISWs are part of the flow of international migration but their experiences have not drawn much scholarly attention in any field, except for two doctoral dissertations (Baldwin 1970; Liu 1992).

Research on gender and migration has been centered on women's participation in paid work and its effect on changing gender relations in immigrant households and communities (Glenn 1986; Grasmuck and Pessar 1991; Hondagneu-Sotelo 1994; Kibria 1993; Lim 1997; Pedraza 1991; Zentgraf 2002). While many scholars have focused on migrant women's participation in paid carework and/or the balancing act between the public and private spheres, only a few scholars have attempted to theorize migrant women's unpaid carework (Salaff 2002; Moon 2003). However, these studies do not take into consideration state policies or legal regulations that demarcate migrant women's activities. The gender division of labor in the private sphere is ostensibly arranged by individual gender ideology. Yet, many studies have shown that there is a well-founded association between state policies and the carework responsibilities that are imposed on women (Litt and Zimmerman 2003; Rosemberg 2003). Therefore it is essential to fill this gap by examining the relationship between state policies and the unpaid carework of women on the move. My research does so by discussing the unpaid carework experiences of migrant women who are prohibited from working for wages because of their legal status as the dependents of "temporary" migrants.

I argue that the experiences of international students' wives (ISWs) are shaped by restrictive immigration laws defining their current legal status and limiting their employment and education, and consequently "forcing" them into carework, which further reproduces unequal gender relations. The experiences of ISWs with a middle-class background are similar to those of temporary professional workers' wives. However, because student husbands' income sources are limited, ISWs' perceptions of their position as a full-time housewife and careworker are likely to be different from those of other migrant women.

Documents provided by the U.S. Citizenship and Immigration Services (the former INS) state that F-2 visa holders are spouses and children of students and their status will be "dependent upon" the status of F-1 visa holders. Even though the gender-neutral term "spouse" is used, F-2 visa status becomes gendered by the meanings of "dependents" in the definition of citizenship. Historically, in the eighteenth and nineteenth century U.S. political rhetoric on citizenship, economic independence was linked with political freedom and became race and gender specific so as to establish the prerogatives of white masculinity; at the same time, all women and Blacks were perceived as dependents (Glenn 2002). Immigration policies, which lump women with children, evoke the conventional middle-class nuclear family structure with a male breadwinner and a female homemaker and reinforce patriarchal ideology.

Based on interviews with Korean international students' wives (KISWs), my exploratory study examines how these women, who generally had paid jobs while living in South Korea, are forced into carework by legal restrictions, although most of them would have preferred to (and expected to be able to) continue their education or be employed while in the United States. I find that KISWs feel that they are in a subordinate position serving their families, but they do not actively challenge the gender division of labor at home because they see their roles as an important part of a family survival strategy. Instead, their feelings of frustration, which stem from being confined at home, are directed, not at their husbands, but mainly toward the restrictive immigration laws.

DATA AND METHOD

The Office of Immigration Statistics (OIS), under the Department of Homeland Security, divides the population into three categories: immigrants, refugees/asylees, and temporary admissions. The last category is "nonimmigrants," including visitors for business or pleasure (tourists), temporary workers and trainees, and students.[1]

According to the *Yearbook of Immigration Statistics, 2003* [U.S. Department of Homeland Security 2004], published by the OIS, of the 27.9 million nonimmigrant admissions to the United States in 2003, 624,917 (2.2%) were students, and 38,049 (about 6% of the combined number of F-1 and F-2 visa holders) are their associated spouses or children. Japan, China, Korea, and India are the leading countries of origin for nonimmigrants admitted as students. Figures by age and gender for F-2 visa holders, who are spouses and children of students, show that adult women "dependents" of F-1 visa holders predominate. That is to say, about 52.3% of F-2 visa holders (about 81% of adult F-2 visa holders over the age of 20) can be considered wives of international students. Korea has the highest number of students' dependents (10,986 or 29% of all F-2 visa holders in 2003) coming to the United States.[2]

My analysis is based on 11 in-depth interviews with KISWs in a medium-size university in the state of New York conducted between March 2004 and November 2004, as well as observations and informal conversations with participants while conducting interviews. I obtained the local directory of a Korean American community organization, which included a subdirectory produced by the Korean graduate student group at the university. I phoned wives of male students listed in the directory and asked if they were willing to participate in the study, and then asked them to refer me to other respondents, using snowball techniques.

Interviews were guided by a semistructured questionnaire covering background information on life in Korea, the process of migrating to the United States, typical daily activities, social networks, division of labor with their husband, and their perceptions of their role as an international student's wife. I met most respondents in their homes. All interviews were conducted in Korean, tape-recorded, later transcribed, translated into English, and coded. The last names used here are pseudonyms.

All the women in my sample held either Bachelor's or Master's degrees and most had held paid jobs in Korea: two middle-school teachers, one copywriter, one freelancer journalist, a computer program designer, a sales director in a fashion company, an English instructor, and two part-time tutors. The other two came to the United States with F-2 visas right after they had graduated from college. Their ages ranged from 31 to 39 with a median age of 35. The length of time during which they have lived in the United States (with F-2 visa) ranged from three to seven and a half years (with a median of four years). Nine women go to or used to go to Korean American churches.

Based on this small sample, I cannot generalize to all KISWs. There are many variables that can differentiate women's experiences, such as how regulations are enforced in different states, the size and characteristics of the international student populations in each school, and school policies or services for international students.[3] Nonetheless, my findings illustrate some of the significant carework-related issues that most KISWs face in the United States.

FINDINGS

Carework at Home

Their legal status constructed KISWs' identity as international students' wives (*yoo-hahk-saeng boo-in*, or simply "wife" within student communities). As a dependent/spouse of an international student who has an F-1 visa, these women have an F-2 visa, which by law makes them ineligible for employment, and virtually erases any opportunities for professional advancement or economic activities in the public sphere. → *a dependent/spouse is what it would say.*

> [F-2 visa status] is completely up to the F-1 visa holder. If the husband loses his status as a student, I lose my status in this country. (Kim)

> You cannot do anything here [with the F-2 visa]. You cannot work, or get the social security number. You have nothing to do except for "staying." (Lee)

ISWs move to the United States with their husbands primarily to keep their family together. A few women said that they had expressed their desire not to move because of their occupations and that they did not want to leave Korea. However, women eventually decided to come after their husbands pleaded or because they saw the potential educational advantages for themselves or for children. Others welcomed the opportunity from the beginning, having their own agenda of studying for a degree or because they had an idealized image of the U.S. life as desirable. Once they arrived in the United States, the social and cultural underpinnings for women's role as wife and mother, compounded with legal restrictions, pressed them to prioritize carework over other agendas. However, they are by no means just "staying," as Lee had implied.

> While my husband studies, I do everything else. . . . I do everything, even men's work, except for making money. I do housework. I am a driver. I bring my child to the hospital. I take care of businesses with insurance companies and the rental office. I did everything when we moved. I get the car fixed. I filed complaints to the police. I take care of bills. (Kim)

However, it is uncommon for women to do all the housework without any husband's involvement. When I asked about the gender division of household labor, women often said that their husbands help them to a certain extent. Three women said that their husbands voluntarily helped with certain tasks like vacuuming or washing dishes. Most women reported that their husbands take out the garbage or vacuum when asked. Unlike the Korean immigrants in Lim's study (1997), where women's paid jobs enabled them to demand men's participation in carework, most KISWs in my sample, even those without paid jobs, did not hesitate to ask men to participate in housework and childcare. This can be explained to some degree by changes in the perception of gender roles among this younger generation. Also, because most women had to give up their jobs and education to support their husbands' education, husbands felt the need to relieve women's workload when requested. However, KISWs do not insist on making these tasks into men's routine chores.

> He at least talks very well. If he doesn't even do that, it could be harder. . . . He always says that he's sorry [that he did not do things she asked], so I just leave it at that [and do things myself.] (Kang)

> My role is a maid. . . . It is to support my husband so that he can have a successful career and he can focus on his study. . . . [Carework] has to be done by somebody. The purpose of coming the United State[s] is the husband's study and the family came with him, so for now I support him [by doing housework and carework]. (Lee)

Most women take up carework responsibilities so that their husbands can concentrate on studying, without being distracted by homemaking and childcare, and receive their degrees in a timely fashion. However, as resonates in Lee's self-identification as a maid, they do not necessarily welcome this role. Instead, they perceive their caregiving roles as part of family life that takes precedence over individual satisfaction. The seemingly lessened conflict over carework responsibilities between men and women is ultimately attributed to the legal restriction imposed on women. That is, by depriving women of options in the public sphere, immigration law normalizes the conventional gender division of carework in the KISWs' households.

Nonetheless, conflicts may arise when women want to pursue a degree but their husbands' education is prioritized or his gender ideology is conservative. In fact, many women schedule their study around childbearing years or with a condition that it would not interrupt men's studying. Cho, who came to the United States as an F-2 visa holder, was the only F-1 visa holder at the time of the interview. When she decided to study, her husband made a condition that he would not change his daily schedule to help her in childcare as a way to accommodate her studying. Eventually after she started to go to school, she managed to include her husband in carework, which she confided with pride, but she still has to balance her life between carework and studying. The dual roles maintained by a small number of KISWs who manage to study is parallel with Korean immigrant women in Lim's (1997) study who resign to the unequal division of family work as immigrant families' survival strategies to ensure familial security.

All but two participants had one or two children. Five of them had infants or toddlers when they came to the United States and four decided to have babies after they realized that "it was about time." Childcare responsibilities are often shared by KISWs' husbands with little pressure, especially when their children are boys. Also, since there is no close female kin network from which KISWs can get help for childcare, their husbands often spend some time with their children in evenings or weekends so that women can take a break. However, it is evident that KISWs are the primary caregivers for their children, which is a problem shared by many first generation permanent immigrant women (Moon 2003).

When asked about daily schedules, most KISWs talked about spending the majority of their time with and for children. Those who can afford to send their children to daycare centers or whose children go to school can have some time for themselves in the morning, going to work out or chatting with friends online. However, their time cannot necessarily be all for their own pleasures.

> [After I sent my child to the daycare center] I just couldn't do anything. I swore to myself that I could not spend these golden hours doing housework. It was just too precious to spend time chatting with friends. Sleeping? No way! Then, I thought of studying but it did not last more than two, three weeks. I just went to take care of things while the baby wasn't with me. I could clean the home in half an hour, which would have taken two hours with the child. And I just went to grocery or shopping. (Choi)

This statement suggests that carework is not something that women actively chose or willingly seek. Rather it is the end result of the fact that other alternatives do not work for them. And few alternatives are available due to the legal restrictions and transient state of the student household.

For most KISWs with children, housework and childcare gradually became their priorities. Most women's afternoons were devoted to children: just spending time with them for children in daycare; helping their reading and writing for those in preschool; or giving rides to soccer clubs or music lessons for those in elementary school.

In addition to childcare at home, when children entered a kindergarten or elementary school, it was the wives who went to the PTA meetings and got involved in other school activities, which are considered important childcare responsibilities. Furthermore, many who go to Korean churches perform carework in an ethnic community setting by volunteering to teach Korean classes at Sunday schools.[4]

Learning to Be a Housewife in the United States

Most the KISWs (9 out of 11) had paid work experiences in South Korea both before and after marriage. So most respondents had relatively limited experiences or skills as homemakers and began to learn how to be a full-time housewife after they moved to the United States. The primary outcome of this can be found in their willingness to improve cooking skills. Many mentioned that they had not been used to cooking because paid employment in Korea exempted them from the responsibility of providing home-cooked meals. Many middle-class professional wives in Korea either buy dishes at stores or often eat out. Those who lived with their husbands' parents only assisted their mothers-in-law who did cooking. After they moved to the United States, with more time on their hands and no assistance available, they tried to learn how to cook Korean meals at home and became accustomed to discussing or sharing recipes with other KISWs.

As migrants, most KISWs spoke of driving a car and speaking English as important skills that they might not have needed to learn in Korea to carry out carework responsibilities. Different public transportation systems in the United States require them to learn to drive a car regularly, and for many, driving is a skill that they have to newly learn or improve in order to perform daily carework. Depending on their financial sources, families may have one car, and in that case, driving their husbands to school is added to the list of KISWs' tasks so that they can use the car to go grocery shopping or drive kids to daycare or schools.

Students who plan to study abroad often resort to private institutions where they can learn to speak in English with native English-speaking teachers, but KISWs accompanying their husbands often come unprepared for living in a foreign country. After they arrive in the United States, through local libraries and the Internet, they find out about private or state programs (e.g., Educational Opportunity Centers [EOC]) that provide classes to immigrants, refugees, and people with low educational attainment and low income. Speaking in English is indispensable because it is needed in every aspect of their lives, such as going grocery shopping or talking to service associates in utility companies. And, when kids go to school, speaking in English becomes more important because they have to consult with their children's teachers and communicate with their children's American friends' parents. Then, it is not about performing a task but building relationships, where a better command of English is critical.

Blocked Alternatives to Unpaid Carework and Women's Carework Perceptions

KISWs hold contradictory perceptions of their carework. On the one hand, most have absorbed the corporate view of full-time unpaid caregivers and think that their contributions are not valuable because they do not help them gain money or power in marital relations. Lee's self-deprecating identification as a maid also resonated in other women's responses. On the other hand, they see their carework as significant because it is indispensable for their husbands' timely completion of his degree. Further, some KISWs felt that being confined to carework enabled them to devote time to rearing their children without being interrupted by work or study. They embrace their motherhood, which otherwise they would not have appreciated. However, when I asked respondents what they would want to do if they could do anything, all of them said that they wanted to either work or study or both.

In this context where women are not given options due to legal restrictions, it is difficult to understand their perceptions of carework without understanding how their legal status "forces" them into carework and its consequences. While getting a job in a U.S. firm that could sponsor a KISW's work visa is technically possible, most women deemed it actually impossible to achieve unless they chose to work undocumented. Going to a graduate school, however, is considered feasible, yet daunting. The infrequent success stories of a KISW getting a post-graduate degree becomes a model for some KISWs to strive for. Even when KISWs had sufficient language preparation, childcare arrangements (or no children), and finances, the current law, which prohibits F-2 visa holders from enrolling in academic institutions as part-time students (which had been allowed before 9-11), circumscribes opportunities for KISWs who have caregiving responsibilities. When her husband decided to come to the United States for a Ph.D. degree, Moon, who had a professional occupation for years in Korea, thought that she also would have an opportunity to improve knowledge and skills in her field by going to a post-graduate school. Her upper-middle-class family was very willing to support her U.S. education. When she finally received a satisfactory score in the TOEFL [Test of English as a Foreign Language] test she got pregnant, so she had to wait for a year until she felt she could leave her child in someone else's hands. Then, when Moon was finally admitted to the school, she found out that she had to change her visa status to F-1, which requires maintaining full-time status. She could not do this because her plan had been to be a part-time student, due to a long commute to school and her childcare responsibilities. Moon then continues:

> If I had known that I am going to stay in the United States, it probably would have been better for me to go to that school because it could help me to find a job here. But, we did not know [whether we will go back to Korea or stay here]. And we do not know that yet.

The transience of a student household, which is a precarious state, also discourages KISWs from getting a degree or looking for career opportunities in the United States. They may or may not stay in the United States, depending on their husband's willingness and/or chance to get a job in the United States, as well as on their children's education and welfare. They feel reluctant to pursue a career in the United States that could be cut short, so they instead remain at home. Under these circumstances, where immigration laws curtail KISWs' opportunities in the public sphere and confine them to carework, women's frustration and resentment derived from the confinement are mostly directed toward the legal restrictions. The regulations strip KISWs of their sense of autonomy, which is frustrating for them, as is well shown in Kim's satirical comment: "Even when I go to the mall, I can't even get a Gap card because I don't have the social security number." Fluctuating changes in U.S. immigration policy after September 11, 2001, were not easy for newcomers to become accustomed to; most respondents who have experienced or seen others go through it voiced discontent with their lives in the United States.

The legal restrictions that constantly remind them of their foreign status and the lack of a sense of autonomy, combined with the other difficulties in immigrant lives, such as cultural differences and language barriers, become overriding factors in forming the women's perceptions of carework. Focusing on KISWs' carework itself, one may presume that what they do is similar to what other middle-class stay-at-home wives in the U.S. do. However, unlike those who voluntarily retreat to full-time homemaking because of the absence of any urgent economic need (Moon 2003), KISWs feel that they are "forced" into carework because state policies limit women's opportunities for public activities such as employment and education and leave little else but unpaid carework.

> In this country where family is considered as an important unit . . . when I look at [it] with that view, I think [allowing wives and children coming with students] makes sense. But not allowing wives to study [part-time] lacks flexibility. I wish they wouldn't do that. (Cho)

Even though Cho does not apply a feminist perspective to the legal restrictions, her comment implies that the current law is outdated in a way that it does not consider the general increase in women's educational attainment and participation in the paid workforce in the last few decades. Since most KISWs had actively participated in or aspired to paid work through postsecondary education, the legal obstacles they encounter and feeling incapacitated in the public sphere can be disheartening. And for KISWs, this lapse may be compensated by their husbands' and children's education. Therefore, KISWs view carework as their familial responsibility, their role in supporting their family, and an opportunity to embrace feminine roles as mothers and wives, but it does not necessarily mean that they actively seek caregiving roles or wish to validate the male breadwinner/female caregiver model of the household division of labor.

CONCLUSION

KISWs are women who come to the United States as dependents of international students and, as F-2 visa holders, they cannot enter paid work or take classes part-time for a degree. With very limited opportunities, they have no other choice but to be confined to carework. KISWs in this study shared similar challenges with the Chinese students' wives described in Liu's (1992) study. They experienced an uncomfortable cultural life in the United States, including language problems, lack of social activities, insecurity due to their transient state, lowered self-esteem compared to husband's advancement, few close friends, and great distance from families. In addition to these problems, KISWs also had some constructive experiences or a positive assessment of their experiences, such as attempting to find opportunities for self-advancement through getting post-graduate degrees, and feeling a sense of achievement in motherhood or improvement in their command of English over the years, as well as a sense of family autonomy through less pressure from dealing with in-laws.

More uniquely, I examined how, under the restrictive immigration laws, international students' wives adjust themselves to carework responsibilities. After moving to the United States, most of them learned to become a housewife in an unfamiliar social environment, including speaking English and driving. As many full-time housewives, they often do double duty, assuming childcare responsibilities as well as household chores, such as cleaning and paying household bills. In addition, they also tend to do carework tasks for husbands, including driving the husband to school and making a lunch for him. Their carework is structured to help their husbands focus on studying to earn a post-graduate degree.

[handwritten margin note: Issues w/ and for KISWs]

I found that KISWs express contradictory views about their current situation. While they speak highly of their roles as indispensable in their families, they feel that they are in a subordinate position serving their families as "maids" and they are blocked from other alternatives besides unpaid carework. However, even when there is an incongruent gender ideology between husbands and wives, KISWs' resentment, which stems from their position of being confined to home, is mainly focused on restrictive immigration laws and they rarely engage in resentment towards their husbands. Thus, the caregiving role is an undesired compromise, but they do their part for the family.

Examining KISWs' experiences enables me to argue that a patriarchal ideology persists in regulations for nonimmigrant populations. By eliminating women's chance for paid work and education, the state immigration policy enforces patriarchal gender roles, which contributes to a husband's more powerful position in conjugal relations and to further reproducing unequal gender relations.

International students, F-1 visa holders, are allowed to work part-time in a designated area (e.g., campus or through school programs) and this can be perceived as a route to recruit immigrant professional workers into the U.S. labor market (Kanjananpan 1995). By prohibiting ISWs from working, state policies began to mold the shape of middle-class families—patriarchal nuclear family structure— at their entry point. Compared to migrant women who come to the United States as temporary workers in secondary labor market sectors, many international students' wives, though not all of them, may afford to live without paid work. However, it is important to recognize that on the social structural level, this arrangement legitimates a deep-rooted patriarchal ideology and practices and inculcates this ideology into vulnerable migrant families, the groups that are often overlooked.

NOTES

I am deeply indebted to Christine E. Bose for her ongoing guidance and support. I am grateful to Mary K. Zimmerman and Jacquelyn Litt for their comments and suggestions, and Angie Y. Chung for her encouragement and advice for this study. I also would like to thank the women who participated in this study.

1. The duration of stay varies among these groups depending on the purposes. For students, it may last from less than six months to more than several years.

2. The current statistics do not tell the specific figures of spouses and of children from any one country. A considerable amount of temporary migration occurs for children's education, and one type of student family consist of F-1 visa holder mothers with children in school.

3. An additional caveat is that I am a female international student, having more options than the wives I interviewed and holding a status closer to their husbands. While this may have influenced the interviews, I believe my status as single and younger than the KISWs created some rapport with them.

4. This is a relatively common practice in Korean American communities where ethnic church networks play a significant role in immigrants' social and cultural, not to mention religious, lives (see Kim 1996; Min 2002). However, KISWs' community carework was often short-lived and intermittent. Many women gradually withdrew from community networks when they felt a gap between the Korean student community and the immigrant community or encountered conflicts with other Koreans. This withdrawal frequently happens because most of them go to church only to receive some assistance in settling down in the area, right after their arrival, or because they are conscious about their temporary status (they will leave eventually for Korea or other areas in the United States), which keeps them from investing too much time and energy in maintaining the network.

Baldwin, Nancy Toman. 1970. "Cultural Adaptations of International Student Wives at the University of Florida." Ph.D. Dissertation. The University of Florida.

Glenn, Evelyn Nakano. 1986. *Issei, Nisei, War Bride: Three Generations of Japanese American Women in Domestic Service.* Philadelphia, PA: Temple University Press.

———. 2002. *Unequal Freedom: How Race and Gender Shaped American Citizenship and Labor.* Cambridge, MA: Harvard University Press.

Grasmuck, Sherri, and Patricia R. Pessar. 1991. *Between Two Islands: Dominican International Migration.* Berkeley, CA: University of California Press.

Hondagneu-Sotelo, Pierrette. 1994. *Gendered Transitions: Mexican Experiences of Immigration.* Berkeley, CA: University of California Press.

Kanjananpan, Wilawan. 1995. "The Immigration of Asian Professionals to the United States: 1988–1990." *International Migration Review* 29(1): 7–32.

Kibria, Nazli. 1993. *Family Tightrope: The Changing Lives of Vietnamese Americans.* Princeton, NJ: Princeton University Press.

Kim, Ai Ra. 1996. *Women Struggling for a New Life: The Role of Religion in the Cultural Passage from Korea to America.* Albany, NY: State University of New York Press.

Lim, In-Sook. 1997. "Korean Immigrant Women's Challenge to Gender Inequality at Home: The Interplay of Economic Resources, Gender, and Family." *Gender & Society* 11 (1): 31–51.

Litt, Jacquelyn S., and Mary K. Zimmerman. 2003. "Global Perspectives on Gender and Carework: An Introduction." *Gender & Society* 17 (2): 156–165.

Liu, Haidong. 1992. "Lives of Chinese Students' Wives in an American University Setting." Ph. D. Dissertation. The Pennsylvania State University.

Min, Pyong Gap. 2002. "Theoretical Frameworks: Ethnicity, Social Services, Race, Gender, Generation, and Transnational Ties." In *Religions in Asian America: Building Faith Communities,* edited by Pyong Gap Min and Jung Ha Kim. Walnut Creek, CA: Altamira Press.

Moon, Seungsook. 2003. "Immigration and Mothering: Case Studies from Two Generations of Korean Immigrant Women." *Gender & Society* 17 (6): 840–860.

Pedraza, Silvia. 1991. "Women and Migration: The Social Consequences of Gender." *Annual Review of Sociology* 17:303–325.

Rosemberg, Fúliva. 2003. "Multilateral Organizations and Early Childcare and Education Policies for Developing Countries." *Gender & Society* 17 (2): 250–266.

Salaff, Janet W. 2002. "Women's Work in International Migration." In *Transforming Gender and Development in East Asia*, edited by Chow, Esther Ngan-ling. New York: Routledge.

U.S. Department of Homeland Security. 2004. *Yearbook of Immigration Statistics, 2003.* Washington, D.C.: U.S. Government Printing Office.

Zentgraf, Kristine M. 2002. "Immigration and Women's Empowerment: Salvadorans in Los Angeles." *Gender & Society* 16 (5): 625–646.

14 CAREGIVING IN TRANSNATIONAL CONTEXT: "MY WINGS HAVE BEEN CUT; WHERE CAN I FLY?"

Denise Spitzer, Anne Neufeld, Margaret Harrison,
Karen Hughes, and Miriam Stewart

These authors explore the experiences of South Asian and Chinese women family caregivers who have migrated to Canada. While caregiving is central to their role as women and members of their community, these migrant women often engaged in paid labor that compressed the time available to fulfill their duties as caregivers. Nonetheless, they were unable to renegotiate their increased caregiving responsibilities in spite of the disruption to family help networks and the increased demands on their time that were caused by migration. This occurs because the gendered nature of caregiving means women's role is to transmit the cultural values that define the boundaries of their ethnic community, and because of the ethnic nature of caregiving, which the Canadian health and other services did not address.

Increasing global migration is one of the prominent demographic features of North American society at the onset of the twenty-first century. While migration studies have expanded dramatically during the past decade, the experiences of female migrants remain under-theorized despite the fact that women compose more than 50 percent of the world's immigrants and refugees (Boyle and Halfacree 1999; United Nations Secretariat 1995).

Migration often requires the reconfiguration or renegotiation of familial and gender roles as immigrants encounter potentially competing values and demands. Our research was undertaken specifically to examine the intersections of gender, carework, and migration in Canada by focusing on immigrant women from two of the most prominent source regions for migrants, Chinese East Asia and South Asia. . . .

Women's carework is central to the practice of culturally appropriate roles that serve to demarcate ethnic boundaries and operate as ballast against the potential onslaught of competing values that threaten transnational communities with dissolution. The role of caregiving in shaping individual, gendered, and group identity is so essential that these activities can be acknowledged as exhausting or constraining but not as burdensome or oppressive. These issues, however, can be weighty for individual women. As Mui (all names are pseudonyms), a 29-year-old Chinese caregiver who joined her husband's family in Canada, said,

I really don't know what to do. I really adjust to a big family. Before I was married, I was happy with my husband. After, I felt there are lots of burden on my shoulder. Well, I am kind of person. I try to change myself to adjust to the environment. Also, what can I say? Can I say I want to get divorced? I want to walk away from my husband? I cannot go anywhere. One expression in Chinese, "My wings have been cut; where can I fly?"

[W]e argue . . . that family caregiving is problematic for immigrant women who attempt to fulfill cultural expectations in a context of altered resources associated with migration. Often, migrant women have fewer kin to rely on and lack access to extra household laborers who would commonly share domestic responsibilities in their home country. A frequently unanticipated decline in socioeconomic status leads to increased participation of immigrant women in the paid labor force, further compressing the time available to conduct household tasks and to fulfill their duties as caregivers. Cultural values such as filial piety, *dharma*, and the relational self remain at the core of women's caregiving activities; subsequently, women's role in the transmission of culture does not allow for any significant renegotiation of these duties. Significant redistribution of caregiving responsibilities fails to occur. . . .

CAREWORK, GENDERED LABOR, AND SOCIAL/CULTURAL CONTEXT

The association of caregiving labor with women's gender roles is widespread, yet cultural and religious values also influence the value and appraisal of carework (Brewer 2001; George 1998; Remennick 1999). . . . In some societies, neglect of caregiving responsibilities—not the burden of the caregiving duties themselves—can elicit negative responses. In Vietnam and Japan, failure to appropriately engage in carework or even seeking the assistance of formal support services can be regarded as a failure that can bring shame to one's family and community (Asahara et al. 2001; Braun, Takamura, and Mougeot 1996). While caregiving may be difficult, for many, the enactment of the role brings self-satisfaction and the recognition of others (Chao and Roth 2000; Gelfand and McCallum 1994; Jones 1996). Some studies suggest that cultural appraisal of the value of caregiving may mediate the effects of caregiving stress (Aranda and Knight 1997; Connell and Gibson 1997), which otherwise contributes to the deterioration of the physical and psychological health of caregivers (Lee 1999). Notably, gender and ethnicity have been found to be more significant than social class in determining obligations felt toward caring for parents (Stein et al. 1998).

Caregiving responsibilities, however, may assume different import abroad. In multicultural societies such as Canada, women serve as symbolic markers of ethnicity and are responsible for securing and maintaining the boundaries between their ethnocultural community and "mainstream" Euro-Canadian society (Yuval-Davis 1997). . . . Our research builds on this current caregiving literature by situating carework within the dynamics of the migration process.

GENDER, GLOBALIZATION, AND MIGRATION TO CANADA

Canadian immigration policies historically have been racialized and gendered, created in response to the economic and social interests or imagined futures of the state (Simmons 1999). . . . Female migration from China was limited by the imposition of a head tax in 1885 rendering it too costly for most families to provide for the migration of spouses (Women's Book Committee 1992). . . . By 1912, only 2,000 South Asian women resided in Canada although 50,000 men had been admitted during the previous half-century (Dua 2000).

Changes in immigration policies beginning in the 1960s and the official embrace of state multiculturalism facilitated the entry of migrants from non-European countries. Moreover, these changes created a policy framework that supports the reunification of families and encourages the entry of skilled labor and entrepreneurs (Simmons 1999). The policy changes have dramatically altered the demographic and social profile of Canada. In less than 40 years, the source of Canadian immigrants has shifted from Europe to Asia, with China, India, and Pakistan serving as the primary source countries in 1999–2000 (Citizenship and Immigration Canada 2001).

THE CONTEXT OF IMMIGRANT WOMEN'S CAREGIVING

Despite its image as a welcoming and tolerant society, discrimination in Canadian society persists. . . . These social realities contextualize immigrant women's caregiving experiences. Economic resources can facilitate women's ability to be a caregiver by reducing the need to work outside the home, by enabling the purchase of services, and by providing access to support services available through the employer; however, immigrant women caregivers are generally disadvantaged economically. Compared with 18.8 percent of Canadian-born women in the study area, 29.2 percent of immigrant women earn wages that are below the low-income cutoff (Lamba, Mulder, and Wilkinson 2000). The discrepancy in socioeconomic status between native and foreign-born women is attributable in part to the reluctance of Canadian officials and professionals to recognize foreign credentials and the demand by employers for Canadian job experience, both of which serve to diminish women's ability to procure remunerative work in their field of expertise (Mulvihill, Mailloux, and Atkin 2001). As a result, immigrant women are concentrated in lower-wage positions in the sales and service industry, although they are often overqualified for these occupations. . . .

In the current Canadian context, government support is provided for health care and some caregiving activities, the range of which is determined at the provincial level. However, the model of care employed by policy makers is still one that depends largely on the carework of immediate female family members (Armstrong and Armstrong 2001). . . . The gap in wages between men and women means that women are more likely than their male counterparts to forgo full-time employment to fulfill caregiving responsibilities (Lee 1999; Luxton and Corman 2001); however, as many immigrant families face downward mobility and economic strain, relinquishing paid employment is increasingly problematic (Gelfand and McCallum 1994; Slonim-Nevo et al. 1995). Furthermore, immigrant women coping with low-waged employment, downward mobility, and caregiving responsibilities, especially those engaged with both children and elder care, have reported increased health problems and stress (Remennick 1999).

Further consequences for immigrant women caregivers stem from the changes wrought by neoliberal policies and the upheaval engendered by health reform. In the past decade or more, cutbacks to government programs and services have contributed to the reprivatization of caregiving work back into the home, thereby increasing the burden on family members, especially women (Armstrong and Armstrong 2001; O'Connor, Orloff, and Shaver 1999). . . . Reduced government support for familial caregiving is particularly problematic for immigrant and refugee families.

THE STUDY

We conducted this study in a large, culturally diverse Western Canadian city, using ethnographic methods, including in-depth interviewing and participant observation. The purpose of the study was to explore the experiences of immigrant women in Canada who are caring for family members with chronic health problems. Chinese and South Asian migrants were selected because they represent the two largest migrant communities in the area.

An advisory committee comprising a diverse group of representatives from immigrant-serving agencies, community health services, and Chinese and South Asian communities was established. This committee met regularly with the investigators and provided input into the parameters of the study and inclusion criteria, aided in the recruitment of participants, provided advice on the design of materials for focus group sessions, and recommended activities for the dissemination of research findings. . . .

A convenience sample of participants was recruited through ethnic media, posters, and flyers; networks of advisory committee member agencies; and the research assistants. . . . Research assistants were members of the Chinese and South Asian communities and were able to serve as both linguistic and cultural interpreters.

Semistructured interviews were conducted with 18 Chinese and 11 South Asian Canadian female caregivers. In addition, 6 women provided a second interview and allowed research assistants to observe them in the process of their routine of caregiving. At the beginning of the first interview, all women were asked to tell the story of how they came to Canada. Then, they were asked to describe how they came to be a caregiver for their family member and what a typical day of caregiving was like for them. Subsequently, they were asked what was difficult or supportive for their caregiving, which services—in addition to physician visits—they had used, what problems they had in accessing services, and how the experience of immigration had affected their ability to be a caregiver.

Four focus group sessions, two with caregivers and two with health professionals and policy makers, were held to allow participants to discuss the program and policy relevance of our findings. Individual and group interviews conducted in the language of the participant's choice were audiotaped and transcribed. . . .

[W]e broadly noted that Chinese and South Asian cultures share certain features including a strong sense of familial loyalty and responsibility, respect for elders, a focus on collectivity, and strong in-group orientation (Chekki 1988; Cohen 1998; George 1998; Lai and Yue 1990). Both Chinese and South Asian immigrants hail from different countries that are within themselves heterogeneous. Nonetheless, each ethnocultural group shares values and histories that reinforce common identities. . . . These shared attributes allowed us to consider recruiting participants from Hong Kong, Taiwan, and China for the Chinese sample and caregivers from India, Sri Lanka, Pakistan, and Bangladesh for the South Asian sample.

FINDINGS AND DISCUSSION

Profile of Participants

Twenty-three of the participants were caring for adult family members suffering from cancer, kidney or heart disease, dementia, or arthritis, and 6 cared for children with conditions such as cerebral palsy and developmental delay. The respondents ranged in age from 29 to 75 and averaged 50 years old. Twelve informants reported household incomes of less than Canadian $39,999, 9 households earned between Canadian $40,000 and Canadian $79,999, and the incomes of 2 families exceeded Canadian $80,000. Six informants declined to provide income information. Three participants resided in Canada for less than 8 years, 4 arrived between 8 and 14 years ago, and the remainder have called Canada home for more than 14 years. At home, 15 women spoke Cantonese, 2 used Mandarin, 8 spoke Punjabi, 2 reported speaking Hindi, and 1 each used English or Urdu. Nineteen women had completed some postsecondary education; 19 were employed outside the home full-time or part-time. Fourteen of the externally employed women were educated beyond a grade 12 level. Twenty-three of the 29 caregivers resided in the same home as the care recipient; of these, 11 cared for additional dependents. The remaining caregivers provided care for a family member who resided in the same Canadian city.

In Canada, all residents are enrolled in the national health care program that ensures free access to physician and hospital services. An array of programs including home care and assistance for independent living are available to help people caring for others at home. However, these services may not be linguistically or culturally appropriate, as they are often predicated on Euro-Canadian standards of care (Neufeld et al. 2002).

Caregiving Beliefs and Women's Roles

Both South Asian and Chinese respondents felt that women were the most appropriate caregivers for elders as well as for children. As in other studies (Asahara et al. 2001; Chao and Roth 2000; George 1998; Sung 1991), daughters and daughters-in-law were the preferred caregivers for our respondents' households. For instance, one 29-year-old Chinese caregiver, Mui, described how the expectations of her in-laws that she provide extensive care for her father-in-law were based on their view that this was the appropriate role for her as the daughter-in-law. "They [husband's family] don't like an outsider to get into the family. They are traditional. They think this is my job and I have to do it." Nav, a university-educated Punjabi woman, commented on her obligation as a daughter and daughter-in-law to care for the elders in her family:

> I have two children of my own, and my mother-in-law is living with me. And on the other hand, I have my own parents who are . . . getting old. . . . I'm not responsible directly, but well, I'm an older daughter. . . . I always feel responsible because if anything happens to them emotionally, they call me. So I feel I'm responsible for that too.

Women were regarded as more sensitive than men to the needs of others. Ming, a university-educated, middle-class, 37-year-old Chinese woman, noted how her five-year-old daughter recognized the strain caregiving placed on her, vowing to be well behaved so as not to burden her mother any further. Her son did not notice her distress.

> I went back to my parents' house, I found out my, uh, my father's sick again. . . . When I went home, I was not happy. And my daughter noticed. She asked me, "Mom, how come you're not happy?" I was so surprised, only five years old! She knows I'm not happy. I said, "Because, your grandpa is . . . sick, . . . so I'm not happy." And she knows. She just told me, "Oh, I'll be good tonight. I won't be fighting with brother, and, uh, I'll be good to you." But my son, he just, he doesn't even notice.

Despite the expectation that daughters-in-law would care for their elders, the women caring for elders often noted that parents longed for the company of their sons. Ming reflected, "They only want their son to be with them. Even though he doesn't do much about it."

As men predominantly had been the recipients of attention and care throughout their lives, they were generally construed as inept in the provision of care. Ming reflected the majority perspective of our informants that men were not suited for carework. Her younger brother was brought from Hong Kong to help with their parents as Ming is employed. He has not, however, found satisfactory work, nor has he been particularly helpful to the family in her eyes:

> I be a full-time mom, a full work . . . taking care of my parents. . . . He [surviving younger brother] is living with my parents. I don't think he can even taking care of himself well enough to [be] taking care of the sick parent.

Both the association of caregiving with women and the construction of men as incompetent in these matters generally prevented both genders from sharing equally in these tasks. Therefore, when a man did offer support to a female relative, it was generally on a limited basis.

Maintaining Cultural Identity

The findings of this study suggest that women, as mothers of the nation and reproducers of society, are increasingly entrusted with the task of maintaining cultural identity through educating the young and modeling their own behavior. According to our respondents, modeling these virtues for their children and others was vital not only for their own standing within their community but also to engage their children in the network of reciprocity that underscored these values. Eunice, a 48-year-old recent Chinese immigrant, is caring for her infirm mother with some support from her brother. From her perspective, the rest of her siblings are disregarding their familial obligations. Eunice explained why she has assumed responsibility for her parent:

> What makes me feel satisfied is that I know how to care for her through filial piety. When I tell the children to treat the elderly nicely, they may say, "What about you?" So there is comparison. I think the most important thing is to accommodate to each other. Sometimes, she takes care of me. When I take bus home after work, she will stand by the window and wait for me. Sometimes, she waits for an hour. So, this is family love.

Ranjit, a 45-year-old, university-educated, middle-class South Asian woman caring for her mother and father, also copes with the demands of paid employment, her children and spouse, and housework duties. She also reinforced these sentiments: "I also think the children will learn from my experience that they should respect and help elders."

Most women rejected the idea of caregiving's being a burden despite reporting exhaustion, ill health, and anxiety due to the overwhelming duties they must complete. Instead, they perceived caregiving as part of their role within the family and community.

> Maybe in our culture, and maybe that's why I am looking after my elderly instead of just throwing them into a nursing home. . . . I had to sell my house to move in with them when they became very old, and I didn't really like doing it. But they need the emotional support as well as the physical support. Maybe in our culture people are more sensitive to the elderly. They are not considered garbage. (Ayesha)

> Well, it's a member of family, and I take it for granted that he is more comfortable when I can get, when I can give him the care he needs. And in our family relations, really, we take it for granted that we care for each other. (Lakshmi)

> Filial piety and caring are what we should do. (Eunice)

Even in cases where the care recipient was unpleasant or hostile, some respondents felt satisfied that they had fulfilled their obligations in a gracious and appropriate manner. This dedication was at times contrasted with Euro-Canadian approaches that seemed to invite greater institutional intervention. When one university-educated, middle-class Chinese caregiver, Ivy, age 49, was offered the option of institutionalizing her in-laws, she responded, "Lady, you don't know what you're talking about. You come from a different culture where [sic] I came from." Nevertheless, some women did experience negative outcomes of caregiving. At age 29, Chinese caregiver Mui described feeling isolated and depressed. A mother of three children, Mui assists her mother-in-law in caring for her cold and demanding father-in-law.

> I am not as happy and free as before. My whole life is around this family. I don't have friends. I feel I am getting older staying at home all day. I look at myself, I feel so old. . . . I feel like falling from the heaven to the hell.

Immigration, Familial Responsibilities, and Employment

The impact of immigration on women's ability to cope with caregiving responsibilities is significant. Migration often means that familial networks are truncated or dispersed, reducing the numbers of kin that can be called on for support. Rina, age 72, compared her experience as a caregiver in India and Canada:

> I was looking after my father in India. It seemed that we had more time there. I used to spend lots of time with him, in his last few days. Even my employer gave me lots of free time to spend with him. My uncle stayed with my father for one and a half month; he was in Canada. All the family came, and we stayed together for few weeks. I don't think you can do it here. In India, there is more closeness.

Sponsoring relatives from overseas to care for infirm family members is not uncommon but requires an investment of time and financial resources as family members who act as sponsors must demonstrate the ability to support incoming relations for a period of 10 years. These efforts may be too costly for low-income households and too time consuming for those who require immediate assistance.

South Asian and Chinese Canadian caregivers found themselves balancing the demands of caregiving with the needs of other family members. Although for some, spousal relations suffered, others said that the presence of a helpful spouse helped ameliorate their distress. Rajinder, a 40-year-old, middle-class Punjabi woman, told us,

I give her [mother-in-law] bath in the evening. . . . Usually my husband helps out. We have no help from friends or any other family member. I come home in the evening, then prepare supper for the whole family, give bath to my small kids, clean the house.

Caregivers like Nav and Ming found that the presence of kin and their competing demands contributed to stress in Canada while similar interactions in their home countries would have been more supportive or less problematic.

The costs of securing paid assistance with family caregiving tasks are higher in Canada. In South Asian countries, for instance, domestic labor is often performed by servants. In China, the work unit system offers support in the form of housing and food services (Bian 1994), and in Hong Kong, Singapore, and Taiwan, foreign domestic workers are frequently employed (Cheng 1996). Economic conditions and the Canadian context made it difficult to procure extrafamilial domestic assistance.

My father was on a very good job back home [India], was in police. We had lots of servants. They did everything. Over here, I have to do everything like cook, clean, work outside the home, look after my children. (Ranjit)

Labor back where I came from is a lot cheaper. I think I would be able to employ someone full-time . . . even if I were, uh, to apply someone to come . . . from overseas, say, for example, a Filipino maid or something. . . . The regulations are not as tough. It would be faster, it would be easier to get one. And cheaper of course. (Ivy)

Many women worked outside the home in low-paying jobs to supplement family incomes. Their employment status further exacerbated their experience of time compression and demanded well-organized plans to cope with the needs of care recipients and other family members. Ivy clearly outlined how her day was organized to combine family caregiving and employment outside the home.

Okay, I get up at 5:00 a.m. Five, every morning, so I have my parents' meal cooked, both breakfast and lunch. I leave the house at 6:30 a.m. for work. I don't come home until 4:00 p.m. Take a shower. That's my best time of the day, myself, I can relax. Maybe a drink of tea. Then I start cooking supper. My supper is at around 7:30 p.m. You know, after wash up everything. Make sure my mom take her pills. Do her night care. Get her up to her room. Make sure she takes all her medication then tuck her into bed, and pray she, that she will sleep the whole night.

As Ivy's employment did not offer supplemental health insurance, family benefits, or flexible hours, it was difficult for her to take time off to accompany her parents to appointments or to provide personal care. Other women like Ranjit also had little time to pursue avenues of treatment or support for their family member because of their need to work outside the home. "I had to make time from my work, housework, and kids to take them [parents] for the fitting of belt and also to check different shops for the walkers to compare their costs" (Ranjit). In summary, the lack of kin support and the demands of often inflexible and poorly waged employment created additional stress for immigrant women caring for family members by increasing their time compression and financial strain.

Extrafamilial Assistance

Commitment to the family and the practice of caregiving in their country of origin shaped and constrained the steps taken by immigrant women to seek help from health and social service agencies in Canada. Both Chinese and South Asian cultures share in a relational sense of self that situates an individual within a set of family relations and stands in contrast to the dominant Western sense of self that focuses on independence. . . . Formal support services for caregiving activities are rare in their countries of origin as the[y] . . . are generally undertaken by kin. Moreover, in many of their home countries, health and social services such as home care, rehabilitative services, or respite care may not be available altogether or are directed to the indigent, making it less likely that newcomers will seek out these programs in Canada (Cohen 1998; Ikels 1993).

With the belief that care is best carried out in the home by providers linked by sentiment and limited traditions of accessing services, many of the women chose not to use available formal services. Ivy, for example, works and cares for two children, her father, and her mother who suffers from diabetes and Alzheimer's disease. Although she feels guilty about attending to the needs of her parents before those of her children, she cannot come to avail herself of services that are culturally and linguistically unacceptable to her parents. "I always tell myself, this is my own parents. You look after them. No one are [sic] going to help you.". . .

As reported in other migrant communities (Braun, Takamura, and Mougeot 1996; Remennick 1999), this reluctance to utilize services is reinforced by elders who feel that caregiving should be delivered by kin who can maintain privacy and are obligated to do so. The status of elders in the family and the obligation of children to be the primary caregiver constitutes a powerful social imperative for the immigrant women in this study. As a result, even with the availability of state benefits, they were unable to renegotiate their significant caregiving demands.

Access to the informal support of friends is also inhibited by an in-group orientation that often confined discussion of care recipients' conditions or caregiving stress to household members. . . .

Interviews with the six respondents who care for children with chronic conditions revealed that immigrant caregivers were more forthcoming in seeking out and utilizing services for their children. Women availed themselves of a variety of services including special education, hospital-based therapy programs, aids for daily living, and home care services for children. Some women became health advocates alongside other parents and actively campaigned for access to specialized services for children in need. One Chinese mother, Li, a 43-year-old university-educated woman, remarked that one formal advocacy group she approached taught her to make demands. "So it was very hard to, to fight, but the teacher help me to . . . how to appeal and fight . . . for the speech [therapy]."

The limited number of cases and types of conditions do not allow us to speculate. However, we suggest that a mother's ability to consider and effect health care decisions pertaining to her children may be an avenue for migrant women to renegotiate caregiving responsibilities with persons or services external to the family. Moreover, the decision-making may be less burdened by concerns over an elder's response to outsiders or the cultural appropriateness of health care as the elderly are often regarded as more rigid in their outlook and behavior.

CONCLUSION: MY WINGS HAVE BEEN CUT; WHERE CAN I FLY?

The caregiving experiences of South Asian and Chinese immigrant women in Canada revealed surprisingly similar responses despite differences in culture and the length of residency in Canada. . . .

The women's stories suggest a number of overarching issues that appear at the intersections of migration, gender, and carework. Caregiving is a holistic activity that may be more costly in a foreign setting (George 1998). We observed that female migrants were afforded fewer options to renegotiate caregiving responsibilities than they possessed at home. They lacked extensive kin support, and their concentration in low-wage employment not only exacerbated time constraints but did not allow them to purchase domestic labor to alleviate their responsibilities. Even in the households with adequate resources to hire external assistance for domestic service, caretaking responsibilities were not transferred to outsiders, confirming our observation that gender is more important than class in shaping these interactions (Stein et al. 1998).

Caregiving, a central focus of kinwork, is embedded in a woman's gender role as wife, mother, and moral being; caregiving responsibilities reinforce gender roles and propagate the values of filial piety and dharma in Chinese and South Asian families. . . . The significance of women's carework to cultural and gender identity is reflected in the fact that our respondents echoed these sentiments regardless of length of residency in Canada. Interactions with elder generations further ensured adherence to appropriate behavior.

For Chinese and South Asian women, family caregiving was problematic as they sought to fulfill cultural expectations with resources altered by migration. Their role in transmitting cultural values did not allow for significant renegotiation of caregiving responsibilities despite disrupted family networks and increased demands. The challenge to Canadian society is to find measures to support women family caregivers from diverse cultural backgrounds.

NOTE

Author's Note: This study was funded by grants from the Prairie Centre of Excellence for Research in Immigration and Integration, Social Sciences and Humanities Research Council of Canada, and the Caritas Health Foundation of Edmonton, awarded to the authors (Anne Neufeld, principal investigator). We wish to recognize the contributions of our research assistants, Chen Chen Shih, Kathy Cheng, Barinder Ghuman, and Tasnim Hirani; the members of our advisory committee; and the community agencies that assisted us. Finally, we are grateful to the caregivers and their families who gave so willingly of their time and their stories.

REFERENCES

Aranda, M. P., and B. G. Knight. 1997. The influence of ethnicity and culture on the caregiver stress and coping process: A sociocultural review and analysis. *The Gerontologist* 37 (3): 342–54.

Armstrong, Pat, and Hugh Armstrong. 2001. *Thinking it through: Women, work and caring in the new millennium*. Halifax, Canada: Maritime Centre of Excellence for Women's Health.

Asahara, Kiyomi, Yumiko Momose, Sachiyo Murashima, Noriko Okubo, and Joan Magilvy. 2001. The relationship of social norms to use of services and caregiver burden in Japan. *Journal of Nursing Scholarship* 4:375–80.

Bian, Yian. 1994. *Work and inequality in urban China*. Albany: State University of New York Press.

Boyle, Paul, and Keith Halfacree. 1999. *Migration and gender in the developed world*. London: Routledge.

Braun, Kathryn, Jeanette Takamura, and Thanh Mougeot. 1996. Perceptions of dementia, caregiving, and help-seeking among recent Vietnamese immigrants. *Journal of Cross-Cultural Gerontology* 11:213–28.

Brewer, Loretta. 2001. Gender socialization and the cultural construction of elder caregivers. *Journal of Aging Studies* 15 (3): 217–36.

Chao, Shu Yuan, and Patricia Roth. 2000. The experiences of Taiwanese women caring for parents-in-law. *Journal of Advanced Nursing* 31 (3): 631–38.

Chekki, D. 1988. Family in India and North America: Change and continuity among the Lingayat families. *Journal of Comparative Family Studies* 19 (2): 329–43.

Cheng, Shu-Ju Ada. 1996. Migrant women domestic workers in Hong Kong, Singapore and Taiwan: A comparative analysis. *Asian and Pacific Migration Journal* 5 (1): 139–52.

Citizenship and Immigration Canada. 2001. *Pursuing Canada's commitment to immigration: The immigration plan for 2002*. Ottawa: Minister of Public Works and Government Services Canada.

Cohen, Lawrence. 1998. *No aging in India: Alzheimer's, the bad family, and other modern things*. Berkeley: University of California Press.

Connell, C. M., and G. D. Gibson. 1997. Racial, ethnic and cultural differences in dementia caregiving: Review and analysis. *The Gerontologist* 37 (3): 355–64.

Dua, Enakshi. 2000. "The Hindu women's question": Canadian nation building and the social construction of gender for South Asian-Canadian women. In

Anti-racist feminism, edited by Agnes Calliste and George Sefa Dei. Halifax, Canada: Fernwood.

Gelfand, David E., and J. McCallum. 1994. Immigration, the family and female caregivers in Australia. *Journal of Gerontological Social Work* 22 (3/4): 41–59.

George, Usha. 1998. Caring and women of colour: Living the intersecting oppressions of race, class and gender. In *Women's caring: Feminist perspectives on social welfare*, edited by T. Baines, P. M. Evans, and S. Neysmith. Oxford, UK: Oxford University Press.

Ikels, Charlotte. 1993. Settling accounts: The intergenerational contract in an age of reform. In *Chinese families in the post-Mao era*, edited by D. Davis and S. Harrell. Berkeley: University of California Press.

Jones, Patricia S. 1996. Asian American women caring for elderly parents. *Journal of Family Nursing* 2 (1): 56–75.

Lai, Magdalene C., and Ka-Ming Kevin Yue. 1990. The Chinese. In *Cross-cultural caring: A handbook for health professionals in Western Canada*, edited by Nancy Waxler-Morrison, Joan Anderson, and Elizabeth Richardson. Vancouver, Canada: UBC Press.

Lamba, Navjot, Marlene Mulder, and Lori Wilkinson. 2000. *Immigrants and ethnic minorities on the prairies: A statistical compendium*. Edmonton, Canada: PCERII.

Lee, Christina. 1999. Health, stress and coping among women caregivers: A review. *Journal of Health Psychology* 4 (1): 27–40.

Luxton, Meg, and June Corman. 2001. *Getting by in hard times: Gendered labor at home and on the job*. Toronto, Canada: University of Toronto Press.

Mulvihill, Mary Ann, Louise Mailloux, and Wendy Atkin. 2001. *Advancing policy and research responses to immigrant and refugee women's health in Canada*. Ottawa, Canada: Centres of Excellence in Women's Health.

Neufeld, Anne, Margaret Harrison, Miriam J. Stewart, Karen Hughes, and Denise L. Spitzer. 2002. Immigrant women: Making connections to community resources for support in family caregiving. *Qualitative Health Research* 12 (6): 751–68.

O'Connor, J., A. Orloff, and S. Shaver. 1999. *States, markets, families: Gender, liberalism and social policy in Australia, Canada, Great Britain and the United States*. Cambridge, UK: Cambridge University Press.

Remennick, Larissa I. 1999.Women of the "sandwich" generation and multiple roles: The case of Russian immigrants of the 1990s in Israel. *Sex Roles* 40 (5/6): 347–78.

Simmons, Alan B. 1999. Immigration policy: Imagined futures. In *Immigrant Canada: Demographic, economic and social challenges*, edited by S. Halli and L. Driedger. Toronto, Canada: University of Toronto Press.

Slonim-Nevo, V., J. Cwikel, H. Luski, M. Lankry, and Y. Shraga. 1995. The caregiver burden among three-generation immigrant families in Israel. *International Social Work* 38:191–204.

Stein, Catherine, Virginia Wemmerus, Marcia Ward, Michelle Gaines, Andrew Freeberg, and Thomas Jewell. 1998. "Because they're my parents": An intergenerational study of felt obligation and parental caregiving. *Journal of Marriage and the Family* 60 (August): 611–22.

Sung, K.-T. 1991. Family-centered informal support networks of Korean elderly: The resistance of cultural traditions. *Journal of Cross-Cultural Gerontology* 6 (4): 431–37.

United Nations Secretariat. 1995. *International migration policies and the status of female migration*. New York: United Nations.

Women's Book Committee, Chinese Canadian National Council. 1992. *Jin guo: Voices of Chinese Canadian women*. Toronto, Canada: Women's Press.

Yuval-Davis, Nira. 1997. Ethnicity, gender relations and multiculturalism. In *Debating cultural hybridity: Multi-cultural identities and the politics of anti-racism*, edited by P. Werbner and T. Modood. London: Zed Press.

III

MOTHERHOOD, DOMESTIC WORK, AND CHILDCARE IN GLOBAL PERSPECTIVE

15 | MOTHERHOOD, DOMESTIC WORK, AND CHILDCARE IN GLOBAL PERSPECTIVE

In ordinary times, it is sometimes hard to see that motherhood is inextricably related to a global economy, government practices, labor force changes, and migration. But as we show in Part 3, motherhood and carework are very much tied to global migration, state resources, and labor practices in both developing and economically prosperous nations. We were reminded of these interconnections as the colossal disasters of the earthquake and tsunami in the Indian Ocean communities and the hurricane Katrina in New Orleans unfolded. News stories circulated on the costs in human lives and the destruction of water, shelter, and food supplies. Fears of widespread and deadly disease were mentioned daily. In this book, we ask questions about motherhood and carework that have not yet been raised in the press or by our politicians. How will the economic disaster created by the events affect traditional forms of livelihood, and how will these, in turn, affect motherhood? How will women's patterns of migration and residence change in response to the loss of traditional income and how will this affect the care of children? Will jobs in paid carework for women figure in the reconstruction of households? What will be the role of international agencies, corporations, and governments to provide care to children? While we have no clear answers to these questions, we show in this part that these are questions that circulate across the globe in regard to motherhood practices and the care of children.

As the following material makes clear, motherhood in globalization is structured by fundamental inequalities among women, between women and men, and across geographic regions. We emphasize scholarship that identifies what Mona Harrington (2000) calls "hardening inequalities" between women that are created and reproduced by the current global reorganization of carework. As we see it, the nascent scholarship on motherhood and globalization that we include in this chapter builds upon the work of U.S. feminist researchers who have challenged the dominant notion that motherhood represents women's essential nature and that in its ideal form, mothers share a universal and natural set of values and experiences. In rejecting biological essentialism, this scholarship has shifted the focus to an analysis of how social resources for mothers are sifted through three main systems of support: family, nation, and market. Women's motherwork takes its structure in response to the shifting resources in these main systems of caring. The focus on women's unequal access to resources, on deep divides between women, shows how material privilege, national location, and transnational policy create what Angela Davis (1998) calls "fragmented maternities."

Part 3 on motherhood and childcare examines the relevance of globalization for the experiences of mothers as they care for children and reflect on their own mothering as well as for the experiences of women who do this labor as paid workers. Here we see a range of mothering experiences: mothers with the financial resources to hire economically and socially vulnerable women to do the tasks of carework and domestic labor, mothers who migrate away from their homes (either long or short distances) for employment as nannies and domestic workers in other women's households, and women who develop new forms of mothering across nations. These differences in mothers' experience reflect inequalities in women's access to resources in caring for their children. We contextualize these disparities by examining how the expansion of global capitalism encourages a market-based and largely exploitative carework economy that builds on and furthers inequalities between race, ethnicity, class, and nations.

We begin by considering the deficiencies in policy support for carework. The wider context of global capitalism undermines public care systems for children even as more of the world's mothers are employed in wage labor. We then consider how inequality among mothers is embedded in an international transfer of carework labor among mothers and paid careworkers. Finally, we examine the experiences of women who become transnational mothers in the search for wages and employment in wealthy economies.

A COLLAPSING CARE SYSTEM

One issue or, better stated, crisis that has emerged since the 1970s in the United States has been the question of childcare. While some mothers have always been employed, it was not until the vast majority of mothers sought employment that concepts like "supermom," "quality time," and "latchkey children" entered into mainstream conversation in the United States and other developed economies. Each of these terms reflects new tensions about mothers' employment. And each implies questions about the nature of responsibility for children: Is motherhood understood as a private activity, done and arranged by individual women for their own children? Is motherhood conceived of as public and governmental responsibilities, activities for which society in general is responsible? Our focus on globalization adds other questions: What are the different forms of mothering activity in the context of globalization? What care deficits are built into globalization? How are mothers affected by interlocking, global economies? Does globalization have the potential to construct mothering activity as a public good that is supported and recognized as valuable?

We define motherhood and carework for children as being concerned with the "physical, cultural, and ideological reproduction of human beings" (Anderson, see Chapter 18). Rather than defined as a public good or resource, our readings show that they are treated as the private responsibility of the family, in particular, of women. In the United States, Mona Harrington argues, the ideology of caretaking is deeply individualized and privatized:

> We don't see a collapsing care system because we don't see care as a system to begin with. We see individuals making private decisions about who takes care of the children or helps [an] arthritis-plagued elderly parent. We see families using the private market for services they don't have time to provide themselves—day care, house cleaning, fast food. We don't add all of this up and call it a system that is working well or badly. (2000, 26)

Our first excerpt, by economist Nancy Folbre, sets the stage for understanding the lack of public investment in carework and the multiple care deficits left in its wake. Folbre presents a cautionary tale of CorporNation, a fictional island nation owned by a multinational company that has purchased its own island to escape labor regulations and taxes. The low wages and scant labor regulations characteristic of CorporNation do not support the reproduction and care of its laborers or their families. The ideal worker is childless, healthy, and literally, carefree (see also Williams 2000 for a discussion of this "ideal worker" model in professional contexts). CorporNation enjoys terrific financial success and remains competitive on an international scale precisely because the responsibilities of bringing up workers from childhood, supporting their families, or caring for their illnesses are outside the scope of corporate responsibility.

Folbre sees this less as fiction than as fact in a global economy increasingly dominated by multinational business corporations. She describes how global capitalism, unfettered by state regulations or a normative ethos that supports the care duties and needs of workers, produces its own care crisis. The new multinational corporations—which account for two-thirds of world trade—now set the stage for weakened supports of social welfare on the part of private companies as well as nation states. These corporations use the human capabilities of its workers without paying for their production or their maintenance. She argues that companies are motivated to decrease the costs of labor by punishing maternity among its workers, forcing birth control on them, and disregarding their mothering responsibilities.

Folbre identifies a reorganization of the process of production in which corporations create and depend upon a class of temporary, ready-made, and disposable workers who travel across the globe for work or who remain home and work for the ubiquitous multinationals. The global reorganization of production has given rise to "footloose" corporations that similarly move around the globe in search of the least expensive labor; these are typically to nations or regions interested in attracting foreign capital and that require virtually no social welfare benefits for workers. Folbre also shows the interconnection between corporate disregard for the carework duties of its workers and the complicity of national governments in disregarding these duties. Here she argues that the expansion of a global capitalist system is deeply implicated in growing carework deficits for children across the globe. While the nature of these crises differ for women situated in different regions and in different social and racial positions, the lack of support for motherhood is fundamentally connected to the expansion of a global capitalist economy that is largely unregulated and exploitative (see Part 2 for a discussion about the carework crises created through structural adjustment programs).

Folbre contends that it is not only multinational corporations but families who are drawn into the challenges of carework and mothering in this new global picture. She refers particularly to the importation and employment of immigrants (both legal and illegal) in wealthy nations to undertake the childcare and domestic work of more economically privileged women. Her work brings us back to the scholarship on women's migration for carework that Sassen and Chang identify (covered in Parts 1 and 2). As we have seen, immigrant women are available as a large and highly exploitable labor pool. While importing careworkers might solve some of the pressing problems of more affluent women employers, it will do little to encourage broader discussion and policy on ways to collectivize the costs of care and protect childcare providers. Nor will it create the conditions by which gender arrangements can change to give fathers more responsibility for care.

Folbre sees a number of scenarios that will be played out in this new global tension over carework. In her most optimistic model, she advocates a new value placed on a "concern for developing human capability not merely increasing the size of our collective GDPs" (see Chapter 16). She calls for rules of minimum taxation for corporations in all countries and punishment of countries that limit workers' rights. She also advocates for investment in the carework responsibilities of workers and envisions a state that is supportive of families, in which values of care and reciprocity are promoted (see also the discussion in Part 4, Chapter 23 on a woman-friendly state).

Currently, however, Folbre argues that we are faced with a choice between two bad scenarios—a return to a "patriarchal society" in which women have few economic and social opportunities and are thus forced to do virtually all the carework, or a market-based system. In the latter scenario—which is more likely given the stability in mothers' labor force participation—"individuals are on their own and nobody provides care unless it is paid for in carefully calibrated low-cost units" (see Chapter 16).

The excerpt from Lynet Uttal's book *Making Care Work* shows what an individualist, market-based system of care looks like in the United States from the perspective of mothers as well as paid childcare workers. The major demographic shift in household labor in the United States labor market since the 1950s has been the change from the male breadwinner model of the mid-century to dual-earner couple and single-parent families by the end of the century. Dual-earner couples are the fastest-growing household type and also reveal the largest increase in time spent at work. According to U.S. census data in 2000, close to 80 percent of single mothers and just over 70 percent of married mothers were employed in the labor force. This compares to just over 58 percent of single mothers and 40 percent of married mothers employed in 1970. No longer able to depend on the unpaid carework of women in households, dual-earner families are struggling with balancing two careers, children, and domesticity. It is these new arrangements—rather than an actual expansion of the work week—that generates what we have come to know as "work-family conflict" (Jacobs and Gerson 2004). We have already shown that, at least in the case of the United States, the new employment patterns of mothers have done little to change the division of carework in households: women continue to assume primary carework responsibility, and it is mothers, rather than fathers, who adjust their work schedule to accommodate carework needs (Jacobs and Gerson 2004). This may be one reason why, in the 1990s, married mothers' labor force participation in the United States has stopped increasing (Cotter et al. 2004).

The rise of women's labor force participation and the lack of public support and policy for childcare have created the conditions for the development of a for-profit market for childcare. In the past, according to Uttal, childcare arrangements were made informally through an underground economy of neighbors and friends who exchanged services. That picture has changed, moving toward the formal market of childcare. In 1994, 61 percent of working mothers used childcare centers or in-home paid family childcare for their childcare arrangements, an increase from 17 percent in 1958. The percentage of care given by nonrelatives almost doubled between 1958 and 1990. Uttal calls this a commodification of childcare (see Part 1 for a full discussion of commodification). This shift means that childcare now takes place outside familiar social networks and inside a market system.

Uttal argues that these trends reflect the "political neglect of employed mothers." This neglect has helped to create a private, "haphazard and diverse system of market-based care" rather than a comprehensive, public child welfare system as in Australia, Sweden, and Japan (2002, 96; see Part 4 for a discussion of state policy and carework). The political neglect stems from persisting assumptions that mother's place is in the home and from policymakers' slowness to acknowledge the legitimacy and necessity of women's participation in the labor force.

Not until the 1990s did the United States witness a shift toward a new acceptance of nonmaternal care of children. According to Uttal, the new work requirement in federal welfare policy (Temporary Assistance for Needy Families [TANF]) is part of the trend toward an acceptance of maternal employment (although in the case of welfare recipients, it is mandatory employment; Litt 2004; Mink 1998). Yet because policymakers failed to respond systematically to new demographic trends of maternal employment, an entirely new market developed—including chains, franchises, and independent businesses—that continues to remain largely unregulated. This is particularly problematic for low-income mothers whose wages barely cover childcare expenses.

Uttal, like Folbre and Harrington, is deeply concerned about the absence of a publicly supported care system for children, the burdens it creates for mothers, and the consequent inequality among women locally and across the globe. She helps us see how the absence of supportive public policy for care positions women in advanced as well as developing nations in a global reorganization of care. As we outlined in Part 1, globalization has intensified the commodification of care by creating increasing supplies of domestic and childcare workers for affluent women and by drawing more First World women into the labor market. Thus, poor women in developing countries are entering into "global survival circuits" (Sassen, Part 1) that support the infrastructure of advanced economies and the lifestyle of the affluent.

Uttal's interviews with mothers who pay for their children's care reveal that they are often uncertain about their carework arrangements. She argues that mothers' uncertainties are created in large part by inadequate public policy that does not regulate, evaluate, or even set ideals for childcare in the private market. The childcare market produces vulnerability for the provider as well. Uttal's work supports the points made by Sassen and Chang (see Part 1) in documenting the use of immigrant and low-wage women laborers to perform carework for more affluent middle- and upper-class women. Uttal helps us to see that systems of race and class intersect with migration practices to form part of the political economy of childcare. (These issues are discussed in more detail in the readings in this part).

From a radically different context, Rebecca Upton shows us the negative consequences of inadequate public provision for children who have been orphaned by the HIV/AIDS crisis in Botswana. Her work helps us to see how poor coordination between the three main sources of welfare—state, family, and market—develop into deeper crises when carework is desperately needed. Botswana has one of the highest HIV infection rates in the world. Upton targets the unsuccessful national public health campaigns as failing to stop the current rapid spread of the virus. The ABC Campaign (Abstain, Be faithful, and Condomise), while ubiquitous, shows little signs of success. In addition, Upton argues that gendered sexual practices are fueling the epidemic. Men's migration for employment, where many engage in casual and unprotected sex, and their subsequent return home make them vectors of transmission. For their part, women feel obligated to reproduce and comply with sexual demands of their partners. But Upton's point is not only that the public health campaign fails to address the AIDS crisis. The campaign has also limited the reach and meaning of public health initiatives. No state agency, she argues, recognizes or addresses the special burdens of caregiving for survivors.

Upton's article documents increasing pressure on the informal system of caregiving. The established system of foster care has traditionally included grandmothers and grandmothers-in-law who provide children and mothers with structures of support. The rising death rate of adult women has stretched the fosterage system to its breaking point: there are greater numbers of children in need of constant care and fewer women to provide it. International religious organizations have been established to care for dependent children, but again, do virtually nothing to alleviate the stress on women whose caregiving responsibilities are intense.

Folbre, Uttal, and Upton all point to what Harrington would call a "collapsing system of care" (2000). They identify the coming together of various crises: globalization that creates the conditions for women to enter global migration chains, the increase in mothers' labor force participation across the globe, and the lack of national- or international-level public recognition and provision of care. Their excerpts show us that what appear to be individual decisions and lifestyle options made by women are in reality embedded in broader global systems. The woman migrant who goes to Folbre's CorporNation makes a seemingly individual decision to seek better prospects in a foreign country, but she is part of a global economy in which workers are used as cheap and disposable commodities rather than as family members. The middle-class American mother Uttal refers to seemingly makes an individual decision about how to care for her children while she is at work; in reality, her choices are governed by and involved in a global division of labor that affects her employment, her options about paying for childcare, and the availability of inexpensive immigrant laborers. And the grandmother in Botswana who is caring for her orphaned grandchildren is also performing carework in the context of global migration chains and national debt that undermines investment in public provision, as well as ideological forces that obfuscate the basis of the AIDS crises. Each reading identifies care crises for mothers that are generated in the context of global forces that undermine public responsibility for care and erode traditional care systems. The resulting solutions that women develop, as we see next, are deeply tied to inequalities among women.

INEQUALITY IN MOTHERHOOD

One of the ironies about studying motherhood is that rather than take us to a set of practices that unite women across social divisions, we are confronted with the reality of profound global and local inequalities. Although much research shows that women continue to have primary responsibility for carework for their children, how they do this labor, the resources they can use, and the supports they can garner vary widely. Research in the United States has documented that differential access to resources (wages, state support, education, etc.) directly affects the ways that mothers are able to take care of their children (Collins 1990; Litt 2000, 2004; Mink 1998). It is only very recently that other scholars have begun to explore the inequalities in motherhood in a globalizing economy. It may well be that this nascent scholarship on motherhood in global context will push us furthest in identifying how power, privilege, and inequality among women function in relation to motherhood.

Our book takes a particular approach to studying inequality among mothers. It follows Mary Romero in identifying and considering macro- as well as microlevel factors that need to be considered. On the macrolevel, we have documented how global capitalism depends on a vast reserve of women's underpaid as well as unpaid care labor. We have identified the social dynamics that create a pool of low-wage and immigrant women workers who increasingly bear the burden of the labor force participation of middle-class women in advanced economies. Macrolevel immigration and welfare policies control the flow of low-wage workers who are available for domestic work and carework. Local as well as global inequalities bring women of the developing economies into the households and nurseries of affluent women in advanced economies.

A microlevel approach examines the relations of care and employer–employee experiences that give daily meaning to inequalities in motherhood. Uttal identifies inequality among mothers as a key contradiction in carework. She asks whether the "liberation of [privileged] women from caring seems to require the creation of a new subclass of women workers" (2002, 92). Many of the articles in Part 3 identify the experiences of low-wage, immigrant women workers who increasingly have come to constitute this "subclass of women workers." The affluent women employers that Bridget Anderson interviewed appear to conceive of their labor force participation in terms of liberation. Yet, Anderson argues, the women they employ to care for their children experience their employment as essential, and fundamentally dominated by exploitation.

Uttal also asks, "How [can an employer] continue to be a caring mother when one is making arrangements that transfer care to others?" (2002, 92). The excerpt from Anderson's study on domestic workers in Europe sheds light on how affluent mothers achieve the status of a "good mother" through their dependence on this situation of inequality. Rather than threaten her identity as a "caring mother," Anderson shows that employers can use their domestic and childcare workers as a way to bolster their own claims to the status of good mother.

Anderson offers a new perspective to understand inequality between women in this context. She asks whether privileged women (i.e., the employers), "like men, enjoy . . . care as emotion freed from labour" (see Chapter 18). She points out that privileged women are able to separate the physical labor of care from the emotional labor of care. By providing the physical labor of caring, paid domestic workers and nannies create the possibility for the disjuncture between "work" and "care" in the mothering lives of the women they work for. Work, in other words, is assigned to racially, ethnically, nationally vulnerable women and care, as emotion and commitment, to higher, more privileged ones.

Mary Romero makes a similar point in her observation that the transfer of childcare and domestic work to paid careworkers enables privileged mothers to maintain the appearance of "good mothers"—that is, to meet the ideology of intensive motherhood (Hays 1996). By paying for childcare, some mothers are able to sustain the ideology of intensive mothering by passing off the labor of children to someone else. Paid childcare workers, by contrast, are forced to confront the contradictions between their own mothering practices and those of their employers.

These bifurcated experiences reflect different forms and status of motherhood. The European employer in Anderson's research fulfills the status of good mother by offering emotional care to her children, while migrant women, who leave their children home, are able to demonstrate care only through their labor: "in remittances, rather than in the cuddles and 'quality time'" (see Chapter 18). As mothers themselves, the domestic workers do not enjoy care as an emotion freed from work. This is not to say that domestic workers and nannies do not develop affection for the children they care for; rather, it is to say that the separation of "work" and "care" serves as an ideological tool that can demarcate those mothers who deserve support in childcare from those who do not.

Anderson offers an astute analysis of how this division of work embodies exploitation not simply of the worker's labor but of her personhood. "The employer is buying the power to command, not the property in the person, but the whole person" (see Chapter 18). Employers, she argues, "want more than labor power." They want a particular caring relationship between the worker and her children, one that renders the mother as essential while accepting her absence from the work process of caring for children.

Anderson locates the assault on "personhood" in a capitalist mentality: the "migrant worker" is conceived of as a "unit of labour" who is available for work without connection to family, friends, and without direct costs to the employer. This ties to Folbre's notion of disposable workers (see also Chang, Part 1) on the fictional island of CorporNation who are treated as socially disconnected. This unfettered individual, "torn from all social contexts" (Anderson 2000, 108), may seem the quintessential dehumanized subject of global capitalism. Yet, according to Anderson, the idea that she is simply "a unit of labour" is a political fiction; her labor cannot be disconnected from her personhood. (See Cheng, Part 2, for an analysis of the dehumanization of domestic laborers by employers.)

Romero's research with children of immigrant domestic workers is groundbreaking in exposing not only inequalities in motherhood, but in childhood itself. She asks the question that is often left unasked: "Who is caring for the maid's children?" On the one hand, Romero shows the special challenges that children face when their mothers migrate to do domestic work. She argues that the children of parents who are employed in domestic service experience "a special stigma and form of exploitation" (see Chapter 19). These children are able to see the contradictions between their own mothers' lives and those of her employers. They are socialized early into relations of class privilege and see, firsthand, that social inequality translates into different access to mothers. While live-in domestic work constitutes only a tiny proportion of paid childcare arrangements (Jacobs and

Gerson 2004), Romero's research reveals wider tensions that are increasingly institutionalized in the globalization of domestic service and new challenges to motherhood. Romero's work ties into a small but growing scholarship on the place of children in transnational practices. The term "transnational social fields" was introduced to indicate the "multi-stranded social relations that link places of origin and settlement" (Orellana et al. 2001, 573; see also Parreñas, Part 1). The care of children is one locus where ties between a mother's "home" and her paid "work" are maintained, constituting yet another new type of global linkage.

TRANSNATIONAL MOTHERHOOD

Another irony in our study of motherhood is that some women leave their children, for days or years at a time, to earn money to help care for them. Because in most wealthy nations immigration law forbids the resettlement of families, immigrant women leave their children at home to be cared for by others. Because of their distance from home, these mothers are forced to create new meanings and practices, what Pierrette Hondagneu-Sotelo and Ernestine Avila call "transnational motherhood."

Hondagneu-Sotelo and Avila document the phenomena of Latina immigrant women who work and reside in Los Angeles while their children remain at home in Mexico and Central America. Since the early 1980s, more and more women from Mexico and Central America have come to the United States in search of jobs. Their essay explores how women are creating new meanings of motherhood that respond to the new spatial and temporal separations from their children.

Hondagneu-Sotelo and Avila identify the macrolevel factors that set the stage for new patterns of migration and the new experience of transnational motherhood: the labor demand for Latina immigrant women in the United States in paid domestic and childcare work, the civil and economic crises and scarce job resources for women and men in Mexico and Central America, and the increasing numbers of women-headed households because of tenuous job opportunities for men. Mothers who embark on immigration are often seen to violate traditional gender expectations, unlike men for whom job seeking supports their "fathering" duties. Moreover, the migration of women differs from men's because of the occupations that women take: rather than production or agricultural work, women immigrants work in "reproductive labor"—paid domestic work or childcare work. The authors argue that this new form of work continues a long legacy of people of color being incorporated into the U.S. economy through coercive systems of labor that do not recognize family rights.

Hondagneu-Sotelo and Avila document the new meaning of motherhood that these immigrant women create. Many who come to the United States leave their own children at home to be cared for by kin, children's fathers, and sometimes, paid caregivers. Employment during motherhood contradicts deeply held traditional beliefs that children should be raised by their mothers. Rather than see themselves as bad mothers, these transnational mothers are trailblazing new constructions of motherhood that can accommodate long physical absences. They are developing new conceptions of motherhood that do not require physical proximity. Wage earning in the United States comes to be defined as a fulfillment of their maternal duties, though they also believe that their absence exacts great costs on their children as well as their own emotional well-being. These findings supplement the work on circuits of migration with a perspective on networks of affection, caring, and financial support. This circuit comes to constitute the basis for new meanings of motherhood forged in a transnational context.

This work resonates with the scholarship on U.S. racial-ethnic minority families that identifies a broad conception of motherhood that includes patterns of paid work. Racial-ethnic minority feminist theory has been at the forefront in identifying the false (and largely white, Western, and middle-class) dichotomy between "love" and "work" and between motherhood and employment. Patricia Hill Collins's (1990) work is essential in helping us see that the "work" component of mothering has been a constant feature of African American women's experiences and practices of motherhood. Rather than represent a threat to or departure from normative motherhood, Collins shows that "motherwork" constitutes the very essence of motherhood. Hondagneu-Sotelo and Avila argue that strong Latina/o traditions and cultural practices support full-time, stay-at-home motherhood, although most Latina's socioeconomic position makes this impossible. Many Latinas work for pay and, like the African American women Collins describes, develop forms of motherhood that combine wage earning with caring for their children. What distinguishes transnational mothers from the mothers documented in earlier scholarship is that they are physically separated from their children for long periods of time and by vast spaces.

Pei-Chia Lan takes the situation of mothers who are employed as domestic workers one step further. She is critical of most studies of domestics and careworkers that create a flawed impression that employers are white and middle class and that domestics are women of color. In an ethnographic study of Filipina domestic workers in Taiwan, Lan develops the concept of the continuity of domestic labor to identity the embeddedness between unpaid household labor and waged domestic labor. Both forms of work, she contends, are feminized and undervalued.

But even more, by focusing on the life experiences of Filipina domestic workers, she is able to reveal the interdependence between their paid labor in Taiwanese households and their unpaid labor of caring for their own families. These women are simultaneously remote madams (i.e., employers of domestic workers), transnational mothers, and substitute mothers. Rather than study domestic workers through a singular lens of paid worker, Lan asks how the simultaneity of the three positions shapes a woman's life trajectory and motherhood activities.

Lan documents how Taiwanese policy has loosened to allow migrants to fill the expanding need for paid domestic workers. In 2003 more than 110,000 foreign workers are legally employed as domestic workers, 90 percent from the Philippines. Lan shows that the decline of male-oriented construction and manufacturing jobs in the Middle East has led to this new demographic pattern in which Filipina wives have more opportunity than their husbands to secure employment abroad. This new pattern has ushered in new gender practices that are structured through women's primary breadwinning obligations. When they move from unpaid housewives in the Philippines to paid workers in Taiwan, they do similar work but in radically different contexts.

Lan positions these women in the "intermediate status in the multitiered international division of reproductive labor" (see also Parreñas, Part 1). While middle- and upper-class women in advanced economies are in the top tier, local women who perform intermittent domestic work in local regions are on the bottom. Migrant workers, more highly educated and possessing more cultural capital than local workers, are in the middle tier.

One particular difficulty, and irony, in the lives of migrant mothers she studied is that they recognize problems in establishing good care for their children at home. Often their grandmothers, aunts, sisters, and in some cases husbands are involved in caring for children. Many migrant mothers hire their own domestic workers who serve as caretakers of her children. Being a madam at home enhances her status and goes some way toward counteracting the degraded status of doing paid domestic and childcare work for others. Despite the obvious similarities in their own lives and those of the domestics they employ, the women Lan interviewed draw clear distinctions between them.

In ways that are identified by Romero, Lan documents the "emotional costs" of family separation. Migrant mothers "perform their labor of love" through letters, phone calls, and money. They interpret their migration not as an act of abandonment but as an extension of caring. But as ties loosen at home, which they sometimes do, migrant mothers may look for emotional rewards in their job as caretakers in Taiwan. Several caregivers spoke with pride about the attachment the children under their care have for them and are often critical of their Taiwanese employers. The fragility of these bonds, however, almost inevitably causes workers to be concerned that they will be separated from these children, which at times intensifies their longing for their own children back home.

CONCLUSION

Part 3 examines motherhood in the context of globalization. We will see the care deficits that have been a consequence of the expansion of global capitalism as well as the rise of women's labor force participation. The dynamics of globalization create care deficits for sending countries at the same time that it "solves" care deficits in receiving countries by commodifying carework as well as care laborers. Thus, the global care deficits and care chains reflect and help to reproduce radical inequalities among women, between women and men, and between advanced and developing economies. Finally, the material documents how mothers employed as careworkers in distant households attempted to manage the contradictions by conceiving of motherhood in new terms.

There is yet another message embedded in the material in this part. That is the deeply privatized and individualized nature of carework. As Mona Harrington argues, we do carework in individualized terms, making seemingly individual and private decisions. In Part 4 we consider how government policy addresses carework and pose new models in which care is defined as a public good, supported through public resources.

1. How are new conceptions of motherhood addressing the reality of mothers' labor force participation?

2. Identify the macrolevel global factors that are creating care deficits in motherhood.

3. What are the tensions between "work" and "emotion" that are expressed in paid domestic and childcare work?

4. What are some ways to minimize the inequality among mothers that is central in globalization?

5. What does it mean to refer to childcare as a public good?

6. Imagine a new CorpoNation that values mothers' carework. What policies would it adopt?

Anderson, Bridget. 2000. *Doing the Dirty Work: The Global Politics of Domestic Labor.* New York: Zed Books.

Collins, Patricia Hill. 1990. *Black Feminist Thought: Knowledge, Consciousness, and the Politics of Empowerment.* Minneapolis: University of Minnesota Press.

Cotter, David A., Joan M. Hermsen, and Reeve Vanneman. 2004. *Gender Inequality at Work.* New York: Russell Sage Foundation.

Davis, Angela. 1998. "Surrogates and Outcast Mothers: Racism and Reproductive Politics in the Nineties." In Annette Dula and Sara Goering (eds.), *It Just Ain't Fair; The Ethics of Health-care for African Americans.* Westport, CT: Praeger.

Harrington, Mona. 2000. *Care and Equality: Inventing a New Family Politics.* New York: Routledge.

Hays, Sharon. 1996. *The Cultural Contradictions of Motherhood.* New Haven: Yale University Press.

Jacobs, Jerry, and Kathleen Gerson. 2004. *The Time Divide: Work, Family, and Gender Inequality.* Cambridge, MA: Harvard University Press.

Litt, Jacquelyn. 2000. *Medicalized Motherhood: Perspectives from the Lives of African-American and Jewish Women.* New Brunswick, NJ: Rutgers University Press.

———. 2004. Women's Carework in Low-Income Households: The Special Case of Children with Attention Deficit Hyperactivity Disorder." *Gender & Society* 18: 625–644.

Mink, Gwendolyn. 1998. *Welfare's End.* New York: Cornell University Press.

Orellana, Marjorie F., Barrie Thorne, Anna Chee, and Wan Shun Eva Lam. 2001. "Transnational Childhoods: The Participation of Children in Processes of Family Migration." *Social Problems* 48: 572–591.

Uttal, Lynet. 2002. *Making Care Work: Employed Mothers in the New Child Care Market.* New Brunswick, NJ: Rutgers University Press.

Williams, Joan. 2000. Unbending Gender: Why Work and Family Conflict and What to Do About It. New York: Oxford University Press.

16 THE INVISIBLE HEART

Nancy Folbre

In this selection, Nancy Folbre examines the crisis of carework from the perspective of two fictional scenarios: first, she describes CorporNation, a fictional country owned by a multinational organization that takes no responsibility for the human needs of its workers. Indeed, it considers the maintenance of human life as conflicting with worker productivity. The second fictional scenario is of middle-class American parents, who, in an attempt to find care for their children, decide to bring cheap laborers (i.e., nannies) into their homes as caregivers, rather than ship their children to other countries to be raised! Folbre uses these scenarios to point to the gaps in care provision for children, the market incentives to disregard care needs of workers and their families, and the individual-level responses that affluent mothers make in the context of poor options for care. By using this response, by privately paying for care, mothers themselves are unlikely to push for national-level changes, or even to argue for more equal division of labor in their households.

I have long dreamed of buying an island owned by no nation and of establishing the World Headquarters of the Dow Company on the truly neutral ground of such an island, beholden to no nation or society.

— Carl Gerstaker, Dow Chemical Executive

Imaginary scenario: A multinational corporation, tired of the frustrations of negotiating over taxation and regulation with host governments, buys a small, uninhabited Caribbean island. Perhaps it is a guano island, previously used only for collecting bird poop for fertilizer. Its new owners write a constitution and announce the formation of a country called CorporNation. Anyone who is a citizen of the new country will automatically receive a highly paid job (minimum salary $50,000 per year). The following restrictions apply to citizenship: Individuals must have advanced educational credentials, be physically and emotionally healthy, have no children, and be under the age of fifty. They need not physically emigrate, but can work from their home country over the Internet. However, they will instantly lose CorporNation citizenship and their job should they require retraining, become ill, acquire dependents, or reach the age of fifty.

*

In short, CorporNation takes advantage of the human capabilities of its citizens/workers without paying for their production or their maintenance when they become ill or old. It can attract the best childless and carefree workers in the world by offering relatively high wages, and do so without threatening the company's own profitability. CorporNation is likely to enjoy unprecedented success in global competition, at least until other corporations adopt the same strategy. (Perhaps some will operate from space stations or previously uninhabited planets, rather than islands.) In the long run, however, the new corporate states will run into problems similar to those created by slash-and-burn farming or overfishing. They are exploiting a natural resource without replenishing it. Their strategy is not sustainable.

This chapter concerns the perverse incentives created by unrestricted global competition. It describes what countries, employers, and even parents have to gain by minimizing the costs of care—making somebody else pay for creating and maintaining other people's productive capabilities. John Gray, Professor of Politics at the London School of Economics, summarizes the problem this way: bad capitalisms drive out good ones. Employers who assume their fair share of social costs by following the rules imposed upon them by democratic governance will operate at a disadvantage. They risk being competed out of existence.[1]

The new global order seems to offer us two equally unattractive choices: we can go back to a patriarchal society in which women are forced to assume the burden of care for others because their other opportunities are severely restricted. Or, we can move ahead to a world in which individuals are on their own and nobody provides care unless it is paid for in carefully calibrated low-cost units. Reasonable alternatives to these extremes are hard to imagine and even more difficult to implement. But they are worth fighting for. . . .

Immigrants are a tremendous boon to advanced economies, because they are literally free. No tax money was spent paying for their production, their maintenance, or their education. From the point of view of developing countries, the migration of highly educated professionals represents a major brain drain. India has supplied the United States with many engineers and doctors. . . . The Philippines exports many nurses. . . . The great advantage of temporary immigrants is their compatibility with last-minute methods of inventory control. If you don't need them, you don't order them. If you accidentally get too many, they can be returned. In the United States, foreign workers are brought in to meet the demand for seasonal labor to harvest fruits and vegetables. Germany sends its contract or "guest" workers back to their home countries when unemployment goes up. In Malaysia, economic crises led to the immediate deportation of non-native workers.

Another reason that temporary immigrants are cost-effective is that they can be denied social benefits. Within the United States, the state of California refuses to provide any social services for illegal immigrants, although they do little to punish employers who hire them. Most Persian Gulf countries provide free medical care to their own citizens, but not to the many Asian workers recruited for one-year contracts of employment. In fact, large employers and employment agencies called *khafeels* wield enormous power over migrant workers.

After a six-month review . . . the U.S. Department of Labor noted that discrimination against pregnant workers violates Mexico's own labor laws.[2] Abuses are common in other countries, as well. The National Labor Committee has charged the *maquila* factories in the Cholomoa region of Honduras with injecting young women with the contraceptive Depo-Provera and handing out packages of contraceptive pills without medical supervision.

The companies' motives are obvious. Mexican law requires firms to provide twelve weeks of paid maternity leave and the option of an additional sixty days at 50 percent salary.[3] The idea, of course, is that employers should help pay for the production of the labor power they utilize. Instead, employers minimize their costs by penalizing maternity among their workers. To eliminate this disincentive, countries need to provide public support for child-rearing (as do Sweden, France, Germany, and other European countries) rather than require individual employers to shoulder the costs. . . .

Not only multinational corporations are tempted to minimize the costs of care. In fact, it's hard to imagine a more telling example than the efforts many affluent parents in the U.S. make to find the cheapest possible high-quality child care. To illustrate this point I've developed a little vignette, based on a cartoon by Norman Dog. I pretend to be looking in a mirror, fussing with my hair, applying lipstick, when I look up suddenly, as though I've just heard or remembered something.

"Oh, bye-bye, darling," I say, throwing a kiss to the child at the door of the room. "Have a wonderful time growing up in Mexico. . . . What's that? You don't want to go? But Sweetkins, Mummy and Daddy have decided that it's no longer cost-effective to raise you in this country. We must be efficient, you know. It's a global economy!" In reality, U.S. parents don't need to send their children to other countries to be raised: they can bring nannies here from more "cost-effective" countries.

Illegal immigrants are generally willing to work for low wages and eager to follow orders. Furthermore, young women who don't have the time or money to develop a personal life of their own may well pour their emotional resources into caring for their wards. In 1993, the honest young mother of new-born triplets looking for a nanny confided to a *New York Times* reporter: "I want someone who cannot leave the country, know anyone in New York, who basically does not have a life."[4] An additional advantage is that you don't have to pay Social Security taxes for illegal immigrants, much less provide them with pensions or health insurance. *They* want to be paid in cash. For obvious reasons, the government does not collect information on the number of illegal nannies in the country. Talking to friends of mine who are highly paid professionals suggests to me that under-the-table nannies can be found easily in Los Angeles, Houston, San Antonio, and New York—an amenity of multicultural cities.[5]

Why not settle for a less-educated American worker? Obstacles loom on both the supply side and the demand side. Most less-educated American workers are women of color who don't want to return to the forms of domestic service that their forebears were condemned to. Besides, most of them are hip to the fact that child care is a lousy career track. . . . At the same time, affluent families prefer not to put women they consider culturally "disadvantaged" in charge of their children. They have been far more eager to hire young European women through the government-sponsored au pair program that, in the 1990s, became a de facto child care service.

The French term au pair literally means "as two people" and implies work as a kind of mother's helper. Most of those who signed up to participate considered it a cultural exchange program. Upon arriving at their new home-away-from-home, however, some of the young women discovered that they were expected to assume virtually full-time child care responsibilities. Many European countries don't allow au pairs to work more than twenty-five hours a week; U.S. regulations allow forty-five. Moreover, there are very few standards for eligibility for applicants and no minimum wage. Earnings of less than $140 a week are typical.

The potential for abuse became so obvious in the 1990s that an interagency government panel reviewed the au pair program and recommended that it be placed under the supervision of either the Department of Labor or the Immigration and Naturalization Service. Congress declined to make the change, bowing—in the words of one journalist—to "constituents' demands for cheap child care."[6] Shortly afterward, the au pair program lost its luster when the death of an infant in Boston was attributed to a young English au pair named Louise Woodward. Suddenly, the idea of regulating the program—requiring, for instance, that any person paid to take care of an infant should be over the age of twenty-one—became more appealing. Largely as a result of the Woodward case, the number of au pairs brought to the U.S. each year has fallen substantially.

A movement is now afoot to create a special temporary visa or permanent-resident category for immigrant nannies. If we can relax our restrictions to bring in agricultural workers to help harvest sugar and oranges, why can't we do the same to help raise our children? It would be incredibly cost-effective. "There are a vast number of women who have had and raised many children who'd be delighted to come to the U.S. and care for children," explains one Washington immigration lawyer.[7] Another activist with the National Organization for Women (NOW) emphasizes how sexist it is to define child-care workers as "unskilled." She's right, and I have no doubt that a major nanny import program would make life much easier for moms in the $80,000–plus salary category—many of whom are loyal members of NOW.

Nanny Imports, Inc., however, suffers from the same limitation as Corpor-Nation. It purchases short-term efficiency at the cost of long-term sustainability. An increase in the supply of women who want to provide one-on-one child care and domestic service will definitely lower the price. But while it may take a long time, that cheap supply will eventually run out. And in the meantime, we might question the desirability of creating a new caste of care workers whose specialization is determined by gender, ethnicity, and nationality, like the Bangladeshis working in Saudi Arabia. Affluent mothers can reduce their child-care costs by increasing the supply of low-cost nannies. If they do so successfully, they will become less likely to participate in broader efforts to redistribute more equitably the costs of care. . . .

A basic recipe [to improve the situation]: Start with a stock of concern for developing human capabilities, not merely increasing the size of our collective GDPs. Skim off the grease; prioritize improvements in the standard of living for the neediest of countries and the most vulnerable within countries. Develop an international system of governance in which poor countries have the same representation as rich ones.

Don't allow a race to the bottom. Impose rules of minimum taxation for all corporations within all countries. Penalize countries that refuse to guarantee basic democratic rights (including the right to organize) as well as those that fail to monitor and enforce environmental safeguards, by restricting access to our consumer markets. Insist on a basic safety net to protect workers from economic insecurity and job losses due to forces beyond their control. . . .

1. John Gray, *False Dawn: The Delusions of Global Capitalism* (New York: New Press, 1998).

2. Sam Dillion, "Sex Bias Is Reported by U.S. at Border Plants in Mexico," *New York Times*, January 13, 1998.

3. Cece Modupe Fadope, "Production vs. Reproduction," *Multinational Monitor* 17, no. 10, October 1996, p. 8.

4. Peter Stalker, *The Work of Strangers: A Survey of International Labour Migration* (Geneva: International Labour Office, 1997), p. 149.

5. For a wonderful elaboration of this point, see Arlie Russel Hoschchild, "The Nanny Chain," *The American Prospect* 11, no. 4, January 3, 2000.

6. Warren Cohen, "Home Wreckers: Congress's Roles in the Au Pair Tragedy," *The New Republic*, November 24, 1997, p. 18.

7. Cited in Eric Schmitt, "Crying Need; Day Care Quandary," *New York Times*, January 11, 1998.

17 | MAKING CARE WORK: EMPLOYED MOTHERS IN THE NEW CHILDCARE MARKET

Lynet Uttal

> Whereas other studies have emphasized how mothers undervalue providers in market-based systems of childcare, Uttal's ethnography paints a more nuanced picture, connecting the personal level of mothers' daily experiences to the larger political, economic, and ideological context of childcare as both paid labor and as intimate carework.

CARE BY OTHERS

There is nothing new about mothers transferring the care of children to others (Michel 1999; Werner 1984). Mothers have always left young children in the care of others both for economic reasons and to pursue social activities for themselves. Historically, many American mothers left their younger children in the care of older siblings while they did household and agricultural work necessary for the family (Werner 1984). Upper- and middle-class women enjoyed a more leisureful lifestyle and privileged social status by engaging other women (both hired and slave) to care for their children (Palmer 1989). Poor immigrant women have left their children in day nurseries so they could take classes about American culture and parenting skills (Wrigley 1989; Wrigley 1990). Mothers across different social classes have always sought out and used alternative caregivers because they have paid jobs outside the home.

What is notably different now is that using child care for employment-related reasons has become more visible, and the types of care that are being used have changed. Employed mothers require childcare services that are reliable and match their regular and often long hours of employment. The childcare needs of employed mothers are different from those of mothers who use child care for occasional maternal absences or child-enrichment purposes. Since childcare providers substitute maternal care for significant periods of time, employed mothers often need child care providers who do more than simply supervise their children. They look for care that provides an approximation of maternal care as well as enrichment opportunities for their children. The quality and nature of the relationship between an individual child and his or her caregiver is an important consideration. Ideally, care is provided by one person who establishes a sincere connection with the child rather than a shifting cast of caregivers.

CHANGING SOURCES OF CARE

In the past, employed mothers primarily obtained child care through noninstitutional arrangements with familiar people such as relatives and neighbors, people who were related to the children through previously existing social networks. For example, an older woman cared for the children of her sons and daughters, or a young mother might have provided care for her neighbor's children while she watched her own. Those who could do so relied on relatives, such as their mothers and sisters, to care for their children (Werner 1984). Many mothers kept child care within the family by working different shifts than their husbands (Presser 1986). Friends were a second-best choice if relatives were not available. Among lower-income and African American families, where rates of maternal employment have historically been higher than among middle-class White families, having other people look out for and care for one's children was and is still a common practice. In some communities, nonrelatives were such important alternative caregivers that they were referred to as "other mothers to the children in their extended family networks, and those in the community overall" (Collins 1994, 55–56). Employed Mexican American mothers reached across the border and hired their relatives from Mexico to come to the United States and provide child care services for them (Lamphere et al. 1993; Zavella 1987).

Such arrangements were (and are) often made through an underground economy. Characteristically, they were hidden from public view, located in the child's or the caregiver's home. Arrangements were made privately, with little or no governmental regulation and licensing. Parents relied on "personal and community-based, first-hand experiences" (Zinsser 1991, 155) to ensure the right choice. Often, child care was found through a personal referral from someone who was familiar with a particular arrangement or caregiver. Even though these were arrangements made with known persons, this care by friends and family was not necessarily unpaid labor: wages, housing, and groceries were often exchanged for the childcare services that were provided. When actual wages were paid, they were seldom formally reported to the Internal Revenue Service, and taxes and social security were not deducted from the payments.

This informal organization of child care within known social networks has allowed for a sense of trust on the part of employed mothers. By keeping the care in the child's private home or under the eyes of friends and relatives, arrangements retained a personalized, family-like character even when money changed hands. Keeping care in the home created a greater sense of security for mothers even when the arrangement was established with nonrelatives who came from outside mothers' social networks and crossed class and racial lines. For example, cross-class and cross-race arrangements were commonly established between economically more privileged White women and African American domestic workers whom they hired to meet both their housework and childcare needs. The wages of African American domestic workers were so low that even less-than-well-to-do White families were also able to afford to hire African American in-home housekeeper/child care providers (Palmer 1989). Today, in-home domestic workers are still often also asked to care for children, especially infants and toddlers (Glenn 1986; Palmer 1989; Rollins 1985; Romero 1992). In spite of the fact that these are wage-based relationships, housekeepers appeared to provide intimate, family-like care in the homes of their employers.

This type of practice persists in regions of the country where women of color and immigrant women make up a significant proportion of the population and discrimination limits their employment options. For example, low income African American and Mexican American women across the South and Southwest and in northern cities have often been limited to domestic work. Other cross-ethnic arrangements are made between Latinas and White employers in the West and Southwest, and between Caribbean and Puerto Rican childcare providers and White employers in the Northeast and Florida (Colen 1989; Palmer 1989; Wrigley 1995). Working-class women, including White women, have always been a major source of low paid childcare work for more economically privileged women. . . .

COMMODIFICATION OF FAMILY FUNCTIONS

The current movement of childcare arrangements out of the child's home and away from familiar social networks is part of a larger trend wherein functions that have historically been provided by family members are now being provided by other institutions, resulting in a reorganization of family caregiving. This shift in care is one of the main reasons that mothers feel less confident about their childcare arrangements.

Family work done by family members to maintain households and their members is increasingly being replaced by consumption activities that make use of mass-produced household goods and services. Many family functions that were historically carried out by family members are now being fulfilled by the purchase of products or services. Not only can ready-to-use products such as clothing and meals be purchased, but many other aspects of family care are also being commodified, such as housecleaning and health care. Even more intimate forms of family care, such as elder care, nursing care, and mental health care, have been commodified in the form of nursing homes, medical services, and therapy. Elder care and child care are the most recent family functions to find themselves shifting into market-based services. . . .

Demographic and economic forces, coupled with public policy decisions and shifts in motherhood ideology, have promoted the rise of market-based childcare services. First, higher rates of women's employment have reduced the availability of family members to provide fully for a child's care or keep care within familiar social networks. Second, because public policy did not acknowledge the legitimacy of maternal employment and failed to respond to the childcare needs employed mothers have, a haphazard and diverse system of market-based child care emerged, much of it in center-based care settings. Finally, multiple reasons for the use of the whole range of childcare settings have contributed to a growing acceptance of children spending time outside their mother's direct care. These historical changes and shifting ideologies explain why the U.S. childcare system is a market-based one rather than a comprehensive child welfare policy as seen in other countries such as Australia, Sweden, Norway, and Japan. . . .

Views about the appropriateness of maternal employment have shifted dramatically in the United States in the last twenty years. The original assumptions that being a mother and an employee are antithetical and that good mothers are always with their children have given way to a greater acceptance of maternal employment and children spending time away from their mothers. The image of the employed mother as a bad mother has faded.

Studies of working-class women's history have shown that poor women, including women of color, have simply not been offered the life circumstances to forego involvement in income-producing activities, either inside or outside their homes (Glenn 1994). Instead, work and family have historically been interwoven for women of color: mothering has included not only caring for their families at home but also laboring for wages in their own homes, in White women's households, and elsewhere outside the home (Collins 1994). Similarly, working-class White women have defined their wage-earning activities as part of their maternal responsibilities rather than in opposition to motherhood (Rose 1998; Segura 1994). Despite this historical reality of maternal employment, employed mothers were rendered invisible until the 1970s (Garey 1999).

Maternal employment became common among middle-class families during the 1970s. As maternal employment moved into the middle class, working-class women's history became the experience of most women, across all classes and racial ethnic groups. During the 1980s, researchers and journalists paid attention to the problems of middle-class women as they learned how to combine work and family. The American public was introduced to the image of professionally employed mothers, and this contributed to the increasing legitimacy of maternal employment.

Recent changes in welfare policy have also contributed to the notion that maternal employment, even for mothers of very young children, is acceptable. When Aid to Families with Dependent Children (AFDC) was first established, African American and Latina women were often excluded from eligibility for welfare benefits because they were defined as "employable mothers" (Chang 1994; Quadagno 1994). More recently, this view of "employable mothers" has been extended to all poor women, including White mothers. The new welfare policy that transforms welfare into Workfare requires mothers receiving benefits to be employed and to place their children in nonmaternal care. Accompanying this policy change has been a significant increase in the provision of childcare services and subsidies. Rather than reinforcing old notions wherein maternal presence trumps self-sufficiency in shaping policy, this new policy is premised on the understanding that maternal income earning can take priority over maternal presence in child rearing.

Whereas in the 1960s the employed mother was viewed as a new social phenomenon, today, the stay-at-home mother is seen as more remarkable. Mothers who have chosen to leave their jobs complain that they receive little cultural support. Middle-class as well as low-income mothers are in the labor force. Mothers are surrounded by other employed mothers. Young women are increasingly planning to be employed even after the birth of their first child, and their plans are supported by an increasingly visible workforce of employed mothers (Machung 1989). Furthermore, the suggestion that "mommy tracks" be established in the corporate workforce (Schwartz 1989) is a public response to private problems that further promotes the acceptability of maternal employment, even if it also promotes a secondary-tier status for professional women. . . .

When a formal market of childcare services emerged in the 1980s, it provided some hope that the childcare needs of employed parents would be publicly recognized and addressed. For-profit childcare centers emerged as big business, corporations received tax incentives from the government to include childcare centers in their new buildings, and full-day care became the norm rather than a special add-on to enrichment programs. U.S. society had turned a corner, from viewing nonmaternal care as deviant to accepting the reality of dual-earner families and single working mothers, and acknowledging that very young children could benefit from exposure to adults outside their own families. Although a wide variety of childcare services is now readily purchasable and acceptable, there is still no workable child care policy for working- and middle-class parents.

Mothers' doubts and worries flow from the structural conditions that privatize the process of selecting and maintaining childcare arrangements, regardless of local support for maternal employment and the development of childcare options. Their worries reflect not only their unconscious awareness of all the social ideas that shape the context within which they make their childcare arrangements but also conscious concerns about how to navigate interpersonal relationships with others when the principles of the relationships (market or care) are not clear. . . .

Several competing social ideas make it extremely difficult for mothers to define their expectations clearly and relinquish the care of their children to others without doubts and worries. First, remnants of the traditional ideology of domestic motherhood remain, and when mothers have doubts about the quality of their care, they also doubt whether they are doing the right thing even to have their children in nonparental care. Second, there are questions about how caring relationships, such as child rearing, can be transformed into market-based relationships: can anyone ever really be hired to "love" their child? Third, although families can easily find child care and leave their children with others, mothers know that they are responsible—and solely responsible—for monitoring that care. The lack of governmental regulations as well as the way in which these new services bring people of very different values and childrearing practices into association means that there is much uncertainty about whether that care fits with the family's ideas of child rearing. Finally, parents are aware that children and childcare providers spend long hours together, and the (possibly conflicting) needs of many, not just their own child, have to be taken into account. For example, a young child might need individual attention from a provider who is responsible for several children at once, or the need to provide constant supervision makes it difficult for the provider to do something as simple as go to the bathroom. So though parents want to be humane about their provider's needs, their young child's needs and well-being are their top priority, making it hard for parents to be confident consumers in the child care market.

In the context of competing ideologies of motherhood, opportunities for employment, economic and social constraints, and value differences, it is not surprising that it is difficult to maintain a concern-free, or "perfect," childcare arrangement. Mothers appear to be behaving strangely, dodging their concerns, and government continues to take a hands-off approach and downplay the seriousness of the childcare needs of employed families. These conditions shift the responsibility for finding strategies to cope to the individual families, requiring mothers to establish ways to ensure the quality of care by themselves. The particularities of individual family childrearing practices and values, combined with the structural conditions of the organization of the work, regulatory neglect, and mothering ideologies, create a volatile mixture—one whose only predictable outcome is confusion, worry, and doubt for individual parents left on their own to navigate different childcare political economies.

Chang, G. 1994. "Undocumented Latinas: The New 'Employable Mothers.'" In *Mothering: Ideology, Experience, and Agency*, edited by E. Nakano Glenn, G. Chang, and L. R. Forcey. 259–286. New York: Routledge.

Colen, S. 1989. "'Just a Little Respect': West Indian Domestic Workers in New York City." In *Muchachas No More*, edited by E. M. Chaney and M. Castro. 171–194. Philadelphia: Temple University Press.

Collins, P. 1994. "Shifting the Center: Race, Class, and Feminist Theorizing about Motherhood." In *Mothering: Ideology, Experience, and Agency*, edited by E. Nakano Glenn, G. Chang, and L. R. Forcey. 45–66. New York: Routledge.

Garey, A. I. 1999. *Weaving Work and Motherhood*. Philadelphia: Temple University Press.

Glenn, E. 1986. *Issei, Nisei, Warbride: Three Generations of Japanese American Women in Domestic Service*. Philadelphia: Temple University Press.

———. 1994. "Social Constructions of Mothering: A Thematic Overview." In *Mothering: Ideology, Experience, and Agency*, edited by E. Nakano Glenn, G. Chang, and L. R. Forcey. 1–32. New York: Routledge.

Lamphere, L. P. Zavella, and F. Gonzales, with P. B. Evans. 1993. *Sunbelt Working Mothers: Reconciling Family and Factory*. Ithaca, N.Y.: Cornell University Press.

Machung, A. 1989. "Talking Career, Thinking Job: Gender Differences in Career and Family Expectations of Berkeley Seniors." *Feminist Studies*. 15:35–58.

Michel, S. 1999. *Children's Interests/Mother's Rights: The Shaping of America's Child Care Policy*. New Haven, Conn.: Yale University Press.

Palmer, P. 1989. *Domesticity and Dirt: Housewives and Domestic Servants in the United States, 1920–1945*. Philadelphia: Temple University Press.

Presser, H. B. 1986. "Shift Work Among American Women and Child Care." *Journal of Marriage and Family*. 48: 551–586.

Quadagno, J. 1994. *The Color of Welfare*. New York: Oxford University Press.

Rollins, J. 1985. *Between Women: Domestics and Their Employers*. Philadelphia: Temple University Press.

Romero, M. 1992. *Maid in the U.S.A.* New York: Routledge.

Rose, E. 1998. "Taking on a Mother's Job: Day Care in the 1920s and 1930s." In *"Bad" Mothers: The Politics of Blame in Twentieth-Century America*, edited by M. Ladd-Taylor and L. Umansky. 67–98. New York: New York University Press.

Schwartz, F. N. 1989. "Management Women and the New Facts of Life." *Harvard Business Review*. (January–February): 65–76.

Segura, D. 1994. "Working at Motherhood: Chicana and Mexicana Immigrant Mothers and Employment." In *Mothering: Ideology, Experience, and Agency*, edited by E. Nakano Glenn, G. Chang, and L. R. Forcey. 211–236. New York: Routledge.

Werner, E. E. 1984. *Child Care: Kith, Kin, and Hired Hands*. Baltimore, Md.: University Park Press.

Wrigley, J. 1989. "Different Care for Different Kids: Social Class and Child Care Policy." *Educational Policy*. 3:421–439.

———. 1990. "Children's Caregivers and Ideologies of Parental Inadequacy." In *Circles of Care: Work and Identity in Women's Lives*, edited by E. K. Abel and M. K. Nelson. 290–312. Albany: State University of New York Press.

———. 1995. *Other People's Children*. New York: Basic Books.

Zavella, P. 1987. *Women's Work & Chicano Families: Cannery Workers of the Santa Clara Valley*. Ithaca, N.Y.: Cornell, University Press.

Zinsser, C. 1991. *Raised in East Urban: Child Care in a Working Class Community*. New York: Teachers College Press.

DOING THE DIRTY WORK? THE GLOBAL
POLITICS OF DOMESTIC LABOUR

Bridget Anderson

Through interviews with domestic workers and their European employers, Anderson identifies the reality that, rather than simply sell her labor, the paid migrant domestic worker is invariably brought into relations with those she is caring for, making a fiction of the capitalist ideology that labor and personhood can be separated. Yet the very acts of labor can bring about feelings of care, challenging the distinction between labor and care. Her work also identifies how the migrant domestic worker's responsibility to perform the carework functions so that her employer can aptly demonstrate her love and commitment as a mother while the paid careworker carries out the actual labor. Her work develops new insights into how "some women exploit others within a general theory of care as women's work."

What is being commodified when employers pay migrant domestic workers? I have argued that the domestic worker is not just doing a set of tasks but is fulfilling a role. This already suggests that it is not simply her labour power that is being commodified. The worker who ha[s] to stand by the door when her employers le[ave] for the evening and remain in the same position until they came home could not really be constructed as selling her labour power.

The migrant worker is framed by immigration legislation as a unit of labour, without connection to family or friends, a unit whose production costs (food, education, shelter) were met elsewhere, and whose reproduction costs are of no concern to employer or state. In this respect, the worker who moves across continents may seem the logical result of capitalism's individual subject, the juridical person, torn from all social contexts, selling her labour power in the global market place. But while states and capitalists want workers, what they get is people.[1] This tension between "labour power" and "personhood" is particularly striking with reference to migrant domestic workers, and I believe it has broader repercussions for migrants and for women (see O'Connell Davidson 1998; Pateman 1988). . . .

COMMODIFICATION AND DOMESTIC WORKERS

According to Marxist theory, workers sell their commodified "labour power" (that is, their property in the person). Marx's theory of surplus value claimed that capitalists profit from this exchange: the value of labour power is determined by the value of the labour time socially necessary to produce it and:

> If their working day or week exceeds the labour-time embodied in their wage, they are creating surplus value: a value over and above the variable capital investment, for which they will receive no recompense. . . . Profit can thus arise. . . . Its premise is exploitation of labour (Sayer 1991: 3).

However, as Pateman (along with Marx) has pointed out, labour power is a political fiction:

> Labour power, capacities or services, cannot be separated from the person of the worker like pieces of property. The worker's capacities are developed over time and they form an integral part of his self and self-identity. . . . The fiction "labour power" cannot be used; what is required is that the worker labours as demanded. (Pateman 1988: 150–1)

Labour power is, in this fiction, not integral to the person and can be traded in the marketplace with buyer and seller constructed as equals. . . .

Are migrant domestic workers selling their "labour power"? [D]omestic work . . . is concerned with the physical, cultural and ideological reproduction of human beings. Paid domestic workers reproduce people and social relations, not just in what they do (polishing silver, ironing clothes), but also in the very doing of it (the foil to the household manager). In this respect the paid domestic worker is herself, in her very essence, a means of reproduction. It is not just her labour power that is being harnessed to the cause of her employer's physical and social reproduction, but it is the very fact that she, the domestic worker, and not her employers, is doing this work, much of which seems invented especially for her to do. The employer is buying the power to command, not the property in the person, but the whole person.

It is this power to command that employers want more than labour power. They often openly stipulate that they want a particular type of person (Gregson and Lowe 1994: 3) justifying this demand on the grounds that they will be working in the home. So employer Anne Marie was emphatic that she would not accept an employee who "smells too strong," because "I cannot stand strong body smells." Or if the worker is to have responsibility for caring work she should be "affectionate," "like old people" or "be good with children." The worker wants to earn as much money as she can with reasonable conditions, but the employer's wants are rather more complicated. This is an oversimplification of the differences between what is being bought and sold by employer and worker, but I think it is an adequate description of how many employment situations begin before more complex interpersonal relations develop. . . . The contradictions and tensions involved in paying for domestic labour are most clearly apparent when the function of that labour includes care. The political fiction of labour power is strained to breaking point—can one pay a care worker for her labour power and be unconcerned with whether she is a "caring person"? Can one pay a person to "be" caring? Can money really buy love? . . .

It is widely accepted that there are two meanings conflated in the term "care": care as labour and care as emotion, and it can be very difficult to disentangle the two. Finch and Groves (1983), in the introduction to their edited volume, write that caring cannot be reduced to "a kind of domestic labour performed on people," but that it always includes emotional bonds. In her contribution to the volume, Graham states that affection and service "can't be disentangled," and Wærness (1984) argues that caring is about labour and feelings, about relations, and that we all need to be cared for. Much of the labour of care is devoted to basic domestic chores. It would be difficult to care for a child and not include cooking her food, washing up her dishes, wiping her face and the table, changing and throwing away her nappy, tidying up her toys and washing her clothes. But once one allows that caring does include some measure of domestic work it is difficult to draw the line—how much of the domestic work is part of caring for one's charge, and when does it become general servicing of the household? And could not domestic work in general be seen as "caring," as looking after one's loved ones and making sure they are comfortable and at ease? As Rose puts it: "It has been both a theoretical and an empirical problem that even where we tried to separate housework from peoplework, they continually merged" (Rose 1986: 168). Indeed, much female-directed advertising is encouraging us in this perception—show your husband how much you love him by buying our brand of powder and washing his shirts really white. The problem is that while X doing something for Y may demonstrate X's love for Y, it may also demonstrate Y's power over X—and these two are not mutually exclusive. And of course, this is heavily gendered. The labour of care for men is usually manifest in the labour involved in "providing for" the family—few are primary carers either of their children, or of their parents. Eighteen percent of older women are cared for by their spouse, as compared with 53 percent of men. As for household chores, in Europe there has been no significant change in men's participation in domestic work despite female employment rates. The labour of care, whatever proportion of it is domestic chores, is chiefly women's work. . . .

The particular danger of viewing care as labour and care as emotion as indistinguishable is that it can lead to an argument that care is not exploitative because women want to do it. . . . It also can lead to an argument that informal care is necessarily better care because it is guided by love, which, as Ungerson has pointed out (1995), has serious implications for unpaid women carers. The negotiating of labour and emotion poses particular problems for women. Much of the literature on care in the 1980s focused on this, and in particular on women's experiences as unpaid carers in the home. Issues around paid care in the home and its relation to gender remain unexplored. One of the most influential recent works on care is Bubeck's *Care, Gender and Justice* (1995) which examines how and why caring work is exploitative of women, and renders women peculiarly and structurally vulnerable to exploitation. Bubeck's definition of "care" emphasises the difference between doing something for someone who cannot do it, and doing something for someone who will not do it (which she calls "servicing"), rather than distinguishing caring from other types of domestic work in terms of tasks performed. So cooking a meal for a bedridden person is "caring," cooking a meal for a husband/able-bodied employer is "servicing." No matter that they have not got time to cook, it is possible for them to cook in a way in which it is not possible for someone who is bedridden. Her definition also seeks to elucidate both why caring work is necessary and its peculiarly human quality:

> Caring for is the meeting of the needs of one person by another person where face-to-face interaction between carer and cared for is a crucial element of the overall activity and where the need is of such a nature that it cannot possibly be met by the person in need herself. (Bubeck 1995: 129)

Even if it were possible for the need to be met by machine, without face-to-face interaction, it is unlikely that this would be deemed desirable—the prospect of totally mechanised old people's homes is a nightmare rather than a utopia. The definition does seem to miss the point, though, that it is only human to show one cares through meeting such needs whether or not the objects of our affections can meet those needs themselves—and, from time to time at least, to meet them in an "excessive" way. This is evident from Bubeck's own example of "care" according to her definition, "cooking her favourite dish for a sick child" (Bubeck 1995: 130). But why "favourite"? Cooking food for a sick child is caring according to her own definition, but cooking her favourite dish suggests labour beyond the strictly necessary. And if one's only consideration is the most suitable, easy and economical dish for the sick child, and what she likes to eat doesn't enter into it, is that really showing "care"? The central difficulty around care as labour/care as emotion has not been resolved. Human beings can labour to demonstrate affection—for the able-bodied and powerful as well as for the weak and vulnerable. Community and human relations, with their ties of power and of affection, are lived and are created through care. . . .

CARE AS LABOUR/CARE AS EMOTION AND PAID DOMESTIC WORK

What implications does this have for the relationship in which one woman pays another to do caring work? While Bubeck states that caring in the sense of providing for the family is "peculiarly male," this is not so. In fact, when a woman is working, the salary for a paid carer is often taken out of the woman employer's wages. Migrant women are themselves usually "providers for" their families, often "providing for" their children back home, who are themselves cared for, paid or unpaid, by another:

> [Y]ou have to look at it from the point of view of necessity, because what they were paying you there (in the Dominican Republic) for doing a job was not even enough to pay for your children's upkeep, let alone pay for someone to look after them for you. On the other hand, when you emigrate to a country, they give you double what you were earning there, you have enough to send back money to your children there, to pay someone else to care for them, and on top of that to live yourself. (Magnolia, Dominicana working in Barcelona)

> The problem in our country is that before men emigrated. Men were going to the US, but the women were staying in the house. Then what happened was that the man emigrated and did not send anything back, he sent back no money. So the woman was a single mother with children, so if she got the chance to emigrate, she emigrated too . . . because she didn't have any other option to find a better future for her children. So it's terrible for her, very difficult, because they are here, they can only send money back home and their children are being brought up and cared for by another, by their relatives. . . . (Gisela, Dominicana in Barcelona)

While most of the migrant domestic workers I met relied on unpaid care by female family members, it is not unusual for domestic workers themselves to employ carers, often rural migrants. Polish women working as domestic workers in Berlin, for example, reportedly often employ Ukrainians to care for their children in Poland. Yet for the majority of migrants interviewed, being a "provider for" rather than carer of their immediate family was not experienced as a liberation, as it is for European female employers, but as another level of exploitation. While the female European employer may continue in her emotional and supportive role, migrant women can have little emotional and moral input into the upbringing of their children. They do not enjoy care as emotion freed from physical labour. Instead the opposite applies: their care for their children is demonstrated in the fruits of hard labour, in remittances, rather than in the cuddles and "quality time" that provide so much of the satisfaction of care.

> It's terrible for us, because we are far from our children, but we are giving them food, education, we are giving them everything, although staying here you are dying because everything depends on you. . . . [F]or this I am saying, I'm spending three more years here, then I'm going back to my children, whatever happens, because like it or not I am keeping my children going, even though it is with this pain and lack of love. (Berta, Peruvian in Barcelona)

It would seem at first glance that in the case of female European employers, the hiring of a carer reflects those distinctions highlighted by Davidoff (1974) of mutually interdependent female stereotypes being worked out in the domestic worker/employer relationship. In this case the stereotypes are the work of servants (the physical labour of care) and the work of wives/mothers (the emotional labour of care). Could it be argued, then, that the hiring of carers facilitates some privileged women buying into Rose's "care-giving myth" (1986), that care involves only emotion and no labour, and like men, enjoying care as emotion freed from labour? In this case, to take up a point mentioned above, it would be possible for someone to care emotionally for a child and do no physical caring work. Female employers therefore are, like men, divesting themselves of the physical labour of care, but are still the "mother" in terms of their responsibility for and involvement in the emotional and moral development of the child. As Rothman (1989) has pointed out, the exultation of genetic links which has its roots in patriarchy and which has now been "modified" to allow for the equal importance of "male and female seed" has led to a downgrading of nurturing, which includes the labour of care. The privileging of the genetic link, and of care as emotion over care as labour, has rendered the importance of the labour of care invisible and unacknowledged. The labour of care is work that anyone can do, as opposed to care as emotion, which is ultimately dependent on some genetic relationship.

This constructs paid domestic labour, then, as simply that: labour. It sometimes seems as if employers are adopting this model, particularly those who hire and fire easily (the carer is "just" a labourer, and the relationship between the carer and the cared-for is of no consequence). It is also made use of when the worker oversteps the mark and gets "too close" to the cared-for. Very occasionally workers, too, attempt this emotion/labour divide:

I'm telling you, on top of what they are paying you for, the physical work, there is also psychological work, that's double work . . . double pay. Sometimes, when they say to me for example, that I should give her lots of love, I feel like saying, well, for my family I give love free, and I'm not discriminating, but if it's a job you'll have to pay me. . . . (Magnolia, Dominicana working in Barcelona)

Those who were more experienced and who had a greater choice of jobs sometimes refused to work as carers or limited themselves to a particular period with any one family. But it was often a hard lesson to learn:

I cared for a baby for his first year . . . the child loves you as a mother, but the mother was jealous and I was sent away. I was so depressed then, seriously depressed. All I wanted was to go back and see him. . . . I will never care for a baby again, it hurts too much. (Ouliette, from Côte d'Ivoire, working in Parma)

But in practice this separation is not maintained. Employers are not only looking for a labourer when they are looking for a carer; they want somebody "affectionate," "loving," "good with children." Sometimes employers attempt to keep workers by appealing to their "finer feelings" (rather than offering an increase in salary):

[I]t's too much. I said, "Madam I am very sorry, I cannot stay here, I have to find another. . . ." "Why Lina, you cannot leave me like this." I said, "Yes, I can, I don't like." "Where is your heart, you will leave me like this? I have no worker." I said, "I'm very sorry. I have to leave you." I cannot stand it. Otherwise maybe I will kill her! (Lina, a Filipina in Paris). . . .

When necessary, however, employers can make use of the labour power fiction, so that any relationship between carer and cared for is not "real" or, if it threatens to be, it can be disrupted immediately without responsibility to the worker. When money does buy care—that is, when care is explicitly commodified—then it is not real care, because real care cannot be commodified: "Money can't buy love," so workers' feelings for their charges are not important. For workers, on the other hand, it can prove impossible to disentangle care as emotion from care as labour: "What they say at the beginning of the job and then what happens, are very different things . . . with old people like it or not it is a job where you have to get to know this old person and take care of them" (Magnolia, Dominicana in Barcelona). For not only may affection be expressed through labour, as has been discussed in the literature, but labour may engender care, and this is particularly true in the case of childcare. As anyone who has been intimately involved with a child can tell, it is often through interaction on the level of basic physical chores—nappy changing, feeding, cleaning, that one develops a relationship with a young child. Workers who are involved in such a relationship and who are deprived of their "own" children may love the child intensely. The difficulty for the worker is that, as Bubeck allows, caring requires "face-to-face interaction"—that is, at the very least, relating. If this face-to-face interaction is repeated on a daily basis in the kinds of conditions experienced by many domestic workers, particularly those who live in, it almost inevitably develops into a relationship. The paid worker loves the child, the child loves the worker, and jealousy and family friction result. . . .

Care involves the whole person. It is bound up with who we are. A worker is not only a worker, she is a woman, a human being, and caring is, as Bubeck puts it, a "deeply human practise," with a particular resonance for women since "Caring as an activity, disposition, and attitude forms a central part of probably all cultural conceptions of femininity" (Bubeck 1995: 160). Employers of domestic workers take advantage of the fiction of labour power but they also acknowledge that care involves the whole person in the personal requirements. The domestic worker is not equated socially with her employer in the act of exchange because the fiction of labour power cannot be maintained: it is "personhood" that is being commodified. Moreover, the worker's caring function, her performance of tasks constructed as degrading, demonstrates the employer's power to command her self. Having allegedly sold her personhood, the domestic worker is both person and non-person. She is, like the prostitute, a person who is not a person, someone for whom all obligations can be discharged in cash (O'Connell Davidson 1998). So, particularly for those jobs which necessarily demand some human interaction, an employer can purchase the services of a human being who is yet not a real human being—with likes and hates, relations of her own, a history and ambitions of her own—but a human being who is socially dead (O'Connell Davidson, 1998: Patterson 1982). Such an exchange further dishonours her before her employer: "I can say that they think about themselves, how to take more money, better conditions for them. They offer because they have to, not because they feel sympathy. Love is silly for them" (Nina, employer in Athens).

The contradictions in the concept of property in the person, apparent from Locke onwards, trap the worker between being a labourer without emotions, selling commodified labour power, on the one hand, and a dishonoured person on the other. . . . So Bertha expressed the contradictions implicit in the attempt to commodify that which cannot be commodified fully:

> Live-in, what are they paying for? Freedom. It's emotional work, and physically you have to be there twenty-four hours, you have to give them your liberty. That is

what they are paying for. To be there all the time. Even if they pay you, give you free time, I think a young person is worth more than the money. There is no amount that they can pay you that can justify you being imprisoned.

"'MEMBER OF OUR FAMILY'—OH REALLY?"

In order to negotiate the contradictions inherent in the attempted commodification of domestic work, and the tension between the affective relations of the private and the instrumental relations of employment, many employers and some workers made use of the notion of the family.

> We are treated as a servant . . . like my employer, they say, "Ah Teresita, we used to treat you as a member of our family." Oh really? But try to observe . . . they will introduce you to their friends as a member of the family, and then they are sitting down, eating with crossed legs, and you will be the one who is running for their needs. Is that, can you consider that a member of the family? It's very easy to say, but it's not being felt inside the house. (Teresita, Filipina in Athens)

"Part of the family." This phrase appears time and again in the literature of domestic work, as it did in my own discussions with domestic workers. This is in part precisely because of the intertwining of domestic work and caring work that I have attempted to tease out (but which employers clearly have no interest in unravelling!) which allows for what Bubeck would count as "servicing" to be portrayed as "care." For employers can argue that domestic workers "love" their employers and show it through action. So while they hire a labourer, gradually the labourer becomes incorporated into the family and has the same kinds of relationship with family members as the kin do.

But which part of the family are they, one is tempted to ask? . . . [T]he phrase suggests becoming part of the special relationship beyond the simple bond of employment, in which the worker will be loved and cared for. . . . For the employer there are clear advantages to the obfuscation of the employment relationship, since it seriously weakens the worker's negotiating position in terms of wages and conditions—any attempt to improve these are an insult to the "family" and evidence of the worker's money grubbing attitude. The worker risks forfeiting "good" relations with her employers by making too many demands. It must be remembered that in these highly individualised work situations, good interpersonal relations can be extremely important, to the extent that a worker will often consider a lower-paying job if she feels happier with the family, since this will have a significant impact on her living and working conditions. For employers of carers, describing a worker as part of the family facilitates the myth that caring is untainted by the market place. They can imagine that the worker is fulfilled by a "real" relationship with the person cared for—while retaining the possibility of terminating the relationship because it was contracted on the labour market and, therefore, can be deemed unreal if necessary. . . .

What the "part of the family" rhetoric obscures is that relations in paid care are, to use Wærness's (1984) term, "asymmetrical." While the worker is expected to have familial interest in the employing family, this is not reciprocated. Cock (1989) found in South Africa that employers were simply unwilling to consider their workers' private lives, and similarly very few employers I spoke to had any idea about the lives of their domestic workers—indeed they resented it if their worker "talked too much." Relations within the family are typically asymmetrical, with women doing more "caring" than men. But paid workers, unlike "wives," "mothers" and "daughters," are not part of a network of obligations and responsibilities (however unequally distributed): all obligations are discharged in cash. "Caring" work requires human beings to do it and cannot be mechanised, but when care is paid for, the person who is paying can avoid acknowledging that the worker is expressing and forming human relationships and community (which is not to say that unpaid care may not be expressing and forming oppressive human relations); her caring brings with it no mutual obligations, no entry into a community, no "real" human relations, only money. So a worker who has cared for a child over many years, who has spent many more hours with her than her "natural" mother, has no right to see the child should the employer decide to terminate the relationship, because the worker is paid. Money expresses the full extent of any obligations.

This reduction of human relations to cash is rendered easier because the emotional relationship is typically not between the carer and the person who is paying her wages (who is, in the final analysis, her employer) but between the carer and the cared-for, and both are relatively powerless before the financier of the care. The growth of this emotional relationship renders the carer vulnerable to exploitation, and the cared for vulnerable to the whims of the person holding the purse strings. As Bubeck points out, some unpaid carers may find themselves empowered by care, their self-esteem enhanced by making others happy and well: "it is this sense of power that underlies the peculiar logic of care, whereby the more one gives the more one is given in return" (Bubeck 1995: 148). This is strikingly inappropriate for paid carers, where even on the level of the individual relationship between carer and cared-for, a genuine affectionate relationship does not bring empowerment but rather its opposite. The care financier is able to manipulate the relationship between the carer and the cared-for to her own ends—to extract more labour from the carer for lower wages for example—safe in the knowledge that the carer will want to do her best for the cared-for. . . .

Becoming "part of the family" is not only a means of maximising labour extracted from the worker. It is an attempt to manage contradictions. For the employer it helps to manage the contradictions of intimacy and status that attach to the role of the domestic worker, who is at once privy to many of the intimate details of family life, yet is also their status giver, their myth maker. It emphasises the common humanity of employers and workers, and explicitly rejects the commodification of human relations while sustaining an illusion of affective relations, and, in some instances, encouraging their formation. The situation of Zenaida, a Moroccan woman working in Barcelona, reveals the vulnerability of carers and the problems for them in being regarded as part of the family. She had cared for an old woman for five years, doing domestic chores as well as caring work. She lived in, was "part of the family," and felt she was treated with respect by her employing family. She was paid by the woman's sons, who even took a holiday in her house in Morocco. Yet she could spend only one night a week with her five children, who lived in Barcelona, and the rest of the time had to leave them to fend for themselves because she lived in. Although he could have obtained a residence permit for Spain, the father of her children remained in Morocco because the first two children were too old to be admitted to Spain under family reunification. The youngest child was six, and she had left her when she was only a baby for six days a week in order to be the old woman's carer. There was no question of her being allowed to sleep with the baby: "You can't do these things. No. Everyone thinks, I don't know, about themselves. You can't do that."

Zenaida's terrible situation points to one of the greatest advantages to the employer of regarding the worker as part of the family, which is the erasure of the worker's own family. While being part of the family may be perceived by the employer as a great favour, for the worker it may be experienced as a denial of their humanity, a deep depersonalisation, as being perceived only in their occupational role, as a "domestic" rather than as a person with her own needs, her own life, and her own family outside of the employers' home (Palmer 1989). By incorporating the worker as "part of the family" employers can not only ignore the worker's other relationships, but feel good about doing so—for it is an honour to be part of the family.

I have highlighted the caring function of domestic work because it brings out the contradictions and tensions in paid domestic labour. But the slippage between labour power and personhood, and the employer's power to command the whole person of the domestic worker, applies whatever function of domestic work the person is hired to perform. It is this slippage that can help us begin to understand what Bubeck sets out to explain, but never fully accounts for: how it is that some women exploit others within a general theory of care as women's work.

1. This comment has stuck in my mind for years, but I can find no reference to it. I only know that I did not originate it.

Bubeck, Diemut (1995) *Care, Gender and Justice.* Oxford: Clarendon Press.

Cock, J. (1989) *Maids and Madams: Domestic Workers under Apartheid.* London: The Women's Press.

Davidoff, L. (1974) "Mastered for Life: Servant and Wife in Victorian and Edwardian England," *Journal of Social History* 7: 406–28.

Finch, J. and Groves, D. (eds) (1983) *A Labour of Love: Women, Work and Caring.* London: Routledge and Kegan Paul.

Gregson, Nicky and Lowe, Michelle (1994) *Servicing the Middle Classes.* London: Routledge.

O'Connell Davidson, Julia (1998) *Prostitution, Power and Freedom.* Cambridge: Polity Press.

Palmer, Phyllis (1989) *Domesticity and Dirt: Housewives and Domestic Servants in the US, 1920–1945.* Philadelphia: Temple University Press.

Pateman, Carole (1988) *The Sexual Contract.* Cambridge: Polity Press.

Patterson, Orlando (1982) *Slavery and Social Death.* Harvard: Harvard University Press.

Rose, Hilary (1986) "Women's Work: Women's Knowledge," in Juliet Mitchell and Ann Oakley (eds) *What Is Feminism?* Oxford: Basil Blackwell: 161–83.

Rothman, Barbara (1989) "Women as Fathers: Motherhood and Childcare under Modified Patriarchy," in *Gender and Society* 3(1) (March): 89–104.

Sayer, Derek (1991) *Capitalism and Modernity: an Excursus on Marx and Weber.* London Routledge.

Ungerson, Clare (1995) "Gender, Cash and Informal Care," *Journal of Social Policy* 24 (1): 31–52.

Wærness, K. (1984) "The Rationality of Caring," in *Economic and Industrial Democracy* 5 (2) (May): 185–211.

19 UNRAVELING PRIVILEGE: WORKERS' CHILDREN AND THE HIDDEN COSTS OF PAID CHILDCARE

Mary Romero

Mary Romero's essay documents the experience of the growing numbers of children whose mothers have moved to other countries in search of wages through carework and domestic work. The essay describes the family disruption that is created by transnational mothering. It also highlights the relations of inequality among children as well as mothers built into the global division of carework.

Much of the workforce began working more hours to make ends meet or to hold on to increasingly scarce "secure" jobs, and others are trying to maintain a certain lifestyle.[1] While these are clearly major social movements and dislocations, they are experienced individually as work and family conflict. Remedies addressing individual solutions to caregiving[2] do not eliminate the conflict but merely shift the burden to more vulnerable and less protected groups.[3] I argue that shifting childcare and other reproductive labor from unpaid female family members to the shoulders of low-wage female (and often immigrant) workers does not bring society closer to eliminating work and family conflict, but actually maintains and strengthens systems of privilege and related values that support masculinity, femininity, whiteness, and citizenship. . . .

Based on her analysis of various work situations, Judith Rollins concluded that employers expecting emotional labor hire women to relieve them from the burden of housework and to enhance their own feelings of superiority.[4] Applying Rollins's analysis to the specific case of live-in nannies, hiring a surrogate is an ideal strategy for maintaining child-centered, emotionally demanding, and labor-intensive mothering, while shifting the burden from one's own shoulders. Domestics and nannies are relegated the more physical and taxing part of child work while employers upgrade their own status to mother-managers.[5]

The structure of the occupation, characterized by the informality of negotiations conducted in the privacy of the employer's home and lacking definitive contract criteria,[6] affords considerable opportunities for employer abuses[7] and makes it difficult or impossible for workers to organize.[8] While employers in domestic service engage in similar self-interests as other employers—increasing the amount of labor and decreasing its value—they resist other dimensions of employment: (1) acknowledging that when a private household worker or caretaker is hired, their home becomes the employee's workplace[9]; (2) accepting the worker as an employee rather than as an extension of the employer's roles as housewife or mother[10]; and (3) actively resisting practices of modern work culture.[11] Domestic labor may be priceless, but employers are unwilling to pay very much for it. . . .[12] By purchasing the low-wage labor of other women in order to substitute for the unpaid labor of wives and mothers, employers are engaged in the social reproduction of their family status; that is, a social reproduction of privileges based on gender, as well as class, race, sexuality, and citizenship. . . .[13]

Both micro- and macro-level analyses demonstrate how racialized-gendered-immigrants and non-migrants[14] are positioned on the continuum of household labor as domestics, nannies, or au pairs; and differentiated by wages, benefits, and overall working conditions. At a micro level, employee and employer social networks[15] and employer preferences[16] shape local domestic labor workforces. Employee and employer networks are evident in the residential clusters of racial ethnic and immigrant domestics and nannies throughout the country.[17] Different populations of workers frequently become stereotyped as ideal employees for housework, childcare, or for live-in positions.[18] Past work experience or skills are less likely to be the basis for hiring private household workers than personality.[19] Racial and ethnic preference for housework versus childcare, as well as their willingness to do the most amount of work for the least amount of pay, are common items on the list of criteria used by employers to hire domestics. Consequently, paid domestic labor is not only segregated by gender, but is stratified by race and citizenship status; higher status individuals are employed at the top of the market and individuals with the lowest status are employed in the least favorable working conditions. Macro-level analysis of labor-market dynamics indicates that areas with the highest levels of income inequality employ the largest number of private household workers in the country.[20] Immigration and welfare policies[21] control the flow of low-wage workers available for domestic and nanny positions.[22] Restricting government subsidies and opportunities for legal work status, or to become citizens, ghettoizes populations of women in domestic service.[23]

Childcare arrangements made by private household workers and nannies are similar to other poor and working-class mothers in the United States: mothers and fathers juggle work hours to allow one parent to be home with the children; they call upon relatives or siblings for help[24]; they give older siblings responsibility for childcare and domestic labor[25]; sometimes they are forced to leave the children alone, or in a few cases, take their children to work.[26] Changes in work and school schedules require flexibility and contingency plans, but the absence of available and affordable childcare greatly limits options for paid laborers.[27]

Live-in positions pose severe restrictions making it difficult and sometimes impossible for domestics to mother their own children. The circumstances forcing working mothers to accept live-in positions underscore the irony that "to be good mothers, women leave their children to migrate."[28] Women accept live-in positions during periods of economic crisis[29] or while transitioning to U.S. residence.[30] Occasionally women find employers who are willing to accept their children (usually one child) as part of the live-in arrangement. Two children of domestic workers that I interviewed described mothers who were employed as live-in workers and had arranged to keep their children with them full-time; one mother kept her daughters with her on weekends.[31] Both children began by sharing the maid's quarters with their mothers as small children and as the employers' children left for college and vacated their rooms, they moved into their own rooms. In both cases, employers were unable to pay a full-time salary thus requiring their mothers to do day work throughout the neighborhood, and then return to clean and pick-up after their live-in employer. The arrangement was maintained throughout most of their working lives because living-in with one employer and doing day work allowed the workers to enroll their children in neighborhood schools which were some of the best schools in the country.[32] However, in each case, the boundaries between family and work were blurred and the distinction between paid and unpaid reproductive labor disappeared.

A growing number of women employed as domestics and nannies are engaged in transnational mothering. The following account of children who spent a number of years with their grandmothers while their mothers were employed as live-in domestics exemplify the conditions, personal sacrifices, and family disruption posed in transnational motherhood. When Sophia Miller was twelve, her mother migrated to New York from St. Vincent, leaving her for four years. Once her mother obtained a green card, she was able to send for her daughter and son. Years later, as a college student, Sophia still felt the loss and rupture in their mother-daughter relationship. The following quote points to the personal cost of transnational mothering:

> Those four years I went through a lot of changes and she wasn't there. I think growing up I didn't really need her as much as I needed her during that four years when she left. So like, I don't know there's things I would've liked to talk to her about and she wasn't there, and now she's around I really don't have that need for

her as much as I did back then, and I that's something I can't get over yet I keep saying, "Well you weren't around. You were never there." I've kind of resented her at first. . . . "Why isn't she coming back [I asked my grandmother]?" "She said she was going to be gone for a month." She was gone for four years. We resented her for that for a while, I really did.[33]

Time spent at work, the demand to work late,[34] and requests to take work home are all factors influencing the rearing and socialization of the workers' children. Circumstances of childrearing for immigrant and poor women employed as household workers differ from their employers. Middle-class children may not spend much more time with their working mothers than the children of domestics, but they are provided a parental substitute.[35] Live-in, as opposed to day work, is the major factor shaping the kind of mothering workers engaged in. Employers' requests for employees to work in their own home changes the quality of time spent with the employees' own children. Cooking,[36] sewing, and childcare may not be entirely opposed by workers because they can care for their own children while earning money. However, these tasks extend the number of hours engaged in paid labor, and shift the cost of equipment and electricity to the worker. Bringing the employer's reproductive labor into the employee's home may also include the children's unpaid labor if they assist their mother in ironing, cooking, and babysitting. . . .

[S]OCIAL REPRODUCTION: LEARNING ABOUT PRIVILEGE

Domestic service involves the social reproduction of class, as well as gender and race privileges in both employees' and employers' families.[37] Ascribing children their parent's social status is a form of social reproduction that links family and work. This takes a peculiar form in domestic service when adolescent children are called upon to augment or replace their mother's paid labor. This is a strategy women doing domestic labor are forced to use to handle family emergencies or illnesses when they fear being fired or losing pay if they miss work. Because they do not receive sick pay or leave, they frequently have no one but family members to call upon. Wages and benefits (or lack thereof) establish the economic conditions that contextualize childrearing and socialization. Like other poor and working class children, the years of dependency are restricted to early childhood rather than extending into adolescence and early adulthood.[38] Children of domestics take their place in the division of household labor with increasing responsibility as they reach adolescence.[39]

The following accounts illustrate how children learn about privilege. Edward Miller's image of the employer's son clinging to his mother as he cried and the knowledge that he was allowed to express such ownership over his mother was a powerful message of class and race domination, as well as privilege.

> I remember going with my father, I guess I must of been four years old, because I could actually physically stand up on the seat, back then they didn't have car seats and seat belts and all of that, so I would drive with him standing up on the seat, the front seat of this forty-seven Chevy we had and we went over to the house where my mother worked, the white family that my mother worked for and this little boy, this little white boy about my age was crying his eyes out because my mother was leaving and I remember feeling a twinge of jealousy and downright anger because I had been taught never to cry when my mother left because that was something she had to do. So I had already been trained not to express that kind of emotion, "get used to it, your mother has to go to work." And here is this little white boy expressing all of this anguish and emotion because my mother was leaving him. My father had gone to pick my mother up from work and she was trying to excuse herself from the little brat and he was crying his eyes out. And I am sitting there watching this and I couldn't cry, I wasn't suppose to cry. So that was the first hint of caste and class differences, and culture and all that.[40]

Recounting the complaints her mother made about an employer's child, Linda Duran learned parents' different class expectations and the extra work that privilege meant for her mother:

> They're too submissive, you know, the kids run wild. One kid has a room full of stuffed animals. Evidently they're all over the dresser and the bed and the floor and this angers her because she's got to pick them up to dust underneath it and that sort of thing. "The kid's too damn old to be having all this stuff in there anyway" and "I don't understand why they have to have so many." "The kid is twelve and why do they have teddy bears." She decided that the kid's not growing up fast enough. So she does talk about it, usually when it affects her work somehow.[41]

Domestic service is a source of knowledge for the workers' children to learn the folkways, mores, norms, values, and racial etiquette of class, gender, whiteness, and citizenship.[42] Rituals and practices of deference that characterize servitude are powerful tools of instruction to teach privilege. Answering evening telephone calls from the employers exposes children to the linguistic deference common in domestic service[43]: e.g., referring to the workers by their first names while formally addressing employers[44]; domestics referred to as "girl," "my girl,"[45] or Maria[46]; and the angloization of first names for easier pronunciation.[47] Workers' children experienced spatial deference when they accompanied their mothers to work as helpers or as domestics themselves.[48] They are frequently the recipients of employers' practice of "gift-giving" of old clothes and other discarded items.[49] The nonreciprocal nature of the interaction and the quality of the exchange is an important lesson in privilege.[50] The systems of gifts and favors that shapes the personalism of the intimate relationship into a strategy of oppression[51] is brought home to the domestics' children when mothers feel obligated to comply with every employer request.[52]

In summary, I found that while the adult children of private household workers did not necessarily understand the class and racial stratification, they learned their place in it. Experiences with employers, their children, the peculiar customs and rituals of deference, and low wages found in domestic service accentuated the significance of class and race in their lives. . . .

Affordable childcare remains a private and family problem rather than a public issue requiring a public solution. Upper-middle-class families can afford the personalized service to augment the limited childcare options. As long as the discussions about reproductive labor remain outside the public arena and are characterized as "a battle between the sexes," our conceptualization of work and family conflict remains stagnant. By contrasting motherhood and childhood in the employer and employee family, the divisions of work and family are revealed as social issues that transcend the purely personal. Both employer and employee families have childcare needs but their purchasing power present completely different options placing the children of domestics at an enormous disadvantage. Stories of domestic service told by workers' children accentuate the unequal distribution of reproductive labor at the societal level. Social scientists have restricted their analysis to the family unit which does not capture the ramifications that poorly paid domestic labor and childcare have on other sectors of society, particularly the workers' families. Maintaining the ideal American family depicted in Norman Rockwell drawings, and later updated with two career families and "Take Your Daughter to Work Day," exist because certain groups pay the price. Caring for children is not priceless in our society but usually relies on the cheapest labor available.[53] Immigration policies and declining welfare benefits assure professionals of a ready pool of low-wage workers.

By hiring private household workers and nannies as substitute mothers under inferior working conditions, employers are purchasing services crucial to both the reproduction of their families and to the social reproduction of privilege. Rather than challenging the everyday rituals that affirm patriarchy in the home, such as the gendered division of household labor, the work is simply shifted to a poorly paid female employee. The system of privileges available to employers and employees determines childrearing and socialization while reproducing class differences. When immigrant mothers employed as live-in nannies are restricted to the most basic "mothering" agenda of sending money home to house, feed, and clothe their children, while they simultaneously sell their labor as caregivers to middle-class women engaged in intensive mothering, "quality" time and activities enhancing cognitive development becomes a privilege, not a right. Childcare policies and programs that are not inclusive of all mothers, regardless of class, race, or citizenship, maintain a system of privileges that relies on subordination.

1. See Juliet B. Schor, *The Overworked American: The Unexpected Decline of Leisure* 107–38 (New York: Basic Books, 1991).

2. Examples include childcare experts' advice to over-extended parents on how to turn limited time with their children into "quality" time, employees seeking flexible and reduced hours, or corporate development of "family-friendly" policies.

3. See Ida Susser, "The Separation of Mothers and Children," in *Dual City: Restructuring New York* 217–20 (John Hull Mollenkopf & Manuel Castells eds., New York: Russell Sage Foundation, 1991) (discussing the contradiction that middle-class women face in juggling the need to be available to children and time commitments to their professional career, and identifying poor immigrants serving as housekeepers, baby sitters, and combination full-time housekeepers to meet the demands).

4. Scott Coltrane & Justin Galt, "The History of Men's Caring, Evaluating Precedents for Fathers' Family Involvement," in *Care Work: Gender, Class, and the Welfare State* 15 (Madonna Harrington Meyer ed., New York: Routledge, 2000) at 31; see also Judith Rollins, *Between Women: Domestics and Their Employers* 183 (Philadelphia: Temple University Press, 1985) at 180 (maintaining that "the presence of the deference-giving inferior enhances the employer's self-esteem as an individual, neutralizes some of her resentment as a woman, and, where appropriate, strengthens her sense of self as a white person").

5. See Barbara Katz Rothman, *Recreating Motherhood: Ideology and Technology in a Patriarchal Society* 198–202 (New York: Norton, 1989) (discussing the managerial mother); see also Dorothy E. Roberts, "Spiritual and Menial Housework," 9 *Yale J.L. & Feminism* 51, 55–59 (1997) (arguing for a division of labor based on spiritual and menial housework); see Susser, 218 (discussing the kinds of planning and arranging that mothers do instead of actually spending time with their children).

6. See Susser, 220.

7. See Mary Romero, "Who Takes Care of the Maid's Children?" in *Feminism and Families* 164–65 (Hilde Lindermann Nelson ed., New York: Routledge, 1997); see also Pierrette Hondagneu-Sotelo, "Regulating the Unregulated?: Domestic Workers' Social Networks," 41 *Soc. Probs.* 50, 55–60 (1994); Maria

Ontiveros, "To Help Those Most in Need: Undocumented Workers' Rights and Remedies Under Title VII, 20 N.Y.U." *Rev. L. & Soc. Change* 607, 610–15 (1993); Mary Romero, "Immigration, the Servant Problem, and the Legacy of the Domestic Labor Debate: 'Where Can You Find Good Help These Days!'" 53 *U. Miami L. Rev.* 1045, 1048 (1999).

8. See Peggie R. Smith, "Regulating Paid Household Work: Class, Gender, Race, and Agendas of Reform," 48 *Am. U. L. Rev.* 851, 918–24 (1999) (discussing current attitudes and conditions impairing unionization efforts).

9. See Mary Romero, *Maid in the U.S.A.* 98 (New York: Routledge, 1992); see also Stephen L. Carter, *The Confirmation Mess: Cleaning Up the Federal Appointments Process* 179–82 (New York: Basic Books, 1994) (arguing that Nannygate is an unconstitutional infringement on the privacy of employing families for example).

10. See id. at 130 (discussing family analogy used by employers to distort relationship); see also Dorothy E. Roberts, "Spiritual and Menial Housework," 9 *Yale J.L. & Feminism* 51 (1997) at 65 n. 72.

11. See id. at 98; see also Suzanne Goldberg, "In Pursuit of Workplace Rights: Household Workers and a Conflict of Laws," 3 *Yale J.L. & Feminism* 63, 100 (1990).

12. See Proposals to Simplify and Streamline the Payment of Employment Taxes for Domestic Workers: Hearings Before the Subcomm. on Social Security and the Subcomm. on Human Resources of the House Comm. on Ways and Means, 103d Cong. 4, 39–40 (1993) (recognizing noncompliance with employment taxes in domestic service).

13. Ritualized cleaning, household management, and other forms of labor servicing life-styles are rooted in the cult of domesticity. See Faye Dudden, *Serving Women: Household Service in Nineteenth-Century America* 140–41 (Middletown, CT: Wesleyan University Press, 1983).

14. See generally Mimi Abramovitz, *Regulating the Lives of Women: The Social Functions of Public Welfare* 3–7 (Boston: South End Press, 1988) (examining the historical role of the state in defining middle-class married women as "fit" and "deserving" and poor single women as "unfit" mothers and thus denied support and forced to seek low-wage). See also Sylvia A. Law, "Women, Work, Welfare, and the Preservation of Patriarchy," 131 *U. Pa. L. Rev.* 1249, 1249–55 (1983).

15. See Romero, 98; see also Carter, 144; Evelyn Nakano Glenn, "Occupational Ghettoization: Japanese American Women and Domestic Service, 1905–1970," 8 *Ethnicity* 352, 380 (1981); Hondagneu-Sotelo, 55–56.

16. See Rollins, 127–31 (discussing employers' preferences based on race and ethnicity); see also Julia Wrigley, *Other People's Children* 5 (New York: Basic,

1995) at 25 (discussing reasons that employers hire or avoid immigrant women as domestics).

17. See Doreen Mattingly, "Making Maids: United States Immigration Policy and Immigrant Domestic Workers," in *Gender, Migration, and Domestic Service* 65 (Jane Henshall Momsen ed., London: Routledge, 1999), at 71–73.

18. See id., at 75.

19. See Romero, 98; n. 50, at 111.

20. See Ruth Milkman et al., "The Macrosociology of Paid Domestic Labor," 25 *Work & Occupations* 483–88 (1998) (finding that in regions in the United States with the highest income inequality among women, domestic service is relatively large; whereas in locations with minimal income inequality, the occupation is of trivial importance or even absent).

21. See id.

22. In her study of childrearing and household formation in New York City, Ida Susser asserted that the "control of migrant entries . . . affects the cost of domestic service and the availability of women to replace those who find well-paid work." Ida Susser, "The Separation of Mothers and Children," in *Dual City: Restructuring New York* 208 (John Hull Mollenkopf & Manuel Castells eds., Philadelphia: Temple University Press, 1991).

23. See Mattingly, 74–76 (discussing the ghettoization effect that the Immigration Reform and Control Act of 1986 has had on immigrant women employed as domestics and nannies in California); see also Chang (2000); Anderson, 25.

24. See Romero (interviewees describing extended family assuming childcare during their mothers' absence).

25. See id., 155.

26. When the option was taking the child to work or leaving the child alone, some mothers were able to obtain their employer's permission to bring the child for the day. Interviewees who were the oldest in the family recall accompanying their mothers to their day jobs. See id.

27. The irregular hours of domestic service resulting from employers' last minute requests placed additional burden on mothers finding adequate childcare. Id.

28. See Shelle Colen, "'Just a Little Respect': West Indian Domestic Workers in New York City," in *Muchuachas No More: Household Workers in Latin America and the Caribbean* 172–73 (Elsa M. Chaney & Mary Garcia Castro eds., Philadelphia: Temple University Press, 1989).

29. An interviewee describes his mother leaving their home in the south during an economic crisis to take a job as a live-in domestic in New York. Since his

father was unemployed, the higher paying live-in domestic position in New York was lucrative enough to warrant separating the family. See Romero, 153–54; see also Elizabeth Clark-Lewis, *Living In, Living Out: African American Domestics in Washington, D.C., 1910–1940*, at 51–65 (1994) (discussing the movement north in search of work in domestic service).

30. Three interviewees were the son and daughters of immigrants. Ricardo Olivas, a Latino growing up in San Francisco in the '50s, was separated from his mother while she took a live-in position in the city. Since she was a single mother and her relatives had not yet immigrated to the United States, she had few child-care options to accommodate her working situation. She was able to enroll her sons in a boarding school in the area. See Romero, 154.

31. One child remembers:
It was extremely hard for her to spend the weekend away from us where we didn't really know anyone here. I spent most of the time during weekends with my father, but so then as she got to know the Patrona we were able to go there with her and spend the weekend with her, and she really liked us and she actually liked us to talk to her two children—the little girl was 5 and the little boy was 2 or 3. She liked us to speak to them in Spanish. They were fluent in Spanish and French and English. She really liked having us around, so we would go. We would go to the park.
Interview on file with author.

32. See Mary Romero, "One of the Family or Just the Mexican Maid's Daughter? Belonging, Identity and Social Mobility," in *Women's Untold Stories: Breaking Silence, Talking Back, Voicing Complexity* 142 (Mary Romero & Abigail Steward eds., New York: Routledge, 1999) (describing a daughter living with her mother in the employer's home, attending school, and participating in the community with the employer's children).

33. Interview on file with the author.

34. See Susser, 218 (describing employers' practice of assuming the availability of nannies).

35. A quote from Edward Miller points to this distinction: "I only experienced her [mother] from I guess 5:30 to 8:00 at night, for three hours of the day, because we had to go to bed at that time, at eight or eight-thirty at night and the little white kids got to benefit from her all day." See Romero, 156.

36. This usually involved employers' requests for cooking particular kinds of ethnic food that were not readily available and took hours to prepare. Sal Lujan remembered his mother cooking Mexican food for her employer's party in Texas.
They've asked her to make Mexican food and they give her a lot of money. They've paid like sixty bucks or something. They give her sixty bucks and she'd make tamales or something like that, and plus she tells them "you have to buy

everything." So they buy everything and she gets to make the whole thing over at their house.

Id. at 157.

37. See Anderson, 30; Rollins, 190.

38. See Frederick Elkin & Gerald Handel, *The Child and Society, The Process of Socialization* 256–59 (New York: Random House, 1984).

39. Unlike upper- and middle-class children, these children were expected to engage in household tasks. For the most part, age was the major determining factor in the amount of work they did; and secondly, was gender. Gender was reported to shape the allocation of tasks in families in cases where the oldest child was female; gender was less a factor in families where the eldest child was a son or when all the children were male. The presence of another adult family member, a father or relative, also affected the redistribution of household chores. Of course, all of this was dependent on the number of hours mothers spent away from home and the family's financial means. See Romero, 159.

40. Interview on file with author.

41. Hays includes a contrasting quote describing intensive mothering:

Why do many professional-class employed women seem to find it necessary to take the kids to swimming and judo and dancing and tumbling classes, not to mention orthodontists and psychiatrists and attention-deficit specialists? . . . Why must a "good" mother be careful to "negotiate" with her child, refraining from demands for obedience to absolute set of rules? Why must she avoid spanking a disobedient child and instead feel the need to explain, in detail, the issues at hand? Why does she consider it important to be consciously and constantly attentive to the child's wishes?

Sharon Hays, *The Cultural Contradictions of Motherhood* 6 (New Haven, CT: Yale University Press, 1996).

42. The following quotes are examples of the sources of knowledge and messages conveyed to domestics' children:

I heard stories of how older people, high school age, interacted with her. The younger children were more like she was a babysitter and they basically had to do what she said. And I think she had more control over them because she took them out of their environment and put them in her house. But the high schoolers I think were a lot more rude to her thinking that she didn't have any power over them.

As they got older their attitude became exceedingly patronizing. That is what I couldn't handle. That was the thing I couldn't handle. . . . And their attitude is just very patronizing. When they really owe her a lot for all she did and sacrificed for them. But I don't know, I guess I don't know how else I would expect them to act. Just a little more respectful that's all.

One of my mom's friends who is young, in her twenties, worked for an employer who had a son around her age. He made a lot of sexual advances at her and

one night when she had to work late, tried to get her to sleep with him. She told his parents and they said it wasn't true, basically said she was lying, and they fired her.
Romero, 151.

43. See id.

44. See id. at 163.

45. See id.; see also Rollins, 194.

46. See Romero, 164.

47. See id.

48. Mothers' low wages frequently resulted in enlisting children into the labor force at an early age. Since many work arrangements are part of the underground economy, child labor restrictions are rarely enforced. See id.

49. See generally Rollins, 190–194; see Romero, 109.

50. The following quote suggests that the child had ambivalent feelings about the old clothes but understood the stigma attached to the practice in domestic service.

I know that a lot of these people [employers] you know as time went by didn't want their clothes anymore. They would want to throw them away. And sometimes she'd (mother) ask for them. After a while they were just given to her. And I wore some of those clothes. Especially when Alice (live-in employer) wasn't paying my mom. And my mom was doing day work. I think that was part of her way to supplement the cost of things that I needed.

I (laugh) had to wear that garbage. That happened quite a bit, hand-me-downs, old clothes, second-hand presents, you could tell that they were things that, ash trays and stuff, that they probably got from their rich relatives and couldn't use them so they rewrapped them and gave them to my mom. My mom would bring that stuff home. . . . You know we did pick through those clothes to see what we could use because we damn sure needed them but it wasn't anything that we were proud of, even back then we had pride, we knew where it was coming from. . . . Salvation Army stuff like that, it wasn't no Buffalo Exchange where it was kind of neat you know like after the sixties to wear these Annie Hall's stuff and you know and to have the kind of worn clothes to identify with the down trodden you know, we were not romanticizing being poor. Not at all. No. That stuff was second-hand. We knew it was second-hand. It was worn. It had the smell of someone else's sweat in it no matter how many times you washed it and you didn't—it was a statement about your class. It was a statement about your economic level and it was a statement about who was keeping you there and so we weren't at all happy about it at all.
Romero, 164–65.

51. See Romero, 123.

52. While many of the interviewees recognized that domestic service offered employment in a labor market that held limited options for their mothers and

attributed employers' generosity for their additional clothing and opportunity, they still felt strongly that their mothers were frequently manipulated. For instance, in the following account, Alex Conrad describes how the employer pressured his mother to work on the holidays by implying she owes a debt.

> This judge [employer] I mentioned, he was instrumental in our lives, my brother got a scholarship to college because he pulled strings. My brother's very bright, but it helped that he could pull some strings. But years later, this woman—the judge was dead—this woman [judge's wife] would call my mother and say, "would you come out on Saturday and work." One time she called, it happened that we were home for the holidays and I got angry and my brothers got angry and, "No. We don't want you to go." And this woman would invoke, "after all the judge did for you." Our response was, "tell her that your son the college professor and your son the lawyer said that we want you home for the holidays and not going out cleaning her house." There was this real tension between just the fact that we felt that early on, but we could play her elitist games now and argue back. My mother felt obligation and she felt bad for this woman.

Mary Romero, "Who Takes Care of the Maid's Children?" in *Feminism and Families* 164 (Hilde Lindermann Nelson ed., New York: Routledge, 1997).

53. See Roberts, 70–75 (arguing that welfare and immigration policies ensure a pool of low-wage workers limited to domestic service).

20 | "I'M HERE, BUT I'M THERE": THE MEANINGS OF LATINA TRANSNATIONAL MOTHERHOOD

Pierrette Hondagneu-Sotelo and Ernestine Avila

Latina immigrants who work as nannies or housekeepers and reside in Los Angeles while their children remain in their countries of origin constitute one variation in the organizational arrangements of motherhood. The authors call this arrangement "transnational motherhood." On the basis of a survey, in-depth interviews, and ethnographic materials gathered in Los Angeles, they examine how Latina immigrant domestic workers transform the meanings of motherhood to accommodate these spatial and temporal separations.

Latina immigrant women who work and reside in the United States while their children remain in their countries of origin constitute one variation in the organizational arrangements, meanings, and priorities of motherhood. We call this arrangement "transnational motherhood," and we explore how the meanings of motherhood are rearranged to accommodate these spatial and temporal separations. . . . Many factors set the stage for transnational motherhood. These factors include labor demand for Latina immigrant women in the United States, particularly in paid domestic work; civil war, national economic crises, and particular development strategies, along with tenuous and scarce job opportunities for women and men in Mexico and Central America; and the subsequent increasing numbers of female-headed households (although many transnational mothers are married). More interesting to us than the macro determinants of transnational motherhood, however, is the forging of new arrangements and meanings of motherhood.

Central American and Mexican women who leave their young children "back home" and come to the United States in search of employment are in the process of actively, if not voluntarily, building alternative constructions of motherhood. . . . Transnational mothers . . . congregate in paid domestic work, an occupation that is relentlessly segregated not only by gender but also by race, class, and nationality/citizenship. To perform child rearing and domestic duties for others, they radically break with deeply gendered spatial and temporal boundaries of family and work. . . .

Transnational mothering is different from . . . other arrangements in that now women with young children are recruited for U.S. jobs that pay far less than a "family wage." When men come north and leave their families in Mexico—as they did during the Bracero Program and as many continue to do today—they are fulfilling familial obligations defined as breadwinning for the family. When women do so, they are embarking not only on an immigration journey but on a more radical gender-transformative odyssey. They are initiating separations of space and time from their communities of origin, homes, children, and—sometimes—husbands. In doing so, they must cope with stigma, guilt, and criticism from others. A second difference is that these women work primarily not in production of agricultural products or manufacturing but in reproductive labor, in paid domestic work, and/or vending. Performing paid reproductive work for pay—especially caring for other people's children—is not always compatible with taking daily care of one's own family. All of this raises questions about the meanings and variations of motherhood in the late 20th century.

Materials for this article draw from a larger study of paid domestic work in Los Angeles County and from interviews conducted in adjacent Riverside County. The materials include in-depth interviews, a survey, and ethnographic fieldwork. . . . For this article, we draw primarily on tape-recorded and fully transcribed interviews with 26 women who work as house cleaners and as live-out or live-in nanny-housekeepers. Of these 26 women, 8 lived apart from their children to accommodate their migration and work arrangements, but other respondents also spoke poignantly about their views and experiences with mothering, and we draw on these materials as well. We also draw, to a lesser extent, on in-depth, fully transcribed interviews with domestic agency personnel. All of the interview respondents were located through informal snowball sampling. The domestic workers interviewed are all from Mexico, El Salvador, and Guatemala, but they are diverse in terms of demographic characteristics (such as education, civil status, and children), immigration (length of time in the United States, access to legal papers), and other job-related characteristics (English language skills, driver's license, cardiopulmonary resuscitation [CPR] training).

While the interviews provide close-up information about women's experiences and views of mothering, a survey administered to 153 paid domestic workers in Los Angeles provides some indicator of how widespread these transnational arrangements are among paid domestic workers. . . .

Just how widespread are transnational motherhood arrangements in paid domestic work? Of the 153 domestic workers surveyed, 75 percent had children. Contrary to the images of Latina immigrant women as breeders with large families . . . about half (47 percent) of these women have only one or two children. More significant for our purposes is this finding: Forty percent of the women with children have at least one of their children "back home" in their country of origin. . . .

How do women transform the meaning of motherhood to fit immigration and employment? Being a transnational mother means more than being the mother to children raised in another country. It means forsaking deeply felt beliefs that biological mothers should raise their own children, and replacing that belief with new definitions of motherhood. The ideal of biological mothers raising their own children is widely held but is also widely broken at both ends of the class spectrum. Wealthy elites have always relied on others—nannies, governesses, and boarding schools—to raise their children (Wrigley 1995), while poor, urban families often rely on kin and "other mothers" (Collins 1991). . . .

Transnational mothers distinguish their version of motherhood from estrangement, child abandonment, or disowning. A youthful Salvadoran woman at the domestic employment waiting room reported that she had not seen her two eldest boys, now ages 14 and 15 and under the care of her own mother in El Salvador, since they were toddlers. Yet, she made it clear that this was different from putting a child up for adoption, a practice that she viewed negatively, as a form of child abandonment. Although she had been physically separated from her boys for more than a decade, she maintained her mothering ties and financial obligations to them by regularly sending home money. The exchange of letters, photos, and phone calls also helped to sustain the connection. Her physical absence did not signify emotional absence from her children. Another woman who remains intimately involved in the lives of her two daughters, now ages 17 and 21 in El Salvador, succinctly summed up this stance when she said, "I'm here, but I'm there." Over the phone, and through letters, she regularly reminds her daughters to take their vitamins, to never go to bed or to school on an empty stomach, and to use protection from pregnancy and sexually transmitted diseases if they engage in sexual relations with their boyfriends.

Transnational mothers fully understand and explain the conditions that prompt their situations. In particular, many Central American women recognize that the gendered employment demand in Los Angeles has produced transnational motherhood arrangements. These new mothering arrangements, they acknowledge, take shape despite strong beliefs that biological mothers should care for their own children. Emelia, a 49-year-old woman who left her five children in Guatemala nine years ago to join her husband in Los Angeles explained this changing relationship between family arrangements, migration, and job demand:

> One supposes that the mother must care for the children. A mother cannot so easily throw her children aside. So, in all families, the decision is that the man comes (to the U.S.) first. But now, since the man cannot find work here so easily, the woman comes first. Recently, women have been coming and the men staying.

A steady demand for live-in housekeepers means that Central American women may arrive in Los Angeles on a Friday and begin working Monday at a live-in job that provides at least some minimal accommodations. Meanwhile, her male counterpart may spend weeks or months before securing even casual day laborer jobs. While Emelia, formerly a homemaker who previously earned income in Guatemala by baking cakes and pastries in her home, expressed pain and sadness at not being with her children as they grew, she was also proud of her accomplishments. "My children," she stated, "recognize what I have been able to do for them."

Most transnational mothers, like many other immigrant workers, come to the United States with the intention to stay for a finite period of time, until they can pay off bills or raise the money for an investment in a house, their children's education, or a small business. Some of these women return to their countries of origin, but many stay. As time passes, and as their stays grow longer, some of the women eventually bring some or all of their children. Other women who stay at their U.S. jobs are adamant that they do not wish for their children to traverse the multiple hazards of adolescence in U.S. cities or to repeat the job experiences they themselves have had in the United States. One Salvadoran woman in the waiting room at the domestic employment agency—whose children had been raised on earnings predicated on her separation from them—put it this way:

> I've been here 19 years, I've got my legal papers and everything. But I'd have to be crazy to bring my children here. All of them have studied for a career, so why would I bring them here? To bus tables and earn minimum wage? So they won't have enough money for bus fare or food?

Transnational Central American and Mexican mothers may rely on various people to care for their children's daily, round-the-clock needs, but they prefer a close relative. The "other mothers" on which Latinas rely include their own mothers, comadres (co-godmothers) and other female kin, the children's fathers, and paid caregivers. Reliance on grandmothers and comadres for shared mothering is well established in Latina culture, and it is a practice that signifies a more collectivist, shared approach to mothering in contrast to a more individualistic, Anglo-American approach (Griswold del Castillo 1984; Segura and Pierce 1993).

Perhaps this cultural legacy facilitates the emergence of transnational motherhood. Transnational mothers express a strong preference for their own biological mother to serve as the primary caregiver. Here, the violation of the cultural preference for the biological mother is rehabilitated by reliance on the biological grandmother or by reliance on the ceremonially bound comadres. Clemencia, for example, left her three young children behind in Mexico, each with their respective madrina, or godmother. . . .

Both Central American and Mexican woman stated preferences for grandmothers as the ideal caregivers in situations that mandated the absence of the children's biological mother. These preferences seem to grow out of strategic availability, but these preferences assume cultural mandates. Velia, a Mexicana who hailed from the border town of Mexicali, improvised an employment strategy whereby she annually sent her three elementary school-age children to her mother in Mexicali for the summer vacation months. This allowed Velia, a single mother, to intensify her housecleaning jobs and save money on day care. But she also insisted that "if my children were with the woman next door (who babysits), I'd worry if they were eating well, or about men (coming to harass the girls). Having them with my mother allows me to work in peace." Another woman specified more narrowly, insisting that only maternal grandmothers could provide adequate caregiving. In a conversation in a park, a Salvadoran woman offered that a biological mother's mother was the one best suited to truly love and care for a child in the biological mother's absence. According to her, not even the paternal grandmother could be trusted to provide proper nurturance and care. Another Salvadoran woman, Maria, left her two daughters, then 14 and 17, at their paternal grandmother's home, but before departing for the United States, she trained her daughters to become self-sufficient in cooking, marketing, and budgeting money. Although she believes the paternal grandmother loves the girls, she did not trust the paternal grandmother enough to cook or administer the money that she would send her daughters. . . .

New family fissures emerge for the transnational mother as she negotiates various aspects of the arrangement with her children, and with the "other mother" who provides daily care and supervision for the children. Any impulse to romanticize transnational motherhood is tempered by the sadness with which the women related their experiences and by the problems they sometimes encounter with their children and caregivers. A primary worry among transnational mothers is that their children are being neglected or abused in their absence. While there is a long legacy of child servants being mistreated and physically beaten in Latin America, transnational mothers also worry that their own paid caregivers will harm or neglect their children. They worry that their children may not receive proper nourishment, schooling and educational support, and moral guidance. They may remain unsure as to whether their children are receiving the full financial support they send home. In some cases, their concerns are intensified by the eldest child or a nearby relative who is able to monitor and report the caregiver's transgression to the transnational mother.

Transnational mothers engage in emotion work and financial compensation to maintain a smoothly functioning relationship with the children's daily caregiver . . . some of these actions are instrumental. Transnational mothers know that they may increase the likelihood of their children receiving adequate care if they appropriately remunerate the caregivers and treat them with the consideration their work requires. In fact, they often express astonishment that their own Anglo employers fail to recognize this in relation to the nanny-housekeeper work that they perform. Some of the expressions of gratitude and gifts that they send to their children's caregivers appear to be genuinely disinterested and enhanced by the transnational mothers' empathy arising out of their own similar job circumstances. A Honduran woman, a former biology teacher, who had left her four sons with a paid caregiver, maintained that the treatment of nannies and housekeepers was much better in Honduras than in the United States, in part, because of different approaches to mothering:

> We're very different back there. . . . We treat them (domestic workers) with a lot of affection and respect, and when they are taking care of our kids, even more so. The Americana, she is very egotistical. When the nanny loves her children, she gets jealous. Not us. We are appreciative when someone loves our children, and bathes, dresses, and feeds them as though they were their own.

These comments are clearly informed by the respondent's prior class status, as well as her simultaneous position as the employer of a paid nanny-housekeeper in Honduras and as a temporarily unemployed nanny-housekeeper in the United States. . . .

Central American and Mexican women involved in transnational mothering attempt to ensure the present and future well-being of their children through U.S. wage earning, and as we have seen, this requires long-term physical separation from their children. . . . For these women, the meanings of motherhood do not appear to be in a liminal stage. That is, they do not appear to be making a linear progression from a way of motherhood that involves daily, face-to-face caregiving toward one that is defined primarily through breadwinning. Rather than replacing care giving with breadwinning definitions of motherhood, they appear to be expanding their definitions of motherhood to encompass breadwinning that may require long-term physical separations. For these women, a core belief is that they can best fulfill traditional care giving responsibilities through income earning in the United States while their children remain "back home."

Transnational mothers continue to state that caregiving is a defining feature of their mothering experiences. They wish to provide their children with better nutrition, clothing, and schooling, and most of them are able to purchase these items with dollars earned in the United States. They recognize, however, that their transnational relationships incur painful costs. Transnational mothers worry about some of the negative effects on their children, but they also experience the absence of domestic family life as a deeply personal loss. Transnational mothers who primarily identified as homemakers before coming to the United States identified the loss of daily contact with family as a sacrifice ventured to financially support the children. . . .

The daily indignities of paid domestic work—low pay, subtle humiliations, not enough food to eat, invisibility (Glenn 1986; Rollins 1985; Romero 1992)—means that transnational mothers are not only stretching their U.S.-earned dollars further by sending the money back home but also, by leaving the children behind, they are providing special protection from the discrimination the children might receive in the United States. Gladys, who had four of her five children in El Salvador, acknowledged that her U.S. dollars went further in El Salvador. Although she missed seeing those four children grow up, she felt that in some ways, she had spared them the indignities to which she had exposed her youngest daughter, whom she brought to the United States at age 4 in 1988. Although her live-in employer had allowed the four-year-old to join the family residence, Gladys tearfully recalled how that employer had initially quarantined her daughter, insisting on seeing vaccination papers before allowing the girl to play with the employer's children. "I had to battle, really struggle," she recalled, "just to get enough food for her (to eat)." For Gladys, being together with her youngest daughter in the employer's home had entailed new emotional costs. . . .

Transnational mothers echoed these sentiments. Maria Elena, for example, whose 13-year-old son resided with his father in Mexico after she lost a custody battle, insisted that motherhood did not consist of only breadwinning: "You can't give love through money." According to Maria Elena, motherhood required an emotional presence and communication with a child. Like other transnational mothers, she explained how she maintained this connection despite the long-term geographic distance: "I came here, but we're not apart. We talk (by telephone). . . . I know (through telephone conversations) when my son is fine. I can tell when he is sad by the way he speaks." Like employed mothers everywhere, she insisted on a definition of motherhood that emphasized quality rather than quantity of time spent with the child: "I don't think that a good mother is one who is with her children at all times. . . . It's the quality of time spent with the child." She spoke these words tearfully, reflecting the trauma of losing a custody battle with her exhusband. Gladys also stated that being a mother involves both breadwinning and providing direction and guidance. "It's not just feeding them, or buying clothes for them. It's also educating them, preparing them to make good choices so they'll have a better future."

Transnational mothers seek to mesh caregiving and guidance with bread-winning. While breadwinning may require their long-term and long-distance separations from their children, they attempt to sustain family connections by showing emotional ties through letters, phone calls, and money sent home. If at all financially and logistically possible, they try to travel home to visit their children. They maintain their mothering responsibilities not only by earning money for their children's livelihood but also by communicating and advising across national borders, and across the boundaries that separate their children's place of residence from their own places of employment and residence. . . .

As observers of late-20th-century U.S. families (Skolnick 1991; Stacey 1996) have noted, we live in an era wherein no one normative family arrangement predominates. Just as no one type of mothering unequivocally prevails in the White middle class, no singular mothering arrangement prevails among Latina immigrant women. In fact, the exigencies of contemporary immigration seem to multiply the variety of mothering arrangements. Through our research with Latina immigrant women who work as nannies, housekeepers, and house cleaners, we have encountered a broad range of mothering arrangements. Some Latinas migrate to the United States without their children to establish employment, and after some stability has been achieved, they may send for their children or they may work for a while to save money, and then return to their countries of origin. Other Latinas migrate and may postpone having children until they are financially established. Still others arrive with their children and may search for employment that allows them to live together with their children, and other Latinas may have sufficient financial support—from their husbands or kin—to stay home full-time with their children.

In the absence of a universal or at least widely shared mothering arrangement, there is tremendous uncertainty about what constitutes "good mothering," and transnational mothers must work hard to defend their choices. . . . Given the uncertainty of what is "good mothering," and to defend their integrity as mothers when others may criticize them, transnational mothers construct new scales for gauging the quality of mothering. By favorably comparing themselves with the negative models of mothering that they see in others—especially those that they are able to closely scrutinize in their employers' homes—transnational mothers create new definitions of good-mothering standards. At the same time, selectively developing mother-like ties with other people's children allows them to enjoy affectionate, face-to-face interactions that they cannot experience on a daily basis with their own children. . . .

Transnational mothering situations disrupt the notion of family in one place and break distinctively with what some commentators have referred to as the "epoxy glue" view of motherhood (Blum and Deussen 1996; Scheper-Hughes 1992). Latina transnational mothers are improvising new mothering arrangements that are borne out of women's financial struggles, played out in a new global arena, to provide the best future for themselves and their children. Like many other women of color and employed mothers, transnational mothers rely on an expanded and sometimes fluid number of family members and paid caregivers. Their caring circuits, however, span stretches of geography and time that are much wider than typical joint custody or "other mother" arrangements that are more closely bound, both spatially and temporally.

The transnational perspective in immigration studies is useful in conceptualizing how relationships across borders are important. Yet, an examination of transnational motherhood suggests that transnationalism is a contradictory process of the late 20th century. It is an achievement, but one accompanied by numerous costs and attained in a context of extremely scarce options. The alienation and anxiety of mothering organized by long temporal and spatial distances should give pause to the celebratory impulses of transnational perspectives of immigration. Although not addressed directly in this article, the experiences of these mothers resonate with current major political issues. For example, transnational mothering resembles precisely what immigration restrictionists have advocated through California's Proposition 187 (Hondagneu-Sotelo 1995).[1] While proponents of Proposition 187 have never questioned California's reliance on low-waged Latino immigrant workers, this restrictionist policy calls for fully dehumanized immigrant workers, not workers with families and family needs (such as education and health services for children). In this respect, transnational mothering's externalization of the cost of labor reproduction to Mexico and Central America is a dream come true for the proponents of Proposition 187.

Contemporary transnational motherhood continues a long historical legacy of people of color being incorporated into the United States through coercive systems of labor that do not recognize family rights. As Bonnie Thornton Dill (1988), Evelyn Nakano Glenn (1986), and others have pointed out, slavery and contract labor systems were organized to maximize economic productivity and offered few supports to sustain family life. The job characteristics of paid domestic work, especially live-in work, virtually impose transnational motherhood for many Mexican and Central American women who have children of their own.

The ties of transnational motherhood suggest simultaneously the relative permeability of borders, as witnessed by the maintenance of family ties and the new meanings of motherhood, and the impermeability of nation-state borders. Ironically, just at the moment when free trade proponents and pundits celebrate globalization and transnationalism, and when "borderlands" and "border cross-ings" have become the metaphors of preference for describing a mind-boggling range of conditions, nation-state borders prove to be very real obstacles for many Mexican and Central American women who work in the United States and who, given the appropriate circumstances, wish to be with their children. While de-manding the right for women workers to live with their children may provoke cri-tiques of sentimentality, essentialism, and the glorification of motherhood, de-manding the right for women workers to choose their own motherhood arrangements would be the beginning of truly just family and work policies, poli-cies that address not only inequalities of gender but also inequalities of race, class, and citizenship status.

1. In November 1994, California voters passed Proposition 187, which legislates the denial of public school education, health care, and other public benefits to undocumented immigrants and their children. Although currently held up in the courts, the facility with which Proposition 187 passed in the California ballots rejuvenated anti-immigrant politics at a national level. It opened the doors to new legislative measures in 1997 to deny public assistance to legal immigrants.

Blum, Linda, and Theresa Deussen. 1996. Negotiating independent motherhood: Working-class African American women talk about marriage and motherhood. *Gender & Society* 10:199–211.

Collins, Patricia Hill. 1991. *Black Feminist Thought: Knowledge, Consciousness, and the Politics of Empowerment.* New York: Routledge.

Dill, Bonnie Thornton. 1988. Our mothers' grief: Racial-ethnic women and the maintenance of families. *Journal of Family History* 13:415–31.

Glenn, Evelyn Nakano. 1986. *Issei, Nisei, Warbride: Three Generations of Japanese American Women in Domestic Service.* Philadelphia: Temple University Press.

Griswold del Castillo, Richard. 1984. *La Familia: Chicano Families in the Urban Southwest: 1848 to the Present.* Notre Dame, IN: University of Notre Dame Press.

Hondagneu-Sotelo, Pierrette. 1995. Women and children first: New directions in anti-immigrant politics. *Socialist Review* 25: 169–90.

Rollins, Judith. 1985. *Between Women: Domestics and Their Employers.* Philadelphia: Temple University Press.

Romero, Mary. 1992. *Maid in the U.S.A.* New York: Routledge.

Scheper-Hughes, Nancy. 1992. *Death Without Weeping: The Violence of Everyday Life in Brazil.* Berkeley: University of California Press.

Segura, Denise A., and Jennifer L. Pierce. 1993. Chicano Family Structure and Gender Personality: Chodorow, Familism, and Psychoanalytic Sociology Revisited. *Signs: Journal of Women in Culture and Society* 19:62–79.

Skolnick, Arlene S. 1991. *Embattled Paradise: The American Family in an Age of Uncertainty.* New York: Basic Books.

Stacey, Judith. 1996. *In the Name of the Family: Rethinking Family Values in the Postmodern Age.* Boston: Beacon.

Wrigley, Julie. 1995. *Other People's Children.* New York: Basic Books.

21 | MAID OR MADAM? FILIPINA MIGRANT WORKERS AND THE CONTINUITY OF DOMESTIC LABOR

Pei-Chia Lan

This article examines the complexity of feminized domestic labor in the context of global migration. Pei-Chia Lan views unpaid household labor and paid domestic work not as dichotomous categories but as structural continuities across the public and private spheres. Based on a qualitative study of Filipina migrant domestic workers in Taiwan, Lan demonstrates how women travel through the maid/madam boundary—housewives in home countries become breadwinners by doing domestic work overseas.

Recently, feminist scholars have paid attention to the gendered division of housework and domestic employment across class and racial lines. Yet as Mary Romero (1992) has pointed out, these studies are still divided into two distinct groups: Most studies of unpaid housework address only white, middle-class women, whereas the literature on domestic service is generally about women of color. To separate these two topics ignores their articulation and embeddedness. The gender battle over housework at home is influenced by the availability of domestic service in the market; those who offer domestic service are often wives and mothers who take care of their own families and households as well. A flawed dichotomy between the terms "maid" and "madam"[1] blinds us to women's multiple roles and fluid trajectories. To explore women's agency in facing the complex organization of domestic labor, we need new ways of conceptualizing domestic labor that "transcend the constructed oppositions of public-private and labor-love" (Glenn 1994, 16).

To fill in this theoretical gap, I view unpaid household labor and paid domestic work not as separate entities in an exclusive dichotomy but as structural continuities across the public/private divide. I develop the concept of the continuity of domestic labor to describe the feminization of domestic labor as multiple forms of labor done by women in both the public and private spheres. These labor activities, situated in different circumstances, are associated with shifting meanings (money/love) and fluid boundaries (maid/madam). I will elaborate this concept using the life experiences of Filipina migrant domestic workers in Taiwan. Some of these workers are housewives in the Philippines, but they, as overseas maids, become breadwinners, transnational mothers, and even domestic employers. . . . The gendered assignment of domestic labor has channeled these women's life chances in both the family and market and in the local as well as in the global context.

THE CONTINUITY OF DOMESTIC LABOR

Domestic labor, which refers to the labor activities that sustain the daily maintenance of a household, is accomplished by a variety of agents, with multiple formats, and in different settings. Family members, mostly women, carry out some household chores and caring labor themselves while transferring other parts of domestic labor to the market economy. For example, people purchase prepared-to-cook foods and mass-produced clothes, and they hire commercial services for duties like child care, cleaning, and gardening. These various arrangements of domestic labor are associated with different forms of compensation. Unpaid labor of female kin is considered a labor of love whose emotional value is related to the ideals of womanhood, such as the cult of domesticity and intensive motherhood among white middle-class Americans (Hays 1996; Palmer 1989). In contrast, the value of domestic service done by nonfamily workers, predominantly minority women, is redeemed through wages. . . .

I develop the concept of the continuity of domestic labor to describe the affinity between unpaid household labor and waged domestic labor—both are feminized work attached with moral merits and yet undervalued in cash. This concept especially sheds light on the life experiences of migrant domestic workers, who are situated in multiple, sometimes contradictory, locations. For them, taking care of the employer's family and taking care of their own family are interdependent activities, and the boundary between madam and maid is fluctuating and permeable. . . . Migrant women sell their domestic labor in the market but remain burdened with the gendered responsibilities in their own families. Although they consistently serve as providers of caring labor to others (their family as well as the employer), these labor activities are nevertheless conducted in segmented spatial settings. In reality, they experience a relation of conflict or disarticulation between these two simultaneous roles. While migrant women stay overseas to assist in the maintenance of another family, those who are mothers have to neglect their own children left behind, and those who are single sacrifice the prospect of starting their own families.

In this article, I illustrate the idea of the continuity of domestic labor with the case of Filipina migrant domestic workers in Taiwan. . . . I ask the following questions: How does the structural continuity between unpaid domestic labor and paid domestic work affect the life trajectories of these women? How do they attempt to maintain or establish their own families while working overseas to take care of others' families? How do they define their womanhood by negotiating the forms and meanings of their domestic labor? Taiwan's government opened the gate to migrant domestic workers beginning in the early 1990s, and since then, it has become a major receiving country in Asia. The government's policy is presented as a solution to the growing demands for housekeeping and care services among the expanding nuclear households and aging population in contemporary Taiwan. Despite employer qualifications being highly regulated under a quota system, the number of Taiwanese households employing migrant domestic workers has rapidly increased within a decade. Currently, more than 110,000 foreigners are legally employed as domestic helpers or caretakers in this country. Ninety percent of them are women from the Philippines and Indonesia, and the rest are from Thailand and Vietnam (Council of Labor Affairs 2002).

My research focuses on migrant domestic workers from the Philippines, which is now the world's second largest labor-exporting country (Asian Migrant Centre 2000). Filipino migrants possess a competitive advantage in the global labor market due to their adequate education and English proficiency. Their predominant destinations have recently switched from North America and Europe to the Middle East and East Asia. Taiwan has now become the fourth major host country, after Saudi Arabia, Hong Kong, and Japan. Domestic workers are a major part of the migrant labor force from the Philippines. Currently, more than half of Filipina overseas workers are placed in service occupations, mainly as cleaners, caretakers, and domestic helpers (National Statistics Office 2002).

This article is based on ethnographic data and in-depth interviews collected between July 1998 and July 1999. . . . To supplement my fieldwork in Taiwan, I made two trips to the Philippines, one in April 1999 and one in February 2002. . . . Among the fifty-six informants, fifty workers were documented, and six were undocumented. The majority (thirty-two) were in their 30s, while fifteen were in their 20s and nine were in their 40s. Their marriage status varied: twenty-three were single, eighteen were married, and fifteen were separated or widowed. One-third of my informants had college degrees, another third received some college education, and the rest were high school graduates. All interviews were done in English, and all the names used in this article are pseudonyms. . . .

Despite the fact that a substantial number of married women hold waged jobs in the Philippines, the ideal Filipino family consists of a male breadwinner and a female housekeeper, and housework and child care are predominantly considered women's duties (Go 1993). The cultural heritages of the Spanish and American co-lonial regimes have inscribed male-centered gender relations that remain influen-tial today (Illo 1995). Paradoxically, the patriarchal logic that governs an unequal division of household labor has created a niche for Filipina women in the global la-bor market. Women have even more advantages over their husbands in seeking jobs overseas. Most Filipino families in my study went through a similar migration pattern: During the 1980s, the husband left the wife and children at home to work in the Middle East. In the 1990s, it became the wife's turn to work abroad, and the husband stayed in the Philippines with the children. This transition happened due to the decline of male-oriented construction and manufacturing jobs in the Middle East during and after the Gulf War, in contrast to the growing demands for domestic workers in other host countries (Tarcoll 1996). . . .

While Filipina migrant workers are mothering others' children overseas, who is taking care of their children? Many rely on grandmothers, aunts, sisters, and other female kin to be substitute mothers; in some cases, the husbands quit their jobs and become full-time homemakers. There are also quite a few migrant mothers who seek non-family members to care for their children. Some consider hired help a better solution than kin caretakers as they find it emotionally difficult to evaluate or criticize the labor performance of relatives. Moreover, kin caregivers are not necessarily cheaper than waged workers because migrant parents are obli-gated to provide relatives with financial return under the cultural norm of *utang na loob* (debts of gratitude). These migrant domestic workers then become remote madams who hire local women to take care of their families while they are main-taining other households overseas. . . .

During interviews, several Filipina migrant domestic workers said to me, in a proud or embarrassed tone, "You know, I have a maid in the Philippines!" One of them is Christina, a college graduate and a former teacher. She hired a live-in domestic to take care of her children while she was working in Taiwan. Despite holding a similar occupation now, Christina drew a clear distinction between herself and her maid: "My sister was laughing, 'You have a maid in the Philippines, but you are a maid in Taiwan!' I said, 'It's different. They are under-educated. Not everyone can work abroad. You have to be very serious, very determined.'"

Migrant domestic workers' ambivalent status, being an overseas maid yet a re-mote madam, indicates their intermediate status in the multitiered "international division of reproductive labor" (Parreñas 2001, 72). On the top tier are middle- and upper-class women in advanced economies who hire migrant workers to mother their children; on the bottom are local women who pick up domestic duties transferred from migrant workers in the middle tier. Other studies have confirmed that the migratory flows from the Philippines are selective: The very poor and chronically unemployed seldom emigrate. The transnational recruitment process has a preference for applicants with high education, skills, working experience, ambition, and economic capital (Alegado 1992). Local domestic helpers are the women who possess less economic and cultural capital; they either are not sufficiently qualified or cannot afford the costs of seeking employment outside of the Philippines.

Migrant mothers received enhanced monetary value for their labor due to higher wage levels in foreign countries; their pecuniary gains enable them to transfer their household labor to poorer women in the Philippines. Becoming a madam at home marks their upgraded social status among village fellows and also brings in psychological compensation for migrants who suffer from class downgrading while working overseas as a maid. To some degree, the feminization of domestic labor has created opportunities for migrant women to improve their life chances, but for local helpers, domestic work remains a dead-end job with little economic value and social recognition.

Still, neither the monetary gains nor the social mobility acquired by migrant mothers cancels out their emotional costs in family separation. Their concurrent duties of unpaid motherhood and surrogate motherhood are segmented by geographic borders. Given the physical distance that hinders migrant mothers from performing their labor of love for their children, migrant mothers now display their love with letters, phone calls, and the money they earn in overseas domestic work. Previous studies have portrayed transnational motherhood with practices like sending children to private schools, purchasing expensive gifts, and remitting generous allowances (Hondagneu-Sotelo and Avila 1997 [see Chapter 20 in this book]; Parreñas 2001). Similarly, migrant mothers in Taiwan rely on the flow of remittances and packages to maintain emotional bonds on the basis of material dependency.

To equate love with money is fuzzy math, especially when one is faced with a shortage of cash. Evelyn, a single mother in her early 40s, has been doing part-time cleaning jobs after "running away"[2] from her contract employer five years ago. Since then, she has not been able to visit her two children in the Philippines. Recently, she was diagnosed with a tumor but has no insurance to pay for further treatment. This physical condition has forced her to reduce her workload as well as the remittances sent to her children. Before I departed for my fieldtrip to the Philippines in 1999, Evelyn excitedly told me, "Maybe you can meet my children there!" During my stay in Manila, I did not get any messages from Evelyn's children but received a phone call from Evelyn one night. She was weeping on the phone:

> My children never called you, right? You know what day is today? It's Mother's Day! They don't remember this day or even my birthday! I am very sad, so I called you in the Philippines. I am not going to send them any more money. I'll see if they will think of me when they have no money.

Evelyn talked about her children in an earlier interview:

> *Evelyn*: I feel very upset about my children. They don't talk to me. This one . . .
> I left her studying in college, but now she got married and has a son already. . . .
> She never told me she got a [boy]friend! She never told me.
>
> *Author*: Why don't they talk to you anymore? Are they mad at you or something?
>
> *Evelyn*: I don't know. . . . Maybe because I don't send them money anymore. . . .
> I am sacrificing my life for *them*! I never never get involved with a man. I need a
> companion also, but I never think of that. I think only of my family. I don't want
> them to become like me. I am suffering for my marriage. But my children, they
> don't understand me. Sometimes I have no job! I have no money to give to my
> landlord. Sometimes I am hungry. I have no food. . . . I never ask them for
> help. . . .

Deeply hurt by her children's suspicion that she had abandoned the family to enjoy life overseas, Evelyn defended herself by underscoring her practices of virtuous womanhood ("I never get involved with a man") and selfless motherhood ("I am sacrificing my life for them"). These practices accord with the cultural prescription of ideal womanhood in the Philippines—*mahinhin* (demure, virtuous, pious, or modest)—embodied by the Virgin Mary as well as the noble figures of Filipinas like the folklore character Maria Clara or the national mother Corazon Aquino (Siapno 1995). Despite Evelyn's efforts to be a virtuous transnational mother, over time, the physical separation obstructed her emotional connections with her children, and her illness hampered her ability to mother them with flows of remittances.

As ties with their children back home are loosening, migrant mothers may find emotional rewards in the job of surrogate motherhood. Scholars have named this situation "diverted mothering" (Wong 1994) or "displaced mothering" (Parreñas 2000 [see Chapter 4 in this book]). Rutchelle, a Filipina mother of two in her 30s, has been working for a Taiwanese household for more than two years. In the church, I frequently saw her along with two Taiwanese children, one girl of five and one boy of four. I assumed that their parents were busy at work, but Rutchelle corrected me: "No, the parents are at home. But the children want to be with me." I asked the boy, Tommy, what his parents were doing that day. He replied, "They're sleeping. Mommy was drinking last night." Rutchelle shook her head and said, "I don't understand why they sleep so much."

Migrant caregivers are often critical of what they perceive as their employers' neglectful and substandard parenting (Hondagneu-Sotelo and Avila 1997, 565). Several Filipina workers told me, with pride or excitement, about their emotional closeness to the children under their care. They blame their Taiwanese employers for spoiling or neglecting their children: "Their parents are too busy. They don't have time to talk to the children." A Filipina worker quoted what the children said to her at the end of her contract: "We don't want to stay here. We want to go to the Philippines with you!" By "being motherly" to the employers' children, migrant caregivers gain self-esteem in negotiating their identities vis-à-vis their employers (Yeoh and Huang 1999, 297). Such evidence that their employers' children prefer them to their biological mothers confirms migrants' motherly capabilities despite the fact that they have left their own children to work as well.

Migrant caregivers are trapped in an emotional predicament at work: They have to assure their madams that their temporary presence will not shake the status of biological mothers, but they also feel traumatized if their emotional ties with the employers' children are only ephemeral. For instance, Rutchelle tried to comfort Tommy's mother, who sometimes feels jealous about the children's attachment to the migrant nanny: "I told her it's OK. I am only a housekeeper. I am here only temporary. The children have two Filipinas before. They forgot them. Helen, the last one, my boss showed him [Tommy] the picture. He doesn't know her." I checked with Tommy, asking, "Who is Helen?" Indeed, he shook his head. I joked with Tommy, "Helen would be upset if she knew you don't remember her." Rutchelle then grabbed the boy in her arms, saying with confidence, "But they will remember me forever!"

The establishment of emotional bonds with the children under their care is a double-edged sword for migrant caretakers. It provides them with some emotional rewards and social recognition for this undervalued carework, but it may also intensify their pain of separation from their own families and cause them additional emotional loss on termination of the job contract (Nelson 1990; Wrigley 1995). In addition, the emphasis on the emotional value in surrogate motherhood sometimes results in a reduction of monetary compensation received by careworkers. Some employers manipulate workers' attachment to the employers' children to extract additional unpaid labor, such as asking the workers to accompany the children on their days off or to give up annual vacations for the sake of the children.

This section has presented multiple roles taken by migrant mothers that cover a wide range of paid and unpaid domestic labor: They are remote madams who hire local helpers at home, they are transnational mothers who manage to deliver their love through overseas remittances, and they are substitute mothers who connect to the employers' children with a cash nexus as well as emotional ties. In all these circumstances, migrant mothers are engaged in a continual bargaining for money and love associated with their paid and unpaid mothering work. They have to pay certain emotional and monetary costs to be a good mother, either a transnational or a substitute one.

In this article, I have sought to unravel the complexity of gendered domestic labor in the context of global migration. The feminization of domestic labor channels women's similar life chances in the family as well as the market. Individual women move across multiple positions involving different forms of domestic labor that are all defined as women's work. Taking on domestic work, a feminized occupation in both the local and global labor market, migrant women become transnational breadwinners but remain burdened by their gendered duties as mothers and wives back home. I underscore the continuity between household labor and waged domestic work to break down a dichotomous categorization between maid and madam. In actuality, women may shift between the status of maid and madam or occupy both positions at the same time.

1. The term "madam," a polite form of address to a woman, implies a proper notion of femininity with a certain class connotation. It is no coincidence that servants and maids usually call their female masters/employers "madam/mum." In this article, I use the term "madam" to refer to housewives as well as domestic employers.

2. Migrant workers in Taiwan are allowed to work only up to six years for the employer specified in the recruitment contract. Transfers of employers are only possible in exceptional conditions such as the death of care recipients. Both Taiwanese and migrants use the term "runaway" to describe those workers who disappear from their contract employers to work without legal documents.

REFERENCES

Alegado, Dean Tiburcio. 1992. The political economy of international labor migration from the Philippines. Ph.D. diss., University of Hawaii, Manoa.

Asian Migrant Centre. 2000. *Asian migrant yearbook: Migration facts, analysis and issues in 1999.* Hong Kong: Asian Migrant Centre Ltd.

Council of Labor Affairs. 2002. *Monthly bulletin of labor statistics.* March. Taipei, Taiwan: Executive Yuan, Republic of China.

Glenn, Evelyn Nakano. 1994. Social constructions of mothering: A thematic overview. In *Mothering: Ideology, experience, and agency,* edited by Evelyn Nakano Glenn, Grace Chang, and Linda Rennie Forcey. New York: Routledge.

Go, Stella. 1993. *The Filipino family in the eighties.* Manila, Philippines: Social Development Research Center, De La Salle University.

Hays, Sharon. 1996. *The cultural constructions of motherhood.* New Haven, CT: Yale University Press.

Hondagneu-Sotelo, Pierrette, and Ernestine Avila. 1997. "I'm here, but I'm there": The meanings of Latina transnational motherhood. *Gender & Society* 11 (5): 548–71.

Illo, Jean Frances. 1995. Redefining the Maybahay or housewife: Reflections on the nature of women's work in the Philippines. In *"Male" and "female" in developing Southeast Asia,* edited by Wazir Jahan Kavim. Oxford, UK: Berg.

National Statistics Office. 2002. Press release of the 2001 survey on overseas Filipinos (SOF). Manila: National Statistics Office, the Philippine Government. Retrieved 24 September 2002 from http://www.census.gov.ph/data/pressrelease.

Nelson, Margaret K. 1990. *Negotiated care: The experiences of family day care providers.* Philadelphia: Temple University Press.

Palmer, Phyllis. 1989. *Domesticity and dirt: Housewives and domestic servants in the United States, 1920–1940s.* Philadelphia: Temple University Press.

Parreñas, Rhacel. 2000. Migrant Filipina domestic workers and the international division of reproductive labor. *Gender & Society* 14 (4): 560–80.

———. 2001. *Servants of globalization: Women, migration and domestic work.* Stanford, CA: Stanford University Press.

Romero, Mary. 1992. *Maid in the U.S.A.* New York: Routledge.

Siapno, Jacqueline. 1995. Alternative Filipina heroines: Contested tropes in leftist feminisms. In *Bewitching women, pious men: Gender and body politics in*

Southeast Asia, edited by Aihwa Ong and Michael G. Peletz. Berkeley: University of California Press.

Tarcoll, Cecilla. 1996. Migrating "for the sake of the family?" Gender, life course and intra-household relations among Filipino migrants in Rome. *Philippine Sociological Review* 44 (1–4): 12–32.

Wong, Sau-Ling. 1994. Diverted mothering: Representations of caregivers of color in the age of "multiculturalism." In *Mothering: Ideology, experience, and agency*, edited by Evelyn Nakano Glenn, Grace Chang, and Linda Rennie Forcey. New York: Routledge.

Wrigley, Julia. 1995. *Other people's children: An intimate account of the dilemmas facing middle-class parents and the women they hire to raise their children.* New York: Basic Books.

Yeoh, Branda S., and Shirlena Huang. 1999. Singapore women and foreign domestic workers: Negotiating domestic work and motherhood. In *Gender, migration and domestic service*, edited by Janet Henshall Momsen. New York: Routledge.

"WOMEN HAVE NO TRIBE": CONNECTING CAREWORK, GENDER, AND MIGRATION IN AN ERA OF HIV/AIDS IN BOTSWANA

Rebecca Upton

In this article, Rebecca Upton highlights the role of gender in the HIV/AIDS epidemic in Botswana, the crisis of care it has unleashed, and the failure of current efforts to stem the rise of HIV infection in the country. Botswana currently has one of the highest HIV infection rates in the world. Deaths among working-age adults have orphaned large numbers of children, producing a crisis of care and undermining a traditional fosterage system that previously helped to support women. Women bear the burdens of the increasing care of dependent children due to cultural patterns in which they remain in villages and bear and raise children while men migrate. Unfortunately, these cultural and deeply personal dimensions in the patterns of men's migration and women's reproduction are too often ignored in current efforts to respond to the spread of HIV/AIDS.

In Botswana, there is an active, public campaign sponsored by the government and known as the ABCs, intended to prevent and stop the current rapid spread of the HIV virus. "Abstain, Be faithful, and Condomise!" are ubiquitous admonishments—printed on billboards, distributed on pamphlets, and broadcast on the radio in this Southern African country. Despite this seemingly widespread attention, the HIV rates continue to rise, and more and more young adults are dying as a result of the epidemic. In addition, cultural understandings about reproductive health as well as historical patterns of migration and child care result in Tswana women's shouldering the greatest burden of caregiving in the era of AIDS in Botswana. Migration is a central aspect of male gender identity and social support in Tswana communities, while reproduction is key in the construction of women's gender identity. These two facets intersect in the changing nature of care for children in the AIDS era.

A historically stable and democratic government and a relatively strong economy have not protected Botswana from some of the highest incidence and prevalence rates of HIV/AIDS infection worldwide. Clinics, hospitals, and the Ministry of Health estimate that approximately one in five individuals is infected (Joint United Nations Programme on HIV/AIDS 2000; Ministry of Finance and

Development Planning 1997), although estimates of one in three in the region are not unrealistic. Without exception, all of the women in my study had a relative or close friend who had died of the HIV/AIDS virus, often a result of a symptomatic illness such as tuberculosis or pneumonia. The increasing death rates as a result of HIV-related illness was a common topic of conversation among women in rural villages as the numbers and the visibility of both those with AIDS and their orphans in need of care increased.

The structures of care in Botswana have changed as a result of these increasing HIV infection rates. Historically, it was not unusual for an older woman to foster children in Botswana (Burman 1996). A daughter would send her children to her mother and even on occasion to the mother of the child's father to provide household assistance and other tasks. The fosterage system provided both children and women with structures of support grounded in reciprocity. Women would receive assistance with household tasks, and children would receive care and training. Today, however, with increasing deaths due to the HIV/AIDS epidemic, greater numbers of children are living with and being supported by women relatives. The fosterage system remains in place but is being stretched to the limit as there are greater numbers of children and fewer older women and resources to take care of them. The crisis of HIV care has resulted in shifts in responsibilities among women and in their available strategies for care and support. The fosterage system has changed from a reciprocal relationship to one where the purpose is largely the care of AIDS orphans.

In this article, I draw on the individual story of Mma Bogadi, a 34-year-old Tswana woman, to illustrate how the broader aspects of migration and reproduction intersect in individual attempts to provide care in the context of HIV. Mma Bogadi, whose name translates as "mother of Bogadi," is one of the women who is a primary caregiver for several children and onto whom these responsibilities have shifted as a result of the HIV epidemic. Mma Bogadi's particular experiences reflect those of many women and highlight some of the most pressing changes in carework in the country. The majority (more than two-thirds) of the women I spoke with were taking care of several children who were not their own biological children, had partners engaged in migration, and were responsible for supporting households. Their lives and that of Mma Bogadi illustrate how the specific issues of migration, reproduction, and the HIV crisis at this individual level are connected to broader issues of gender and carework.

Mma Bogadi, who lives in a rural area with limited amenities, has three children of her own but now cares for her late niece's two children as well. She provides them with clothing, food, and school fees and worries about their health given her niece's death from tuberculosis, a clear indication to Mma Bogadi that her niece was HIV positive. The costs of caring for these children are mounting, and rather than the children assisting her in the household, she worries about her resources and abilities to provide for them. Sitting in her three-room cement block home in a rural village in Northern Botswana, Mma Bogadi watches the five young children living in her household as she works on a portable sewing machine, her main source of income. She tells me that "when you follow the ABCs, you aren't thinking about what will happen if you have to take care of someone else's children." As she said, "Before you might have one, maybe two children sent to you, they would help you out. . . . Today, you are the ones helping them, and it is not just two—you might get five that you have to support. . . ."

Networks and systems of support have shifted, and even seemingly reversed, as a result of the HIV/AIDS health crisis. Previously, children would be sent to older women for support, and those women could rely on some remittances and financial support from men migrants, usually their sons and husbands. These remittances varied in amount according to what men could or would send back but in general accounted for less than half of a woman's source of income. As a result of illness, remittances have become more uncommon, and fewer men are actually able to support family members; thus, women today find themselves the primary and unpaid caregivers for children of AIDS victims.

Despite some remittances, support of children by men has historically been rare among the Tswana. Men were the ones primarily involved in migration processes throughout Southern Africa and, as a result, were not the main caregivers in the home. It is important in the cultural construction of men's identity for them to say that in addition to migrating, they have fathered a child; however, financial support and acknowledgment by men for those children has been difficult to obtain for the majority of women in the country (Garey and Townsend 1996; Molokomme 1991).

Mma Bogadi's daughter Onalena has two children whom she raises on her own. She explained, "I worry about what will happen to me, who will care for my children if anything was to happen, my mother is already so overwhelmed"; she has begun to pursue other avenues for child maintenance to receive more money for the family. She said, "Everything has changed. Of course, you would care for your children, you want children, but now you have to think about who else might care for them." Mma Modise, 49 and caring for three grandchildren and two others from her brother's family, recalled the significance of migration in the construction of men's identity and its interconnectedness with the contemporary HIV/AIDS epidemic. She said,

> It was common for men to send back money to women, at least something. . . . Today, things have changed and [women] have to look out for themselves, work to provide for all of these children because the men who have left, they may have families [elsewhere] and maybe they just die.

For Mma Bogadi, Onalena, and others, the lived experience of those changes is directly related to the cultural significance of and interconnectedness between systems of migration and reproduction. Previously unreliable remittances from men are even more unreliable as HIV/AIDS death rates increase and women are faced with greater numbers of children to support. . . .

While child fosterage has long been a part of Tswana culture, so too has the phenomenon of migration, both internal and transnational to other parts of Southern Africa. During much of the latter half of the twentieth century, men of reproductive age (approximately 75 percent of men aged 18 to 40) migrated to other parts of Botswana or to South Africa as part of the diamond and coal mining industries. In addition, men and boys were expected to travel to and maintain the cattle kraals outside of villages and towns. Participation in migration, both within the country and to other parts of the region, was often an important part of the life cycle for men, part of the definition of personhood and often entailing migrating for several years at a time before returning home.

While participation in migration processes is central to men's identity, one result is that women are rendered socially invisible. Ironically and even illogically, because women are the primary caregivers, partly as a result of this male out migration, there is a Tswana proverb that states that "women have no tribe." This negates any recognition that women and their young children compose the majority of households[1] and maintain community identity. *Mosadi*, or woman, literally translates as one who stays or remains. By extension, those who stay or remain have no tribe, and by definition, tribes or groups of people in Botswana were nomadic and migration was normative. But as is evident with the advent of the contemporary HIV/AIDS crisis, it has become increasingly the case that those who have remained, the women who are the primary caregivers, are the ones who are responsible for Tswana communities throughout the country. The invisibility of women as reflected in the proverb points to a pervasive cultural gender hierarchy where women are seen as less significant. The advent of the HIV/AIDS crisis, however, shifted greater burdens of care onto women and reinforced many of these gender inequalities (Baylies and Bujra 2000). . . .

For men who migrate . . . the risk of HIV infection and transmission is high, and eventually, by extension, the risk to women is high. While this is certainly not a new observation, what is significant is that many of the educational materials aimed at HIV/AIDS prevention may not be reaching these men on the move or adequately addressing the intertwined cultural imperatives for men and women to have children. The questions become, Who are the ABCs aimed at? How culturally appropriate are they if the impetus to have a child to be considered an adult person remains socially significant? How are they to be acted on if condomizing, while intended to protect one from illness, may in fact be understood as contributing directly to it?. . .

Public and global attention to the HIV/AIDS crisis in Botswana is high and has rapidly increased in recent years as both governmental and international aid agencies have donated large sums of money to increasing awareness and family planning programs.[2] Much of the foci of these initiatives center on educating youth about HIV and reinforcing the need to use condoms and other barrier methods of protection. The problem of AIDS in Botswana is increasingly visible, yet for many Tswana individuals, AIDS remains a "radio disease," something ubiquitous in advertising ("Everyone knows what the ABCs are; you even hear about on the radio," Onalena says) but not necessarily in the forefront of individual practices.

Government and international aid agencies recognize the growing HIV/AIDS crisis with initiatives aimed at educating people about the disease and the importance of using condoms. However, no agency has recognized the actual crisis of care and the role of women's caregiving as key elements in this context. One facet of the growing crisis of care that has garnered public awareness as a result of the AIDS epidemic is the care of dependent children. In addition to the active, visible campaigns supported by the government for education about HIV/AIDS, orphanages, largely supported by international religious organizations have sprung up in answer to this issue. In Mma Bogadi's village, for example, the Lutheran church has established an orphanage, in some sense formalizing the fosterage system in the AIDS era and attempting to address the problem of these dependent children. Less attention is given to the plight of the women who are actually caring for these children and the cultural factors that have contributed to the rise of this crisis of care. Caring for AIDS orphans is just one aspect of the growing crisis, one that highlights gender inequalities and shifting responsibilities for care.

The cultural allegation that women have no tribe reflects a larger structure of gender inequality in Botswana. This gender hierarchy, which has rendered women socially invisible despite their maintenance of children, has become reinforced in the recent HIV/AIDS era. By focusing on preventing further infection, visible, educational campaigns that emphasize abstinence, being faithful, and condomizing ignore the less visible, cultural, and gendered significance of women's reproduction and the role of men's migration in Tswana society. Both these strategies place women at increased risk for HIV infection.

In addition, while traditional fosterage systems afforded both women and children structures of support, in an era of increasing HIV infections, those systems have become undermined, and women now shoulder the greatest responsibilities in caring for the increasing numbers of children and individuals affected by the HIV/AIDS epidemic. With respect to the Tswana proverb, in the face of the current epidemic women have even less of a tribe as their health and systems of support diminish. As the current crisis of care in Botswana continues to escalate, gender and carework, as they are related to cultural systems of migration and identity, are changing. Only through culturally appropriate means of prevention, however, where women's roles as caregivers and the centrality of reproduction are recognized in context, will the HIV/AIDS crisis begin to be successfully redressed.

1. The Botswana government and the National Development Plan estimate that approximately 44 percent of households are headed by women.

2. The Botswana government has created an AIDS unit within the Ministry of Health, and agencies such as Joint United Nations Programme on HIV/AIDS, the World Health Organization, the Centers for Disease Control, and others have invested in AIDS prevention programs throughout the country. Most recently, the Bill and Melinda Gates Foundation has contributed enormous amounts of money to the country in an effort to stem the spread of, and educate people about, HIV.

REFERENCES

Baylies, Carolyn, and Janet Bujra. 2000. AIDS, sexuality and gender in Africa. London: Routledge.

Burman, Sandra. 1996. Intergenerational family care: Legacy of the past, implications for the future. *Journal of Southern African Studies* 22 (4): 585–98.

Garey, Anita Ilta, and Nicholas Townsend. 1996. Kinship, courtship and child maintenance law in Botswana. *Journal of Family and Economic Issues* 17 (2): 189–203.

Joint United Nations Programme on HIV/AIDS/World Health Organization. 2000. UNAIDS/WHO epidemiological fact sheet update. New York: United Nations.

Ministry of Finance and Development Planning, Central Statistics Office. 1997. National development plan VIII. 1997/8–2002/03. Gaborone, Botswana: Government Printer.

Molokomme, A. 1991. Children of the fence: The maintenance of extra-marital children under law and practice in Botswana. Research report no. 46. Leiden, the Netherlands: African Studies Centre.

IV VALUING CAREWORK THROUGH POLICY AND CULTURE: COMMUNITIES, STATES, AND SUPRANATIONAL INSTITUTIONS

23 | VALUING CAREWORK THROUGH POLICY AND CULTURE: COMMUNITIES, STATES, AND SUPRANATIONAL INSTITUTIONS

In Part 4 we shift focus to examine carework in the context of communities, nations, and supranational policymaking bodies such as the United Nations and the European Union. As we have demonstrated throughout this book, the policy influence of supranational organizations is growing. We think it important to consider how these developments affect national sovereignty and the ability of single states to resist global policy trends to which they are opposed, to recognize and compensate carework, and to pursue the goal of what Helga Hernes (see Chapter 25) has called a "woman-friendly state." We are interested in how various levels of policy regimes and institutional arrangements orchestrate carework, and how this, in turn, impacts gender relations. Of particular concern is how the policies of individual states interface with the policies of supranational organizations, and the consequences when these policy orientations either conflict or reinforce each other. Do these dynamics alter gender relations? What effects will changes in policy regimes have on the empowerment of women and ethnic minorities? What will happen to the gender and family-friendly policy agendas toward which some European welfare states have been moving? What are the chances for a "culture of care" (see Hernes) or a "universal caregiver" model for the gender division of labor (see Fraser, Chapter 24) to be embedded in future policies of developing and newly democratic states?

The readings we selected for Part 4 introduce a rich array of concepts, theoretical issues, and intriguing questions to help us explore carework in this broader context (see Fraser, Hernes, and Herd and Harrington Meyer). The readings also include excerpts from several empirical studies presenting research conducted in

Azerbaijan (Najafizadeh), Bangladesh (Anwary), as well as European and other advanced economy countries (Christopherson and Valiente). These examples help to link the concepts and issues presented in this part of the book to everyday life in locations around the globe.

Together, these selections accomplish three primary objectives. First, they introduce the notion of "care of the community" and explore how this concept is distinct from the more common notion of carework as one-on-one support and assistance given to individuals and families. Care of the community, just like individually oriented forms of carework, is gendered activity that often supports hierarchal gender relations. Social policy both shapes and reflects cultural ideas about care. This observation leads us to our second objective in Part 4, which is to examine how community and individual forms of carework are interpreted, appreciated, and valued. The social valuation of carework involves the extent to which carework is seen as a responsibility or duty of citizenship, as well as the degree to which citizens are guaranteed having access to and receiving care when they need it. Another issue concerning the value of carework is whether it tends to be hidden within the private sphere of family life or whether it is publicly recognized as making a civic contribution to the well-being of communities and societies. Just as in other forms of work, long-standing historical and cultural interpretations affect how carework is valued and whether it is understood as paid or unpaid, private or public.

Our third objective is to examine the role of the state in adjudicating carework and the gender relations related to carework. A central purpose here is to show that social policy regimes play a fundamental role in setting the parameters within which men and women engage in paid and unpaid labor and negotiate their competing demands. We begin this discussion by considering the various policy alternatives for conceptualizing the gender division of labor with respect to carework. In particular, we are interested in the question of what constitutes an ideal solution for allocating carework and at the same time assuring gender equity. With these ideals in mind, we focus on existing state policies in relation to gender and carework. In addition, we shift attention beyond the state to consider how globalization is altering the autonomy of nations and how multinational governance bodies are assuming an increasingly important role in shaping carework and gender. As part of our consideration of this third objective, we examine current changes in state policies affecting carework and prospects for the immediate future.

If there are, in fact, multiple crises of care emerging globally that are profoundly changing gender relations throughout the world—as we have argued in this book—then a key question that remains concerns the role of governmental policies in these changes. Do such policies support or attempt to redirect these crises of care? What is the nature of the relationship between carework in the new world economy and the increasingly complex network of national and international governance structures that together wield considerable global influence and decision-making authority? Will the forces of exploitation in paid carework that are disproportionately directed toward disadvantaged groups—low wages, risky and overly demanding work conditions, and few civil and economic rights for migrants—receive carte blanche in multinational policy regimes? Or, will supranational structures take responsibility for ensuring basic levels of social welfare and social care to these workers, and in turn extend social citizenship across borders? What are the implications of these developments for gender equity and for the empowerment of women?

CARE OF THE COMMUNITY

Community care, as individual carework, is more likely provided by women than men, especially when it is unpaid (Cancian and Oliker 2000). In recent years, this gender gap has narrowed as women's time has become more limited due to their increasing participation in the labor force (Stolle and Lewis 2002). Nonetheless, U.S. women continue to provide and are still expected to provide considerable community carework in addition to their "double shift" as employed workers and as those primarily responsible for household work and family care. Despite the triple burden of home, job, and community care, women are often targeted for blame as the level of community volunteering and civic engagement decline:

> Schools, churches, and local charities still recruit women for volunteer caring work and do not often recruit men. Peer into elementary school classrooms or church kitchens and you will still see mostly mothers or female parishioners, some dressed in their work clothes, tutoring children or donning aprons to prepare the food. Teachers and ministers send the calls for help out to "mothers," as though their time is more available than fathers' time. And, where these calls meet with too little success, disappointed organization members blame women's employment rather than employed fathers' lack of adaptation to new realities. . . .
> (Cancian and Oliker 2000)

Community care serves to reinforce gender inequality. This occurs in part because community carework, like one-on-one carework, is shaped by beliefs that women are "natural" caregivers (devoted, nurturing, empathetic, etc.), and because it occupies women in ways that limit their access to conventional sources of power and status. When women fulfill citizenship obligations through community volunteering and service, time and energy are diverted away from activities that otherwise might provide status and economic independence. A key dilemma for women has been that they are positively rewarded for doing socially beneficial work that ultimately reinforces their subordinate position in the gender hierarchy.

Global economic changes create new and unique contexts within which to examine the contradictions between community care and women's empowerment. Two of the excerpts included in Part 4 provide examples from the developing world where care needs are significant and neither state-sponsored nor market-based services are available or accessible. In these two very different countries, women joined together in voluntary nongovernmental organizations (NGOs) and responded directly to address key gaps in their respective countries' human services systems. Both examples also illustrate the critical role of community careworkers in countering ineffective state services. The neglect in Bangladesh is exacerbated by globalized employment patterns and also reflects historical and cultural gender bias; while in Azerbaijan, the lack of services could be attributed more to the effects of dramatic economic and social transitions combined with the effects of war. These examples draw attention to the particular difficulties of asking women in developing countries to add community care to a day already overloaded with both paid and unpaid labor.

In Azerbaijan, several nongovernmental women's advocacy organizations studied by Mehrangiz Najafizadeh have grown as a grassroots response led by women professionals to meet the multiple needs of Azeri women in the wake of the transition to democracy. As Najafizadeh points out, not only do these organizations care for the community by offering needed services, they also are attempting to protect the opportunities for women's empowerment by acting as a buffer against the spread of Islamic fundamentalism.

Afroza Anwary focuses on Bangladesh, where a voluntary organization of women's advocates rose up in the face of governmental neglect. Their activism drew international attention and assistance for the medical care needs of local women who had been victims of acid attacks. Her report draws attention to the connections between globalization and violence toward women and illustrates the agency and value of community carework through NGOs. Care of the community, her account suggests, can be carried out as a global effort. For an excellent discussion of such efforts among international women's organizations, see Valentine Moghadam's (2005) *Globalizing Women: Transnational Feminist Networks.*

CAREWORK AND THE CIVIC ENGAGEMENT DEBATE

In their excerpt, Pamela Herd and Madonna Harrington Meyer take up the relationship between carework, individuals, and the community, examining the meaning and value of carework within a sociohistorical and policy context. They question why community carework has been defined culturally and politically as civic activity, celebrated for contributing "social capital" toward the stability and well-being of the nation, while at the same time individual carework is taken for granted, its societal benefits disregarded. They offer a compelling case for rethinking our assumptions about civic engagement and its relationship to carework. In their view, "the daily physical and emotional labor of feeding and nurturing citizens" is itself a form of civic engagement because it enables citizens to exercise their rights and perform their civic responsibilities (see also Folbre, Chapter 16). As they point out, "Mothers often stay home cooking dinner and helping the children with their homework, while fathers, freshly fed and dressed, attend town finance meetings." Seen in this way, women's carework makes civic life possible.

While they acknowledge that family carework encroaches on the time available for community carework, Herd and Harrington Meyer argue that both are forms of civic engagement. Especially important in their argument is that family carework not be considered private activity, but rather be recognized as the way that many women (and some men) meet their citizenship obligations. This point is particularly relevant to the current debate among scholars mainly in the United States over the decline in civic engagement and the reasons for it.

At issue in this debate is the alleged differential decline in women's and men's participation in voluntary community organizations in Western countries. This decline is seen as lowering communities' "social capital" (Stolle and Lewis 2002). A loss in social capital, in turn, results in a myriad of social problems based on lack of trust and interpersonal reciprocity (Putnam 2000). At its core, declining social capital means community instability and disintegration (Coleman 1988). Gender and carework enter the picture because leading proponents of the declining social capital approach have implicated increases in dual-earner families and families headed by single mothers as the primary reasons why civic participation has decreased. According to theorists such as Putnam and Coleman, women do not have the time or energy for the triple demands of job, family care, and community participation, especially when caught in a single-parent family structure that itself erodes the formation of social capital.

Herd and Harrington Meyer suggest that women, far from causing the problem due to their increasing labor force participation, actually add to the level of civic activity through their unpaid carework. They argue that voluntary organizations provide services very similar to those provided by individual caregivers—for example, food, medical care, transportation, and interpersonal comfort. They ask a compelling question: how can a volunteer hospice worker be considered engaged in civic activity while a woman caring for her elderly aunt is not? The two authors offer a fresh point of view, highlighting the gendered assumptions built into the way that conventional scholars conceptualize and differentially value community versus individual forms of carework.

Herd and Harrington Meyer conclude by discussing the role of state policy in shaping the nature of carework. They hypothesize that state policies to help families balance work and family will, in turn, lead to increases in civic activity whether conducted inside or outside the family. For example, policies that encourage a more equitable distribution of carework between men and women will give women more time to become involved in politics and in civic organizations; policies that enable parents to better coordinate home and work responsibilities will increase time for both family and community carework; policies that increase compensation for paid carework and other undervalued jobs will help lift women and minorities out of poverty and allow them resources so that they can further increase their participation outside the home and workplace.

CAREWORK IN THE CONTEXT OF SOCIAL POLICIES AND WELFARE REGIMES

Perhaps the single most important contribution of the feminist literature on comparative welfare states—with the potential for similar import in the growing feminist literature on supranational governmental bodies—is the uncovering and problematizing of unpaid family carework. Nancy Fraser (see Chapter 24) discusses the need for a new model for the gender division of labor. She argues that the male breadwinner/female caregiver model is obsolete and that we must develop more equitable ways to distribute paid employment and unpaid carework between husbands and wives. Presenting and critically evaluating several models, Fraser helps us understand the assumptions that are embedded in social policy regimes and how these regimes, in turn, shape the nature of carework. Fraser identifies two approaches that she considers currently possible for a new gender division of labor—the "universal breadwinner" model (where both husband and wife are breadwinners and carework is purchased in the market) and the "caregiver parity" model (where men remain breadwinners and women receive compensation and societal benefits for carework). Neither model meets Fraser's criteria for gender equity and fairness, however, in part because neither adequately shifts responsibility for family carework from women to a more equitable arrangement. The caregiver parity approach better supports carework, yet at the same time fosters inequality by perpetuating women's lower incomes and social marginality. Fraser concludes by offering a third solution, centered on the idea that men and women should both be workers as well as carers. Her analysis helps us understand the connection between social policy and carework and clarifies how critical social policies can be in determining the nature of the work we do in our daily lives.

Fraser's analysis is theoretical; however, she cites Sweden as an example of a working social policy regime that presents "a good statement" of her model solution. We can see the principles of Fraser's "universal caregiver" solution in the following statement from the Swedish Institute (2004), "Swedish gender equality policy is fundamentally concerned with the ability of each individual to achieve economic independence through gainful employment. Just as important are measures to enable both women and men to combine jobs with parenthood . . . and participate in all aspects of community life according to their capabilities" (p. 2). Based on the fundamental premise that men and women should share both parenthood and employment and be relieved of major barriers to combining job, family, and community participation, Sweden has enacted a number of specific policies. For example, family care for infants and young children is supported by a universal government program of paid family leave that extends for nearly 16 months, compensated at 80 percent of qualifying income for 390 days and at $8.50/day[1] for the remaining 90 days. (Parents not employed prior to the birth receive approximately $21.50 a day for the first 390 days.) In a further effort to achieve gender equity there has been an increased policy emphasis in recent years to encourage fathers to spend more time with their children (Hobson 2001). Thus, current Swedish policy reserves 60 nontransferable parental leave days for the father and 60 for the mother, with the remaining days to be divided between the parents at their discretion. Fathers, in addition, are entitled to 10 days of leave when the child is born. These policies are based on the goal of shared parenting and carework between men and women.

Other policies are designed to help families coordinate jobs and family life as well. For example, parents of young children have the right to choose to work a six- as opposed to an eight-hour day; they are entitled to paid temporary leave to care for a sick child up to 60 days each year; and the government guarantees a place in preschool for all children ages 1–6 and after-school care for children ages 7–12. Swedish childcare is subsidized, based on the parents' income. Together, these policies create the financial and social conditions for parents to be both workers and carers, with their responsibilities divided within a framework of gender equity.

The examples underscore that time availability for daily tasks is a significant consequence of social policy. Though often unrecognized by the average citizen, government policies can either free parents from the time squeeze of combining both job and home responsibilities (through family-friendly labor policies and economic protection for family caregiving) or leave these conflicts untouched (by enacting policies that ignore family needs), forcing individuals and families to find ways to cope on their own. The fact that social policies arrange and shape time use in this way has been largely invisible to American scholars but constitutes a hall-mark of Scandinavian feminist theorizing of the welfare state. Helga Hernes, for example, in Chapter 25, uses the term "chronopolitics" to explain how time de-mands are determined by the social politics of the state. We can see how the Scan-dinavian state tries to ease the time conflicts of families with children. In Sweden, employed mothers and fathers of infants and toddlers are protected from many of the double demands of a paid job and daily childcare and household work by a so-cial policy regime that cushions them from a time bind. Zimmerman (1993) com-pared the experiences of parents with seriously ill children in Finland (which has a policy regime similar to Sweden's) and the United States. She found that health-care and welfare policies created significantly different carework experiences in each country. Universal and affordable health care in Finland combined with paid parental leave and additional subsidized services such as transportation, childcare, and housekeeping enabled Finnish families to experience less disruption than their counterparts in the United States. As a result, Finnish parents generally had an eas-ier time arranging to stay with their sick child and reported far less concern with the financial impact of the illness than did parents in the United States.

In contrast to the generous family leave policies in Sweden and the other Nor-dic countries, parents in the United States may, if they are fortunate, get a few weeks of paid leave after the birth of a child. If they want to continue to protect time for parenting and carework, however, they may have to give up their job and reduce the family income. In low-income or single-parent families, this rarely is an option. Because childcare and domestic work have not been made a public re-sponsibility at the national level—that is, beyond the 1993 Family and Medical Leave Act, which provides job protection during twelve weeks of unpaid leave for slightly more than half of employed women in the United States—the excessive time demands for employed parents remains a challenge that individuals must manage for the most part on their own through the private market (see Part 3 for further discussion).

The comprehensive array of benefits available to parents in the Nordic countries reflects the premise that citizens are entitled to a public safety net to assure their basic welfare needs during times when they are unable to provide for themselves. This approach to social policy has been defined by Gøsta Esping-Andersen (1990) as "social democratic," and analyzed as one of three types of contemporary welfare states or "regimes" (the other two are the "corporatist" and "liberal"). The basis for Esping-Andersen's typology is the chance in each regime type for the decommodification of workers. In other words, classification of welfare regimes is based on the extent to which, in that particular regime, a worker can maintain a livelihood without reliance on the market. For example, if a worker cannot work due to illness or disability or job loss, a decommodified worker will be able to maintain the basic necessities for living through receiving state benefits. Commodified workers, on the other hand, depend on the market for basic necessities and, in this case, would be unable to buy them and would, therefore, decline into poverty. Decommodification (by definition) is greatest in social democratic welfare regimes such as in the Nordic countries.

Feminist theorists have taken issue with Esping-Andersen for his gendered assumption that workers are male (Orloff 1993; Sainsbury 1994). They argue that his theory does not adequately consider the situation of women and the conditions under which they would have the resources to live independently. Decommodified male workers may be married to women who are economically dependent. For these scholars, one criterion to use in evaluating social policies would be the ability of women to live outside of marriage. As Hobson (1991) puts it, Esping-Andersen uses a framework for determining equality that focuses on the state-market rather than the state-market-family nexus. Male workers may receive state benefits that allow them (and their families) to live outside the market under certain conditions (an example of decommodification); however, Esping-Andersen does not consider the gender division of labor within families. Despite state benefits that decommodify workers, wives may well remain dependent on male breadwinners. To be truly independent, they would need benefits that would allow them "de-familialization," that is, resources so that they could live outside the family (see Hobson, Lewis, and Siim 2002 for an excellent discussion of de-familialization).

Helga Hernes (see Chapter 25) contends that the Scandinavians' social democratic approach to social policy has the potential to create a "woman-friendly state." The example of Swedish benefits just discussed is a case in point—generous paid family leave following childbirth, guaranteed and affordable childcare, and programs to support caregiving by fathers. In such a state policy regime, the ability for an individual to move between public (labor force participation) and private (unpaid carework) is eased in order to reduce the conflict between family life and employment demands. In the excerpt from her classic work on women and the welfare state, Hernes analyzes how the social democratic state shifts the division of responsibility for the citizens' welfare among state, market, and family, so that the state takes on some of the carework that traditionally has been left to the family. Referring to such policies as "state Feminism," Hernes argues that this type of welfare state is friendly to women because it "enable[s] women to have a natural [sic] relationship to their children, their work, and public life" and "would not force harder choices on women than on men." Ideally, then, a woman-friendly state would provide opportunities for de-familialization as well as decommodification, allowing women to be able to live independently if conditions within the family cannot meet their needs.

It is important to point out, however, that scholars have been of two minds about how the state is related to women's empowerment and advancement. Nordic feminists beginning with Hernes have accepted the power of the state to compensate for and redistribute the burdens of carework and have seen the state as a potential partner and ally in moving toward the goal of a woman-friendly state. Thus, Simonen (1991) discusses the state's contribution to carework in Finland as "social mothering." Other feminists in Europe and the United States, however, have written about the coercive consequences of state welfare policies in terms of gender inequity. This view sees the state as a patriarchal force, as a potential oppressor or adversary and not necessarily a friend (see, for example, Pateman 1988; Bashevkin 2002). We keep these opposing views regarding state policies and their impact on women in mind as we turn to consider another level of social policy—multilateral, supranational institutions—and their implications for gender and carework.

SUPRANATIONAL ORGANIZATIONS AND THE WOMAN-FRIENDLY STATE

The idea of a woman-friendly state is incompatible with most interpretations of global economic forces. Neoliberal economic policies, which have dominated the thinking of decision-makers in key global economic organizations such as the World Bank, insist on minimizing social spending and scaling back welfare state programs. Research is limited on the effects of such supranational governance structures on national social citizenship rights and benefits and their impact on gender relations and carework. Part 4 addresses some of the key issues involved. We ask: How has the interconnection among national economies affected the progressive social policies in European states that have recognized carework? As affluent nations undergo economic and policy restructuring to meet the presumed demands of the global economy, will the movement toward a universal caregiver model for the gender division of labor find support, or will this direction be reversed? Are woman-friendly policies compatible with the demands of the new global economy? How are states and supranational organizations responding to care deficits? Will restructuring of social policy regimes improve the lives of global migrants, particularly those following in the wake of deficits created by global care chains? Or, will national stratification systems based on constructions of race, ethnicity, social class and gender be further inscribed into new and more intractable global structures of inequality?

The readings in Part 4 address how the forces of globalization, including the policies imposed by increasingly powerful supranational institutions, are affecting carework and gender relations in both First and Third World contexts. Circumstances in the developing world are illustrated by both Najafizadeh (Azerbaijan) and Anwary (Bangladesh), as well as by Rosemberg's research on Brazil, presented in Part 1. In developing countries, survival itself dictates that there may be as many breadwinners per family as can find work. Nonetheless, the cultural values and meanings attached to family, work, and gender relations in these countries remain embedded in ideologies of male breadwinner dominance. The contradictions between these gender expectations, carework demands, and the economic realities of daily life create significant tension. These contradictions are also reflected in policy ambiguities as a result of competing internal interests intersecting with the pressures exerted by supranational organizations.

The recent history of early childcare and education policy (ECCE) in Brazil as discussed in Part 1 provides a case in point. As Rosemberg observes,

> The process of establishing contemporary Brazilian ECCE . . . could not manage to write its own national history since it suffered strong pressure from multilateral organizations, which found national allies (including governments). Developed countries have been able to construct their own history with little outside interference. They constitute the majority stockholders in the multilateral organizations and exert pressures rather than suffering them. The history of contemporary ECCE policies in the developing countries is quite different. (Rosemberg 2003)

Brazil's own internal strategy to upgrade the care and education of young children went counter to the recommendations of outside multilateral organizations, such as UNICEF, UNESCO, and the World Bank. These organizations developed and disseminated a nonformal, community-based model for childcare and education.

Instead of educational centers with increased training for teachers and caregivers, this approach involved lower-cost public investment and centered on the use of voluntary or semivoluntary (low-paid) work by women without professional training. Rosemberg argues that these externally imposed policies have depressed the life conditions and life chances for many Brazilian women and children.

The economic demands of globalization imposed by debt regulations and the social policies that support the carework of women and the lives of children are often incompatible, as evidenced in the example from Brazil. Economic demands can also create tension with respect to traditional gender norms, especially those that govern breadwinner and caregiver roles in the family. Excerpts from Azerbaijan and Bangladesh illustrate this aspect of globalization, gender, and carework. In both these developing countries, state policies neglect to provide adequate care services for women, and, as a result, women have organized their own care services. Their efforts illustrate once again the significance of carework for the community as discussed at the beginning of this essay.

In Azerbaijan, local professional women found the resources to form a variety of NGOs, whose work is described in the excerpt by Najafizadeh. In Bangladesh, circumstances were different, requiring local women to look outside their country for support to force national officials into offering improved care services for the women victims of acid violence. Local women enlisted the support of international humanitarian NGOs such as Amnesty International and UNICEF. These supranational organizations encouraged the Bangladesh government to enact more woman-friendly policies; they worked together with local women to address the care deficit and promote greater gender equity. Thus, it is important to distinguish humanitarian supranational organizations from those that are primarily economic in purpose; their roles and impact on carework and gender can differ considerably.

Rosemberg's study of early childhood education in Brazil shows how the structural adjustment agenda of supranational organizations influenced the scaling back of social citizenship benefits (in childcare and education) for women and children. Woman-friendly policies that had been previously adopted were overturned as a result of policies from the World Bank. These examples suggest a sort of ongoing global challenge, with more economically oriented supranational organizations (International Monetary Fund, World Bank) encouraging developing nations to reduce spending on carework and related social citizenship programs, while humanitarian and social change oriented supranational organizations, such as those who joined forces with local women's organizations in Bangladesh and Azerbaijan, work to develop and strengthen social care programs.

In advanced economy nations, carework is more likely to be recognized in formal social policy. This has occurred primarily in Western Europe, especially in the Nordic countries, and to a much lesser extent in the United States. Because carework and social citizenship issues overall have been more prominent in European social policy, they are also increasingly at issue in the policies of the European Union (EU). In her analysis of EU policies in relation to gender and the welfare state, Borchorst (1994) argues that Western European welfare regimes are increasingly influenced by supranational organizations, and in particular by the EU. She points out that the EU was formed by right-wing, Christian democrats who instilled social policies reflecting the principle of subsidiarity, a conservative approach toward carework and the family, which views the family as the primary provider of care with the state assisting only when necessary. On the other hand, she calls attention to the fact that the EU Court of Justice has also taken more direct stands on gender relations through its equal pay and equal treatment directives. Those initiatives, in addition to the EU directive calling upon member states to provide fourteen weeks of paid maternity leave, support a woman-friendly policy approach. This apparent contradiction raises the question of whether the EU has had a beneficial or detrimental impact in terms of promoting gender equity, especially in relation to its work–family policies. According to Borchorst, this is a very difficult question. She predicts that EU regulations "will magnify the differences between women, supporting those who can compete directly with men. This is especially true for women with higher education; more marginalized women will not benefit from the free mobility of labor and the prohibition on sex discrimination. These women might also carry a heavier burden of unpaid work in the family and they cannot afford to pay others to perform it" (1994, 39–40).

The excerpt from Susan Christopherson presents an analysis of what is actually taking place as individual European countries adapt to the global economy and restructure their policy regimes into a unified policy. Far from the woman- and family-friendly ideals presented in the readings by Fraser and Hernes, Christopherson's research suggests that just the opposite is actually taking place. She finds in her study of ten advanced economy countries (mostly in Western Europe) that carework is becoming more decentralized and privatized, shifting from national to local governments or from public to family responsibility. Such changes constitute a process of devolution. Both of these excerpts add an important dimension to Part 4 because they carry forward the analysis of woman-friendly policy regimes, first introduced by Fraser and Hernes, into the current period of globalization and welfare state restructuring.

Celia Valiente's analysis of recent childcare policies in Spain supports Christopherson's conclusions regarding the perpetuation of carework as a family responsibility. Spain provides a contrast to many other European countries in that childcare has been receiving increasing attention (as opposed to devolution). Yet, at the same time, it has evolved in ways that work against women's participation in the labor force. Spain's social policy regime in this area thus reflects an educational rather than a woman-friendly logic. We can apply other concepts introduced in this book to suggest that these policies fail to address the care deficit in Spain while supporting a male breadwinner/female carer model of the gender division of labor.

CONCLUSION

All of us as individuals depend on the carework of others. The social value given to carework, however, has to do with societal arrangements such as how time for carework is allocated, whether carework is compensated, how carework fits with paid employment, and how carework is divided by gender. Social policy regimes govern these matters. Thus, we can say that carework is socially constructed in relation to communities, nations, and (increasingly) supranational institutions. Carework that is unpaid and hidden within the family as a task largely assigned to women signals and promotes gender inequity. As we have seen, on the one hand, national and supranational policy regimes often support such arrangements. On the other hand, gender equity is encouraged in policy regimes where the importance of carework is recognized, and where woman-friendly policies exist to help citizens coordinate employment with family responsibilities. In today's global economy with major care deficits in single-parent, dual-earner, and transnational families, it is especially important to see the connections between social policy regimes and the gender division models implicit in them. Will there be progress toward the universal caregiver model? Or, will the neoliberal assumptions of supranational policy bodies continue to gain influence and eclipse the promise of a woman-friendly state?

1. What does it mean to refer to a nation's social policies as promoting a "woman-friendly state"?

2. Describe some ways that social policies influence gender and carework. How is globalization making a difference in this relationship?

3. What is an ideal arrangement for the gender division of labor that is also gender equitable?

4. Why do you think there is more public recognition (for example, the idea of "social capital") in the case of carework directed toward communities than for carework performed on a one-on-one basis for individuals?

5. How can multilateral or supranational organizations influence the internal policies of nations that govern carework? What are the implications for gender?

1. Calculated at 7 Swedish kronor per 1 U.S. dollar.

Bashevkin, Sylvia (ed.). 2002. *Women's Work Is Never Done: Comparative Studies in Caregiving, Employment and Social Policy Reform.* New York: Routledge.

Borchorst, Annette. 1994. "Welfare State Regimes, Women's Interests and the EC," pp. 26–44 in Diane Sainsbury (ed.), *Gendering Welfare States.* London: Sage.

Cancian, Francesca M., and Stacey J. Oliker. 2000. *Caring and Gender.* Thousand Oaks, CA: Pine Forge Press.

Coleman, James S. 1988. "Social Capital in the Creation of Human Capital." *American Journal of Sociology* 94: 95–120.

Esping-Andersen, Gøsta. 1990. *The Three Worlds of Welfare Capitalism.* Cambridge, U.K.: Polity Press.

Hobson, Barbara. 1991. "Decommodification in Gender Terms: An Analysis of Esping-Andersen's Social Policy Regimes and Women's Social Citizenship." Unpublished paper. Stockholm University.

Hobson, Barbara (ed.). 2001. *Making Men into Fathers: Men, Masculinities and the Social Politics of Fatherhood.* Cambridge, U.K.: Cambridge University Press.

Hobson, Barbara, Jane Lewis, and Birte Siim (eds.). 2002. *Contested Concepts in Gender and Social Politics.* Northampton, MA: Edward Elgar.

Moghadam, Valentine M. 2005. *Globalizing Women: Transnational Feminist Networks.* Baltimore: Johns Hopkins University Press.

Orloff, Ann Shola. 1993. "Gender and the Social Rights of Citizenship: State Policies and Gender Relations in Comparative Research," *American Sociological Review* 58 (3): 303–28.

Pateman, Carole. 1988. "The Patriarchal Welfare State," pp. 231–260 in A. Gutmann (ed.), *Democracy and the Welfare State.* Princeton, NJ: Princeton University Press.

Putnam, Robert D. 2000. *Bowling Alone: The Collapse and Revival of American Community.* New York: Simon and Schuster.

Rosenberg, Fúlvia. 2003. "Multilateral Organizations and Early Child Care and Education Policies for Developing Countries." *Gender & Society* 17 (2): 250–266.

Sainsbury, Diane. 1994. *Gendering Welfare States.* London: Sage.

Simonen, Leila. 1991. *Feminist Social Policy in Finland: Contradictions of Municipal Homemaking.* Aldershot, England: Avebury.

Stolle, Dietland, with Jane Lewis. 2002. "Social Capital—an Emerging Concept," pp. 195–229 in Barbara Hobson, Jane Lewis, and Birte Siim (eds.), *Contested Concepts in Gender and Social Politics.* Northampton, MA: Edward Elgar.

Swedish Institute. 2004. "Equality between Women and Men." Fact Sheet 82. Stockholm, Sweden.

Zimmerman, Mary K. 1993. "Caregiving in the Welfare State: Mothers' Informal Health Care Work in Finland." *Research in the Sociology of Health Care* 10: 193–211.

AFTER THE FAMILY WAGE: A
POSTINDUSTRIAL THOUGHT EXPERIMENT

Nancy Fraser

Building on the central point that social policy regimes shape the gender division of labor, Nancy Fraser points out that the male breadwinner/ female caregiver model based on a single family wage is no longer feasible. Using principles of gender equity, Fraser identifies and examines two approaches to reconceptualizing the division of labor that characterizes current policies in postindustrial, capitalist countries. She analyzes the implications of these approaches for women and suggests a third alternative— the universal caregiver model—that she considers to be more equitable.

The gender order that is now disappearing descends from the industrial era of capitalism and reflects the social world of its origin. It was centered on the ideal of the family wage. In this world people were supposed to be organized into heterosexual, male-headed nuclear families, which lived principally from the man's labor market earnings. The male head of the household would be paid a family wage, sufficient to support children and a wife-and-mother, who performed domestic labor without pay. Of course countless lives did not fit this pattern. Still, it provided the normative picture of a proper family. . . .

Today, however, the family-wage assumption is no longer tenable—either empirically or normatively. We are currently experiencing the death throes of the old, industrial gender order . . . rooted in part in the collapse of the world of the family wage, and of its central assumptions about labor markets and families. In the labor markets of postindustrial capitalism, few jobs pay wages sufficient to support a family single-handedly; many, in fact, are temporary or part-time and do not carry standard benefits.[1] Women's employment is increasingly common, moreover—although far less well-paid than men's. . . . Gender norms and family forms are highly contested . . . [and] many people no longer prefer the male breadwinner/female homemaker model. . . . In short, a new world of economic production and social reproduction is emerging—a world of less stable employment and more diverse families. Though no one can be certain about its ultimate shape, this much seems clear: the emerging world, no less than the world of the family wage, will require a welfare state that effectively insures people against uncertainties. It is clear, too, that the old forms of welfare state, built on assumptions of male-headed families and relatively stable jobs, are no longer suited to providing this protection. We need something new; a postindustrial welfare state suited to radically new conditions of employment and reproduction. . . .

Two different sorts of answers are presently conceivable . . . which qualify as feminist. The first I call the Universal Breadwinner model. It is the vision implicit in the current political practice of most US feminists and liberals. It aims to foster gender equity by promoting women's employment; the centerpiece of this model is state provision of employment-enabling services such as childcare. The second possible answer I call the Caregiver Parity model. It is the vision implicit in the current political practice of most Western European feminists and social democrats. It aims to promote gender equity chiefly by supporting informal carework; the centerpiece of this model is state provision of caregiver allowances. . . . Which expresses the most attractive vision of a postindustrial gender order? Which best embodies the ideal of gender equity?

UNIVERSAL BREADWINNER MODEL

How would [the universal breadwinner] model organize carework? The bulk of such work would be shifted from the family to the market and the state, where it would be performed by employees for pay.[2] Who, then, are these employees likely to be? In many countries today, including the US, paid institutional carework is poorly remunerated, feminized and largely racialized and/or performed by immigrants.[3] But such arrangements are precluded in this model. If the model is to succeed in enabling all women to be breadwinners, it must upgrade the status and pay attached to carework employment, making it, too, into primary labor force work. Universal Breadwinner, then, is necessarily committed to a policy of "comparable worth"; it must redress the widespread under-valuation of skills and jobs currently coded as feminine and/or "non-white," and it must remunerate such jobs with breadwinner-level pay. Universal Breadwinner would link many benefits to employment and distribute them through social insurance, with levels varying according to earnings. In this respect, the model resembles the industrial-era welfare state.[4] The difference is that many more women would be covered on the basis of their own employment records. And many more women's employment records would look considerably more like men's.

Not all adults can be employed, however. Some will be unable to work for medical reasons, including some not previously employed. Others will be unable to get jobs. Some, finally, will have carework responsibilities that they are unable or unwilling to shift elsewhere. Most of these last will be women. To provide for these people, Universal Breadwinner must include a residual tier of social welfare that provides need-based, means-tested wage replacements.

Universal Breadwinner is far removed from present realities. Not surprisingly, Universal Breadwinner delivers the best outcomes to women whose lives most closely resemble the male half of the old family-wage ideal couple. It is especially good to childless women and to women without other major domestic responsibilities that cannot easily be shifted to social services. But for those women, as well as for others, it falls short of full gender equity.

THE CAREGIVER PARITY MODEL

Caregiver Parity is also extremely ambitious. On this model, many (though not all) women will follow the current US female practice of alternating spells of full-time employment, spells of full-time carework, and spells that combine part-time carework with part-time employment. The aim is to make such a life-pattern costless . . . a program of caregiver allowances to compensate childbearing, child-raising, housework and other forms of socially-necessary domestic labor . . . must be sufficiently generous at the full-time rate to support a family—hence equivalent to a breadwinner wage . . . [with] continuity of all the basic social-welfare benefits including health, unemployment, disability and retirement insurance.

This model organizes carework very differently from Universal Breadwinner. Whereas that approach shifted carework to the market and the state, this one keeps the bulk of such work in the household and supports it with public funds. Caregiver Parity's social-insurance system also differs sharply. To assure continuous coverage for people alternating between carework and employment, benefits attached to both must be integrated in a single system. In this system, part-time jobs and supported carework must be covered on the same basis as full-time jobs. . . . Years of supported carework would count on a par with years of employment toward eligibility for retirement pensions. Benefit levels would be fixed in ways that treat carework and employment equivalently.

Caregiver Parity, too, is far from current US arrangements. It requires large outlays of public funds to pay caregiver allowances, hence major structural tax reform and a sea-change in political culture. . . . Caregiver Parity stops short of affirming the universal value of activities and life-patterns associated with women. It does not value caregiving enough to demand that men do it, too; it does not ask men to change. . . . In general, Caregiver Parity improves the lot of women with significant carework responsibilities. But for those women, as well as for others, it fails to deliver full gender equity.

TOWARD A UNIVERSAL CAREGIVER MODEL

Both Universal Breadwinner and Caregiver Parity are highly utopian visions of a postindustrial welfare state. Either one of them would represent a major improvement over current US arrangements. Yet neither is likely to be realized soon. Both models assume background preconditions that are strikingly absent today. Both presuppose major political-economic restructuring, including significant public control over corporations, the capacity to direct investment to create high-quality permanent jobs, and the ability to tax profits and wealth at rates sufficient to fund expanded high-quality social programs. Both models also assume broad popular support for a postindustrial welfare state that is committed to gender equity. If both models are utopian in this sense, neither is utopian enough. Neither Universal Breadwinner nor Caregiver Parity can actually make good on its promise of gender equity—even under very favorable conditions. Although both are good at preventing women's poverty and exploitation, both are only fair at redressing inequality of respect: Universal Breadwinner holds women to the same standard as men, while constructing arrangements that prevent them from meeting it fully; Caregiver Parity, in contrast, sets up a double standard to accommodate gender difference, while institutionalizing policies that fail to assure equivalent, respect for "feminine" activities and life patterns. . . . Neither model, in sum, provides everything feminists want. Even in a highly idealized form neither delivers full gender equity. . . .

A third possibility is to induce men to become more like most women are now—viz. people who do primary carework. Consider the effects of this one change on the models we have just examined. If men were to do their fair share of carework, Universal Breadwinner would come much closer to equalizing leisure time and eliminating androcentrism, while Caregiver Parity would do a much better job of equalizing income and reducing women's marginalization. Both models, in addition, would tend to promote equality of respect. If men were to become more like women are now, in sum, both models would begin to approach gender equity. The key to achieving gender equity in a postindustrial welfare state, then, is to make women's current life-patterns the norm for everyone. Women today often combine breadwinning and caregiving, albeit with great difficulty and strain. A postindustrial welfare state must ensure that men do the same, while redesigning institutions so as to eliminate the difficulty and strain.

We might call this vision *Universal Caregiver*. What, then, might such a welfare state look like? Unlike Caregiver Parity, its employment sector would not be divided into two different tracks; all jobs would be designed for workers who are caregivers, too; all would have a shorter work week than full-time jobs have now;

and all would have the support of employment-enabling services. Unlike Universal Breadwinner, however, employees would not be assumed to shift all carework to social services. Some informal carework would be publicly supported and integrated on a par with paid work in a single social-insurance system. Some would be performed in households by relatives and friends. . . . Other supported carework would be located outside households altogether—in civil society. . . .

A Universal Caregiver welfare state would promote gender equity by effectively dismantling the gendered opposition between breadwinning and caregiving. It would integrate activities that are currently separated from one another, eliminate their gender coding and encourage men to perform them too. This, however, is tantamount to a wholesale restructuring of the institution of gender. The construction of breadwinning and caregiving as separate roles, coded masculine and feminine respectively, is a principal undergirding of the current gender order. To dismantle those roles and their cultural coding is in effect to overturn that order. It means subverting the existing gender division of labor and reducing the salience of gender as a structural principle of social organizations.[5] At the limit, it suggests deconstructing gender.[6] By deconstructing the opposition between breadwinning and caregiving, moreover, Universal Caregiver would simultaneously deconstruct the associated opposition between bureaucratized public institutional settings and intimate private domestic settings. Treating civil society as an additional site for carework, it would overcome both the "workerism" of Universal Breadwinner and the domestic privatism of Caregiver Parity. Thus, Universal Caregiver promises expansive new possibilities for enriching the substance of social life and for promoting equal participation. . . .

Much more work needs to be done to develop this third—Universal Caregiver—vision of a postindustrial welfare state. A key is to develop policies that discourage free riding. Contra-conservatives, the real free riders in the current system are not poor solo-mothers who shirk employment. Instead they are men of all classes who shirk carework and domestic labor, as well as corporations who free-ride on the labor of working people, both underpaid and unpaid. . . . The trick is to imagine a social world in which citizens' lives integrate wage-earning, caregiving, community activism, political participation, and involvement in the associational life of civil society—while also leaving time for some fun. This world is not likely to come into being in the immediate future. But it is the only imaginable postindustrial world that promises true gender equity. And unless we are guided by this vision now, we will never get any closer to achieving it.

NOTES

1. David Harvey, *The Condition of Postmodernity. An Inquiry into the Origins of Cultural Change* (Oxford: Blackwell, 1989); Scott Lash and John Urry, *The End of Organized Capitalism* (Cambridge: Polity Press, 1987); Robert Reich, *The Work of Nations: Preparing Ourselves for 21st Century Capitalism* (New York: Knopf, 1991).

2. Government could itself provide carework-services in the form of public goods or it could fund marketized provision through a system of vouchers. Alternatively, employers could be mandated to provide employment-enabling services for their employees, either through vouchers or in-house arrangements. The state option means higher taxes, of course, but it may be preferable nevertheless. Mandating employer responsibility creates a disincentive to hire workers with dependents, to the likely disadvantage of women.

3. Evelyn Nakano Glenn, "From Servitude to Service Work: Historical Continuities in the Racial Division of Paid Reproductive Labour," *Signs—Journal of Women in Culture and Society* 18, no. 1 (Autumn 1992): 1–43.

4. It, too, conditions entitlement on desert and defines "contribution" in traditional androcentric terms as employment and wage deductions.

5. Susan Moller Okin, *Justice, Gender, and the Family* (New York: Basic Books, 1989).

6. Joan Williams, "Deconstructing Gender," in *Feminist Legal Theory: Readings in Law and Gender*, (eds.) Katharine T. Bartlett and Rosanne Kennedy (Boulder, Colorado: Westview Press, 1991).

25 | WOMAN-FRIENDLY STATES AND A PUBLIC CULTURE OF CARE

Helga Maria Hernes

The following excerpt is taken from the classic work, *Welfare State and Women Power*, in which Norwegian sociologist Helga Hernes discusses the role of the state in relation to carework and gender and introduces the concept of the woman-friendly state. Hernes articulates the state's fundamental role in deciding boundaries between public and private carework and in orchestrating women's time availability and time use. She sees time constraints as fundamental in producing gender stratification and inequity and policies that address these constraints as empowering women. A key aspect of the Scandinavian welfare state's friendliness to women is the prospect for development of a culture of care.

[A] woman-friendly state would enable women to have a natural relationship to their children, their work, and public life (Hernes 1982: 32–40). I wish to make the claim here that Nordic democracies embody a state form that makes it possible to transform them into woman-friendly societies. This claim rests on an analysis of these countries' history and potential for development, as well as assumptions about the needs of women that are not uncontroversial. Most feminists would deny that states can be non-repressive and non-violent, and thus be friendly to women (or children and men for that matter).

A woman-friendly state would not force harder choices on women than on men, or permit unjust treatment on the basis of sex. In a woman-friendly state women will continue to have children, yet there will also be other roads to self-realization open to them. In such a state women will not have to choose futures that demand greater sacrifices from them than are expected of men. It would be, in short, a state where injustice on the basis of gender would be largely eliminated without an increase in other forms of inequality, such as among groups of women. . . . What makes it difficult to achieve is the fact that gender is a basic principle of social organization, and that the requirement of not increasing other forms of inequality will mean that most men will lose some of their present privileges, i.e. their unjust advantages. This process will in other words involve power struggles . . . [yet] Scandinavian development has created the potential for evolution towards woman-friendly states and societies. The questions that arise in regard to this development concern the boundaries between public and private responsibility for reproductive tasks, and the acceptance of legitimate gender differences in societies that have equality as an over-riding and long-standing policy aim. There is no normative agreement on these issues among feminists, among women in general, or among political decision-makers. Nor is there any theoretical agreement. While their relevance is perhaps especially evident in Scandinavia, and while the empirical references [here] are Nordic, questions of the balance between private and public, and of re-conceptualizations of equality are shared by colleagues in many countries. . . .

The division of labor between family, market, and state is decisive for the welfare of women and for their social power. . . . In contrast to many other Western countries, where traditional "family work" has been marketized, the Nordic solution has been its incorporation into the public sector administered by the state and municipalities. One of the weaknesses of much of the feminist literature, especially from a Northern European point of view, is a persistent overemphasis on women's dependence on the kinship system. . . . If one looks at the recent history of the articulation of women's interests, their demands have been as much for gaining control over their own destinies within private settings, as about institution building. Women's claims have for example been for longer maternity leaves and shorter working hours per day rather than institutional facilities in order to be able to take care of their own children and other social responsibilities. Public responsibility lies of course in the acknowledgement that this kind of work is deemed to be socially necessary labor, and should be rewarded (O'Brien 1979, Dahl 1985). In terms of policy this has meant that the strict division between social policy and labor market policy is not in the interests of women. . . . The new boundaries between private and public involve in other words both the acknowledgement that certain values, such as care for the young and the elderly, are a public concern, and their institutionalization in humane organizational forms. . . .

My main thesis is that women's lives are more dependent on and determined by state policies than men's. . . . Market and state can thus in some ways be regarded as gender-specific arenas for action and problem-solving. Yet this is also an oversimplified picture, since the "men's" market is heavily dependent on state subsidies in order to survive. The tension between the productive and reproductive spheres is both primitive and complicated. It can be explained most simply by pointing out that the activities of one sphere are regarded as a contribution, while those of the other are regarded as costs in relation to the national product. Roughly speaking, one can say that men dominate on the income side and women on the expenses side, partly because much of women's work, both paid and unpaid, is either not counted in the national product or because it also counts as public expense in the form of transfers. This is further underlined by neo-liberal economic theory, which misrepresents the public sector's contribution to and large investment in the private sector, and strongly overestimates the private and the industrial sector's contributions to the public good. The invisibility and misrepresentation of women's work is thus both a question of unpaid work . . . and of paid work in the public sector—carried out predominantly by women—as a contribution to the producing sectors' productivity and efficiency. . . .

CHRONOPOLITICS

Cyclical time is often considered to be the "timeless" dimension, the world of un-changing cycles of "life itself." Linear time is man-made, historical time, the time we shape. Not surprisingly, different social institutions are associated with each of these: the family—and traditionally the life of women—mainly with cyclical time; the economic, professional, and political sphere—and largely the life of middle-class men—with linear time. These two time-ordering principles, cyclical and lin-ear, impute to us and socialize us into different logics of action. . . .

Yet there are limits to the extent that linear and clock time can encroach upon the biological and social rhythms of infants or on the needs of the sick or the very old. The difference in velocity in the two time modes or segments is felt when they collide. . . . And profound changes in the organization of daily life have caused women to experience these inner and outer conflicts between time cultures more strongly than men. . . . The combination of daily routines and life cycles that char-acterizes family life constitutes one specific time system. The time schedules of dif-ferent professions such as medicine, of large organizations or of bureaucracy are more fixed and less flexible. Their internal coordination requirements are so strict that there is great resistance to making their timing and scheduling even more complex. The temporally rigid way in which . . . professional commitments are defined today is one of the key characteristics of modern social organization (Zerubavel 1979, p. 52). . . . A good time policy should aim at making transitions from one time segment to another less costly. . . . The temporal structures of vari-ous social and economic subsystems have changed and need new modes of syn-chronization. . . .

There are many important ways in which the state . . . affects the use of time and the attitude towards it in the working and the non-working population. There are a number of ways in which the state affects individual life courses, and thus indi-vidual working lives. If we consider work time policies, not in terms of work hours, but in terms of the investment of time spent in paid work over a lifetime, the state's role is considerable, both as it affects individual strategies, and as it determines the boundaries for individual action. There are too many different tasks that need to be done, which, for a variety of reasons, are difficult to provide through the labor market. There are also too many tasks and activities that require cyclical rather than linear time cultures and that are therefore not easily converted into money and paid labor. This does not mean that such work could not be credited towards various aspects of social citizenship that are provided through life course policies, such as old age insurance. . . . More importantly, though, from the public policy perspective the public sector of health care and social services is by no means capable of meeting the needs and demands for which it is responsible. A great deal of unpaid or grossly underpaid work is being done to meet these needs. Yet, it does not give the same entitlements as work in the traditional labor market. . . .

THE FUTURE OF CAREWORK

The aging process that most central and northern European welfare states are undergoing has taken its toll in terms of various signs of conflict between generations and between old and new political opponents. This is especially true of the mature corporate welfare states of Scandinavia, where the state's intervention in our formerly private lives has taken the form of a silent revolution. . . . The children of the silent revolution have no sense of the problems the welfare state was created to solve; they see it rather as a creator of problems. . . .

It is in this light that we must view the current centrality of the issue of time and the conflicts about the use of time. This is a conflict not only between labor and capital . . . but also a generational issue, where the public/private split reappears in very palpable forms. The children of the silent revolution have accepted that the state attends to their so-called private needs. They have accepted that public and private goods and needs are so closely intertwined and interwoven that their parents' concepts of what is public, private or personal have little to do with the reality in which they live. The welfare state as we know it in Scandinavia has undermined and deflected the traditional dividing lines between public and private spheres, between state family, market, and civil society as separate and distinct spheres of activity. Debates about the new balance are not only concerned with issues of paid and unpaid work and the social values they represent, but with the time spent on these activities and the civil, social, and economic entitlements we attach to time spent in paid and unpaid work and activities. The extent of these entitlements is today still largely determined by status in the labor market. The perceived injustices created by this situation have become even more obvious since research has uncovered the large amount of unpaid work that is an integral part of the modern welfare mix. The issue for many is thus that this new welfare mix must accept the consequences of the social changes it has itself created: one of which is the destruction of traditional views on the public and private use of time, which is now central in questions of care . . . the major topic of this paper. Public use of time creates rights and benefits for the person carrying out the relevant activities, which private use of time does not bestow. . . .

The specifically Scandinavian blend of social and labor market policy has found its physical expression in the public sector, which makes the bodily concerns and needs of families its own: childbirth, physical and mental handicaps, illness, old age become the object of public concern. In contrast to the classical liberal state, which had institutionalized the private-public split and made it partly coincide with the body-mind dichotomy, the Scandinavian welfare state has brought "hidden concerns" into the open. To put it somewhat loftily, the body-mind dichotomy, which had been basic to Western civilization since Plato, found its most highly developed institutional expression in the liberal state. It is severely undermined in the mature welfare state. . . .

A CULTURE OF CARE

Can one thus speak of a public "care culture" that is basic to the organization of daily life? Few Scandinavian observers would so far agree to such a description of reality (Lagergren 1984). Yet for purposes of international comparison one might say that the Scandinavian blend of commitment to public risk-sharing in connection with personal health and welfare and long traditions of volunteer work at a local level contain the seeds for such a culture. . . .

A care culture would have to refer to the institutionalization of a shared value system. At this point in history it is difficult to imagine shared values when it comes to the actual personal provision of care, mainly because women's roles are undergoing such rapid transition without corresponding changes in men's roles. There seems to be more of a collision of interests than a sharing of values. . . .

There are some well-founded reasons for hope. Social democracy is being changed from within by women activists and feminists. New political forces emphasize values and virtues based on care and compassion, and insist on their relevance to public life. . . . Feminist ideology thus presupposes a political system that translates the values of compassion and care into political principles of justice and equality which in turn can inform social policies and forms of social organization.

Even though feminist theory tells us little about how, where, and by whom its values are to be institutionalized, it rejects hierarchy and concentrations of power . . . [and] might well be highly relevant for the creation of a new public care culture. . . . Social democratic tradition . . . might . . . well be renewed from within and pave the way for the creation of a care culture of solidarity between generations. Creating solidarity between women and men will require other forces of change. For it is equal participation in the culture of care and the culture of more traditional work by men and women that will be the clearest expression of a new gender solidarity. . . .

Dahl, T. S. 1985. *Kvinnerett I.* Oslo: Universitetsforlaget.

Hernes, H. M. 1982. *Staten—kvinner ingen adgang?* (The State—No Access for Women?) Oslo: Universitetsforlaget.

Lagergren, M. (ed.) 1984. *Time to Care.* London: Pergamon Press.

O'Brien, M. 1979. Reproducing Marxist Man. In Clark and Lange (eds.) *The Sexism of Social and Political Theory.* Toronto: University of Toronto Press.

Zerubavel, E. 1979. Private Time and Public Time: The Temporal Structure of Social Accessibility and Professional Commitment. *Social Forces,* 58: 38–59.

26 WOMEN AND THE RESTRUCTURING OF CARE WORK: CROSS-NATIONAL VARIATIONS AND TRENDS IN TEN OECD COUNTRIES

Susan Christopherson

In recent years, global economic pressures have encouraged advanced economy countries to seek ways to cut costs and be more efficient in their support of welfare. As a result, countries in the north—even those with well-developed welfare states—are currently restructuring their social policies. In the following excerpt, Susan Christopherson examines current restructuring efforts in ten advanced economy countries in order to assess the implications for carework and gender. She concludes with a call for more advocacy and activism on the part of women to stop the erosion of their rights as citizen workers and carers.

As policy makers attempt to devise politically safe ways to restructure the welfare state and reduce expenditures, the care question looms as a particularly difficult one. . . . On the one hand, policy makers can and do use the ideology of family responsibility to shift the cost of care to family members and to make it appear that that is the preferable solution. On the other hand, the increasing reliance on female employees creates an interest among employers to reduce the cost (disruptions, absences) associated with a dual responsibility for caring and full-time wage work. Flexible time schedules have been the preferable solution, but they do nothing to alleviate the total burden. They do make it easier to juggle multiple responsibilities with less cost to the employer. Consequently, women are still stuck with the "double shift" as Arlie Hochschild dubbed it.

A third factor entering the equation is the predominance of women in paid caring occupations, more than 95 percent across OECD [Organization of Economic Cooperation and Development] countries. Women's employment is intertwined with the provision of caring services in complex ways. The loss of informal family care givers as women enter the workforce affects both child and elderly care sectors . . . at the same time, the demand for waged carers, jobs that women primarily hold, increases. . . .

A recent set of national care studies focused on women's employment patterns in childcare and elderly care work provides perspective on how the responsibility for caring is being redistributed even as the need for it increases. The case study countries include the Netherlands, Canada, the United States, the United Kingdom, Germany, Belgium, France, Finland, Norway, and Spain (Christopherson 1997) and provide evidence that demonstrates how the increasing demand for female labor and the drive to decrease state responsibility for a basic need is being resolved. . . .[1]

CROSS-NATIONAL TRENDS

1. Separation of Care Financing from Care Provision

Among the prominent cross-national trends is increasing separation of care financing from care provision. For example, while care for the elderly and children may still be financed via national taxes, the actual service is provided by local government, private providers or subsidized family members. In one politically popular variant of this trend, the public resources to provide for caring are redistributed in the form of a cash benefit to families. This strategy shifts the burden of providing for or managing care (and accountability) directly to family members and those whom they employ. It creates competition in the caring labor market, potentially driving down the wages of those carers still employed in the public sector. In some cases, the benefit is needed to supplement family income, creating pressure on family members to supply care rather than employ a carer.

2. Decentralization and Devolution of the Provision of Care

A second, closely related, trend is the decentralization and devolution of responsibility for the provision of caring services to the local government, community, and family. The welfare state has historically been conceived of as a national set of institutions, one purpose of which was to ameliorate differences in access to basic social needs (adequate food, education, health care, security in old age) across regions and places within the country. Decentralization, which has been carried out under the banner of efficiency and public choice theory, has undermined this evening out function, constructing ever-greater differences in the cost and quality of basic needs provision from place to place. Decentralization and the differentiation that accompanies it also makes it difficult, if not impossible, to replicate effective training practices, credentialing, or "best practice" across a national or even subnational regional terrain. . . .

As a consequence of policies to restructure health and social service provision, localized, community care in some countries has evolved into a system in which care in the community is, in reality, care by female relatives (Wærness 1990). The use of relatives or self-employed workers to carry out caring functions is a very different concept than that of community care, which emphasizes coordinated care that brings the recipient of care as well as the providers into a community of care.

As community care has become the preferable policy in OECD countries, a critical literature has developed, particularly in Scandinavia, which recommends that policy makers recognize the extent to which community care means care by female family members and orient policy to support these informal carers (Wærness 1990). In countries with already high levels of community care, such as Denmark, there is pressure for more support because of the expectation that such care substitutes for both family-member-provided care and institutional care. In other countries, increasing support for informal carers is intended to dampen demand for institutional care, which is much more expensive. It is important to note that support for home-based "community carers" is more extensive in those countries with social welfare state commitments to provide for people in their old age. Where care for the elderly has remained unchanged as a family (i.e., a female) responsibility, for example in Southern Europe, family members who care for elderly relatives have fewer community resources to assist them. This may possibly help account for the dramatic fall in birthrates in countries such as Spain and Italy, where the demands of caring work fall even more heavily on women than they do in the European countries of the north. . . .

Despite the implementation of policies that limit the role of the state in the financing and provision of caring services, the nation state continues to play an active role in social policy provision—in the guise of regulator. There is still an important influence on the structure of employment in caring occupations emanating from national and local regulation. This regulation may determine: (a) the number and skills of workers in caring institutions (staffing norms); (b) standards of care for individual and institutional care; and (c) occupational qualifications. In many cases, these regulatory frameworks have been reworked to respond to the increasing demand for care. Either directly or indirectly, changes in regulation, especially the move to local or micro level regulation (in the firm or family) have served to increase the private provision of care, to weaken governmental controls over the qualifications of some workers (particularly in home care), and to weaken the influence of collective bargaining on the conditions of work. Changes in staffing patterns, increasing the ratio of unqualified to qualified staff in childcare centers, for example, are one result. Another is the increase in the use of unqualified homecare workers in elderly care. . . . As caring activities become increasingly individualized and devolved to family and community, however, the ability to enforce this expanding regulatory regime comes into question. There is little enforcement capacity accompanying the new regulatory welfare state. . . . Standards are honored only nominally. Why then, the regulation? . . . Regulation is a cheap way out of responsibility and accountability.

The evidence from these country case studies is not definitive, but it does give an "on the ground" feel for how the provision of social services in the welfare state is being restructured and raises some provocative questions.

First, it suggests that social service work is becoming more decentralized and employment more fragmented both geographically and with respect to work site, the differences among women are likely to increase. Those women with educational credentials and in favorable local labor markets situations are likely to be able to use their potential mobility to advantage. Women without credentials and in noncompetitive labor markets are likely to lose even the small amount of economic power that employment in public sector social services once conveyed. Second, the evidence suggesting that more caring responsibilities are being transferred from the public sector to family members, particularly women, raises questions about care-based (as opposed to citizenship-based) rationales for public assistance. The assumption that women hold primary, if not exclusive, responsibility for care has made it easier to engage that responsibility to reduce public costs. . . .

That women remain an unorganized and incoherent interest group when it comes to their rights as citizen-workers is a too often neglected legacy of the postwar welfare state. Welfare state reformers have used that historical weakness and a traditional family ideology to justify and implement changes in welfare services. The increased emphasis on family (or community) responsibility for care is almost exclusively defined as a female responsibility. . . . It is the strength of this ideology that has allowed for the surreptitious and politically non-controversial shift of the costs of socially necessary care to women both in families and as workers.

1. The studies, organized by the Working Party on Women's Role in the Economy of the Organization for Economic Cooperation and Development, vary considerably in the extent of information provided. Because of significant differences in publicly available information and definitional problems, it is difficult to make direct cross-national comparisons. But because the researchers were responding to the same questions, however, the case studies are able to broadly illuminate changing patterns in financing and provision of care and in the situation of the caring worker.

REFERENCES

Christopherson, Susan. 1997. *Child care and elderly care: What occupational opportunities for women?* Labor Market and Social Policy Occasional Paper no. 27. Paris: OECD.

Wærness, Kari. 1990. Berufsbildung, Beschäftigung, und Karrieremöglichkeiten von Frauen in der Alterpflege in der Bundesrepublik Deutschland. Bundesministerium für Familie, Senioren, Frauen, und Jugend. *Materialien zur Frauenpolitik*, no 60, Bonn.

CARE WORK: INVISIBLE CIVIC ENGAGEMENT

Pamela Herd and Madonna Harrington Meyer

This analysis extends the ideas of Helga Hernes and other recent feminist theorists who have discussed the important impact of social policies on care work and gender. Where Hernes theorizes the centrality of time and the incompatibility between the cyclical demands of care work and standard corporate linear time, Herd and Harrington Meyer show that this incompatibility also affects civic engagement through limiting voluntary work in organizations. They echo earlier feminist writers by highlighting the importance of invisible care work and challenging conventional ideas of public–private boundaries. Care work, they argue, is itself a civic responsibility and a major contribution to social capital. In the context of globalization, these ideas have profound implications.

The burgeoning literature on the decline of civic engagement has been largely gender blind. The debate about the cause of its decline provides a rich example of the invisibility of women and women's unpaid care work. Scholars and politicians observe that Americans have increasingly withdrawn from community organizations, reduced their political activity, placed their individual self-interest over the common social good, and more generally failed to fulfill their citizenship obligations, thus threatening our democracy (Elshtain 1999; Putnam 1995). Explanations for lackluster participation in civic activities vary, including women's increasing participation in paid labor, a declining public morality, and excessive reliance on welfare programs (Galston and Levine 1998; Putnam 1996). Rarely can we find anything acknowledging how women's disproportionate responsibility for care work interferes with or enhances traditional forms of civic activity.[1] Rarer still is any mention of how care work, in and of itself, constitutes civic activity. . . .

Feminists explore the experiences and meanings of unpaid care and place gender at the center of the debate. In response to those who might suggest that care work is not a form of civic engagement because it occurs within a private family sphere rather than a more public political sphere, we suggest that the public–private dichotomy is challenged by civic engagement scholars themselves who argue the family is a key part of civil society. Civic engagement scholars argue that families, like civic engagement, are critical to a healthy democracy. Here, we lay the theoretical groundwork to incorporate the unpaid care work provided within families into standard definitions of civic engagement. . . . In contrast to those who suggest that strong federal policies inhibit civic activity, we suggest that policies that help families balance paid and unpaid responsibilities will encourage and revitalize civic engagement (Mettler 1999). Our concern is less with why participation in civic life has declined over time and more with the extent to which the concept has been defined in away that fails to recognize care work as the way many women and some men meet their citizenship obligations. . . . Feminist scholars have demonstrated that care is work and that care work should be both a right and an obligation of social citizenship. We infuse gender into the civic engagement debate by arguing that care work, defined as the daily physical and emotional labor of feeding and nurturing citizens, is an active form of participatory citizenship with far-reaching civic benefits. . . .

In framing debates about the causes of and solutions for the decline in civic activity, social capitalists, moralists, and historical institutionalists have looked at nearly every kind of unpaid activity—including voting, tutoring, fund-raising, and even bowling. Notably absent from their definitions of civic activity is care work, the daily tasks related to raising and caring for citizens. Care work is generally overlooked in these three theoretical perspectives because they are derived from political traditions that define citizens as male breadwinners and voters who are sustained by the women who cared for them and their children, the future generation of citizens (Hernes 1987; Lister 1997). Social capital, moralist, and historical institutionalist approaches have largely failed to take the power of gender as a social force seriously. . . . We argue that caring for spouses, children, the disabled, and the elderly has paradoxical effects on civic engagement. Care work both limits and enhances traditional forms of civic engagement. Furthermore, we argue that unpaid care work, in and of itself, constitutes a vital form of civic activity. Thus, we make gender central to the debate about the causes of and solutions for the decline in civic engagement.

UNPAID CARE WORK AS AN OBSTACLE

Care work is often the most satisfying work that many women and some men do during their lifetimes. But there is no question that it usurps care providers' time, money, health, and other resources. Thus, it often interferes with traditional civic activities. After all, there are only 24 hours in the day. For women, more so than for men, unpaid care work leaves less time and fewer financial resources for participating in politics, social movements, civic or voluntary groups, or other traditional forms of civic activity. Social capitalists, historical institutionalists, and moralists pay little direct attention to the role unpaid care work plays in inhibiting traditional forms of civic participation. Social capitalists acknowledge that mothering, which removes many women from the paid labor force, can lead to social isolation, which in turn negatively affects civic participation. But they do not make the direct link between performing the work of caring and having little time left for membership in organizations (Putnam 2000). Historical institutionalists and moralists have had little to say with regard to how unpaid care work could limit civic engagement.[2] Here we rely on feminist analyses to link care work and civic engagement.

Decades of previous feminist analyses have shown that women shoulder a disproportionate responsibility for unpaid care work, limiting their employment and citizenship. Women perform the majority of unpaid care work within families for children, people with disabilities, and the elderly (Cancian and Oliker 2000; Hochschild 1989; Hooyman and Gonyea 1995). For example, 80 percent of long-term care for the elderly and people with disabilities is provided within families, and 75 percent of that is done by women (Hooyman and Gonyea 1995). Scholars interested in citizenship have emphasized how women's caring interferes with the citizenship right to participate in paid labor, which in turn leads to loss of their basic social rights as citizens due to economic vulnerability (Knijn and Kremer 1997; Lister 1997; Mink 1998). Others have pointed out how this disproportionate responsibility for unpaid care work limits women's political participation and power (Hernes 1987; Lister 1997).

Disproportionate responsibility for unpaid care work, particularly when combined with paid work responsibilities, often limits the time women have to participate in traditional civic activities. Mothers spend about 36 hours per week doing household labor, while fathers spend 16 hours per week (Voydanoff and Donnelly 1999). A married woman, with children, working full-time can expect to see a reduction of 50 percent in her volunteering (Putnam 2000). Moreover, the substantial increase in white women's labor force participation—even when they are mothers of young children—further tests their ability to find time to participate in traditional civic activities (Rubin 1994). Paid work, particularly work done out of financial need as opposed to choice, negatively affects participation in traditional civic activities. Americans are in the paid labor force 163 hours per year.... Among developed nations, the United States has the highest percentage of labor force participants working 50 or more hours per week (Hochschild 1997; Leete-Guy and Schor 1993). Furthermore, vacation time, sick leave, and paid absences, already less than in most European countries, have decreased for many American workers (Leete-Guy and Schor 1993). The consequent time demands on family life limit citizens' potential to join the local school board or volunteer on a political campaign.

The evidence is quite clear that limited economic resources hinder participation in traditional civic activities (Burns, Lehman Schlozman, and Verba 2001; Verba, Lehman Schlozman, and Brady 1995). Women's disproportionate responsibility for unpaid care work limits earnings and demands resources, thereby reducing women's civic engagement. Mothers earn less because they work less than both men and non-mothers. But even mothers working full-time have lower wages than men and women without children, in part due to the time demands associated with caring for children (Harkness and Waldfogel 1999). . . . Years spent out of, or with limited participation in, the labor force interfere with savings and investments, as well as private pension and social security benefits. Ultimately, the higher poverty rate among older women, which is not expected to change for the baby boomer generation, is due to a lifetime of unpaid care work (Smeeding, Estes, and Glasse 1999). . . .

The demands of care and paid work threaten women's health and consequently their ability to be active citizens. Care workers often have poorer physical and mental health than their peers (National Alliance for Caregiving 1997). Mothers providing full-time unpaid care work, along with women who have disproportionate burdens of household labor, have high levels of stress and depression (Adam 1999; Bird 1999). In addition, studies show that caregivers for the developmentally disabled and the elderly have poorer self-reported health, including higher levels of depression, exhaustion, lack of exercise and higher rates of chronic illnesses and drug misuse (Brody 1990; Hoyert and Seltzer 1992). Being sick, tired, and depressed stifles people's ability to focus on anything other than their most immediate responsibilities.

Just as care work has limited women's ability to be fully engaged as employees, it has limited their capacity as citizens. Some might quibble with the argument that the time demands associated with care work limit one's ability to participate in civic activities because of evidence that busy people actually participate more (Burns, Lehman Schlozman, and Verba 2001; Freeman 1996). But there is evidence that care work pressures, in particular balancing paid and unpaid work, have taken their toll on civic engagement (Putnam 2000). However, we are not suggesting that the impact of care work on civic activity is the same for all women. Indeed, care work is often outsourced to paid nurses, nannies, housekeepers, cooks, and laundry services, reinforcing race and class inequities among women. Rather, we are suggesting that for women who perform the care work themselves, being too busy, too poor, and too drained by care work may interfere with their traditional civic activity. These drains are invisible in the gender-blind accounts of the decline in civic engagement—or, if they are visible, analysts blame women's lack of moral values instead of analyzing the gender dynamics of civic participation as revealed through care work.

CARE WORK AS A CATALYST

While families are not invisible to civic engagement scholars, the care work that women perform within families is invisible in this debate. For example, while Putnam (2000) addressed the importance of family dinners in fostering social capital, he never acknowledged the fact that someone must shop, cook, and eventually clean up after the meal. This kind of care work, performed mostly by women, has long provided the necessary support for other family members to maximize their own civic engagement. Families provide the basic necessities required to develop, and exercise, the rights and demands of citizenship. Mothers often stay home cooking dinner and helping the children with their homework, while fathers, freshly fed and dressed, attend town finance meetings. When mothers do take on political duties, such as attending a hearing about a local garbage incinerator, they often do so with children in tow. Moreover, when children are able to participate in volunteer activities through their schools and on their own time, they do so only because their mothers, and occasionally their fathers, shuttle them to and from these activities.

Care work often activates those who had been previously politically inactive citizens, expanding their boundaries because of the care they provide for their families. In fact, feminist analyses of citizenship have made it clear that women's care work often stimulates women's political activity (Gordon 1994; Lister 1997; Mink 1995; Skocpol 1992). By not addressing or examining unpaid care work and how it affects civic engagement, the present-day debate about civic engagement is incomplete. In a limited manner, social capitalists and moralists have noted the family's role in precipitating civic engagement. Social capitalists have shown how being married and being a parent are correlated with increased participation in school-, youth-, and religious-related activities and acknowledged the family as a form of social capital (Putnam 2000). And moralists have noted how the family is the primary place where civic virtue and morality are developed (Elshtain 1982b). But these scholars have not addressed how it is that care work, as opposed to certain family forms, precipitates civic engagement. Moralists remain fixated on family structure as opposed to the care work. Similarly, social capitalists ignore the fact that it is not being a parent that leads to Parent-Teacher Association participation; it is the parenting or the active work of caring that leads to involvement in children's schools. In the same way that the focus on paid work in poor communities ignores the practice of unpaid care, the focus on family structure at the expense of care work misspecifies the gender dynamics of key mechanisms of civic engagement. . . .

CARE WORK AS CIVIC ENGAGEMENT

In the two previous sections, we demonstrated how care work interferes with, and at other times facilitates, traditional forms of civic activity. In this section, our aim is to redefine civic engagement to include unpaid care work provided within families. While most civic engagement scholars recognize political activity, such as participating in the Parent-Teacher Association, as civic engagement, they have not defined more traditional types of unpaid care provided within families as civic engagement.[3] In both the labor market and the welfare state citizenship literature, care was unacknowledged until feminists brought it to the forefront and made arguments for the value of care.[4] Here, we bring care work to the forefront of civic engagement debates by making the case for why unpaid care provided within families should be considered a form of civic action.

To be defined as a form of civic engagement, civic activity must be voluntary and altruistic in nature, while simultaneously nurturing reciprocity, social ties, and social trust (Putnam 2000). Moreover, it must be unpaid and only indirectly related to the state. Thus, these activities will improve the health of a democracy. What could possibly fit these definitional requirements better than care work? We suggest that the unpaid care work provided within families, like other traditional civic activities, fosters the attributes of democratic citizens. . . . While civic engagement theorists have never specifically excluded care work from their definitions of civic activity, neither have they ever included it. . . . [W]e argue that civic engagement scholars have already laid the groundwork for including care as civic engagement. Not only does care work meet the guidelines of what defines a civic activity, but civic engagement scholars have included the family in both civil society and key measures of the civic engagement that occurs within that civil society. . . . Voluntary organizations such as hospices and the Red Cross provide the exact same services that families provide: food, shelter, medical care, transportation, and a shoulder to cry on. But unpaid care work performed by family members is generally not recognized as a form of civic engagement, while nearly all of the same tasks performed by anyone but family members are regarded as forms of civic activity. A woman spending hours at her mother-in-law's bedside is a dutiful daughter-in-law, while a stranger or neighbor sitting beside the same bed is a hospice volunteer. Hospice and respite care providers often provide the care work that some families do not have the time, money, or other resources to provide. How can we argue that a hospice volunteer caring for a neighbor is engaged in a civic activity, while a woman caring for her elderly aunt is not? Regardless of where the care work is provided and who provides it, the work, the emotional and financial costs to the care provider—and the rewards for the care recipient and the society at large—are the same.

We argue that unpaid care work within families is as voluntary or as altruistic as other forms of civic engagement. Care work is gendered, and tremendous social pressures push women to perform it (Harrington Meyer 2000). . . . For both men and women, the decision to care or not to care is made within a social context shaped by the intersection of gender, race, and class (Harrington Meyer 2000), but by and large, women continue disproportionately to provide care, despite the enormous costs they pay to do it. We argue this is just as altruistic, if not more altruistic because of the higher costs associated with it, as unpaid care work provided by hospice or respite services. . . . While voluntary and altruistic are two important descriptors of civic activity, fostering social and reciprocal ties between individuals is arguably the most important outcome of civic engagement, particularly for social capitalists (Putnam 1995, 1996, 2000). One might even infer from social capitalists that the whole point of volunteering is to expand particularistic family ties and develop social trust. But while civic engagement scholars, notably social capitalists, have focused heavily on how the development of ties between families and the larger community is important, they pay less attention to the work that must go on within families for these expanded ties and trust to germinate. Studies by social psychologists find that children develop the ability to trust only if they can count on having their basic needs met, such as being fed and clothed (Holmes 1995). Perceptions of being cared for emotionally also have been found to be a strong component of trust (Peters, Covello, and McCallum 1997). And the development of trust within families is correlated with a more generalized trust of others, similar to social trust (Couch, Adams, and Jones 1996; Couch and Jones 1997). Furthermore, nearly all unpaid family care work involves a dizzying degree of reciprocity between extended family members, neighbors, and friends. Many scholars have documented how neighbors and extended family rely on informal care exchange networks (Edin and Lein 1997; Oliker 2000). A mother picks up her neighbor's children, along with her own, from school or sports practices, knowing that in exchange she can count on her neighbor to oversee both of their children playing in the driveway a couple of afternoons per week. A neighbor takes out an older woman's garbage every Thursday morning so that her daughter does not have to make a special trip. Thus, unpaid care provided within families overlaps with unpaid care provided in other families. Both within and between families, reciprocities form as a result.

The final way civic engagement scholars lay the groundwork for calling family care civic engagement is the attention they pay to the family in civic life. . . . [C]ivic engagement scholars' discussion of the family has mostly focused on its form, as opposed to the work that goes on within it. In the process, they have demonized countless women who provide enormous amounts of care work but do it outside of marriage. Moralists, in particular, have been quick to link the decline in civic engagement to the disintegrating family (Elshtain 1999; Galston and Bennett 1999). Elshtain (1999) pointed to a woman's deciding to have a baby without getting married as evidence of the moral decline that pervades civil society. Galston and Bennett (1999) included the family as one of five measures to evaluate America's civic health, but they quantified it based on divorce rates and illegitimate births. These scholars defined the family in terms of marriage, as opposed to the care work involved in keeping a family together, be it a one-parent, two-parent, grandparent, or same-sex family model.[5] Consequently, these scholars are more focused on maintaining traditional family structures and regulating women's lives as opposed to acknowledging the care work that mostly women provide.

Our point is that care work meets all the standards of other civic activities and thus should rightly be called civic engagement. It is generally voluntary and altruistic, and it fosters social trust and reciprocity. Moreover, it occurs within an institution of civil society, the family. It is a tremendous irony that civic engagement scholars have so specifically focused on the importance of family in civil society and its impact on civic engagement but have mostly ignored the unpaid care work provided within families, largely by women, that maintains those families. . . . We have a hard time understanding why unpaid care work within families has generated so little attention within the civic engagement debate when everything from bird-watching to bowling has merited the attention of these scholars. Its exclusion makes clear the limited understanding of gender inequality in the civic engagement literature. . . .

THE STATE'S ROLE IN CIVIC ENGAGEMENT

The role of state policy in civil society is hotly contested among civic engagement scholars. . . . [W]e argue that supporting unpaid care work as a civic activity, and attempting to redistribute the responsibility for it, can actually improve civil society and consequently the civic engagement that occurs within it by improving health and income security, particularly for marginalized groups of citizens.

Moralists and social capitalists overlap in their views of the role of government, and particularly the federal government, in fostering an active civil society. Their perspectives are rooted in the idea that the state that governs best governs least. . . . [M]oralists expect a very limited role for the federal government in regards to unpaid care work and more general welfare needs. They expect churches and small, local, grassroots organizations to fulfill welfare needs. . . . Social capitalists oppose federal policies that support unpaid care work in families, despite emphasizing the need for families to help reinvigorate civic activity. . . . The social capitalist agenda, which rests on a refusal to use government policies to support unpaid care work, pushes the burdens of unpaid care work onto families, specifically women (Fraser 1994; O'Connor, Shola Orloff, and Shaver 1999). The lack of formal services is linked to "coercive" gender inequality (Zimmerman 1993). When welfare states fail to relieve existing inequalities in the distribution of unpaid care work, they reinforce those inequalities (Hobson 1990). Both moralists and social capitalists are rooted in a liberal ideology that demands a weak state with limited federal policies. Consequently, including unpaid care work in their definition of civic engagement would have little impact on their view of the role of social policy because they already see almost no role for federal policy in improving civic engagement. Moralists in particular believe that government can only harm civic engagement, regardless of the type.

By contrast, historical institutionalists see a larger role for the government, specifically the federal government, in improving civil society and civic engagement. They challenge the distinctions between local organizations and the government and claim that big government cannot be blamed for civic disengagement (Skocpol 1998). . . . Historical institutionalists often note the gendered character of supposedly universal benefits (Mettler 1999; Skocpol 1992). National policies, such as universal postsecondary education or even universal health care, would give positive supports to those providing the bulk of unpaid care. But historical institutionalists have generally not counted family care work as civic engagement. Thus, while the universal policies historical institutionalists usually support would indirectly improve the condition of family care work, they would likely not ameliorate gender inequalities in the provision of unpaid care work. . . . If historical institutionalists acknowledged the unpaid care work provided within families as a form of civic engagement, they would come closer to a social feminist view of the state's role in fostering civic engagement.

Unlike civic engagement scholars, feminist scholars have attended carefully to how women's unpaid care work has contributed to women's dependence, poverty, and exclusion from civic activities (Daly 2000; Knijn and Kremer 1997; Mink 1995, 1998).Women who perform care work in welfare states with weak social policies tend to be poorer and to have less representation in elected offices (Esping-Andersen 1999; Korpi 2000; Siaroff 2000). U.S. citizens do not have access to universal health care, universal childcare, paid parental leave, or any other ways of packaging welfare that would help balance paid work and care work demands. As a result, the relative poverty rate, which is the percentage of persons below 50 percent of median income, among single mothers in the United States is nearly 60 percent (Korpi 2000). In addition, women constitute less than 30 percent of Congress, 10 percent of governors, and 25 percent of state legislatures in the United States (Center for American Women and Politics 2000). In the United States, men with young children are more likely than women with young children to hold elected office (Dodson 1997). Moreover, women tend to enter public office later in life than men due to child care responsibilities (Dodson 1997). Women in the United States are not alone. France and Germany have greater supports than the United States does for women who provide care work, but the available supports tend to push women out of, rather than enable them to remain in, the labor force (Sainsbury 1999). As a result, relative poverty rates for single mothers in France and Germany are 20 and 25 percent, respectively (Korpi 2000). Countries such as France and Germany, with low women's labor force participation rates, tend to have low elected representation among women (Siaroff 2000). In 1998, France's parliament was just 11 percent women, while Germany's was less than 30 percent (Siaroff 2000). Feminists argue that for women to participate fully in paid work, politics, and civil society, they need to have a greater choice about whether and how much to care (Harrington Meyer 2000).

Most feminist scholars see the state as having the potential to spread the burdens of unpaid care work and consequently improve the provision of it, though there is disagreement among them as to how this should be done so as to improve gender equity (Harrington Meyer 2000; Hobson 2000; Lister 1997; Sainsbury 1994; Zimmerman 1993). As Fraser (1994) argued, achieving gender equity is a difficult task because it is a complex notion fraught with inherent contradictions that make a clear policy solution difficult to achieve (see also Lewis 1992). Striking a balance between the equality versus difference perspectives, that is, treating women like men on one extreme and essentializing women's differences on the other extreme, is ultimately a difficult task (Lister 1997, 2000). In calling care work a form of civic engagement, we need to be careful to value and redistribute unpaid care work to undermine the traditional gendered division of labor and enhance women's participatory citizenship simultaneously (Lister 2000). To this end, we support public policies that redistribute unpaid care work largely provided by women. Such redistribution would improve the quality of and access to care and also increase women's participation in the traditional political process. After all, women in elected office are more likely than men to be supportive of policies that support unpaid care work (Boles 1991; Dodson 1997; Thomas 1994). The goal is to value care work as civic engagement while simultaneously reducing the burden of care women shoulder. We point to the Scandinavian welfare states as examples of welfare regimes that support unpaid care work and encourage civic activity and thus promote gender equality. Scandinavian policies are heavily geared toward providing citizens' social rights. They emphasize universal policies that support women's unpaid care work through income and employment support policies without enforcing their economic dependence on men (Korpi 2000; Leira 1992; Sainsbury 1999). Key policies include universal health care; universal income support; public day care services, particularly for young children; paid maternity and paternity leave; and public home health services for the disabled elderly. These policies allow women to maintain independent households and provide care without living in desperate poverty or being forced to be economically dependent on men (Orloff 1993; Sainsbury 1999). Relative poverty rates among single mothers in Norway and Sweden are the lowest in the world, at less than 5 percent (Korpi 2000).

Generous health and income support policies make the tasks associated with caring easier and consequently lead to better care. Unlike in the United States, Scandinavian single parents are not forced to choose between the income security of a job and worrying that their children are being inadequately cared for, if at all (Edin and Lein 1997). As Scheiwe (1994) argued, policies need to support "care times," time spent out of paid labor to provide care, in the way that they support periods of unemployment or disability. In a study comparing the experiences of parents caring for chronically ill children in the United States and Finland, Zimmerman (1993) showed how policies such as universal health insurance, income support, parental sick leave, and formal care services allowed parents to focus more on their sick children and less on health care bills and their jobs. Moreover, these countries have taken policy steps to redistribute care work between men and women, though these attempts have been less successful (Lister 2000).

Policies that facilitate women's social citizenship, which redistribute care work, have had an enormous impact on women's participation in the formal political sphere. The women who live in these countries are far more likely to have equal representation in elected office (Siaroff 2000). About half of Norway's and Sweden's parliaments are composed of women. Nowhere else in the industrialized world do women enjoy such high levels of participation in elected office. Women have a powerful and relatively equal voice in these democracies. Thus, while scholars such as Leira (1992) point to the continued elusiveness of gender justice even in Scandinavia, Scandinavian social policies effectively accomplish the explicit goal of increasing gender equity—in both economic and political arenas. . . .

DISCUSSION

Social capital, historical institutional, and moralist perspectives fail to address the importance of gender as a social force in the civic engagement literature. We address this limitation by identifying the role of care work in participatory citizenship. For women, in particular, unpaid care work often competes with paid work for resources such as time, money, and health. Cooking, cleaning, and caring may limit participation in traditional forms of civic activity. But by providing citizens with food, clothing, nurturing, and shelter, care workers also facilitate civic involvement from one generation to the next. In some instances, care work even prods citizens to become highly political; legions of women have joined environmental and disability reform movements because of their commitments to their children or frail elders.

In contrast to androcentric political theorists, we argue that care work is often, in and of itself, a fundamental form of civic engagement. It meets all of the criteria that define other forms of civic activity. It is generally voluntary and altruistic, while fostering reciprocity and trust. Furthermore, many civic engagement scholars focus on the importance of the family. Thus, care work's exclusion from the definition of civic activity is not because it takes place within the private family. The exclusion of unpaid care is theoretically inconsistent given the attention paid to family in the literature. . . .

Care work affects the health of civic life and is a fundamental component of participatory citizenship. Welfare regimes that support the right to give and receive care enhance participatory citizenship and welfare for all citizens. Although historical institutionalists have addressed ways in which welfare states may stimulate civic engagement, they have not addressed how women's care work might fit into this. We argue that a strong centralized welfare state can relieve class and gender inequities that inhibit democratic participation. Although some civic engagement thinkers argue that strong welfare states hinder traditional civic engagement, evidence suggests that social program spending can enhance social trust and group membership, critical outcomes of civic engagement (Andersen 1999). Universal programs that spread the risks and costs of caring across all taxpayers can strengthen feminist goals, social cohesion, and consequently civic participation by making everyone responsible for an activity from which we all benefit.

1. Burns, Lehman Schlozman, and Verba (2001) did look at the impact of women's disproportionate responsibility for domestic labor on their political participation. However, they looked at gender differences in participation as opposed to considering how unpaid care (regardless of who performs it, though it is mostly women) affects civic engagement.

2. It is important to point out that historical institutionalists have dealt extensively with the maternalist movement, which provides an example of where mothering precipitates women's civic participation (Skocpol 1992). Similarly, moralists have stressed how certain family forms provide moral and emotional foundations for civic engagement. However, moralists ignore the gendered work and attitudes on which traditional families rest. We take up both of these points in the Care Work as a Catalyst section.

3. Some scholars, particularly moralists such as Elshtain (1998), do not think that participating in social movements should be considered civic engagement. Social capitalists also are sometimes uncomfortable with social movements if they hurt social trust, which is an important part of social capital.

4. Feminist literature relating to the labor market has been able to show that providing care, bearing and raising children, cooking, cleaning, and caring for the elderly is just as important to society as paid work; it has simply been unremunerated (Laslett and Brenner 1989; Mink 1995, 1998; Oakley 1974; Secombe 1974). The citizenship literature has also validated the societal necessity of care work by incorporating it into a definition of citizenship that views care as a social right and in some cases a social obligation (Harrington Meyer 2000; Knijn and Kremer 1997; Lister 1997).

5. Elshtain (1982a) has made a career out of bringing the family into political thought and theory, emphasizing nurturance, love, and morality as representative of women's contribution within the family. Simply put, she reminds feminists that the "new woman" should not be the "old man." Her writings on the civic engagement debate, however, have mostly focused on the "decline" of the family ("illegitimate" births, divorce and so on) (Elshtain 1996, 1999). In this debate, she emphasizes how the decline in traditional family forms undermines civil society.

REFERENCES

Adam, Emma K. 1999. The effects of relationship style, hours of paid work and division of child rearing labor on emotional and physiological stress in working mothers. American Sociological Association Paper. *Sociological Abstracts* 047.

Andersen, Kristi. 1999. The gender gap and experiences with the welfare state. *PS: Political Science and Politics* 33 (1): 17–19.

Bird, Chloe E. 1999. Gender, household labor, and psychological distress: The impact of the amount and division of housework. *Journal of Health and Social Behavior* 40 (1): 32–45.

Boles, J. K. 1991. Advancing the women's agenda within local legislatures. In *Gender and policymaking: Studies of women in office*, edited by L. Dodson. New Brunswick, NJ: Center for the American Women and Politics.

Brody, Elaine. 1990. *Women in the middle: Their parent care years*. New York: Springer.

Burns, Nancy, Kay Lehman Schlozman, and Sidney Verba. 2001. *The private roots of public action: Gender, equality, and political participation*. Cambridge, MA: Harvard University Press.

Cancian, Francesca, and Stacey Oliker. 2000. *Caring and gender*. Thousand Oaks, CA: Pine Forge Press.

Center for American Women and Politics. 2000. *Election 2000: Summary of results for women*. New Brunswick, NJ: Rutgers University Eagleton Institute of Politics.

Couch, Laurie, Jeffrey Adams, and Warren Jones. 1996. The assessment of trust orientation. *Journal of Personality Assessment* 67 (2): 305–23.

Couch, Laurie, and Warren Jones. 1997. Measuring levels of trust. *Journal of Research in Personality* 31 (3): 319–36.

Daly, Mary. 2000. *The gender division of welfare*. Cambridge, UK: Cambridge University Press.

Dodson, Debra. 1997. Change and continuity in the relationship between private responsibilities and public office holding: The more things change, the more they stay the same. *Policy Studies* 25 (4): 569–84.

Edin, Katherine, and Laura Lein. 1997. Work, welfare and single mother's survival strategies. *American Sociological Review* 62 (2): 253–66.

Elshtain, Jean Bethke. 1982a. *The family in political thought*. Amherst: University of Massachusetts Press.

————. 1982b. Feminism, family, and community. *Dissent* 29 (4): 442–49.

————. 1996. Democracy at century's end. *Social Service Review* 70 (4): 507–15.

————. 1998. Not a cure all: Civil society creates citizens, it does not solve problems. In *Community works*, edited by E. J. Dionne. Washington, DC: Brookings Institution.

————. 1999. A call to civil society. *Society* 36 (5): 11–19.

Esping-Andersen, G. 1999. *Social foundations of postindustrial economies*. Oxford, UK: Oxford University Press.

Fraser, Nancy. 1994. After the family wage: Gender equity and the welfare state. *Political Theory* 22 (4): 591–618.

Freeman, Richard B. 1996. Working for nothing: The supply of volunteer labor. No. 5435. Cambridge, MA: National Bureau of Economic Research.

Galston, William, and William Bennett. 1999. *National Commission on Civic Renewal: Update to "A nation of spectator's report."* College Park: University of Maryland.

Galston, William, and Peter Levine. 1998. America's civic condition: A glance at the evidence. In *Community works*, edited by E. J. Dionne. Washington, DC: Brookings Institution.

Gordon, Linda. 1994. *Pitied but not entitled: Single mothers and the history of welfare, 1890–1935*. New York: Free Press.

Harkness, Susan, and Jane Waldfogel. 1999. The family gap in pay: Evidence from seven industrialized countries. Luxembourg Income Study working paper no. 219, Syracuse University, New York. Retrieved from http://lisweb.ceps.lu/publications/liswps/219.pdf.

Harrington Meyer, Madonna, ed. 2000. *Care work: Gender, labor, and the welfare state*. New York: Routledge.

Hernes, Helga Maria. 1987. *Welfare states and women power*. London: Norwegian University Press.

Hobson, Barbara. 1990. No exit, no voice. *Acta Sociologica* 33 (3): 235–50.

————. 2000. *Gender and citizenship in transition*. New York: Routledge.

Hochschild, Arlie. 1997. *The time bind*. New York: Metropolitan Books.

Hochschild, Arlie, with Annie Machung. 1989. *The second shift*. New York: Basic Books.

Holmes, Eva. 1995. Educational intervention for young children who have experienced fragmented care. In *The emotional needs of children and their families*, edited by J. Trowell. London: Routledge.

Hooyman, Nancy, and Judith Gonyea. 1995. *Feminist perspectives on family care: Policies for gender justice*. Thousand Oaks, CA: Sage.

Hoyert, Donna L., and Marsha M. Seltzer. 1992. Factors relating to well being and life activities of family caregivers. *Family Relations* 41 (1): 74–81.

Knijn, Trudie, and Monique Kremer. 1997. Gender and caring dimensions of welfare states: Toward inclusive citizenship. *Social Politics* 4 (3): 328–61.

Korpi, Walter. 2000. Faces of inequality: Gender, class and patterns of inequalities in different types of welfare states. Luxembourg Income Study working paper no. 224, Maxwell School of Citizenship and Public Affairs, Syracuse, NY. Retrieved from http:/lisweb.ceps.lu /publications/liswps/224.pdf.

Laslett, Barbara, and Johanna Brenner. 1989. Gender and social reproduction: Historical perspectives. *Annual Review of Sociology* 15:381–404.

Leete-Guy, Laura, and Juliet Schor. 1993. Assessing the time-squeeze hypothesis: Hours worked in the United States, 1969–1989. *Industrial Relations* 33 (1): 24–43.

Leira, Arnlaug. 1992. *The welfare state and working mothers: The Scandinavian experience*. NewYork: Cambridge University Press.

Lewis, Jane. 1992. Gender and the development of welfare state regimes. *Journal of European Social Policy* 2:159–73.

Lister, Ruth. 1997. *Citizenship: Feminist perspectives*. Washington Square: New York University Press.

———. 2000. Dilemmas in engendering citizenship. In *Gender and citizenship in transition*, edited by Barbara Hobson. New York: Routledge.

Mettler, Suzanne. 1999. Promoting the general welfare: Reflections on the consequences of social policy for civic life. Paper presented at Improving Civic Life: Symposium on Citizenship and Civic Engagement, 22–23 October, Syracuse, NY.

Mink, Gwendolyn. 1995. *The wages of motherhood: Inequality in the welfare state*. Ithaca, NY: Cornell University Press.

———. 1998. Welfare's end. Ithaca, NY: Cornell University Press.

National Alliance for Caregiving. 1997. *Family caregiving in the U.S.: Findings from a national survey, final report*. Washington, DC: National Alliance for Caregiving and AARP. Retrieved from http://www.caregiving.org/content/repsprods.asp.

Oakley, Ann. 1974. *The sociology of housework*. New York: Pantheon.

O'Connor, Julia S., Ann Shola Orloff, and Sheila Shaver. 1999. *States, markets, families: Gender, liberalism, and social policy in Australia, Canada, Great Britain and the United States*. Cambridge, UK: Cambridge University Press.

Oliker, Stacey. 2000. Examining care at welfare's end. In *Care work: Gender, labor and the welfare state*, edited by Madonna Harrington Meyer. New York: Routledge.

Orloff, Ann Shola. 1993. Gender and the social rights of citizenship: The comparative analysis of gender relations and welfare states. *American Sociological Review*, 58, 303–328.

Peters, Richard G., Vincent Covello, and David McCallum. 1997. The determinants of trust and credibility in environmental risk communication. *Risk Analysis* 17 (1): 43–54.

Putnam, Robert. 1995. Bowling alone: America's declining social capital. *Journal of Democracy* 6 (1): 65–78.

———. 1996. The strange disappearance of civic America. *American Prospect* 7 (24). Retrieved from http://www.prospect.org/archives/24/24putn.html.

———. 2000. *Bowling alone: The collapse and revival of American community*. New York: Simon & Schuster.

Rubin, Lillian. 1994. *Families on the fault line*. New York: Harper Collins.

Sainsbury, Diane. 1994. *Gendering welfare states*. London: Sage.

———. 1999. Gender, policy regimes and politics. In *Gender and welfare state regimes*, edited by Diane Sainsbury. Oxford, UK: Oxford University Press.

Scheiwe, Kirsten. 1994. German pension insurance, gendered times and stratification. In *Gendering welfare states*, edited by Diane Sainsbury. London: Sage.

Secombe, Wally. 1974. The housewife and her labour under capitalism. *New Left Review* 83 (January/February): 3–24.

Siaroff, Alan. 2000. Women's representation in legislatures and cabinets in industrial democracies. *International Political Science Review* 21 (2): 197–215.

Skocpol, Theda. 1992. *Protecting soldiers and mothers*. Cambridge, MA: Belknap.

———. 1998. Don't blame big government: America's voluntary groups thrive in a national network. In *Community works*, edited by D. J. Dionne. Washington, DC: Brookings Institution.

Smeeding, Timothy, Carroll Estes, and Lou Glasse. 1999. Social security reform and older women: Improving the system. Income Security Policy Series paper no. 22, Maxwell School, Center for Policy Research, Syracuse, NY.

Thomas, Sue. 1994. *How women legislate*. New York: Oxford University Press.

Verba, Sidney, Kay Lehman Schlozman, and Henry Brady. 1995. *Voice and inequality*. Cambridge, MA: Harvard University Press.

Voydanoff, Patricia, and Brenda Donnelly. 1999. The intersection of time in activities and perceived unfairness in relation to psychological distress and marital quality. *Journal of Marriage and the Family* 61 (August): 739–51.

Zimmerman, Mary K. 1993. Caregiving in the welfare state: Mothers' informal health care work in Finland. *Sociology of Health Care* 10:193–211.

28 | ACID VIOLENCE AND MEDICAL CARE IN BANGLADESH: WOMEN'S ACTIVISM AS CAREWORK

Afroza Anwary

Acid attacks on women are increasing at alarming rates in Bangladesh, but the government has failed to provide medical care to the victims. Easily available sulfuric acid, which can mutilate a human face in moments, has emerged as a weapon used to disfigure a woman's body. In this excerpt, Anwary illustrates another aspect of the interface of globalization, gender, and carework: how local and international nongovernmental organizations join forces to develop medical care services for women that were previously seriously deficient.

This is a study of how carework for women victims of acid attacks has been developed since the 1980s. It is also a study of how feminist groups have generated regional as well as international support for victims. In other words, it is a study of activism as carework. I examine how women activists in Bangladesh amplify their concerns for acid victimization to reach the international arena and how they mobilize civil society toward its full potential as an agent of healing and health care. I also demonstrate how local and international organizations pressured the government of Bangladesh into providing necessary and crucial medical care for victims. This article illuminates the multiple sites of carework by highlighting the importance of international networks. I explain how people who care for a vulnerable group can promote gender justice in the context of a strong patriarchal society like Bangladesh.

Acid violence is a particularly vicious form of aggression against human beings. Sulfuric acid, thrown on a human body, causes skin tissue to melt, often exposing bones below the flesh, sometimes even dissolving the bones. Most attacks, made by men, are directed at the faces of young women to destroy their physical appearance (Swanson 2002). Recovering from the trauma takes considerable time and, because of the disfigurement, victims' psyches are debilitated, negatively affecting every aspect of their lives. Survivors of acid attacks experience social isolation, encounter great difficulty finding work, and if unmarried, lose the opportunity to marry.

Acid attacks are a classic example of how gender conditions the responses of civil society, especially private, voluntary, and nongovernmental organizations (NGOs). The world has shrunk due to globalization, allowing an instant flow of information between nations. Consequently, when human rights abuse is overlooked by a national government, an outcry from local activists who want to help the victims can be communicated globally, causing wide public awareness. When the government of Bangladesh failed to provide basic medical care to acid survivors, local activists were able to contact international activists using new technology and pressure the Bangladesh government into providing necessary and crucial medical care to victims. Interaction between the state and NGOs has made international resources available to acid survivors in domestic social struggles. I begin by considering the social contexts and meaning of acid attacks and explain why acid victimization has become highly sensationalized in a global world. Then I examine the effects of globalization on acid violence, demonstrate how existing gender divisions are contested by new labor demands embedded in globalization, and argue that this may precipitate a rise in acid attacks. Finally, I explain the importance of activism and international networks on social policy related to health care work.

ACID ATTACKS: SOCIAL CONTEXT AND MEANING

The Western world seems to hold a common myth that acid violence only occurs in the Third World and may be related to Islamic fundamentalist men's throwing acid in the faces of women who are not veiled. Historical and current evidence on acid attacks is inconsistent with this perception. Acid violence does not occur in Bangladesh alone. It occurs in Pakistan (A matter of honor 1999), China (Acid test 2000), Ethiopia (SWIPNET 1998), and historically, in Europe (Davis 1984).... Acid attacks are a modern problem partially related to global development. In Bangladesh, daily economic struggles take precedence over attempts to win legal rights for acid victims. The lack of medical care, the absence of alternative institutions for victims rejected by their families, the failure of the government to enforce laws against the attackers, and rapid globalization have facilitated local feminist groups' efforts to effectively publicize and sensationalize acid victimization. The publicity also created space for building political coalitions around concern for human rights among groups living in vastly different political and cultural conditions.

Obtaining accurate statistics on acid attacks is difficult because most Bangladeshis live in isolated rural communities and mechanisms to collect such information are weak. In addition, police reports significantly under-represent the number of annual acid attacks. Many victims do not report attacks to police because they fear reprisals from offenders' friends and families (Nasreen Haq, personal communication, 3 March 2001). However, new evidence suggests that reported cases of attacks are increasing at an alarming rate. According to Swanson (2002), there are approximately 300 cases reported each year.

Motivated by a variety of situations, men throw acid on women much like men rape, to keep women in their place. As in many patriarchal cultures, masculinity in Bangladesh refers to the ability of men to protect, defend, and sustain their property, including their homes and families. Furthermore, recent high levels of poverty and unemployment in Bangladesh contribute to attacks on women because of family feuds over property. Destroying female relatives' faces is the worst type of humiliation performed by men. The following example of a young man named Kuddus illustrates this point. Kuddus's cousin, who claimed the ownership of a disputed fruit tree, attacked Kuddus's wife and sister. Earlier that day, Kuddus claimed his ownership of the tree (Acid attack on sister-in-laws 2002).

The tremendous emphasis on women's appearance is also responsible for acid attacks. Parents have a primary responsibility to protect their daughters from sexual temptations, thereby preserving their marriageability. In a society where marriage is the only way to maintain the social status of women and ensure their economic security, virginity and appearance are the only resources women have in the marriage market. Women are not expected to get involved in romantic relationships before marriage. Sometimes, men victimize women who reject their marriage proposals. The men know they can avoid direct responsibility for their acts because the government fails to prosecute acid attackers. By destroying women's appearance, attackers try to bolster the political power that they feel was threatened when the women rejected their proposals. The men use women's appearance and sexuality to mark the boundaries between themselves and the women. Therefore, appearance seems to be a map of power for men and women. The following case illustrates this point. Majeda's parents refused a marriage proposal for her from one man, and Majeda was married to someone else. The angry suitor attacked her. Her eyeballs were badly burnt and hung from their sockets. Her attacker is still at large (Help victims of acid violence 2001).

In summary, the national context of Bangladesh is partially responsible for acid attacks, and the devastating effects of acid attacks on the victims require emergency medical carework. In the next section, I explain how globalization may precipitate acid attacks in Bangladesh.

THE IMPACT OF GLOBALIZATION

The new labor demands embedded in globalization may precipitate a rise in acid attacks because they contest the existing gendered division of labor. Globalization of the national economy has had a significant effect on Bangladeshi government policy. To attract multinational corporations into taking advantage of cheap labor in Bangladesh, the government developed new policies that led to the growth of the export-oriented garment industry (Rozario 2001). However, the garment industry prefers to hire semiskilled or unskilled women, which has led to a dramatic increase in women's employment in the secondary sector of the economy.

Such encroachment from women into paid employment poses a challenge to male supremacy in Bangladesh, and women who achieve increased economic autonomy are apt to experience resistance and hostility from men. Nonetheless, deteriorating economic conditions, high unemployment rates among male breadwinners, the increasing number of landless households, and the lack of agricultural work for male laborers has forced some men to allow their wives, daughters, and mothers to participate in the paid labor force. In urban centers, women are often the sole wage earners, and they are expected to take care of their household responsibilities as well (Rozario 2001).

Women who are burdened with both housework and paid labor and who fail to perform their traditional gender roles often are victimized by their husbands. For example, Ashma Begum worked in an export-oriented garment factory and was the sole breadwinner of the family. She returned home late from work. Her unemployed husband who gained some financial privilege from her income was irate because his dinner was not prepared by her. Later, he threw sulfuric acid on her face, disfiguring her (Acid attacks 1998a). Ashma Begum's victimization reflects a reactionary backlash against women's increasing autonomy caused partly by the process of globalization. It also reflects men's increasing insecurity about the erosion of patriarchal privilege in Bangladesh at the entrance to the twenty-first century.

In sum, globalization and the structural adjustment policies of the government of Bangladesh reinforce gender violence. In the next section, I show how globalization also initiated a new pattern of activism. I highlight the importance of international networks in helping to bring global resources to acid survivors and in pressuring the government of Bangladesh to provide medical care for them.

SOCIAL POLICY AND GENDER ACTIVISM

Acid attacks became a major issue of debate amid a resurgence of women's activism in the early 1980s. Early organized responses to acid attacks stemmed from internal mobilization instigated by women's organizations such as Naripokkho, a national, voluntary membership organization working to build resistance to violence against women. Many staffers are university educated, having the ability and knowledge to interact with governmental, nongovernmental, and international agencies. Many have personal ties with local and global civil society organizations. The key resources of knowledge and know-how of the staff and the active participation of victims in programs like Naripokkho help activists link victims' experiences with all global injustice that women face. Naripokkho has four working groups: reproductive rights and women's health, violence against women and human rights, gender issues in the environment and development, and the representation of women in media and cultural politics (Nasreen Haq, personal communication, 3 March 2001). Programs and activities include research, campaigns, protest work, discussions, lobbying and advocacy, cultural events, alliance with other human rights organizations, and monitoring of state interventions to combat violence against women. The group organizes workshops for survivors and their families, helping to rebuild their confidence, returning them to an active life within their communities, and allowing victims to come together and realize that they are not alone (Asian Women's Resource Exchange 2002).

Many international organizations located in Bangladesh, such as the British Council (BC), responded to the call of women's groups to help the victims. The BC is the United Kingdom's international organization for educational and cultural relations. By using its global network of offices, the BC promotes, among other things, gender equality in a global world. The BC works closely with national governments, local NGOs, private agencies, and international organizations. The BC of Bangladesh formed Supporting Survivors of Acid Attacks, a project that helps survivors access quality medical care, legal assistance, rehabilitation, and education. Using posters, flyers, and stickers twice a year, the BC organizes weeklong festivals, seminars, and workshops, including drama related to women's issues and acid attacks (Farah Kabir, personal communication, 30 July 2002).

Naripokkho persuaded the United Nations Children's Fund (UNICEF) and Amnesty International to recognize the plight of the acid survivors. The group convinced UNICEF that most acid survivors are young girls, who should be considered children who need emergency health service from organizations like UNICEF (Naripokkho 2001). UNICEF works in close partnership with the Bangladesh government, the Ministry of Public Health, and other national and international NGOs to eliminate violence against women and girls. For example, with economic support from UNICEF's Bangladesh Child Protection Section, the Ministry of Women's and Children's Affairs made a video that documents case studies of men helping female survivors of violence to seek justice (Acid Survivors Foundation [ASF] 1999). UNICEF, with financial assistance from the Canadian

International Development Agency, formed ASF. A board of 15 trustees representing national and international NGOs, international donors, and acid survivors governs ASF. The goal of ASF is to provide ongoing help in the treatment, rehabilitation, and reintegration of the victims of acid attacks. With the help of other NGOs, ASF ensures that victims receive treatment at the hospital within three days of their attacks, and it provides survivors with better access to legal justice systems (ASF 1999). ASF established Thikana House, which is the only health care facility service in the country for acid victims with less serious burns (Swanson 2002). The BC provided support for the positions of two case managers responsible for acid victims and supported transportation of victims to Thikana House (Farah Kabir, personal communication, 30 July 2002).

The BC in Bangladesh showed a documentary called Ayana, which revealed that attacks did not stop victims and their families from surviving. Women's groups and national and international organizations used advocacy and lobbying to demand that the Bangladesh government provide necessary medical support for the victims and enforce laws against acid attacks (Farah Kabir, personal communication, 30 July 2002).

Activists also approached foreign NGOs worldwide. Italian NGOs Cooperazione Internationale and Associezone Onlus provided treatment for acid burn victims. Corporation Darmeyestekika, a Spanish NGO, funded the treatment of six survivors who were featured on television, which led to wide support from the Spanish society (Acid attacks 1998b). Two survivors were featured on the popular American television programs 20/20 and Oprah. These programs invoked hundreds of sympathetic Americans to help the survivors (Naripokkho 2001). British Airways worked closely with ASF to provide free roundtrip tickets for some survivors to travel abroad where they received reconstructive surgery (Faces of hope 1999).

In the early 1990s, newspapers reported a rash of disfigurement due to acid attacks on young women. By the mid-1990s, documentation of acid attacks recorded by activists and protests in Dhaka were followed by demands for better care for acid victims. Although the outside world was unaware of these acid attacks, knowledge started to spread outside Bangladesh after 1995. In 1999, the World Press Club gave an award to Shafiqul Alam for his photo of an acid survivor whose head, except for one eye, was completely covered by a veil. The victim was ashamed to show her face in public because of her severe scars. The award drew the attention of the Western world to acid attacks.

A few activists visited the United States to speak publicly about the plight of acid victims and to appeal to human rights organizations to provide medical care to the victims. In the United States, a Bangladeshi physician and an advocate for children's rights approached Healing the Children (HTC), a nonprofit organization that secures donated medical care for children around the world whose families cannot afford medical expenses. The doctor also requested that HTC sponsor acid survivors for reconstructive surgery (Naripokkho 2001). Friends and families of the advocates for children's rights in Bangladesh traced the young victims of acid attacks; then HTC approached the American embassy in Bangladesh to help with immigration-related issues for the victims (HTC 2002).

In 1999, two survivors of acid attacks were brought to the United States by HTC. HTC contacted Shriners Hospital, a 30-bed pediatric burn unit that provides cost-free acute care and reconstructive surgery to children having burns that cause deformity to their faces. In 1999, the government of Bangladesh responded to the demands of the women's groups and national and international organizations by building a new 50-bed burn unit in Dhaka, Bangladesh. Until 1999, Dhaka Medical College Hospital was the only public hospital in the country that had a burn unit. Dhaka Medical College Hospital had only 8 beds for female patients, whereas 300 reported female victims needed urgent care each year (Swanson 2002).

In early 2001, HTC sent a medical team to Bangladesh to provide surgical services for victims of acid violence and to share skills and techniques with local physicians. With the help of local hospitals, HTC performed surgeries to excise scar tissue, release contracted skin, and graft skin to cover scarred areas. By 7 April 2001, 31 patients underwent surgery (HTC 2002).

In November 2001, two universities in Bangladesh and the University of North London jointly organized a two-day workshop on violence against women. An international seminar on violence against women was held in the BC auditorium in Dhaka in January 2002. The public was encouraged to participate in the seminars. Seminars and workshops provided an opportunity to promote networking among local organizations and between local and international organizations engaged in improving the status of women and their human rights (Farah Kabir, personal communication, 30 July 2002).

Now, because of assistance from national and international organizations, the spirit of cooperation and collegiality predominates among organizations and individuals providing medical care to acid survivors. In the center of this cooperation are women's groups that strategically mobilize information about acid attacks, successfully motivate different organizations to provide medical care to acid survivors, and gain some leverage over the much more powerful government that tries to ignore the human rights abuses in Bangladesh.

International networks also have affected the implementation of laws against acid attacks. The government of Bangladesh developed a law that legislated the death penalty as the maximum punishment for perpetrators of acid attacks. However, perpetrators largely go unpunished. Naripokkho has investigated 217 cases of acid attacks from October 1998 to September 2000. Of 217 cases, only 27 suits were filed against attackers, and only 18 cases were under investigation by the courts (Naripokkho 2000).

Recently, pressure from British dignitaries who attended meetings organized by the BC and pressure from the U.S. State Department, the U.S. Agency of International Development, and other international organizations have led high-ranking Bangladeshi officials and the prime minister of Bangladesh to direct the court to pay attention to acid attack cases that receive high international visibility (Swanson 2002).

In sum, international networks have been important in shaping the health care needs of acid survivors of Bangladesh. The role of women activists has been crucial in bringing international resources that help meet the physical and social needs of everyday life for acid survivors.

CONCLUSION

Using dramatic personal testimonies of acid survivors, a network of women's groups was the first to broaden its concerns for acid victimization to reach the international arena by regular communication. It linked Bangladesh and international human rights activists through the frequent exchange of publications, visits, e-mails, letters, and postings on the Internet. New technology in a global world rapidly increases the number of individuals who are aware of the problems and strengthens the mobilization that is underway. A network of transnational human rights organizations then lobbied the government of Bangladesh and international organizations to provide medical care for victims. High visibility of acid victims in the international arena, protest in the cities, and pressure from international donor organizations to whom the government routinely turns for financial help forced the government to provide medical care to acid victims.

International organizations that work closely with local NGOs and other indigenous organizations sought appropriate and acceptable ways to provide medical care. In the absence of universal normative evaluations of acid victimization, international organizations provide universal normative evaluations of human rights abuses. Prestigious organizations such as UNICEF help build activists' credibility by publicly speaking on behalf of the victims. Such support is crucial for attracting public attention. In addition, support from international agencies is crucial because resources for the victims are shrinking significantly and assistance from outside organizations increases the resources of victims/local activists appreciably. On one hand, alignment with agencies has broadened the power base of local feminist groups and provided innovative tactics, which are particularly important for achieving the major goal of the victims: receiving medical care. On the other hand, by providing necessary medical care to the victims of acid attacks, local and international organizations met their social responsibilities.

Acid attack on sister-in-laws. 2002. *Daily Ittefaq*, 13 July.

Acid attacks. 1998a. *Daily Star*. Retrieved 1 January 1998 from http://www
.dailystarnews.com/200101/14/n1011410.htm.

———. 1998b. *Daily Star*. Retrieved 16 November 1998 from http://www
.dailystarnews.com/200101/14/n1011410.htm.

Acid Survivors Foundation (ASF). 1999. Acid Survivors Foundation: An important new initiative. Retrieved 16 October 1999 from
http://www.bicn.com/ezino/features/lifeinbgd/htm.

Acid test. 2000. *Time*, 11 December.

Asian Women's Resource Exchange. 2002. National partners: Bangladesh. Retrieved 12 July 1997 from http://www.arrow.org.my/docs/partners.html.

Davis, Jennifer. 1984. A poor man's system of justice: The London police courts
in the second half of the nineteenth century. *Historical Journal* 27:309–35.

Faces of hope. 1999. Teen launches crusade to stop acid attacks against women in
Bangladesh. *20/20*, 1 November.

Healing the Children (HTC). 2002. Healing the Children: Bangladesh. Retrieved
23 July from http://www.htcne.org/Bangladesh.html.

Help victims of acid violence. 2001. *New Nation*, 4 January.

A matter of honor. 1999. *Nightline*, 16 February.

Naripokkho. 2000. Brochure. 3 March.

———. 2001. Brochure. January–September.

Rozario, Santi. 2001. Claiming the campus for female students in Bangladesh.
Women's Studies International Forum 24:157–66.

Swanson, Jordan. 2002. Acid attacks: Bangladesh's efforts to stop the violence.
Harvard Health Policy Review. Retrieved 6 July 2002 from
http://hcs.harvard.edu/~epihc/currentissue/swanson.php.

SWIPNET. 1998. Ethiopian woman victim of acid attack. Retrieved 28 November 1998 from http://home.swipnet.se/~w~26522/Home.

29 WOMEN'S EMPOWERING CAREWORK

IN POST-SOVIET AZERBAIJAN

Mehrangiz Najafizadeh

In this article, Mehrangiz Najafizadeh focuses on the Republic of Azerbaijan, which has experienced major social, political, and economic upheaval since declaring independence from the Soviet Union in 1991. Najafizadeh examines the transition into the global economy as well as the Nagorno-Karabakh war with Armenia in terms of how these events have affected Azeri women's carework activities. Her analysis highlights the women's advocacy associations that have emerged and function both to provide direct care services and as a mechanism for assisting women to be more effective caregivers to their own families and communities.

Since declaring independence from the Soviet Union in 1991, the Republic of Azerbaijan has undergone major social, political, and economic transition. The transition to democracy, privatization, and a free market economy has opened Azerbaijan to many opportunities—including integration into the global economy—that were not available under the Soviets. At the same time, Azeris now confront many new challenges and hardships posed by the transition, with women particularly marginalized and adversely affected. The situation is further exacerbated by the Nagorno-Karabakh Conflict with Armenia, which has had devastating human and economic costs: about 20,000 Azeri deaths, nearly 1 million Azeri refugees and internally displaced persons (IDPs), the loss of roughly 20 percent of Azeri territory, and economic damage estimated at U.S. $53.5 billion.

Both Azeri women and Azeri men have been subject to negative aspects of the economic transition, to detrimental consequences of war, and to the dramatic reduction in the social security and protection previously provided by the state. Especially women, however, have been burdened both with an increase in various facets of family caregiving responsibilities and with the need to assume essential economic roles in the family. Thus, when the state no longer provides all of the necessary social services, who will assume that role has become a critical question. I argue that one answer is found in the emergence of the Azeri women's advocacy movement, which is composed of women's nongovernmental organizations that have arisen in response to the caregiving crisis. These organizations, sparked by the challenges of economic restructuring and war, play an important role in opening a space and giving a voice to Azeri women.

In the following discussion, I construe caregiving broadly: ranging from highly skilled medical care, school teaching, and other social services to traditional caregiving within the family, including providing material care for elderly parents. . . . My analysis is informed by fieldwork that I conducted in Baku, Azerbaijan, in the summers of 2001 and 2002 with individuals from women's advocacy associations, as well as from government and international agencies and organizations, and universities in Azerbaijan.

THE IMPACT OF TRANSITION ON WOMEN'S EMPLOYMENT AND PAID CAREWORK

The Soviet era in Azerbaijan was characterized by collectivization and by state industries, including state-supported caregiving services such as health and education. In contrast, as reflected in my interviews conducted in Azerbaijan as well as in current national and international reports, the transition to privatization and to a free market economy during the 1990s resulted in the closure of many Soviet factories—that as yet have not been replaced by private sector industries—and in increased unemployment among women and men. The transition to privatization also resulted in the elimination of free health care provided by the state and in the restructuring of the state health care and education systems. These changes led to decreases in state caregiving services and, consequently, to increases in unemployment in areas where women constituted the predominant labor force. . . . [T]he transition period has produced significant increases in the proportion of Azeris living in poverty. . . . Although the transition has led to significant economic benefits for a relatively small number of Azeris, about 60 percent of the population is at the poverty level, and about 20 percent of all households are considered "very poor" (International Monetary Fund 2000, 33–34; UNDP 2000, 22).

Women and men share "equal rights and freedoms" under the constitution of the Republic of Azerbaijan, yet employment and caregiving are highly gendered. Azeri women have been especially adversely affected by post-Soviet privatization and economic transition (Najafizadeh 2001). Ibrahimbekova (2000a, p. 7) noted, for example, that "privatization has obtained a male 'image' and . . . 90 percent of owners are men." Furthermore, the participation of women in high-paying jobs and in political decision-making has declined considerably. In industry and services, for example, women earn only 53 percent of men's earnings, and they hold only 12 percent of the seats in Parliament, compared to the Soviet era when women deputies constituted 39 percent of the Supreme Soviet of Azerbaijan (Sabi

1999, p. 117; State Statistical Committee of Azerbaijan Republic [SSCAR] 2000b, 108; UNDP 2000, p. 79). . . .

Azeri women tend to occupy more government jobs and positions in caregiving sectors—such as teaching, social work, and health services—where salaries have declined significantly (UNICEF 1999, p. 77). For example, health care workers and social workers average U.S. $12 per month, and education workers average U.S. $28 per month (SSCAR 2000a, pp. 70, 78; 2000b, p. 103). Furthermore, salaries in these jobs are gendered. Specifically, women constitute 77 percent of all employees in health and social work caregiving positions (61 percent of all physicians) and 68 percent of those employed in education. Yet women earn only 60 percent of what men earn in the health care/social work sector and 70 percent of what men earn in the education sector. . . .

THE IMPACT OF TRANSITION ON WOMEN'S ROLES IN THE FAMILY

While men often have remained unemployed for extended periods of time during the transition, women have tended to seek income through the informal economy. Indeed, my interviews indicate that although an informal economy also existed under the Soviets, it has increased dramatically during the post-Soviet transition. . . . These women have added the role of sole or primary breadwinner to their traditional responsibilities as the main family caregiver. Similarly, in other instances, the unemployed husband has left his wife and children and migrated to another region of Azerbaijan or to Russia, Iran, or Turkey in hopes of securing a job. In these situations, too, the wife retains her family caregiving role but assumes the breadwinner role—most commonly in the informal sector—to meet the needs of the family while she waits for funds to be sent from her migrant husband. The transition has affected women's caregiving roles in other ways. For example, the elimination of state services—such as day care centers and kindergartens— has placed additional caregiving demands on working mothers, and the elimination of state medical services (and the lack of resources to pay for fee-based medical services) has placed much of the burden of medical care on women. As such, family members with health problems commonly are cared for at home by mothers or grandmothers using traditional home remedies. Similarly, reductions in state-funded pensions for the elderly now often require family members—typically female members—to provide caregiving for parents and grandparents (Abdulvahabova 2000; Arnould 2001; Lieven 2001; Sabi 1999; UNDP 1999, pp. 40–45).

Furthermore, the economic transition and the Nagorno-Karabakh Conflict have taken a psychological toll on many Aerzi families, where increased levels of stress and anxiety have resulted in increased substance abuse, domestic violence, and family conflict (Abdulvahabova 2000, p. 27; Ibrahimbekova 2000b, p. 15; Seifullaghizi 2000, p. 30). Indeed, a survey in four regions of Azerbaijan revealed that 37 percent of adult women had experienced violence (32 percent in their natural family and 58 percent in their husband's family) and that 75 percent of these women viewed "lack of money" during the transition as central to the problem of violence (United Nations Development Programme Gender in Development Unit 2000, pp. 30–41).

Although the Nagorno-Karabakh Conflict has been under a cease-fire since 1994, the lives of many Azeri women continue to be dramatically altered by the war. Some women suffered the loss of their husbands or sons during the war, while other women are among the nearly 1 million Azeris who are either refugees or IDPs. Indeed, 71 percent of IDPs are women, and 60 percent live in tents in refugee camps or in railroad boxcars, with the remainder living in abandoned buildings and other temporary housing. As the UNDP (2000, p. 61) noted, "The worst affected are children and women belonging to families that face unemployment, physical insecurity, stress and above all, enormous loss of dignity and self respect. . . ."

AZERI WOMEN'S ASSOCIATIONS: AGENTS OF CARE AND EMPOWERMENT

Since national independence in 1991, more than 20 nongovernmental Azeri women's advocacy associations have emerged in this context of social, political, and economic transition. These are associations that are organized by women and for women, in large part because the government is unable to adequately address the pressing needs of women. Nor can it serve and oversee caregiving functions, as was the case under the Soviet regime. Instead, women's associations are now providing particular types of caregiving services. . . .

My various interviews in Azerbaijan, as well as published documents, suggest that the removal of the Soviet totalitarian political system was a necessary element for the emergence of women's caregiving associations but not a sufficient one. Several other conditions and events must also be included to explain the rise of such associations. First is the existence of a strong base of highly educated women professionals. Under the Soviet system, education of men and of women was a major priority. Thus, when independence was declared in 1991, Azerbaijan already had a substantial core of highly educated women. Some of these women had developed not only technical expertise in their professions but also leadership skills, social consciousness, and commitment to social reform. . . . They began the process of developing a new national identity and redefining the role of Azeri women. Second, the Nagorno-Karabakh Conflict, which started in 1988, resulted in massive waves of refugees and IDPs, large numbers of whom were women and children. In the early 1990s, several Azeri women's associations emerged to provide humanitarian assistance in direct response to the refugee/IDP crisis. Third, during the early 1990s, Azeri women were increasingly exposed to the international context. In 1994, a committee was established to coordinate the attendance of Azeri women's associations (approximately 70 women in total) at the 1995 Fourth World Conference on Women in Beijing. One objective of attending the conference was to bring the Azeri refugee/IDP crisis and its impact on women to the international arena. At the same time, participation in the conference helped Azeri women's associations articulate other women's needs and issues, and it stimulated the formation of additional Azeri women's associations in the years following the conference. Fourth, external international agencies and organizations . . . have been instrumental in providing material support, as well as organizational mentoring, to encourage and assist in the establishment and continuation of women's associations. In 1998, the president of Azerbaijan established the State Committee on Women's Issues as a government agency to foster women's rights and also to develop relations with Azeri women's associations. Finally, during the 1990s and into the 2000s, linkages between Azeri women and international agencies and organizations—as well as international women's networks—have diversified the foci of Azeri women's associations. Whereas the refugee/IDP situation continues as a central concern for many associations (more than a decade after the start of the war), there also has been a distinct broadening of the scope of association activities to encompass a myriad of women's issues (see Lemberanskaya and Mamedova 2001; Najafizadeh 2001; UNDP 1999, pp. 8–12, 61–65).

Azeri women's associations tend to be self-supporting and to rely very heavily (and sometimes totally) on the voluntary, unpaid efforts of their members . . . providing a network of care and support for Azeri women . . . similar to what Cancian and Oliker (2000, pp. 136–37) refer to as "community care." To illustrate the activities and functions of these associations, I focus on three . . . which I selected for study in consultation with colleagues from universities and international organizations in Azerbaijan as exemplifying the diversity of Azeri women's advocacy associations.

Azerbaycan Qadin va Inkishaf Markazi (Azerbaijan Women and Development Center [AWDC]), established by Elmira Suleymanova, doctor of chemistry, is a leading advocate of women's rights in Azerbaijan. AWDC has played a significant role in identifying and addressing important issues for women from various backgrounds, including those from rural and urban areas, those who are economically disadvantaged, and refugees and IDPs. Founded in 1994, AWDC was the first research center in Azerbaijan to focus on gender and women's issues, and it played a central role in Azerbaijan both in preparations for the Beijing World Conference on Women in 1995 and in post-Beijing Azeri women's development efforts. As Suleymanova put it, "AWDC practically became the clearinghouse for disseminating information on the Beijing Platform for Action and lobbying local Azeri women's and youth NGOs [nongovernmental organizations] on implementation." In subsequent years, AWDC has focused on various women's issues and has worked in cooperation with national government entities, such as the Ministry of Health and the Ministry of Education, as well as with international agencies and networks, including UNDP, UNICEF, and the United Nations Population Fund, to enhance Azeri women's well-being and to bring Azeri women's issues to the forefront of national and international dialogue. Examples include women's health, family planning, gender-based violence, and women's social and political rights, especially the rights of women refugees and IDPs. Indeed, Suleymanova noted that "networking initiatives have placed Azeri women's concerns on the international women's movement agenda." And by putting these issues on the public agenda, AWDC has played a significant role in the empowerment of Azeri women.

AWDC also conducts gender-related research, such as research on the status and needs of women and children refugees and IDPs, which has given additional public visibility to women's issues. It has issued various publications including *111 Stories of Refugee Women*, a compilation of oral histories. With UNICEF support, AWDC, together with the Child-to-Child Network, created an alliance of nongovernmental organizations to advocate for children's rights. Furthermore, with the assistance of UNICEF and other international organizations, AWDC works closely with health care workers and counselors to implement health-related projects, including family planning and the child immunization programs, the distribution of vitamins and iodized salt, and psychological counseling for those suffering from war trauma. AWDC's activities . . . educate women to function more effectively as careworkers, including a program for training women teachers in rural areas and a publication, *Manual for Kindergarten Care Providers*. As Suleymanova has commented, in reflecting on the plight of Azeri women, "We are Azerbaijan. We are together like five fingers on a hand. We are for Azerbaijan. . . ." And therein is the social consciousness and commitment both to address the immediate needs of women and to empower women to help create a more humane and egalitarian society. . . .

Another association, *D. Alieva adina Qadin Huquqlarini Mudafia Camiyyati* (Association for the Defense of Women's Rights [ADWR]), is headed by Novella Jafarova, a chemist and former head of the State Committee of Geology and former faculty member at Baku State University. ADWR includes members from various professions, such as teachers, lawyers, and physicians. As the transition and the war have imposed many difficulties on families, ADWR seeks to protect the rights of women in various arenas, to foster women's political participation, and to implement educational and humanitarian programs. Jafarova has emphasized, for example, that "we have many, many laws that supposedly protect women's rights, mainly laws from the Soviets. Yet many Azeri women are not really protected." ADWR has working relations with international organizations, such as the Oxford Committee for Famine Relief, the Initiative for Social Action and Renewal in Eurasia, and the Open Society Institute, as well as with national government entities, and it has established various working groups with specific objectives. For example, in this period of transition and economic austerity, one working group conducts workshops, trains women in a variety of skills, and assists them in finding employment or in developing their own small businesses. Another working group provides women refugees and IDPs with various forms of aid and counseling. Yet another group focuses on raising women's consciousness about their legal and political rights through seminars and public lectures.

ADWR activities also extend into the realm of legal consultation and representation for women who confront problems such as child custody and support, family violence, and spousal abuse and who lack funds to provide their own representation. Other working groups focus on issues and rights pertaining to religion, to minorities, and to the elderly and handicapped. There are still other working groups: one that conducts sociological research on gender-related issues, one that concentrates on leadership training for young women, and one that focuses on problems associated with prostitution, the trafficking of women, HIV/AIDS, and women's health. . . . [T]hrough its many and diverse activities, ADWR provides caregiving and also promotes empowerment. . . . These activities emphasize the development of leadership skills and building self-confidence for participation in the public arena, and they have been effective in helping women become elected to political office.

A third association, *"Simmetriya" Azerbaycan Cender Assosiasiyasi* (Azerbaijan Gender Association "Symmetry"), is headed by Kamilla Dadasheva, a medical doctor, and is the first and the major women's association in Azerbaijan focusing specifically on violence against women. The association's name—Azerbaijan Gender Association "Symmetry"—is indicative of its emphasis on fundamental principles of gender equality—gender symmetry—within the family as well as within the broader Azeri society. Symmetry was founded by medical professionals who had personal experience in treating victims of gender-based abuse. As Dadasheva has noted, "Working as doctors and nurses, we had often come across women patients who had been subjected to violence, especially domestic violence, and we had witnessed the fear and hopelessness in their eyes."

Responding to the increase in family violence during the transition, Symmetry works to raise awareness about the causes and consequences of physical, sexual, and psychological abuse and violence against women and children. Azeri women frequently do not report abuse because of fear, shame, or dependence, and therefore, Symmetry has developed workshops and seminars for women and men that promote gender sensitivity and that teach techniques for dealing with family issues in nonviolent ways. During spring 2000, Symmetry organized, jointly with the Organization for Security and Co-operation in Europe, a major conference in Baku where issues pertaining to violence against women were the focus. . . . Reflecting on the success of the conference, Dadasheva commented that it "was a very important event for Azerbaijan, a country where traditions and mentalities are very much dominated by the role model of male dominance over women" (Organization for Security and Co-operation in Europe 2001, pp. 35–36). In another cooperative activity, in 2001, Dadasheva, with the support of the Initiative for Social Action and Renewal in Eurasia, participated in an internship in the United States where she met with various individuals and organizations to learn more about American domestic violence programs. Although spousal rape is illegal in Azerbaijan, it is seldom prosecuted, and there are no laws pertaining to other forms of spousal abuse. Rather, for the police, which tends to be male dominated (with only roughly 2 percent women officers), domestic violence is an issue that typically is left to be resolved as a private matter by the family and within the family. As a consequence, Symmetry has produced various brochures, including "Police Against Domestic Violence," and is engaged in innovative workshops and training sessions to sensitize law enforcement personnel about issues of violence against women. . . . Most recently, it started operating a crisis center where female victims can call a hotline and receive emergency aid at the center or at the hospital where volunteer physicians and other staff can provide medical and psychological consultative assistance. Furthermore, while many of Symmetry's activities focus directly on providing support and care for victims of gender-based violence, the association's broader function, as a mechanism of women's empowerment, is found in its efforts to work with the Ministry of Justice on legislation to make violence against women a public issue and to protect the rights of women.

CONCLUSION

Most Azeris believed that independence would bring both political freedom and economic well-being. However, exacerbated by the Nagorno-Karabakh Conflict, the transition has not produced the expected results. To the contrary, the quality of life for many Azeris—particularly women—actually has deteriorated. With the Soviet social security safety net no longer in place, Azeri women's advocacy associations now play important caregiving and empowering roles for Azeri women. The three Azeri women's associations discussed in this article represent diversity of activities and functions. . . . Yet while they differ in terms of specific objectives and target populations, they share . . . a common bond both as women's associations and as nongovernmental organizations, and they also are characterized by very high levels of social consciousness and commitment to enhancing the position of women in the new Azeri society. . . . By placing women's issues—such as women's social and political rights, the plight of refugees and IDPs, and gender-based violence—on the public agenda, these associations' caregiving activities have had an empowering effect that extends beyond humanitarian and material aid. Their activities raise women's consciousness and seek to alter traditional, gendered social relations and consequently to give Azeri women more power and control over their own well-being.

These associations empower women at two levels: at the micro level, when women gain support and knowledge that gives them greater control over their position and well-being within the family, and at the macro level, when women gain greater public recognition of their issues and their rights and gain increasing access to higher-level positions. They seek to create an environment in which women can actually and fully exercise their fundamental rights of equality as proclaimed in the national constitution. Azeri women's advocacy associations represent a women's movement that plays an important role in opening a space and giving a voice to Azeri women in post-Soviet Azerbaijan.

Abdulvahabova, Sajida. 2000. The necessity of the women's movement. *Genderology: Azerbaijan International Scientific Journal* 4:27–28.

Arnould, Francoise. 2001. Where has the life gone? Spring cleaning in Baku. *Azerbaijan Today: The International Journal* 2:14–15.

Cancian, Francesca M., and Stacey J. Oliker. 2000. *Caring and gender.* Thousand Oaks: Pine Forge Press.

Ibrahimbekova, Rena. 2000a. Gender aspects of economy. *Genderology: Azerbaijan International Scientific Journal* 2:6–8.

———. 2000b. Gender problems during the transition period in Azerbaijan. *Genderology: Azerbaijan International Scientific Journal* 1:13–15.

International Monetary Fund. 2000. *Azerbaijan Republic: Recent economic developments and selected issues.* Washington, DC: International Monetary Fund.

Lemberanskaya, Larissa, and Gulnara Mamedova. 2001. *Documentation and evaluation project: Open Society Institute—Azerbaijan Women's Program.* Baku, Azerbaijan: Open Society Institute.

Lieven, Anatol. 2001. The Caucasus and Central Asia ten years after the Soviet collapse. *Eurasia Insight* 8 (October): 1–4.

Najafizadeh, Mehrangiz. 2001. Gender and change in societies in transition. Paper presented at the 19th annual meeting of the Association for Third World Studies, Savannah, GA, 12 October.

Organization for Security and Co-operation in Europe/Office for Democratic Institutions and Human Rights. 2001. *Ten years of ODIHR: Working for human rights and democracy (1991–2001).* Warsaw, Poland: Organization for Security and Co-operation in Europe.

Sabi, Manijeh. 1999. The impact of economic and political transformation on women: The case of Azerbaijan. *Central Asian Survey* 18:111–20.

Seifullaghizi, Zarifa. 2000. Some aspects of the use of force against women. *Genderology: Azerbaijan International Scientific Journal* 4:27–28.

State Statistical Committee of Azerbaijan Republic (SSCAR). 2000a. *Azerbaijan in figures 2000 (statistical yearbook).* Baku: State Statistical Committee of Azerbaijan Republic.

———. 2000b. *Women and men in Azerbaijan 2000.* Baku: State Statistical Committee of Azerbaijan Republic.

UNICEF and the Republic of Azerbaijan. 1999. *Children and women in Azerbaijan: A situation analysis.* Baku: United Nations Children's Fund and the Republic of Azerbaijan.

United Nations Development Programme (UNDP). 1999. *Azerbaycan qadinlari—Women of Azerbaijan: The report on the status of women of Azerbaijan Republic.* Baku, Azerbaijan: United Nations Development Programme.

———. 2000. *Azerbaijan human development report 2000.* Baku, Azerbaijan: United Nations Development Programme.

United Nations Development Programme Gender in Development Unit and Symmetry. 2000. *Women and violence.* Baku, Azerbaijan: United Nations Development Programme and Symmetry Gender Association.

CENTRAL STATE CHILD CARE POLICIES

IN POST-AUTHORITARIAN SPAIN:

IMPLICATIONS FOR GENDER AND

CAREWORK ARRANGEMENTS

Celia Valiente

The impact that state policies have on carework is illustrated by the specific case of public preschool programs in Spain. Such programs have continuously expanded in the past three decades; however, this policy has done little to support increases in the proportion of women in the paid workforce. Preschool is not the same as childcare because the former does not address the care needed by children younger than three years old and offers programs with short hours and long holidays.

Child care can be thought of as a labor market, gender equality, or education policy. [I]n post-authoritarian Spain, the educational rationale has been the predominant one, and it has succeeded in expanding the supply of places in free public preschools. Nevertheless, the very definition of these institutions as schools rather than child care centers has limited their utility for working mothers. Preschool programs provide solid educational services for children three to five years old. Addressing the educational needs of young children (from all social classes) is a laudable goal. . . . However, preschool programs ignore care required by infants and toddlers as well as the child care needed by mothers to ensure employment access.[1]

In many advanced industrial societies, social provisions like child care have been reduced or eliminated in the recent trend toward welfare state retrenchment (Clayton and Pontusson 1998; Garrett 1998; Pierson 1998; Stephens, Huber, and Ray 1999). However, in Spain, public provision of central state child care has increased steadily since the end of the right-wing authoritarian regime in 1975. Since 1975, conditions in Spain have been less favorable toward childcare policy rationales other than the educational approach. Childcare provisions have often been expanded in other countries during periods of labor shortage to facilitate the employment of women with children—the most important available reserve of labor. In Spain, however, there have been no such labor force shortages for the past three decades. Indeed, the unemployment rate hovered above 13 percent between 1981 and 2001, and it is unlikely that labor shortages will develop in the foreseeable future.[2]

At the same time, after 1975, the political and social actors who might have defined childcare measures as programs that benefit working mothers... have not consistently advanced this definition in practice for two reasons. First, in post-authoritarian Spain, feminists have been overwhelmed by the amount of other demands... already... achieved in other Western countries, among them the equality of women and men before the law, the decriminalization of the sale and advertising of contraceptives (achieved in 1978) or abortion under some circumstances (accomplished in 1985), the establishment of divorce (obtained in 1981), and the criminalization of violence against women. Second, between the late 1930s and 1975, the existence of a right-wing authoritarian regime contributed to moving Spanish feminists away from issues such as motherhood and child care later on. The official doctrine of the dictatorship defined motherhood as women's main duty toward the state and society and affirmed that the role of mothering was incompatible with others, such as that of waged worker (Nash 1991, 160). After almost 40 years of being literally bombarded with the idea of mothering and caring as the most important task in women's lives, the last thing Spanish feminists wanted to do after the dictatorship was to pay a lot of attention to the issues of motherhood and child rearing. Women's liberation was then understood as opening the range of concerns that define women's lives, such as waged work, political participation, or control of their bodies. This definition carefully eludes the place of motherhood and child care in the life of the newly liberated female Spaniards.[3]

Instead, policy makers active in the area of child care (mainly from the Ministry of Education) have relied primarily on the educational logic, focusing on measures explicitly intended to benefit children. Since 1975, the main central state childcare policy has been to supply an ever increasing number of free educational preschool programs for children between the ages of three and five (mandatory schooling starts at six).[4] As a result of this policy, in the academic year 2001–2002, school attendance rates for three-, four-, and five-year-olds were comparatively high in Spain at 98 percent.[5] In contrast, the proportion of Spanish children aged two or younger cared for in public or private centers is one of the lowest in the European Union: 1.3 percent for children younger than one year, 5.7 percent for children aged one year, and 13.7 percent for those two years old (Ministerio de Educación y Cultura 2001, pp. 69, 122–23; my calculations).[6]

In Spain, child care has always been an education policy independent of the different types of political regimes that governed the country during the twentieth century. Since the dictatorship, the supply of places in free public preschools has been expanded by parties of different ideological colors while they have held office (although for different reasons): a Center-Right coalition of parties up to 1982, a Social-Democratic party between 1982 and 1996, and a Conservative party since then. These three governments have understood the increasing access of children to preschool services as a necessary step for Spain to catch up with surrounding countries since most European Union member states are economically more developed. All three governing groups have thought that one of the reasons for the relative backwardness of Spain was an education deficit. . . .

CHILD CARE POLICIES AND THE GENDERED LABOR FORCE

Public preschool programs cannot be used by mothers as perfect substitutes for child care, since preschool hours are shorter than the work hours for full-time jobs (and sometimes much shorter and interrupted by a break). It is necessary to stress that even if women's employment rate (34 percent in the first quarter of 2002) is comparatively very low, most Spanish women who work for wages (83 percent in the last quarter of 2001) have full-time jobs (Instituto Nacional de Estadística 2002). Preschool holidays (usually three months) are much longer than paid work holidays (one month).

The acute scarcity of child care for children aged two or younger and the fact that available child care is preschool education for children between the ages of three and five helps explain the comparatively low Spanish female employment rate. Other reasons include the general scarcity of employment in Spain for both men and women (men's employment rate was also unusually low at 61 percent in the first quarter of 2002) (Instituto Nacional de Estadística 2002), the lack of incentives provided by authorities to create part-time work up until the 1990s, gender discrimination in hiring, and the shortage of care services for other people in need such as the frail elderly, the sick, and the handicapped. Because of its limitations, child care policy in Spain has not significantly contributed to reversing the historical pattern of low levels of women's participation in the labor market. In 1976, the female employment rate was 27 percent, and since then, it has fluctuated to reach the current 34 percent (Instituto Nacional de Estadística 2002).

In this context, it is not surprising that some Spanish mothers of working age conceptualize the combination of work and family responsibilities as an impossible mission and do not even try. Other mothers try it by using not only preschool services but also help from female relatives (usually grandmothers) and to a lesser extent from the children's fathers and, for the middle-class, paid carework from domestic servants (Tobío 1999). Therefore, the transformation of childcare policy into a useful resource for women to participate in the Spanish labor market is a policy goal still pending achievement in the future.

1. This report draws heavily on Valiente (2001, 2002).

2. The unemployment rate is the proportion of registered unemployment in the active population (which is the employed and the registered unemployed).

3. For more in English on the Spanish women's movement and Spanish feminist approaches to public policies (including child care), see Durán and Gallego (1986), Kaplan (1992, 191–210), and Threlfall (1985, 1996).

4. While preschool programs in public centers enrolled 347,026 children younger than six in the academic year 1975–1976, by 2001–2002, this figure had more than doubled (798,565 children; provisional data for 2001–2002) (Instituto Nacional de Estadística 1977, 101; Ministerio de Educación y Cultura 2002).

5. Approximately two-thirds of children aged three, four, and five years old are now enrolled in public preschools, while the remaining third is enrolled in private preschools (Ministerio de Educación y Cultura 2002).

6. In social science research, Spain is often compared with other European Union member states, even in studies like this on issues such as child care, for which no mandatory European Union regulation exists.

Clayton, Richard, and Jonas Pontusson. 1998. Welfare-state retrenchment revisited: Entitlement cuts, public sector restructuring and inegalitarian trends in advanced capitalist societies. *World Politics* 51 : 67–98.

Durán, María A., and María T. Gallego. 1986. The women's movement in Spain and the new Spanish democracy. In *The new women's movement: Feminism and political power in Europe and the USA*, edited by Drude Dahlerup. London: Sage.

Garrett, Geoffrey. 1998. *Partisan politics in the global economy.* New York: Cambridge University Press.

Instituto Nacional de Estadística. 1977. *Estadística de la enseñanza en España: Curso 1975–76* (Statistics on education in Spain: Academic year 1975–76). Madrid, Spain: National Institute of Statistics.

———. 2002. *Encuesta de población activa* (Active population survey). Madrid, Spain: National Institute of Statistics. Available from http://www.ine.es.

Kaplan, Gisela. 1992. *Contemporary Western European feminism.* London: UCL Press and Allen & Unwin.

Ministerio de Educación y Cultura. 2001. *Estadísticas de la educación en España 1998–1999: Resultados detallados, series e indicadores* (Statistics on education in Spain 1998–1999: Detailed results, series and indicators). Madrid, Spain: Ministry of Education and Culture.

———. 2002. *Estadísticas de las enseñanzas no universitarias: Series e indicadores 1992–93 a 2001–02* (Statistics on nonuniversity education in Spain: Series and indicators 1992–93 to 2001–02). Madrid, Spain: Ministry of Education and Culture. Available from http://www.mec.es.

Nash, Mary. 1991. Pronatalism and motherhood in Franco's Spain. In *Maternity and gender politics: Women and the rise of European welfare states, 1880s–1950s*, edited by Gisela Bock and Pat Thane. London: Routledge.

Pierson, Paul. 1998. Irresistible forces, immovable objects: Post-industrial welfare states confront permanent austerity. *Journal of European Public Policy* 5 (4): 539–60.

Stephens, John D., Evelyne Huber, and Leonard Ray. 1999. The welfare state in hard times. In *Continuity and change in contemporary capitalism*, edited by Herbert Kitschelt, Peter Lange, Gary Marks, and John D. Stephens. New York: Cambridge University Press.

Threlfall, Monica. 1985. The women's movement in Spain. *New Left Review* 151:44–73.

———. 1996. Feminist politics and social change in Spain. In *Mapping the women's movement: Feminist politics and social transformation in the North*, edited by Monica Threlfall. London: Verso.

Tobío, Constanza. 1999. Solidaridad y cambio entre generaciones de mujeres (Solidarity and change among generations of women). In *Género y ciudadanía* (Gender and citizenship), edited by Margarita Ortega, Cristina Sánchez, and Celia Valiente. Madrid, Spain: Autonomous University of Madrid.

Valiente, Celia. 2001. Do political parties matter? Do Spanish parties make a difference in child care policies? In *Promoting evidence-based practice in early childhood education: Research and its implications*, edited by Tricia David. Amsterdam: JAI.

———. 2002. The value of an educational emphasis: Child care and restructuring in Spain since 1975. In *Child care policy at the crossroads: Gender and welfare restructuring*, edited by Sonya Michel and Rianne Mahon. New York: Routledge.

CONCLUSION

Carework can be thought of as the glue that holds societies together. Like glue, carework often is transparent, and serves its supportive function largely hidden from public view. Looking through the lens of globalization, however, as we have done in this book, makes visible how vital carework is to individual lives and families. In addition, this lens clarifies how carework is embedded in the organization of the global economy, civil society, and political systems.

At the beginning of this book, we anticipated that our focus on carework and gender would lead to new understandings of *globalization*. We hope readers can now see that globalization involves much more than economic exchange; it reflects and generates broad social reorganization as well. Global forces are influencing nations to decentralize and privatize their social policy regimes, reducing social citizenship and potentially retreating from (or never developing) the ideal of woman-friendly states. These same forces are reaching into the realm of gender relations and family life, reinforcing gender divides, and fragmenting families as grandmothers, mothers, wives, aunts, sisters, and daughters enter into new and stressful dual roles as breadwinners and caregivers. As Saskia Sassen cautions, the economic growth behind globalization offers as much risk for exploitation as it does opportunity for advancement, especially for vulnerable women from developing countries.

In our introduction to this book, we promised that our focus on gender and globalization would yield a fresh approach to the study of *carework*. Accordingly, we have examined the transnational and global economic conditions under which carework has become ever more critical to regenerating, reproducing, and sustaining human labor. Carework, as Helga Hernes argues, disproportionately consumes women's time and drains their energy. The contents of this book underscore how growing demands for care in the new global economy continue to channel predominantly women into carework roles. This leads, in turn, to more deeply entrenched gender, race, and class divisions and inequalities—hierarchical systems that are increasingly global in addition to local in scope. In documenting the fundamental connection between carework and gender equity, we have also addressed the third promise of this book—that through our focus on carework and globalization we would arrive at a better understanding of contemporary gender dynamics and structures.

We are consistently struck by the contradiction that carework is both vital for society and at the same time overlooked, invisible, and devalued. As the materials in this book have demonstrated, carework, like other forms of work, is essential for the common good and for individuals in their daily lives as care providers and care receivers. We hope that readers will now find more visibility of and social significance in the daily tasks of care they have previously taken for granted. Moreover, we are struck by the fundamental inequalities of carework—within households, across local regions, and between nations around the globe. We hope that our readers will also pay greater attention to these inequalities as they come to recognize how their daily lives depend routinely upon the accomplishment of inequalities in carework.

Sociologist David Smith (2001) argues that we get the best view of globalization by considering how the current global situation works. Our book has looked at globalization in reference to how carework operates through particular issues such as gender, race, migration, childcare, domestic labor, labor rights, and labor exploitations. Each of these is embedded in the organization and transformations of care as it exists and travels around the globe. By looking at carework in particular contexts, we have been able to bring personal stories together with the larger social, political, and economic dynamics of globalization.

We organized our examination of the relations between gender, carework, and globalization around four crises of care. We now reflect on these crises in light of the approaches and material in Parts 2, 3, and 4. We do not provide an exhaustive overview, but rather identify key points that will be useful in future considerations of carework.

CRISIS 1: THE CARE DEFICIT

This book has defined the care deficit to refer to a lack of paid care (or affordable paid care) and a lack of or insufficient informal, unpaid, family care. Much of the material has identified the macrolevel forces that generate the conditions for deficiencies in care. For example, we have shown that the transnational migration of women has provided a large labor pool of underpaid workers who obtain employment in more privileged women's households in affluent societies. This dynamic creates new care deficiencies in immigrants' countries of origin. At the same time, women's increased labor force participation around the globe creates new demands for paid carework, domestic work, and services. Rebecca Upton's analysis of the carework crisis brought about by HIV/AIDS similarly shows the implications of inadequate public policy for women's carework practices and obligations. Rather than accidental or random patterns, the challenges and resources that women confront as careworkers are deeply tied to wider social forces.

Government policy, market capitalism, supranational organizations, local worker activism, and international corporations directly affect the provision and availability of care as well as the cultural value assigned to care activity. We have documented this in examples as wide-ranging as the Scandinavian social democratic models for woman-friendly, universal carer states (Hernes, Fraser) and the realities at the opposite end of the spectrum in countries where publicly provided care resources are absent (Najafizadeh) or biased against the current needs of women (Anwary, Valiente). We have also documented care inadequacies within the more politically and economically conservative yet affluent United States. Uttal shows how the private childcare market fills gaps that could be met by adequate public provision. Mary Blair-Loy and Jerry Jacobs and Terry Repak illustrate the care deficits and various strategies used by affluent U.S. families in relation to global economic forces. Moreover, we have shown that the growth of supranational organizations can undermine national efforts to protect and support women's carework (Rosemberg, Christopherson).

Care deficits for families left in immigrant women workers' counties of origin are illustrated in many articles. The situation of Filipina domestic workers in Taiwan (Lan), immigrant minorities in Europe (Anderson), and Latina domestics in the United States (Hondagneu-Sotelo and Avila and Romero) all show the costs when women search for employment that takes them far from home. Further, the research presented in this book identifies how all women, in their daily lives and practice, negotiate the deficiencies in the care they can provide. Affluent women purchase the care of other women, as developed in the articles by Lynet Uttal,

Rhacel Salazar Parrennãs, Pei-Chia Lan, and others, while women with greater economic need take jobs filling these care deficits. We have also examined the microlevel experiences and perceptions of women as they respond to pressures of carework. We have seen that mothers create new meanings of motherhood as a long-distance enterprise (Hondagneu-Sotelo and Avila) and the costs it exacts on children (Parreñas, Romero).

Care deficits also occur for women who migrate with their husbands, but without other adult female members of their extended families. Minjeong Kim's research on the wives of Korean international students in the United States and the research of Denise Spitzer and her colleagues on Asian immigrant wives in Canada show how migration increased the amount of carework that needed to be done, whether or not the women held paid employment. Wives experienced a deficit of help as they performed family carework because they no longer had mothers-in-law or other female relatives available to share in cooking, cleaning, and dealing with health-care problems, as they had in their home countries. Carework was an extended family effort in their countries of origin, but became a nuclear family effort after they migrated, increasing their burden. In these examples, both the cultural discontinuities and contradictions of migration and the social policies in receiving countries that regulate immigration intersect in powerful ways to shape and constrain women's carework patterns.

CRISIS 2: THE COMMODIFICATION OF CARE

The commodification of care refers to the increasing trend in which carework services have been transformed into services and products that are sold and exchanged in a market. Activities that were previously carried out in the unpaid, informal sector (among kin, friends, or other groups) have been developed into different carework occupations. The readings in this book have shown that globalization has led to greater, rather than less, commodification of carework. In many of our readings we saw that immigrant women's carework was a commodified task to be bought and sold like any market product (Raijman, Parreñas, Repak, Chang, Cheng, Romero, Lan, Hondogneu-Sotelo and Avila). Our book also documents the mixed consequences of commodification. Affluent consumers can purchase a degree of flexibility in their daily lives by purchasing the work of others. Yet the consequences are not always positive for those whose labor is purchased, the paid careworker. While these jobs bring in needed wages, paid careworkers also face exploitative work conditions as well as challenges to personal integrity and their own family responsibilities.

Perhaps more significantly, the legal, political, and social contexts within which immigrant women sell their labor is often highly regulated. In Israel, because overstaying a tourist visa to enter paid carework is illegal and punishable by deportation, Latina domestics were easily cheated of their pay and rarely complained about this unequal labor transaction. In Taiwan, Filipina domestics' labor was controlled by regulations that not only limited the duration of their contracts but required deposits from employers for their labor (as if they were returnable bottles), and regular health inspections—not to test the quality of their work, but in order to assure that they remained as full-time workers who had no local family responsibilities. While immigrant status was highly regulated, the conditions of their work settings were not. Thus many immigrant women labored in degrading work conditions (Anderson), and worked in private households where they had few, if any, labor protections.

Governmental context is critical in assessing how commodified carework affects women. Carework can be supported as one dimension of a woman-friendly state—that is, within the context of a state responsive to citizens' care needs through financing carework as a state obligation. From this standpoint, rather than lead to the exploitation of workers, the commodification of carework assists women and families by providing support for carework. Thus, commodification can be constructed in very different ways: as part of a state policy regime that takes responsibility for carework or as part of a profit-oriented global marketplace with little regulation. Overall, the examples and analyses presented in this book suggest that global forces are working to increase the latter form of commodification—the marketization of carework and the exploitation of careworkers.

CRISIS 3: SUPRANATIONAL ORGANIZATIONS AND THEIR IMPACT IN SHAPING CAREWORK

In this book, "multilateral" has referred generally to organizations and corporations that involve two or more nations. Supranational organizations are multilateral organizations with the added feature of governance structures with the potential to supercede national policies. We can see the struggle between national policy and the imposition of external regulations in the ongoing development of and current resistance to the European Union (EU) as a (supra)governmental body. From a global perspective, we have seen the effect of the impact of supranational economic bodies, such as the IMF and World Bank, and their policies of structural adjustment. As Saskia Sassen and Grace Chang have explained, these policies serve neoliberal economic interests, which have subordinated social programs and social citizenship policies to economic development. Here we can refer to the tension that we described in Part 2 between "globalization from above" and "globalization from below." An example of the tension between local and supranational initiatives was clear in Fúlvia Rosemberg's study of Brazil where first the United Nations (UNICEF) and later the World Bank imposed policies at odds with those enacted by the Brazilians themselves. Nongovernmental organizations (NGOs), UN commissions, EU regulations, and so on increasingly appear as major actors in international law, labor, and markets.

The articles on migration and carework illustrate the role of multilateral organizations in creating the push factors that drive Latinas to Israel and Filipinas to Taiwan in search of work. More importantly, all the migration-related articles show how national citizenship and labor regulations shaped carework arrangements, and reduced careworkers' empowerment. United States citizenship laws prohibited international student wives from paid employment and channeled them into unpaid carework (Kim). The lack of culturally appropriate institutions in Canada forced Asian wives to take on more carework than they would have at home (Spitzer et al.). Illegal carework by South American women in Israel meant they needed to be hired by word of mouth, stay with one employer or in housing away from police surveillance, and feared negotiating good contracts (Raijman et al.). And, Filipina workers in Taiwan were recruited from only a few countries explicitly to do highly regulated domestic work, as described in Chapter 11.

CRISIS 4: REINFORCING RACE AND CLASS STRATIFICATION GLOBALLY

All of the articles in this book document the relationship between gender, race, nation, and class inequalities in carework. In Part 1 we asked a key question: "To what extent is globalization helping to move humanity toward a global stratification system of haves and have-nots that is built upon hierarchies of race, class, and gender?" Our book has considered that question through a sustained analysis of how carework functions in relation to global and local inequalities.

The research highlighted in this collection reveals that gender inequality is not only central to the organization of carework, but that it is taking on new forms in relation to globalization. Women undertake the majority of the world's carework, even as wider social forces are overturning traditional gender and work practices. New, transnational households hold the possibility of empowering women, but as Sassen points out, jobs in some sectors of the global economy are, in reality, exploitive dead ends. More research is needed to document how and whether empowerment occurs. At the same time, current research is concerned with documenting how the household, with its new and changing functions in globalization, can also represent empowerment and new forms of solidarity among women.

A number of the articles in this book document the gendered as well as racialized or nationalized nature of different carework occupations and practices. Some jobs—those requiring less direct labor—Sassen characterizes as "valorized" in contrast to others that are "devalorized." Our selections illustrate the processes through which that inequality and differentiation occur, on the microlevel in individual households and on the macrolevel through national immigration and labor policies. As pointed out earlier, the readings document that rather than leading women toward collective empowerment, immigration has often disempowered women.

Gender intersects with other hierarchies in producing inequalities in carework. Thus Parreñas, Romero, and Lan document the inequalities between women across developing and developed economies in their different relations to carework. Our essays have covered the difficult question of what it means for the more affluent mother to shift carework to nannies and domestic workers. We have revealed the contradiction that hiring a surrogate can be an ideal strategy for maintaining the myth of the "good mother" (that is, emotionally attentive) while actually shifting the work to another woman. Bridget Anderson and Mary Romero showed the essential exploitation of personhood that is built into the condition of doing domestic work for others. Their articles provide a theoretical understanding of the inequalities between women that are structured into the daily transfer of carework. In identifying an undercurrent and central dimension of mothering in globalization, their work helps us to see that divisions and inequality among employers and domestics both symbolize and reproduce divisions among women.

The articles focused on migration and citizenship illustrate the intensifying and interlocking global stratification systems of gender, class, and race or ethnicity (nation). Kim shows how middle-class Korean wives are forced into unpaid carework in the United States. In contrast, the studies by Shu-Ju Ada Cheng and Rebecca Raijman and colleagues illustrate how labor and citizenship laws channel migrant women into low-paid carework jobs in Taiwan and Israel, respectively. In the latter two cases, governments are consciously refusing to change the national racial-ethnic composition, or ethnoscape, in any permanent manner, and state laws actively stereotype careworkers as socially inferior.

In his classic work, *The Three Worlds of Welfare Capitalism*, Gøsta Esping-Andersen argues that social policy regimes function as systems of social stratification. One of the key objectives of this book has been to highlight the centrality of carework as a basis through which social policies can either promote gender equity or exacerbate gender divisions and inequality. Our selections have confirmed the ways that national social policy regimes as well as supranational governance structures solidify and reinforce gender, race, and class hierarchies. Moreover, applying the global lens allows us to see that these hierarchies are rapidly expanding from national to global. This suggests that globalization, through its impact on carework, is creating deeper divisions among women and between individuals based on their race and class.

More attention needs to be paid to carework for the elderly. As economic restructuring disrupts traditional employment arrangements and as populations age, we expect heightened concern for elderly care. Health-care systems will face new tensions. We anticipate deepening care crises in the global south as more women migrate to do this form of carework.

LOOKING TOWARD THE FUTURE

The future of carework is not preordained. People are not only victims of globalization, they are active agents on their own behalf. Thus, social movement groups and NGOs have tried to improve the situation of paid careworkers by challenging national and supranational governments and organizations, pushing them to enhance citizenship and employment rights. Individuals foster globalization from below by creating successful organizations like the National Union of Domestic Employees (NUDE) in Trinidad and Tobago or Intercede (The International Coalition to End Domestics' Exploitation) in Canada. Cross-national efforts, like the International Wages for Housework campaign, or alliances created by groups and NGOs around UN-sponsored international conferences, also try to link carework-improvement struggles around the globe. Such efforts, especially when led by women from the global South, ought to be encouraged.

In addition, we cannot assume that the crises of global carework will be static. We have identified the current problems as a care deficit, the commodification of care, the role of multilateral and supranational organizations, and the strengthening of race and class stratification globally, but we should keep our eyes open for new problems or opportunities as global political or economic conditions change. For example, if nations tightened their immigration regulations, migration for carework and the carework deficit might decrease, but there would be less opportunity for women to earn wages to support their families. If there were a global economic recession, carework might be decommodified and pushed back into the home as unpaid family work. Clearly, the relations between gender and carework in globalization are contradictory and complex. We hope that this book has sensitized you to these complexities as you forge carework in your own lives. We also hope that this book has encouraged you to step outside of your local context to position yourself as "global citizens."

REFERENCE

Smith, David. (2001). Globalization and Social Problems. *Social Problems.* 48 (4): 429–34.

COPYRIGHT ACKNOWLEDGMENTS

INDEX

Page numbers followed by "n" indicate notes.